Administrative Law

SAGE was founded in 1965 by Sara Miller McCune to support the dissemination of usable knowledge by publishing innovative and high-quality research and teaching content. Today, we publish more than 850 journals, including those of more than 300 learned societies, more than 800 new books per year, and a growing range of library products including archives, data, case studies, reports, and video. SAGE remains majority-owned by our founder, and after Sara's lifetime will become owned by a charitable trust that secures our continued independence.

Los Angeles | London | New Delhi | Singapore | Washington DC

Administrative Law

The Sources and Limits
of Governmental Agency Power

Daniel L. Feldman
John Jay College of Criminal Justice,
City University of New York

Los Angeles | London | New Delhi
Singapore | Washington DC

Los Angeles | London | New Delhi
Singapore | Washington DC

FOR INFORMATION:

CQ Press

An Imprint of SAGE Publications, Inc.

2455 Teller Road

Thousand Oaks, California 91320

E-mail: order@sagepub.com

SAGE Publications Ltd.

1 Oliver's Yard

55 City Road

London EC1Y 1SP

United Kingdom

SAGE Publications India Pvt. Ltd.

B 1/I 1 Mohan Cooperative Industrial Area

Mathura Road, New Delhi 110 044

India

SAGE Publications Asia-Pacific Pte. Ltd.

3 Church Street

#10-04 Samsung Hub

Singapore 049483

Printed in the United States of America

Library of Congress Cataloging-in-Publication Data

Feldman, Daniel L., author.

Administrative law: the sources and limits of governmental agency power / Daniel L. Feldman, John Jay College of Criminal Justice, City University of New York.

pages cm
Includes bibliographical references and index.

ISBN 978-1-5063-0854-8 (pbk.: alk. paper)

1. Administrative law—United States. I. Title.

KF5402.F45 2016
342.73'06—dc23   2015028148

This book is printed on acid-free paper.

Acquisitions Editor: Sarah Calabi

Editorial Assistant: Katie Lowry

Production Editor: Bennie Clark Allen

Copy Editor: Janet Ford

Typesetter: C&M Digitals (P) Ltd.

Proofreader: Catherine Forrest

Cover Designer: Scott Van Atta

Marketing Manager: Amy Whitaker

Certified Chain of Custody
Promoting Sustainable Forestry
www.sfiprogram.org
SFI-01268

SFI label applies to text stock

15 16 17 18 19 10 9 8 7 6 5 4 3 2 1

BRIEF CONTENTS

DETAILED CONTENTS

I started teaching administrative law to Master of Public Administration (MPA) students in 1977, taught the course to law students for several years, and now once more teach MPA students. No one, including myself, has ever been satisfied with the available textbooks. Each has very good qualities, but almost all overwhelm the students with much too much material and tedious prose.

I wanted a book that my students would really like; a book that was deep, but short, accessible, and conversational. So I wrote it.

Standard administrative law casebooks include too much material for any student to absorb in a one-semester course, or even in a yearlong course. This text presents information that a student can understand and absorb within a semester. Of course, as the author, it reflects my preferences and priorities as to what to include. Each chapter presents a problem and asks the reader to assume the role of a government official faced with that problem. Administrative law provides guidance, and walks the reader through the kind of logic necessary to apply in that situation, regardless of whether or not the official has a law degree. Each chapter also includes practice problems, generally taken from real-life examples with no answers provided so that instructors have ready-made assignments for their students. The book's extensive index and tables of cases and statutes also help instructors and students to locate key points quickly and easily.

Most administrative law texts include in an appendix either the whole of the very lengthy federal Administrative Procedure Act, or much of it, or force the reader to go to some other source to find it. The present book conveniently provides short but relevant excerpts wherever the reader would otherwise need to search for them, and also on necessary occasions provides excerpts from the Model State Administrative Procedure Act, the Code of Federal Regulations, and sample state administrative procedure acts and regulation codes.

Administrative law presents some daunting challenges to its students, but repays the effort needed to master it with a much clearer understanding of the logic of American government. Probably the major difficulty is psychological: people tend to resist rather than assimilate material that generates ambiguity and reflects clashes between equally legitimate values. For example, it may be hard to accept that the interests of taxpayers in the aggregate justify denying relief to a citizen who relied to his or her detriment on bad advice from a government employee; or that some procedural guarantees of fairness to individuals in agency hearings may cost too much in terms of efficiency or even fairness to a larger group of beneficiaries, or to other groups. It is not merely a failure of implementation that stands between us and a system of perfect justice: even in principle, such a system exceeds our reach. People dislike this reality, and try to resist internalizing it.

Another difficulty is intellectual: issues of administrative law transcend particular agencies and particular topics of substantive law, but necessarily arise and the issues are couched in such agencies and their topics. Therefore, students learn about *Chevron* deference (the concept that judges should not second-guess interpretations of unclear statutes by agencies that administer those statutes) in the context of a case about pollution control; or learn why due process sometimes requires agencies to give joint hearings to pairs of applicants seeking government licenses, in the context of a case about the assignment of radio frequencies to broadcasters. So, students must penetrate some of the substantive law of environmental protection and of communications regulation in order to understand the underlying administrative law principles. These are merely two examples: a thorough review of administrative law draws on examples from virtually every one of the enormous range of substantive law areas administered by agencies.

Perhaps instead of responding to these challenges with enthusiasm, some students of administrative law have just skimmed the surface. If they never really engaged with the deeper issues, issues that challenge the heart as well as the mind, they may have experienced the field as boring. It has long been my goal to show that administrative law, on the contrary, is *interesting*. I must confess that I have not always succeeded, but at least some of the blame goes to the existing textbooks. A few years ago, a student lingered after the first administrative law class of the semester to ask me a question. As she did so, a student who had taken the course from me in a previous semester happened to pass by. Recognizing the student as a friend, he came into the classroom and proceeded to tell her that I was a very good teacher. While naturally I was grateful for the compliment, the precise way he offered it disappointed me: he said that I had taken very boring material and made it interesting. My goal, of course, had been to persuade students that the material itself is interesting.

That night, I gave my wife, a former federal prosecutor, a brief description of the encounter. At first she tried to reassure me, noting that so long as the student thought that I had made the material interesting, I should be satisfied. Then she stopped herself and asked me to remind her again which course I was talking about. "Administrative law," I said. "Oh," she responded, "but that *is* boring."

As noted, I have not always succeeded in persuading those I encounter that administrative law is interesting. I do believe, however, that I have succeeded with the majority of my students, although not with my wife.

This book reflects those efforts.

Chapter 1 first establishes the overwhelming primacy of agencies, as opposed to legislatures or courts, in the daily lives of citizens, and thus introduces the central role of administrative law. Then, setting out the troubled evolution of the non-delegation doctrine, it gives the "big picture" view of the sources and boundaries of government agency power. Chapter 2 delves somewhat deeper into "sources and boundaries," but more theoretically so that readers who wish to devote more attention to practical issues may choose to skip it. Further, it presents an opinionated and possibly controversial defense of administrative legitimacy, accusing the two most recent presidential administrations—those of George W. Bush and Barack Obama—of insufficient regard for the constitutional role of Congress in policies they pursued through their agencies.

Chapter 3 recounts struggles for power over agencies between Congress and the presidency, mostly fought in the courts, for example focusing on the legislative veto, special prosecutors, and executive orders. Chapter 4 introduces the Administrative Procedure Act, the model State version of the Act, and the modern organizing vehicles of regulatory law, the *Federal Register* and state registers, and the *Code of Federal Regulations* and state codes. It also reviews some of the major issues that emerge from discretionary and informal agency action, including street-level decision-making, investigations, and interpretive rulemaking. Chapter 5 explains the process of rulemaking, the role of bias and *ex parte* contacts in that context, and the painful refusal of courts to allow estoppel against government agencies. Chapter 6 reviews federal regulatory preemption and *Chevron* deference, but includes a section at least as controversial as Chapter 2 in taking sharp issue with Justices Scalia and Thomas's argument that courts should defer to agency interpretations of ambiguous statutory provisions even to the point of vast expansions of the agency's own jurisdictional boundaries. Although for most part I believe this book reflects an effort to be objective, other aspects of the book reflect my idiosyncrasies and biases as well. Readers will find more value if they look for and identify statements that merely reflect my opinions, and challenge and test those opinions. Very respectable scholars disagree on many issues; readers should feel free to do so as well.

Chapters 7, 8, and 9 all address aspects of adjudication. Chapter 7 explains the justification for adjudication by agencies, and sets forth the legal evolution from "privilege" to "entitlement," eventually constrained by the *Matthews* balancing test. Chapter 8 surveys the range of entitlements that grew out of the *Kelly v. Goldberg* "rights revolution," and some of the costs thereof. Chapter 9 gives readers a taste of agency adjudication in one example of an administrative hearing process concerning state pension appeals.

Why and how some agencies (notably the Securities Exchange Commission and the National Labor Relations Board) try to use rulemaking to avoid adjudication; how some states have responded to their own agencies' similar efforts; how sometimes private parties feel oppressed by the opposite choice as well—an agency's choice of adjudication instead of rulemaking; and the courts' reactions to all of these interactions ground the discussion in Chapter 10. Chapter 11 covers the technical, but important, issues that determine whether a private party gets the chance to challenge an agency's decision in a regular Article III court with a discussion of standing, ripeness, exhaustion of administrative remedies, and so forth. Chapter 12 offers the history, justification, and evolution of sovereign immunity and officer tort liability in the United States. Chapter 13 expands on Chapter 8 in providing a fuller discussion of rights of government employees against adverse agency action, since that topic is of special interest to government employees and their managers. Chapter 14 covers the Freedom of Information Act, Open Meetings Law, and related state and federal statutes, along with other issues in transparency, such as the role of electronic rulemaking.

Please tell me you found it interesting.

ACKNOWLEDGMENTS

I t is a pleasure to acknowledge those whose advice and inspiration contributed to this book. Several such debts go back a long way; some are to those now gone. The legendary Clark Byse taught my Administrative Law class; the equally legendary Louis Jaffe, another great architect of American administrative law, taught another class I took, but I had the pleasure of seeing his mind at work. Lance Liebman, the former dean of Columbia Law School, was my boss in John Lindsay's mayoral administration in 1969 to 1970. Both of us young men then, we moved on to Harvard Law School the following year—I as a student, he as a professor—and have stayed friends since. He was kind enough to recruit Peter Strauss, a living giant of administrative law and Lance's colleague at Columbia Law School, to provide immensely valuable responses to an earlier draft. My good friend Rose Mary Bailly, an adviser to the drafters of the 2010 Model State Administrative Procedure Act and a distinguished professor of administrative law at Albany Law School, generously gave my manuscript a line-by-line edit and vastly improved it. I hope I have adequately reflected the thoughts of Professors Bailly and Strauss in this book. The book's faults will correspond to my failure to do so.

My dear friend Louis Bochette introduced me to Eli Silverman, then chair of the government department at John Jay College, who hired me to teach my first administrative law class in the MPA program there starting in 1977. After a few years there, I taught that subject and other courses at various other universities. Louis, then, started me on my administrative law teaching path. Sadly, he passed away during the fall of 2014. Some years later, my good friend David Trager, then dean of Brooklyn Law School, invited me to teach the course there, which I did throughout the early 1990s. David later become a highly respected federal district court judge in Brooklyn, but left us far too soon in 2011. John Feerick, then dean of Fordham Law School and a perennial generous servant to the people of New York as unpaid chair of various ethics bodies, invited me to teach at Fordham. Although I taught other law courses throughout most of the first decade of the current millennium that experience nonetheless helped inform my thoughts on administrative law. When I switched my full-time occupation from government service to teaching in 2010 and returned to John Jay College, my friend and Public Management Department chair Ned Benton allowed me to persuade him to revive the Department's administrative law class, which I now teach every semester.

Alison J. Hankey, a fine editor at a different publishing house, suggested the "What am I supposed to do?" feature. Suzanne Flinchbaugh, my former editor, recommended the use of excerpts from the APA and other documents, and provided much enthusiastic support, and my current editors at SAGE/CQ Press, Sarah Calabi, Bennie Clark Allen, Janet Ford, and Katie Lowry, have been equally and wonderfully helpful.

I dedicate this book to all of the aforementioned, whether still with us or sadly now gone.

Daniel. L. Feldman
John Jay College of Criminal Justice, City University of New York

SAGE Publications wishes to thank the following reviewers:

Peter Bergerson, Florida Gulf Coast University

Mark Iris, Northwestern University

Mitchel Sollenberger, University of Michigan–Dearborn

Robert Howard, Georgia State University

Joseph Smith, University of Alabama–Huntsville

Eric Fink, Elon University School of Law

ABOUT THE AUTHOR

Daniel L. Feldman teaches for the City University of New York in the Master of Public Administration (MPA) program at John Jay College of Criminal Justice as Professor of Public Management. His fifth book, *The Art of the Watchdog*, coauthored with David R. Eichenthal (SUNY Press, Albany, New York), was released early in 2014. A state legislator for eighteen years, he wrote more than 140 laws, including New York's Organized Crime Control Act and Megan's Law; and as chair of the Assembly Committee on Corrections, led the effort to repeal the Rockefeller drug laws. Both prior and subsequent to his career in elective office, he conducted major investigations during sixteen years in high-level appointed offices. He holds degrees from Columbia College and Harvard Law School.

GLOSSARY

Note: This glossary does not include definitions of words or phrases explained at length in the text, except for those frequently used words whose meaning might not become clear early on in the book.

Adjudication: 1. The process of hearing and resolving a dispute when the parties to it subject its outcome to resolution by a judge or judges or a person or persons acting in a judge-like capacity, used here primarily in the context of government agency personnel acting in a judge-like capacity. 2. The result or resolution of such a dispute.

Attractive nuisance: A term from tort law referring to hazards such as swimming pools without fences or other barriers, or deserted open mine shafts, that might entice vulnerable persons, generally children, to enter and suffer injury in consequence.

Color of law: Used in the phrase "acting under the color of law": acting with the appearance of official power, although, for example, the government employee does not have legal authority to take the action in question; or the individual appears to be a government employee, but is not.

Deference: Used here to mean the stance of a court when instead of relying on its own best judgment as to the meaning of an unclear statute or regulation, it accepts the interpretation of an agency responsible for carrying out the mandate of that statute or regulation.

Delegation: Used here to mean a transfer of power, sometimes understood as the transfer of lawmaking power, sometimes as the transfer of policymaking power; often as part of the phrase "non-delegation doctrine."

Dicta: Comments in a judicial ruling not necessary to the decision of the precise issue in controversy.

Discretionary: 1. Action by a government agency or its personnel when its enabling statute gives the agency a choice of approaches to carry out its responsibilities. 2. Agency action undertaken to carry out mission responsibilities other than rulemaking or adjudication.

Estoppel/"equitable estoppel":   The principle that a party to a dispute may be barred by the decision-maker from asserting a claim when such party had previously made an inconsistent claim on which the opposing party had relied; more generally, the principle that a court will refuse to enforce a claim based on unfair behavior.

Ex parte: On or from one side only; communications between a decision-maker and one participant in a dispute without notice to an opposing participant or participants.

Expressio unius est exclusio alterius: A statute's inclusion of certain items in a list implies the exclusion of other items.

Habeas corpus: Literally, that you have the body; the power of federal courts to compel the attendance of a prisoner to judge whether that prisoner has been justly incarcerated.

Hearsay: A statement, not his or her own or substantiated, but heard from another and quoted by a witness.

Immunity: Used here to mean protection of government officials from liability, whether the party claiming injury seeks a remedy against the government ("sovereign immunity") or seeks a remedy personally against the official (usually "qualified immunity," where the official must show that he or she did not violate a clearly established right) rather than "absolute immunity."

Judicialization: Used here to mean the tendency to import standard courtroom trial procedures into agency adjudications.

Legal positivism: In its dominant modern form, a variety of legal philosophy or jurisprudence holding that to be legitimate, law must emanate from a body or institution generally recognized as authoritative in the society in which it functions.

Legislation: 1. A statute. 2. Statutes.

Legislature: An elected representative body of persons that enacts laws in the form of statutes.

Managerialism: Pursuit of efficiency; in extreme forms, also the pursuit of market goals, such as increased market share and profit.

Non-delegation doctrine: That a legislative body like Congress cannot transfer its lawmaking power or policymaking power to some other entity.

Overbroad: A term applied to a statute that lacks sufficient standards, guiding principles, or constraints to channel the actions of the agency charged with its implementation.

Preemption: Used here to mean that the law of the superior jurisdiction prevails, e.g. federal law prevails over state law, state law prevails over local law.

Pro se: Literally, for oneself; a person who represents himself or herself in court, without an attorney.

"Regime" values: 1. The dominant aspirational values in a political culture. 2. The values for which the political entity was established to pursue.

Regulation: 1. A law not enacted by a legislature, nor the outcome of a dispute resolved by adjudication judge or judges or a person or persons acting in a judge-like capacity, but issued by a government agency so authorized by a statute enacted by an elected representative body. 2. Any statement issued by a government agency clarifying the meaning or guiding the implementation of a statute enacted by a legislature.

Respondeat superior: Literally, "let the master answer," the principle under which the employer is held legally responsible for the actions of the employee.

Rule/"regulation": Used interchangeably with the second definition. Usage varies, however. For example, the Michigan Civil Service Commission distinguishes rules as having "the force and effect of law," from regulations, which "implement the rules issued by the commission." [http://www.michigan.gov/mdcs/0%2C1607%2C7-147-6877---%2C00.html, 2015]

Statute: A law enacted by a legislature (see "legislation").

Tort: Other than in the context of a contract, a wrongful act or violation of rights for which a civil remedy, usually money damages, may be had, whether or not the act or violation may also engender criminal liability.

Ultra vires: Literally, beyond strength, power, or force; used here to mean outside or beyond the legal power of a particular agency or agent (generally, of government).

Non-Delegation Doctrine: "Agencies Cannot Make Laws" (Ostensibly)

WHY STUDY ADMINISTRATIVE LAW?

Citizens and students who want to understand American government tend to look first to courses on constitutional law or to Congress. But agencies execute most of the governing. So, in order to understand most of our government, look at administrative law, the law that sets forth the logic of agency power: the sources of that power, and the limits of that power.

Many readers of this book will spend a good part of their professional lives working in government agencies. If you are among that group, you will find that administrative law explains many of the procedures you follow and creates the framework of law that structures much of your work. Indeed, you may find yourself turning to administrative law to explain why you cannot do something your political leadership has commanded.

Government operates primarily through agencies. When you attend a public school or university, pay your taxes, get protected or arrested by the police, look for "grade A" beef or eggs, you are interacting with the work of a government agency. Since administrative agencies serve so many different purposes—from delivering the mail; to fighting wars; to issuing parking tickets; to educating children; to sending social security checks—they necessarily vary in structure. Except for a small minority mandated by the U.S. Constitution, a state constitution, or the charter of a local government, these agencies owe their origin to laws enacted by Congress, state legislatures, or local legislative bodies (i.e., "statutes"). All agencies have some leadership format: a Cabinet secretary, a director, a commissioner, or some other officer or group of leaders, like a board or a commission. Most state and federal agencies employ civil servants who may have done well on merit examinations or survived some other kind of competitive process, and enjoy some degree of job protection under civil service laws that, for example, prevent them from being fired solely to make room for political patronage hires. All have units that perform executive functions, for instance any of the tasks listed at the beginning of this paragraph, among thousands of other tasks. Sometimes, the leadership of the agency devises rules ("regulations") to clarify or implement the mandate of the legislation originally empowering the agency; often an office of counsel or another unit of the agency will prepare such regulations. Many agencies also have units that hear and resolve arguments ("adjudications") between the executive personnel of the agency and individuals, businesses, or other entities who challenge their decisions.

One way or another, elected executive officials, such as presidents, governors, county executives, and mayors appoint agency leaders, and usually can replace them as well, giving those officials power and influence they can exercise over those agency leaders. Elected legislators can enact, repeal, and amend the legislation that empowers the agencies. Citizens who may feel that they have been abused can appeal agency adjudicative decisions. Citizens, businesses, and other government officials may also bring the judicial power to bear on questionable agency rulemaking or other agency actions, which often entails using the federal Administrative Procedure Act (APA), first enacted in 1946 and amended often thereafter. In later chapters, we explore in detail how the APA requires agencies to adhere to certain principles of fairness and due process in their adjudications, to a lesser extent in rulemaking, and to an even smaller extent in their executive functions. Every state also has an administrative procedure act, usually mirroring, at least to some extent, one of the Model State Administrative Procedure Acts (MSAPAs), especially that of 1961. Later chapters include frequent reference to the 2010 MSAPA, and one can presume that over time more states will adopt provisions of this more current MSAPA.

Survey results released in 2010 showed that about a fifth of American adults "faced a legal issue that could have involved hiring a lawyer" in the past year.[1] Another statistic is that less than half of American adults have "contacted a U.S. Senator or Representative" between 2004 and 2008[2]; however, virtually every adult American deals with government agencies many times a year.

While Congress in recent years[3] enacts three or four hundred bills each two-year session, and Pew Research suggests even fewer are meaningful,[4] federal agencies issue ten times as many rules and regulations in the same period.[5] Internal Revenue Service regulations determine far more decisions on individuals' tax returns (albeit usually smaller decisions), than Internal Revenue Code provisions enacted by Congress. National Labor Relations Board (NLRB) rulings determine the outcome of thousands more labor cases than the National Labor Relations Act itself.[6] A federal statute that is four pages limits compensation to executives of financial institutions "bailed out" in 2008; yet, there are 123 pages of Treasury Department regulations in the *Federal Register* detailing those limitations.[7]

The federal courts decide about 400,000 cases a year.[8] One law professor has claimed that "federal agencies complete more than 939,000 adjudications" annually, while "federal judges conduct roughly 95,000 adjudicatory proceedings, including trials."[9] The Social Security Administration alone completes about twice as many hearings in an average year as all the federal courts put together.[10] At the state government level as well, agencies generate far more rules and decisions than courts or legislatures.

The point is that agencies, not courts or legislatures, are responsible for most of the governance in the United States (as well as in other nations). For any citizen, and especially for citizens who look toward careers in government, administrative law answers many fundamentally important questions[11]: By what right do government agencies exercise power? What are the sources of their powers, and the limits on those powers? If they exceed those limits, what can citizens do about it?

At its core, administrative law is about basic value conflicts: fairness versus efficiency versus representativeness. Do you want to complain that the bureaucracy moves so slowly that it is driving you out of business, or do you want to complain that it does not give you a sufficient chance to prove that you are right? Do you want your taxes to go up, or your Social Security check or Medicare payments to go down so that government can afford the personnel cost of giving everyone an opportunity to fight agency decisions in court; or do you want to be told that you don't meet the technical legal requirements to get a court to listen to your argument about why the government agency should not have done what they did to you? Do you want all policy judgments to be made by your elected representatives—people you can fire if they don't represent your point of view—or do you want the bureaucracy to continue to operate? How much representative democracy do you need? Let's start with the last question.

THE NON-DELEGATION DOCTRINE

The second sentence of the Constitution reads "All legislative powers herein granted shall be vested in a Congress of the United States, which shall consist of a Senate and a House of Representatives."[12] Therefore, in effect in a document agreed to by their representatives in 1789, the people of the United States said "The first rule is that Congress does the lawmaking."

Also in 1789, however, Congress said that veterans' benefits should be based on service in the Revolutionary War "under such regulations as the President of the United States may direct."[13] Immediately, this produced certain problems: what if the veteran had been hurt tripping over a sack of flour, off duty, not in uniform? Congress did not have the time to pass a different law for each such question; soon, judges realized that they also had too many other things to do.[14] In 1820, after the press had exposed various scandalous abuses, Congress finally fully handed such decisions to the Secretary of War.[15] A bureaucrat began making policy decisions.

Theory versus Practice

But, didn't this contradict the principle that Congress was supposed to do the lawmaking? The Secretary, and then his clerks, began to make rules as to who was eligible for veterans' benefits and who was not. This would seem to have been in direct violation of the 1789 constitutional agreement that Congress would make the rules, and "the Government of the United States, or . . . any Department or Officer thereof,"[16] would merely carry them out.

The people gave up their own power to Congress to make laws. They elect Congress to represent them, and can replace Congress every two years (with one-third of the Senate also replaceable every two years). If they don't like what their representatives in Congress do, they can replace them. But, if Congress gives its power to someone else (i.e., a civil servant, a bureaucrat, a clerk), the people might not even know, and certainly cannot fire them the way they could "fire" Congress. Clearly, the people have less control over this third party than they have over Congress.[17]

Thus, legal tradition says that when the people choose to give, or "delegate," their powers to someone, that individual or entity cannot then give the powers to someone else. This dates back to ancient Roman law, and passed down to John Locke in the 17th century. The Supreme Court first cited the principle, presumably based on Locke, in a decision in 1831.[18] Consequently, how could Congress so casually have delegated its power to make rules to the president, or in reality to his agents in the War Department?

This seemingly nit-picking debate, which has provided grist for the administrative law mill for a long time, in fact has serious reverberations, and probably lacks a fully satisfactory resolution.

The obvious response is that Congress could not possibly make every petty rule needed to guide every bureaucratic decision. The theory used to justify the grant of authority to agencies to make such rules was that agencies were merely to "fill up the details"[19] (i.e., that Congress would set out the broad policies with its legislation, and that agencies' rules would simply fill in the necessary administrative details).

It was not such a long step from the theory that agencies could "fill up the details" to the theory that Congress could actually delegate legislative authority so long as it prescribed "standards" to limit the agency's use of the power. The Interstate Commerce Commission (ICC) imposed certain requirements on a railroad company undergoing reorganization before they allowed it to issue stock. The Court, once again, gave lip service to the non-delegation doctrine, but this time explicitly okayed actual delegations as long as they were limited by a "prescribed standard," such as if the ICC's enabling statute said that it should protect the public against financial failure by railroads.[20]

Broader Delegations

The Court approved broader and broader delegations imposing such "limits" or so-called standards as prohibiting "unfair" competition,[21] and regulating the airwaves as the "public convenience, interest or necessity requires."[22] With the vast expansion of federal agency power in the National Industrial Recovery Act (NIRA), in 1935 the Court at last saw standards it found impermissibly broad. In *Panama Refining Co. v. Ryan*,[23] the Court rejected as no real restriction the "limit" on the President's power to ban interstate shipments of oil produced in violation of state law to when the oil was shipped in an "unfair competitive practice" or failed to "conserve natural resources." Justice Cardozo, dissenting, pointed out broader delegations the Court had permitted.[24]

But, no one dissented in *Schechter Poultry Corp. v. United States*, famously known as the "sick chicken" case.[25] NIRA gave the President the power to prescribe "codes of fair competition" for any industry if the President thought the industry's own code was anticompetitive, or the power to approve industry codes. Under NIRA's Live Poultry Code for the New York City area, wholesale chicken dealers were not allowed to let their customers (butchers and retailers) select individual chickens; rather, they were required to accept whichever chickens came out of the coops.[26] The Schechter brothers were charged with criminal offenses (!) for permitting their customers to select individual chickens and thereby avoid buying sick ones. They challenged the constitutionality of Congress giving the President the power to tell them how to sell chickens. (In reality, dominant forces within industries often wrote codes to their own liking, with New Deal officials often unable to monitor or even understand the implications of some of these types of codes). The Poultry Code, for example, favored wholesalers over retailers. (The Schechters were trying to attract retailers with the fairer deal that they had historically offered.[27])

Justice Cardozo, concurring this time, agreed that here Congress had given the Executive, in effect, a "roving commission to inquire into evils and then, upon discovering them, do anything he pleases."[28] Since the President, on recommendation of a trade association, could impose codes that could do "anything that Congress may do within the limits of the Commerce Clause for the betterment of business," Cardozo agreed that "This is delegation running riot. No such plenitude of power is susceptible of transfer."[29]

In the second and last time the Supreme Court threw out a delegation of power to the federal executive, Joseph Schechter and his brothers, chicken dealers from Brooklyn, had overturned the cornerstone of the National Industrial Recovery Act.[30]

AGENCY POWER POST-*SCHECHTER*

Since *Schechter*, no congressional delegation of power to a government agency has been held too broad, although at least some of the delegations that have been upheld arguably have been at least as broad as the delegation in *Schechter*. In *National Broadcasting Co. v. United States*,[31] the Court upheld the Communications Act of 1934, which gave the Federal Communications Commission (FCC) the power to grant broadcast licenses "if the public convenience, interest, or necessity will be served thereby." The Court claimed that if the standard were more specific, the FCC could not accomplish the task intended for it. How such a standard could serve as an "intelligible principle," the Court did not explain. In *FCC v. RCA Communications, Inc.*,[32] the Court went even further when the FCC attempted to figure out the policy direction Congress wanted, and therefore based a decision "in favor of competition." The Court actually objected to the FCC's effort to determine congressional intent, scolding the FCC for failing to rely on its own judgment instead! Apparently, not only did Congress not need to supply a guiding principle, the agency need not even attempt to discern one.

Delegation to a Private Organization

The Court has never explicitly backed away from a 1936 decision rejecting a congressional delegation of power to a private organization, *Carter v. Carter Coal Co.*,[33] despite the fact that outsourcing of formerly government work has meant in reality that plenty of policy decisions affecting the public are now made by private entities.[34] The private identity of the recipient of delegated power seems to make the delegation worse, but "if legislative standards exist, the individual's private status does not come into play."[35] Rather, the test of constitutionality should be: first, whether the government (Congress *or* the president) has granted powers whose extent, importance, or nature exceed an appropriate private role; and second, "whether the actors in question are subject to enough governmental checks to guard against arbitrary or self-serving conduct."[36] As "the Constitution does not authorize private parties to exercise decisional authority over their peers," if the delegation fails these tests, it should be struck down."[37]

State courts have generally been somewhat more willing to strike down statutes as violating the non-delegation doctrine, as noted in a leading Texas case, *Texas Boll Weevil Eradication Foundation Inc. v. Lewellen.*[38] Beyond informative *dicta* as to delegations to government agencies, the Texas decision also offered tests to determine whether a statute violates the prohibition against delegating government powers to a private entity: (1) Does the government exercise significant review power over the entity's decisions? (2) Are the interests of the affected public represented in the decision-making process? (3) Does the entity enforce its decisions against individuals? (4) Do the entity's interests conflict with those of the public? (5) Can it establish or impose criminal penalties? (6) Is the delegation broad or narrow? (7) Does the entity enjoy special expertise for its assigned role? (8) Does the delegation include guidelines or standards channeling the entity's behavior?[39] Federal courts should perhaps consider applying the Texas tests as well.

Ultra Vires: "Outside the Power"

And despite occasional obituaries to the contrary,[40] the non-delegation doctrine lives on. In *Kent v. Dulles*, the Court held that Congress did not really mean to give the Secretary of State unlimited power to withhold passports on the basis of "beliefs or association," because that would have violated both the non-delegation doctrine and the Fifth Amendment right to liberty.[41] In a 1980 Supreme Court decision, Justice Stevens opined that if a safety standard allowed the Secretary of Labor to limit benzene without a meaningful quantitative showing that it was dangerous, then the statute "might be unconstitutional under the Court's reasoning in *A.L.A. Schechter Poultry Corp. v. United States* [citation omitted] and *Panama Refining Co. v. Ryan* [citation omitted]. A construction of the statute that avoids this kind of open-ended grant should certainly be favored."[42] Justice Rehnquist, concurring, argued that the statute did not justify the majority's interpretation, that it therefore clearly violated the non-delegation doctrine, and that the Court should therefore have invalidated it on that basis, not reinterpreted it.[43]

State courts have invoked the non-delegation doctrine to strike down statutes far more often than federal courts, but such use of the doctrine is in decline even at the state level.[44] More typically, state courts sidestep the non-delegation doctrine, as did the Supreme Court in *Kent v. Dulles*, on the argument that the underlying statute would be overbroad if it allowed for the particular rule the agency had issued. The court then called the agency's action "*ultra vires*," or "outside the power" given to the agency.

Case in Point: New York City Ban on Sugary Drinks

For example, when Michael Bloomberg was Mayor of New York City, he seems to have felt a heavy responsibility for safeguarding the health of the people of his city. Thomas Farley, appointed by Mayor Bloomberg as his second Commissioner of Health and Mental Hygiene, strongly supported the Mayor's efforts in this regard. Bloomberg and Farley persuaded the New York City Council to restrict smoking—even outdoors, on public beaches, and in public parks.[45] Apparently pleased with the progress the City had made in reducing that major cause of illness, Bloomberg decided to take on what was becoming known as "the obesity epidemic," aiming his influence at one of its most publicized causes, sugary drinks. First, in 2009 and again in 2010 he sought a state tax on such drinks,[46] but the Legislature refused to enact it. Then, in 2011, he tried to persuade the federal government to prohibit the use of food stamps to purchase them, but failed.[47] Finally, in May, 2012, he proposed to ban the sale of sugary drinks of 16 ounces or more in any establishment subject to health inspections by the City of New York.[48] The New York City Board of Health adopted his proposal four months later, in the face of a huge and expensive public relations campaign against it by the soda industry.[49] The regulation did not cover grocery stores and convenience stores, since the City Board of Health has no jurisdiction over such establishments. Had the State legislature or the New York City Council been amenable to a law banning the sale of large sugary drinks, of course they could have included all sources.

The Court of Appeals, New York's highest state court, invalidated the regulation as beyond the agency's powers.[50] Using a four-part test, it found that the agency had violated three of those parts, which was enough for the court to strike it down. The regulation's "Portion-Cap Rule" prohibited the sale of a sugary drink in a container that can hold more than sixteen ounces of liquid, and defined "sugary drink" to exclude beverages with certain ingredients, such as those that are more than fifty percent milk or milk product. The court first explained that the Board of Health cannot make laws, but can only issue regulations carrying out laws that the City's lawmaking body, the City Council, has enacted. Then, it applied the first part of the test: did the regulation merely relate to the Board of Health's powers under the New York City Charter to advance public health? The court held that by restricting portions instead of banning the drinks, the Board of Health was factoring in "the economic consequences associated with restricting profits by beverage companies and vendors,"[51] among other policy choices, and was thus making policy on its own, not just exercising the health-related powers it had been given. Furthermore, in limiting consumer choice the regulation reflected a policy choice on a range of compromises between personal autonomy and health protection. The court recognized that this test posed difficulties, in that almost any health-related regulation would also have *some* other social and economic consequences; for example, the non-health-related consequences of some health regulations would be relatively minor, but the economic consequences of this regulation were significant. Even so, failing this test alone might not invalidate a regulation.

Accordingly, it then turned to the second factor: had the City Council or the State legislature enacted any laws that the regulation might reasonably be thought to have implemented? Again, the court recognized some difficulty: the very reason legislatures establish agencies is to allow them to determine the detailed choices needed to achieve broad policy goals. Those detailed choices may be hard to differentiate from the kind of policy choices that elected legislators should be making themselves. But neither the City Council nor the State legislature had enacted any laws whatsoever concerning the ingestion of sugary beverages: "Devising an entirely new rule that significantly changes the manner in which sugary beverages are provided to customers at eating establishments is not an auxiliary selection of a means to an end; it reflects a new policy choice,"[52] said the court. Thus, the regulation failed the second test as well.

The court adopted the analysis of the reviewing court below, the Appellate Division of New York's Supreme Court, in noting that the City Council and the State legislature had "repeatedly tried to reach agreement in the face of substantial public debate and vigorous lobbying by interested factions."[53] In the face of their failure to do so, the Board of Health, in deciding to issue its regulation, ignored the clear message of lawmakers that regulation in this regard was unwarranted. In general, the law remains that legislative failure to enact legislation is not a statement of policy,[54] but when circumstances suggest that the legislature has affirmatively decided against enacting a particular law at present, courts may treat that apparent decision as a factor in determining whether an agency acted *ultra vires* in issuing a regulation.

The court suggested that the regulation might fail the test of the fourth factor as well, specifically whether the regulation at issue reflected the exercise of the agency's special technical competence, in light of "the fact that the rule was adopted with very little technical discussion."[55] However, it regarded analysis under that factor as unnecessary, since the regulation failed the basic test on which the various factors merely shed light: "an administrative agency exceeds its authority when it makes difficult choices between public policy ends rather than finds means to an end chosen by the Legislature. . . ."[56]

The decision illustrates the greater willingness of state courts to invoke the non-delegation doctrine, even in using it to interpret legislation narrowly to find that executive action exceeded a legislative mandate. For example, however unlikely it might be for the Surgeon General to attempt to ban the sale of large sugary drinks nationally; if that had occurred, it would be equally unlikely that the Supreme Court would invoke the non-delegation doctrine to invalidate the ban.

GIVING AGENCIES JUDGE-LIKE POWERS

Giving agencies judge-like powers, like giving them rulemaking powers, also raises a question of legitimacy. When Congress gives agencies adjudicative powers, it is not exactly delegating, because Congress itself has no such power (except under unusual circumstances like impeachment). But, at least since 1828, the Supreme Court has recognized the power of Congress to include such adjudicative duties within an agency's general mission when it explained that such agency "Courts" are not under Article III (the Judiciary article) of the Constitution, but Congress can create them "in the execution of those general powers which that body possesses. . . ."[57]

More generally, the Court allows Congress to vest such powers in agencies when "Government sues in its sovereign capacity to enforce **public rights** [emphasis added] created by statutes within the power of Congress to enact."[58]

The Constitution says "The Trial of all Crimes, except in Cases of Impeachment, shall be by Jury . . .," so agencies cannot impose criminal penalties.[59] They can seek and impose civil penalties. When Congress has enacted a law that imposes criminal penalties for violation of rules issued by an agency, because the agency is not an Article III court, it cannot hear cases under that statute. For criminal prosecution the agency must refer such cases to the Department of Justice, and a federal court may impose a sentence of imprisonment if it finds an individual guilty.[60] The Department of Homeland Security, through its Immigration and Customs Enforcement bureau, may seem to be an exception, but for technical reasons, it is not: it can "detain" people for years, but not "imprison" them. . . . [61]

Even at the state level, generally agency hearing officers do not exercise contempt powers, so state agencies, like federal agencies, cannot impose deprivations of liberty on citizens.[62]

CONCLUSION

Agencies do operate within some limits. But, under the practical constraints of time and expertise Congress often cannot reach the level of detail necessary to clarify what it wants agencies to do; and often, when it can, it *chooses* not to do so in order to avoid arousing the antagonism of one faction or another. American law has evolved to track the consequent sometimes steady and sometimes dramatic increase in the power of agencies over the generations, and has accommodated the necessary shift of power away from direct control by the legislative branch, especially at the federal level and even in the states. For government to provide the services most Americans appear to want—even those who complain about the growth of government[63]—inevitably Americans must sacrifice a significant degree of representativeness.

WHAT AM I SUPPOSED TO DO?

State Public Health Council and Smoking Restrictions: Interpretation of a Statute's Absence

Let's say you were the director of your state's Public Health Council in the mid-1980s. By then, the public had been well informed that secondhand smoke from cigarettes contributed to lung cancer and other diseases. Your state legislature had, many years earlier, authorized the Public Health Council to issue and enforce such regulations as would improve the health of the citizens of the State. In the 1970s, the legislature had restricted smoking in some public places like libraries and museums. But, in the past few years, some liberal Democratic members of the State Assembly, passionate crusaders against the ill effects of tobacco smoke on health, had introduced legislation that would have greatly extended restrictions on smoking to many other workplaces and indoor areas. In the Assembly, with a Democratic majority, for several years in succession such legislation was reported out of committee to be voted on by the entire body. However, perhaps because of the influence of lobbyists for the cigarette manufacturers, and lobbyists for the bar and restaurant industry who thought such restrictions would keep some customers away, the bill was soundly defeated with a combination of Republican and conservative Democratic Assembly members. In the other House, the State Senate, the Health Committee refused to report the bill to the floor for a vote.

You are well aware that the Governor, who appointed you, supported the legislation, but would be even more pleased to see the change in law made by his administration—more specifically, by the agency you run—rather than by the legislature. The Governor surely would like to get credit for protecting the health of the public in this manner.

A well-established principle of statutory interpretation—perhaps more appropriately denominated as a principle of "non-statutory interpretation"—holds that legal inferences should not be drawn from legislative inaction on a piece of legislation.[64] That is, too many diverse reasons could explain the failure of a legislature to enact a law so that such failure cannot be the basis for assuming a particular motive like antipathy to the substance of the bill. For example, most of the opposition to a bill might come from legislators who thought it did not go far enough, and didn't want its enactment to "take the wind out of the sails" of the support for a stronger law.

Therefore, should you, as the Public Health Council director, draft, propose, and promulgate a regulation carefully balanced to take into account the reasonable concerns of bar and restaurant owners that would require restaurants that can seat more than fifty people to establish smoke-free areas for customers who want to avoid tobacco smoke?

From a practical point of view, going forward with the regulation might seem the wiser course. You would probably please your boss, the Governor. The lobbyists would have to concede that you made an effort to accommodate their concerns in a reasonable way, and in any event, while they can complain, their actions have far less practical impact on you than they might have on legislators. The legislators who opposed the legislation themselves might object on principle, but so long as someone other than themselves annoyed the lobbyists, their friendly relationships with the lobbyists would remain undisturbed. This does not seem the kind of policy decision that might enrage the legislature enough for it to cut your agency's funding or narrow its jurisdiction. Of course, you would probably please the legislators who supported the legislation. And in terms of your own peace of mind, advancing public health would give you satisfaction—the very kind of satisfaction you wanted when you sought this job in the first place.

What are your legal responsibilities? The enabling legislation for your agency encourages such legislation, so arguably the legislature has almost commanded you to go forward. You report to the Governor, know that he would want you to issue the regulation, and therefore arguably have some duty to advance his policy agenda, since the public chose to elect him. The courts, in explaining that agencies should not draw legal inferences from legislative inaction, seem to have given you the green light, despite the legislature's rejection of tighter restrictions on smoking.

So why do you hesitate?

Something about the non-delegation doctrine bothers you. You know very well that the courts, for decades, have mostly treated it as a dead letter, allowing Congress and state legislatures to give agencies extremely broad powers—as your state legislature gave you: what *can't* you do in the name of advancing the health of the citizenry?

But, on some level you know that in a democracy, the people's elected representatives are still supposed to have the final word, not those who staff the agencies created and empowered by those elected representatives. And here, what the legislature did was not exactly "inaction": rather, it explicitly rejected the legislation several times, or at least one house did, while the other house did not give it a vote at all.

In *Boreali v. Axelrod*, the New York Court of Appeals justified your hesitation. The New York Public Health Council had not hesitated to issue such a regulation. The court said, "Unlike the cases in which we have been asked to consider the Legislature's failure to act as some indirect proof of its actual intentions [citations omitted], in this case it is appropriate for us to consider the significance of legislative inaction as evidence that the Legislature has so far been unable to reach agreement on the goals and methods that should govern in resolving a society-wide health problem . . . Manifestly, it is the province of the people's elected representatives rather than appointed administrators, to resolve difficult social problems by making choices among competing ends."[65]

Thus, your point about legislative inaction was a valid one, but the Court of Appeals thought that the facts of this case demanded a different result. The fact that one house of the Legislature voted down the legislation several times recently—legislation that was the model for the Public Health Council's regulation—at least suggested something outside the category of "legislative inaction."

The court also invalidated the regulation on the basis of a weaker argument, claiming that in limiting its reach only to certain restaurants, the Council had entered into the realm of economic policy, which the court thought exceeded the boundaries of its public health powers. The court did not find overbroad, or a violation of the non-delegation doctrine, the original legislative delegation of power to the Public Health Council. Rather, it found that in issuing the regulation, the Public Health Council had acted *ultra vires*, or "outside the powers" granted to it by the legislature by that delegation.

You should know that in the sugary drink case discussed above, the four-factor test used by the court came from *Boreali*.

In later years, the legislature itself enacted the kind of law it had earlier rejected; a law that the Public Health Council had tried to implement on its own. The lesson for public servants in government agencies may be one of patience: Notwithstanding the strength of your commitment to the particular policy goals of your agency, your overriding commitment must be to the fundamental principles of democratic self-government. The trial judge in *Boreali* may have overstated the matter somewhat, but his comment, criticizing those who would allow agency personnel to override legislative preferences when they are not explicit, but are nonetheless clear, still resonates for those of us who value representative democracy: "Defendants' view of the executive power would have us come full circle from the old days of rule by benevolent autocrat to a modern rule of the benign bureaucrat."[66]

PRACTICE PROBLEMS

PROBLEM 1: It is 1990, when the AIDS epidemic terrified much of the public. Imagine that Congress passed a law giving the director of the Public Health Service the power to adopt "appropriate and necessary" rules to contain the AIDS epidemic. Violation of any such rule is a criminal offense. The Director finds that at least a million Americans are HIV-positive; cannot estimate how many will develop the disease; and knows that sex and blood contact and needle-sharing spread AIDS. The Public Health Service promulgates the following regulation: Every federal job holder and job applicant must take a blood test. All who test HIV-positive must be fired or rejected. You are the Director's deputy. Does your oath to "support and defend the Constitution" require you to refuse to carry out his order for the firings and rejections on the basis that his directive is *ultra vires*, or "outside his powers," because the statute itself violates the non-delegation doctrine? Why or why not?

PROBLEM 2: A state statute permits cities of a certain size to transfer all parking violations out of Criminal Court into agencies they may establish, to lessen congestion in the courts and to expedite such cases. While prosecutors must prove guilt "beyond a reasonable doubt," agencies need only find liability by a preponderance of the evidence (and their rulings will be upheld by courts so long as the courts believe they are supported by the even weaker standard of "substantial evidence," a matter we explain more thoroughly in Chapter 9), and they may impose a penalty of up to $1,000 per violation. The Deputy Mayor, your boss, instructs you to take the necessary steps to create such an agency for your city. Should you object that the statute constitutes an unconstitutional delegation of power to an administrative agency?

ENDNOTES

1. *One in Five Americans Had a Legal Issue This Year That Could Have Involved Hiring a Lawyer,* Says New FindLaw.com Survey, (press release, *FindLaw* website, 1/6/10, http://company.find law.com/pr/2010/010510.lawyer.html).

2. Kathy Goldschmidt and Leslie Ochreiter, *Communicating with Congress: How the Internet has Changed Citizen Engagement* (based on survey research by Zogby International), (Washington, DC: Congressional Management Foundation, 2008, 10, http://nposoapbox.s3.amazonaws .com/cmfweb/CWC_CitizenEngagement.pdf). Some studies covering the same time period found that less than one-quarter of the public communicated with *any* federal government official within a year; Benjamin I. Page, Larry M. Bartels, and Jason Seawright, Democracy and the Policy Preferences of Wealthy Americans, 11 *Perspectives on Politics* 51, 69, n.19 (March 2013).

3. 460 bills in the 110th Congress (2007–2008), Mark Murray, 113th Congress Not the Least Productive in Modern History, *NBC News*, 12/29/13, http://www.nbcnews.com/politics/first-read/113th-congress-not-least-productive-modern-history-n276216; 383 in the 111th Congress, A Summary of the Record of the 111th Congress of the United States, *id.* and http://www.congress-summary.com/A-111th-Congress/Laws_Passed_111th_Congress_Seq.html; 283 in the 112th Congress, A Summary of the Record of the 112th Congress of the United States, Murray, *id.* and http://www.congress-summary.com/B-112th-Congress/Laws_Passed_112th_Congress_Seq.html; as of December 29, 2014, 296 in the 113th Congress, Murray, *id.*, accessed 1/13/15.

4. Apparently using different metrics, the Pew Research Center reported that the 110th Congress enacted only 300 bills, the 111th, 215, and the 112th, 151, and of those, 121, 72, and 41, respectively, were merely ceremonial; Drew DeSilver, Congress Continues Its Streak of Passing Few Significant Laws, *FACTANK*, Pew Research Center, 7/1/14, http://www.pewresearch.org/fact-tank/2014/07/31/congress-continues-its-streak-of-passing-few-significant-laws/, accessed 8/4/14.

5. "On average, Federal agencies and departments issue nearly 8,000 regulations per year." Regulations.gov: Your Voice in Federal Decision-Making, http://www.regulations.gov/#!siteData, Site Data, website, accessed 12/3/14; This figure probably includes interpretive and procedural rules, accounting for the disparity between it and the following figure: Between FY2003 and FY2012, the Federal Register published 37,786 final and interim final rules, an average of about 3,800 rules a year. U.S. Office of Management and Budget, 2013 Draft Report to Congress on the Benefits and Costs of Federal Regulations, 10, available at http://www.google.com/url?sa=t&rct= j&q=&esrc=s&source=web&cd=25&ved=0CDoQFjAEOBQ&url=http%3A%2F%2Fwww .whitehouse.gov%2Fsites%2Fdefault%2Ffiles%2Fomb%2Finforeg%2F2013_cb%2Fdraft_2013_ cost_benefit_report.pdf&ei=9mV_VKi9LMH2yQSxrYD4Bg&usg=AFQjCNGixbx1vHS1mvy8 TTopqOP_9do1bA&sig2=WR-P41kvLETkPuoF6jE1nQ&bvm=bv.80642063,d.aWw, accessed 12/3/14; The latter figure is similar to that estimated by Clyde Wayne Crews, Ten Thousand Commandments 2014, Competitive Enterprise Institute, available through http://cei.org/studies/ ten-thousand-commandments-2014, accessed 9/16/15; about "seven thousand rules and policy statements each year" as of 2009, according to Christine Harrington and Lief Carter, *Administrative Law and Politics*, 4th ed., (Washington, DC: CQ Press, 2009), 9; over one thousand "significant regulations in each of several two-year periods preceding 2011, Final Rules Issued by Year, Regulatory Studies Center, George Washington University, http://www.regulatorystudies.gwu .edu/images/pdf/04_20_12_annual_final_rules.pdf, not counting regulations with "an annual effect on the economy" of under $100 million a year or that do not raise certain other issues. Section 3(f) of Executive Order of the President 12866, Regulatory Planning and Review, 9/30/93, http://www.whitehouse.gov/sites/default/files/omb/inforeg/eo12866/eo12866_10041993.pdf, published in Federal Register Volume 58, Number 190, 10/4/93.

6. Daniel L. Feldman, *The Logic of American Government*, (New York: William Morrow & Co., 1990), 40 (citations omitted).

7. Cornelius M. Kerwin and Scott R. Furlong, *Rulemaking*, 4th ed., (Washington, DC: Sage/CQ Press 2011), 2.

8. The U.S. Supreme Court decides about 160 to 170 cases a year. Table A-1: Supreme Court of the United States—Cases on Docket, Disposed of, and Remaining on Docket at Conclusion of December Terms, 2008 Through 2012, available at Statistical Tables—Supreme Court, United States Courts website, http://www.uscourts.gov/Statistics/JudicialBusiness/2013/statistical-tables-us-supreme-court.aspx, accessed 1/13/15; The federal Circuit Courts of Appeals closed 55,803 cases in the year ending on June 30, 2014, a typical recent year. Table B, U.S. Court of Appeals—Cases Commenced, Terminated and Pending During the 12-Month Periods Ending June 30, 2013 and 2014, available at Statistical Tables June 2014, United States Courts website, http://www.uscourts.gov/Statistics/StatisticalTablesForTheFederalJudiciary/june-2014.aspx, accessed 1/3/15; The federal district courts disposed of 327,467 cases in the year ending on June 30, 2014. The total figure is the sum of the civil and criminal cases from the two different tables: Table C, U.S. District Courts—Civil Cases Commenced, Terminated and Pending During the 12-Month Periods Ending June 30, 2013 and 2014 and Table D, Criminal Cases Commenced, Terminated and Pending During the 12-Month Periods Ending June 30, 2013 and 2014, available at Statistical Tables June 2014, *id.*

9. Jonathan Turley, The Rise of the Fourth Branch of Government, 5/24/13, *The Washington Post*, http://www.washingtonpost.com/opinions/the-rise-of-the-fourth-branch-of-government/ 2013/05/24/c7faaad0-c2ed-11e2-9fe2-6ee52d0eb7c1_story.html, accessed 1/25/14; See also Administrative Decisions and Other Actions—by Agency, University of Virginia Library: Government Information Resources, http://www2.lib.virginia.edu/govtinfo/fed_decisions_ agency.html. Accessed 1/13/15.

10. Table 2.F9, Annual Statistical Supplement 2013, U.S. Social Security Administration Office of Retirement and Disability Policy website, http://www.ssa.gov/policy/docs/statcomps/ supplement/2013/2f8-2f11.html, accessed 1/13/15.

11. This is not to denigrate other fields of study in any way. Indeed, in a later chapter I argue strongly for serious engagement with constitutional values and tradition to enable administrative agency personnel to meet their responsibilities more fully.

12. Article I, Section 1.

13. 1 Stat. 95, Act of September 29, 1789, Chapter 24. The next year Congress enacted a law licensing "traders with the Indians" and requiring them to obey applicable laws, including, similarly, "such rules and regulations as the President shall prescribe"; 1 Stat. 137, Act of July 22, 1790, Chapter 33, cited on page 97 of the Attorney General's Report on Administrative Procedure, Senate Documents, no. 8, 77th Congress, 1st Session, (Washington, DC: Government Printing Office, 1941), cited in John Rohr, *To Run a Constitution*, (Lawrence, Kansas: University of Kansas Press, 1986), 167; and see page 253, n.1 and page 257, n. 59.

14. James D. Ridgway, The Splendid Isolation Revisited: Lessons from the History of Veterans' Benefits Before Judicial Review, 3 *Veterans Law Review* 135, 145 (2011), http://www.bva.va .gov/docs/VLR_VOL3/3-Ridgway-TheSplendidIsolationPages135-219.pdf; William Henry Glasson, *Federal Military Pensions in the United States*, (New York: Oxford University Press, 1918), 62, http://books.google.com/books?id=EsOEAAAAIAAJ&printsec=frontcover& source=gbs_ge_summary_r&cad=0#v=onepage&q&f=false.

15. Glasson, *supra* at 63–71.

16. Article I, Section 8, Clause 18 (the "Necessary and Proper" Clause).

17. At best, the next Congress, if it included a majority so inclined, could do the firing (by defunding or repealing the authority for the agency in question). Or, a sympathetic president, perhaps a new one, could simply fire the civil servant unless Congress had arranged for civil service protection shielding the civil servant. John Stuart Mill anticipated modern (and at least somewhat unfair) complaints about bureaucracy: "having no longer a mind acting within it, [bureaucracy] goes on revolving mechanically though the work it is intended to do remains undone." *Representative Government* [1861], forgottenbooks.org, 2008, Chapter 6: Of the Infirmities and Dangers to Which Representative Government is Liable, 73, http://books .google.com/books?id=JlwiZ19_TfMC&printsec=frontcover&source=gbs_ge_ summary_r&cad=0#v=onepage&q&f=false.

18. *Shankland v. Washington*, 30 U.S. (5 Pet.) 390, 395.

19. *U.S. v. Grimaud*, 220 U.S. 506, 31 S. Ct. 480 (1911).

20. *U.S. v. Chic., M., St. P. and P.R. Co.*, 282 U.S. 311, 324, 51 S. Ct. 159, 162 (1931).

21. *Federal Trade Commission v. Gratz*, 253 U.S. 421, 431, 40 S. Ct. 572, 576 (1920)

22. *Federal Radio Commission v. Nelson Bros. Bond & Mortgage Co.*, 289 U.S. 266, 273, 53 Sup. Ct. 627, 631 (1933).

23. 293 U.S. 388, 55 S. Ct. 241

24. Dissent, 293 U.S. at 433ff., 55 S. Ct. at 255ff.

25. See *Schechter Poultry Corp. v. United States*, *TheFreeDictionary* by Farlex, http://legal-dictionary .thefreedictionary.com/The+sick+chicken+case. At one time, I owned a tee shirt sold by the NYU bookstore displaying the name of the case and its citation over a picture of a chicken with a bandaged leg.

26. Article VII, § 14 of the Live Poultry Code, cited at 295 U.S. 495, 526, 55 S. Ct. 837, 842 (1935).

27. See discussion of the Schechter case in Amity Shlaes, *The Forgotten Man: A New History of the Great Depression*, HarperCollins ebooks, no date indicated, http://www.scribd.com/ doc/22737739/Amity-Shlaes-The-Forgotten-Man-A-New-History-of-the-Great-Depression, 214–225, 239–245.

28. Concurrence, 295 U.S. at 551, 55 S. Ct. at 852.

29. 295 U.S. at 552-3; 55 S. Ct. at 853.

30. I have a personal connection to the Schechter case. In the late 1970s, my widowed father and I lived together in Rockaway, Queens. From time to time he brought home roast chickens for dinner. Since I was teaching administrative law at the time, one day I noticed that the bag the chicken came in said "Schechter Poultry," with the address on Brighton Beach Avenue in Brooklyn. Out of curiosity, I stopped in one day after work. It was no longer a live poultry market, of course, but a store selling cooked chicken. I asked the lady behind the counter if, by any chance… She said "He's in the back." Joseph Schechter, probably in his nineties at the time, came out front. Someone had a camera, and a few weeks later I showed my class photographs of me with the man who brought down the National Industrial Recovery Act. Unfortunately, the pictures are lost in the mists of time.

31. 319 U.S. 190, 219, 63 S. Ct. 997, 1011 (1943).

32. 346 U.S. 86, 94, 73 Sup. Ct. 998, 1004 (1953).

33. 298 U.S. 238 (1936).

34. See., e.g., Daniel Feldman, The Legitimacy of Government Agency Power, 75(1) *Public Administration Review*, pp. 75–84, January/February 2015, DOI: 10.1111/puar.12279.

35. Harold Krent, The Private Performing the Public: Delimiting Delegations to Private Parties, 65 *U. Miami L. Rev.*507, 510–11 (2011).

36. 65 U. Miami L. Rev. at 538.

37. 65 U. Miami L. Rev. at 554.

38. *Texas Boll Weevil Eradication Foundation Inc. v. Lewellen*, 952 S.W. 2d 454, 468, 40 Tex. Sup. J. 523 (1997).

39. 952 S.W. 2d at 472.

40. See, e.g., William T. Gormley Jr. and Steven J. Balla, *Bureaucracy and Democracy*, 3rd ed., (Los Angeles, California: Sage/CQ Press 2013), 106: "a moribund tenet of administration law known as the nondelegation doctrine." In the very decision cited as support for this declaration of death of the doctrine, Justice Scalia wrote, "The scope of discretion § 109(b)(1) [the section of the Clean Air Act in question] allows is in fact well within the outer limits of our nondelegation precedents." *American Trucking Association v. EPA*, 531 U.S. 457, 474, 121 S. Ct. 903, 913 (2001). While the decision certainly can be cited as an example of the very wide limits the Court allows before it will find a violation of the non-delegation doctrine, quite clearly the Court continues claim adherence to it, and as I have noted elsewhere, wide limits are still limits.

41. *Kent v. Dulles*, 357 U.S. 116, 129–130, 78 S. Ct. 1113, 1119–1120 (1959).

42. *Industrial Union Department, AFL-CIO v. American Petroleum Institute*, 448 U.S. 607, 646, 100 S. Ct. 2844, 2866 (1980).

43. 448 U.S. at 671–688, 100 S. Ct. at 2878–2887.

44. Gary J. Greco, Survey: Standards or Safeguards: A Survey of the Delegation Doctrine in the States, 8 *Admin. L. J. Am. U.* 567–603 (Fall 1994).

45. Javier C. Hernandez, Smoking Ban for Beaches and Parks is Approved, *The New York Times*, 2/2/11, http://www.nytimes.com/2011/02/03/nyregion/03smoking.html, 7/8/14.

46. A.G. Sulzberger, Bloomberg Says a Soda Tax "Makes Sense," *The New York Times*, 3/7/10, http://www.nytimes.com/2010/03/08/nyregion/08soda.html?_r=0, accessed 7/8/14.

47. Patrick McGeehan, U.S. Rejects Mayor's Plan to Ban Use of Food Stamps to Buy Soda, *The New York Times*, 8/19/11, http://www.nytimes.com/2011/08/20/nyregion/ban-on-using-food-stamps-to-buy-soda-rejected-by-usda.html.

48. Michael M. Grynbaum, Bloomberg Plans a Ban on Sugary Drinks, *The New York Times*, 5/30/12, http://www.nytimes.com/2012/05/31/nyregion/bloomberg-plans-a-ban-on-large-sugared-drinks.html?pagewanted=all, accessed 7/8/14.

49. Michael M. Grynbaum, Health Board Approves Restriction on Sale of Large Sugary Drinks, *The New York Times*, 9/13/12, http://www.nytimes.com/2012/09/14/nyregion/health-board-approves-bloombergs-soda-ban.html, accessed 7/8/14.

50. *New York Statewide Coalition of Hispanic Chambers of Commerce v. New York City Department of Health and Mental Hygiene*, 2014 NY Slip Op. 4014, 2014 N.Y. LEXIS 1442 (June 26. 2014).

51. *Id.* at **6, *18.

52. *Id.* at **8, *22.

53. *Id.* at **2, *6–7.

54. *Clark v. Cuomo*, 66 N.Y. 2d 185, 486 N.E. 2d 794, 495 N.Y.S. 2d 936 (1985); *Flanagan v. Mt. Eden Gen. Hospital*, 24 N.Y. 2d 427, 248 N.E. 2d 871, 301 N.Y.S. 2d 23 (1969).

55. 2014 NY Slip Op. 4014 at **9, 2014 N.Y. LEXIS 1442 at *24.

56. *Id.* at **8, *23–4.

57. *American Insurance Company v. 356 Bales of Cotton*, 26 U.S. (1 Pet.) 511, 545, 7 L. Ed. 242, 257.

58. *Atlas Roofing v. Occupational Health & Safety Review Commission*, 430 U.S. 442, 450, 97 S. Ct. 1261, 1266 (1977).

59. Article III, Section 2.

60. *U.S. v. Grimaud*, 220 U.S. 506, 521, 31 S. Ct. 480, 484–5 (1911).

61. Deportation "has been consistently classified as a civil rather than a criminal procedure." *Harisiades v. Shaughnessy*, 342 U.S. 580, 594, 72 S. Ct. 512, 521 (1952); *Fong Yue Ting v. United States*, 149 U.S. 698, 730, 13 S. Ct. 1016, 1028–1029 (1893); Detention pending deportation would be classified as civil as well.

62. *Wright v. Plaza Ford*, 164 N.J. Super. 203, 218, 395 A. 2d 1259, 1266 (App. Div. N.J. 1978).

63. See, e.g., Press Release, Many Americans Ambivalent Over Laws Aimed at Healthy Living: Poll, *Harris Interactive*, 3/20/12, http://www.harrisinteractive.com/NewsRoom/PressReleases/tabid/446/ctl/ReadCustom%20Default/mid/1506/ArticleId/986/Default.aspx.

64. See, e.g., "congressional silence 'lacks persuasive significance,'" *Brown v. Gardner*, 513 U.S. 115, 121, 115 S. Ct. 552, 557 (1994), quoting *Pension Benefit Guarantee Corporation v. LTV Corp.*, 496 U.S. 633, 650, 110 S. Ct. 2668 (1990); "Legislative inaction is a weak reed upon which to lean in determining legislative intent [citation omitted]"; *Flanagan v. Mt. Eden Gen. Hospital*, 24 N.Y. 2d 427, 433, 248 N.E. 2d 871, 874, 301 N.Y.S. 2d 23, 28 (1969).

65. 71 N.Y. 2d 1, 13, 523 N.Y.S. 2d 464, 471 (1987).

66. *Boreali v. Axelrod*, No. 47-304-87 at 5 (Sup. Ct. Schoharie Co. 1987).

The Legitimacy of U.S. Government Agency Power[1]

T he first chapter described how citizens delegate their lawmaking power to Congress, and Congress delegates some of that power to agencies, although courts tried to find other ways than "delegation" to describe that grant of power. But, students of administrative law have discredited government agencies' claims to logical integrity and legitimacy on that basis, and have also discredited two other theories attempting to justify such power.[2] I propose two new justifications, in order to persuade you that the various theories, applied together, do indeed justify government agency power. The federal level has necessarily dominated the discussion, but the principles involved apply to state agencies as well. As noted in the previous chapter, however, courts have been more sanguine in applying the traditional form of non-delegation theory at the state level. In *Boreali v. Axelrod*, for example, the New York court even went so far as to weigh the Legislature's refusal to enact legislation as evidence supporting its decision to invalidate an agency regulation as an attempt to impose a policy decision inconsistent with the will of the Legislature.[3]

THE "TRANSMISSION BELT" THEORY[4]

School children think that the President is the "boss" of federal government employees, and citizens without the interest in or opportunity for further inquiry generally leave it at that. Somewhere between elementary school and a graduate degree, some people learn what we covered in the last chapter: that citizens lend their inherent lawmaking power to the representatives they elect to the House and Senate, and those representatives, in turn, transfer some power by creating agencies, defining their missions, and authorizing them to make decisions necessary to carry out their subscribed missions.

When I ask you to run an errand for me, I trust and entrust you, not someone else, to perform that task. I don't ordinarily authorize you to give the task to someone else. Thus, if the American people give Congress the task of lawmaking, Congress cannot then ask agencies to undertake that task[5] without some fancy footwork. Nevertheless, clearly agencies really do make laws with major policy implications. This makes it hard to say that only the people's elected representatives make laws.

Sometimes when the need for agency expertise and/or its inability or unwillingness to make hard choices prevailed,[6] Congress could not even manage to devise plausible constraints, and still the Supreme Court allowed the delegation of power.[7] To this day, the Court has never deemed a delegation of power to a federal agency as too broad,[8] with the exception of two famous decisions in 1935, *Panama Refining Co. v. Ryan* and *Schechter Poultry Corp. v. United States.*[9] The first "provided literally no guidance for the exercise of discretion, and the [second] conferred authority to regulate the entire economy on the basis of no more precise a standard than stimulating the economy by assuring 'fair competition.'"[10]

The idea that the lawmaking power of Congress can properly be transmitted to agencies, whether or not it is still called "lawmaking" power when agencies exercise it, has been characterized as the "transmission belt" theory for several decades now.[11] It has lost persuasive power as it became increasingly clear that agencies really do make laws with major policy implications, a realization that seriously undermines the notion that only the people's elected representatives legitimately exercise that power.

Early on, the Supreme Court defended the "non-delegation doctrine" by holding that agencies did not really make laws, but just "fill[ed] up the details" of the legislation Congress enacted to define their missions,[12] and the Court continued to preach that "a delegated authority cannot be delegated."[13] Woodrow Wilson, a leading political science professor before he became president, reflected that same view, arguing in 1887 that true lawmaking involves political decisions, which should be left to legislators, not bureaucrats: "Administrative questions are not political questions. Although politics sets the tasks for administration, it should not be suffered to manipulate its offices."[14]

However, bigger government, especially in "the middle fifty years of the twentieth century,"[15] made it harder to sell that fiction, so even before Roosevelt's New Deal, the Supreme Court acknowledged that agencies did and could make laws, so long as Congress, in letting them do so, set forth "intelligible principles" to limit such agency lawmaking.[16] Congress had authorized the Federal Communications Commission to grant broadcast licenses "if the public convenience, interest, or necessity will be served thereby;"[19] the Court upheld delegations barely even recognizable as "intelligible principles."

OTHER JUSTIFICATIONS FOR AGENCY POWER: EXPERTISE, PUBLIC PARTICIPATION, REPRESENTATIVE BUREAUCRACY

With Congress establishing agencies like the Federal Communications Commission, government under the New Deal had grown even bigger, so to protect the idea of representative democracy, theorists argued that agencies merely applied their technical expertise to the missions set by Congress, and therefore did not actually usurp the lawmaking power.[20] Public administration scholars supported this view by defending the "efficiency" of government agencies. This attempt to separate "administration" from politics had deep and old roots, back to Woodrow Wilson and our English forebears. Nonetheless, as with all such attempts, it was less than entirely persuasive. Too obviously, politics guided "expert" agency decision-making.[21]

So, some theorists came up with a third justification.

Section 4 of the Administrative Procedure Act[22] "guarantees the public the right to participate"[23] in rulemaking. Congress is not required to hold hearings or invite public debate prior to legislating on any given issue, but agencies before they can make rules have to give notice to the public, explain the factual basis they used to decide the rule, let the public comment on it, and explain if they disagree with the public comments.

Indeed, in the 1970s, environmental and consumer groups vigorously strove to involve themselves in agency decision-making. They got very involved in the public hearings where interested members of the public, including such groups, can present testimony.

Some theorists saw this development as the "democratization" of government agencies, infusing them with a new kind "representative" legitimacy.[24] But, this effort also ran into trouble since lobbyists representing well-organized economic interests could exercise far more influence than consumer and environmental groups more broadly reflective of the public. The more powerful interest group participants in this version of "agency democracy" did not serve to represent the public interest.[25]

In view of the weaknesses of the legal theories, public administration scholars argued that demographic diversity among government employees, rendering agencies more "representative" of the population, could help to justify agency power in a democracy. However, members of the same racial, religious, ethnic, or other demographic groups may have widely differing points of view, and may be subject to bureaucratic self-interest and/or regulatory capture just as if they shared demographic characteristics.[26]

Anton Chekhov, a doctor as well as a writer[27] once noted that when doctors offer many different remedies for the same disease, most likely none of them is any good and the disease is incurable.[28] As an analogy, his comment does not quite apply here, because in my view with the addition of two more theoretical justifications, the various theories together do sufficiently support the legitimacy of U.S. government agency power.

BUREAUCRATS' OATH AND AGENCY POWER

John Rohr,[29] a greatly respected professor at Virginia Polytechnic Institute until his death in 2011, in his classic writings on public administration,[30] taught us that the obligations of a public servant, whether bureaucrat or government employee, are not primarily to their immediate supervisor, nor to Congress or the President, nor even to the public, but to the Constitution. That is why each and every American government official takes an oath to "support and defend the Constitution of the United States."[31]

A former student of the late Professor Rohr worked at the Treasury Department. She delayed submitting an assignment because she had constitutional doubts about it. After several reminders, the Treasury Secretary finally demanded fiercely in a meeting in front of other high-level officials of the Department: "The President expects this to be done. I took an oath to support the President, and so did you." She said, "Actually, I took an oath to support the Constitution, which means the assignment you gave me should involve seeing what Congress and the courts have said about this matter." Professor Gary Wamsley, a colleague of Professor Rohr's, who told me the story, said "There was a stunned silence," and the young staff member remembered, "You could have heard a pin drop." At last, the Secretary growled, "Well, get on with it and get it in as soon as you can."[32]

Rohr's insight offers us considerable comfort. In our representative democracy, when bureaucrats tell us what to do, they govern legitimately if they act within constitutional limits, never mind that the Constitution says nothing about the bureaucracy.

Impact of Constitutional Culture

You might ask whether this answer "begs the question." What are those constitutional limits? Professor Laurence Tribe of Harvard Law School calls "the invisible Constitution" the unstated, important, if sometimes controversial points we have to infer from the constitutional commitments to the rule of law, republican form of government, and other basic premises.[33] This makes Rohr's advice even harder to interpret. How is the bureaucrat supposed to decide among the various values the Constitution brings to bear?

- Obeying the law, however clear or unclear it may be;
- Deferring to the President's responsibility (and his appointees' responsibilities) to execute the laws the way in accordance with their Election Day mandate; and among other things, guaranteeing liberty, equality, and property rights even against majority preferences?

As Rohr explained in an earlier work, however, the "soft power" (my phrase here, not his) of political culture matters greatly. When bureaucrats understand that their duty to the Constitution comes first, such understanding shapes their behavior. Rohr dispatched earlier skeptics with his vivid illustration from Vichy France: does anyone doubt that replacing the free French motto of "liberté, égalité, fraternité" with Vichy's "travail, famille, patrie" both reflected and triggered real changes in behavior?[34]

As a good illustration of an American agency head's loyalty to constitutional principle, Rohr offered Thomas Cooley, the first chair of the Interstate Commerce Commission. Congress had enacted a law empowering the ICC to force railroads to award money to a citizen who showed, at a hearing at the ICC, that the railroad's improper action had hurt the citizen. Congress clearly wanted the ICC to do so. Cooley, the leading constitutional scholar of his day, refused, because he thought it would violate the spirit of the Seventh Amendment, which requires a jury trial when "the value in controversy" in a civil lawsuit "exceeds twenty dollars."[35]

Even for public servants who may not be constitutional scholars, more consciousness of the oath would shape behavior. By itself, that doesn't guarantee that difficult bureaucratic decisions would be resolved more easily. But, as Rohr suggests, "suppose" that an agency bureaucrat must decide "whether to resist, support, or ignore" the following orders to facilitate

1. President Nixon establishing a system of warrantless wiretapping for purposes of national security; or

2. President Jefferson considering the Louisiana Purchase; or

3. President Lincoln suspending the writ of habeas corpus without congressional authorization; or

4. President Franklin Roosevelt planning during World War II to establish "relocation centers" for West Coast citizens of Japanese origin; or

5. President Truman seizing the steel mills during the Korean War.[36]

It is clear that the bureaucrat cannot "rigorously deduce[]" the correct behavior from the Constitution. However, by "the careful study of each of the situations given above," as one possible avenue toward "professional competence in the constitutional heritage," not necessarily a "lawyer's competence in constitutional law," provides "an initiation into a community of disciplined discourse in which one learns the ways of the constitutional heritage," leading the administrator toward "a *sense* of what is constitutionally appropriate."[37]

Bureaucrats as Balance Wheel

The constitutional oath enables bureaucrats to operate as an essential "balance wheel" for the three proper branches of government to which they owe loyalty: executive, judicial, and legislative. When duties toward those branches conflict, the bureaucrat's ultimate loyalty—to the Constitution—may determine which duty should prevail.[38]

Thus, the Constitution itself may legitimize bureaucratic behavior so long as administrative agency personnel try to understand how it limits their behavior, and try to stay within those limits to the best of their ability.

Such an effort goes beyond the literal requirements of the law: "the Constitution provides a floor, not a ceiling, for moral aspiration."[39] Rohr strengthened appreciation of the role of values and not just law that is reflected in and perpetuated by the American constitutional tradition. He identified liberty, equality, and property as the American "regime values."[40] These values combine variously to generate representativeness, the kind of fairness we know as due process, and freedom of expression.[41] Those values incorporate, but also go beyond specific points of law so that while the law prevents only government from restricting freedom of speech, American culture discourages such restrictions by private entities, like universities as well.[42] Similarly, the Constitution allows the detention of enemy combatants at Guantanamo "for the duration of the particular conflict in which they were captured,"[43] but President Obama referenced "our Constitutional ideals" as the justification for his plea to Congress to "lift[] the remaining restrictions on detainee transfers [so] we [can] close the prison at Guantanamo Bay."[44]

This Rohr-inspired theory may disappoint those who feel they need a clearer chain of logic. But, as Holmes famously said, "the life of the law is not logic, but experience."[45] Now, we must take a closer look at our underlying assumptions about law.

PEOPLE CREATE THE LAW THEY NEED

Many or most of us instinctively imagine law as coming from "the top, down," with Congress and the President, or whoever constitutes the ruling body or bodies in a society, issuing edicts for all to follow (i.e., all of us and our government agencies). The jurisprudential theory called "legal positivism" roughly reflects this view,[46] and the "transmission belt" theory we discussed earlier fits well with it. That is, we imagine law as coming from "the top, down," with Congress handing down laws for the agencies to follow.

As we have seen, however, the "transmission belt" theory suffers serious inconsistencies; law need not flow from "the top down." As the great American jurisprudential scholar, Lon Fuller,[47] taught us, law can emerge "from the bottom up."[48] Custom, he said, hardens into law. Man creates law to "facilitate [human] interaction,"[49] not to build some logically consistent theoretical structure.

Modern governments, not only that of the United States, generally had to give agencies broader and broader powers both to counterbalance increased concentrations of private power and to organize government's response to increasingly complex societies.[50] The U.S. Supreme Court, as we have seen, twisted itself into knots trying to accommodate administrative law theory to that reality. Fuller supplies a clearer explanation: law develops "out of the activity that sustains it."[51] In other words, people create the law they need.

In Fuller's view, the common law, over time, by trial and error gradually rejects bad ideas in favor of better ones, and builds an ethos "founded on reason, natural justice, and enlightened public policy."[52] Further, "those who actually created our republic and its Constitution [tried to make them] suit the nature of man."[53]

Constitutional Values and Managerial Values

Thus, our national culture adds to the regime values that Rohr identified, which may also be designated "constitutional values." There are two universal values: efficiency, in the sense of maximizing whatever goods have cultural priority; and security, in terms of safety from damage to persons or property either from domestic or foreign attack. For many generations, the geographic reality of two oceans meant that Americans could give less attention to security, and prosperity and the frontier meant that they could give less attention to economic efficiency. Therefore, what we define here as managerial values—values prioritizing efficiency and security—played a weaker role in the United States, but still played an important role.

Lon Fuller's jurisprudence warns against excessive tilts in either direction, managerial or constitutional. Fuller certainly would not have countenanced the weakening of constitutional values as exemplified by the unitary-executive theory of the Bush-Cheney administration of "virtually unlimited presidential power, unchecked by congressional or judicial oversight." At least at one point, this theory was apparently applied by the Obama administration as well in withholding surveillance program documents from Congress and from the FISA (Foreign Intelligence Surveillance Act) court.[54] Similarly, Fuller would have objected to the massive contracting out of government functions that also threatens those values.[55] Such developments undermine adherence to several of his eight canons of law's "inner morality," such as consistency and application as formulated.[56] Those eight principles significantly overlap constitutional principles of due process. Their excessive violation not only abandons fairness, but ultimately renders commands ineffective and thus not even "law."[57] Thus, for Fuller, loyalty to the constitutional oath would have to incorporate not only the law per se, but also the "regime values" that Rohr identified as intrinsic to the American constitutional tradition.

On the other hand, Fuller criticized what he saw as an excessive tilt toward constitutional values when judicial institutions attempted to deal with "managerial" problems, as in some instances of institutional litigation. Fuller noted that courts "declar[] rights, and rights to be meaningful must in some measure stand firm through changing circumstances."[58] But, institutional litigation can result in such massive dollar outcomes as to alter state budgets radically; for example, the Bryce Hospital litigation that threatened to divert sixty percent of Alabama's expense budget, excluding education, to the support of its mental patients.[59] Legislatures, at least in principle, can weigh the needs of every sector of a state and allocate benefits and burdens accordingly. Judges, in contrast, should not even take into account the needs of parties not before them. Therefore, "fairness," the essential judicial value, must in such circumstances bow to efficiency, the essential managerial value.

Fuller applied the same logic to agencies, in decrying the excessive judicialization of agency procedures. Due process, he argued, should not always define agency decision-making. He questioned the use of adjudication, with the attendant application of constitutional values, for allocative tasks, such as the Federal Communications Commission's adjudication of competing claims for radio and television frequencies.[60] "[I]n a baseball team," he noted, "no one has a right to left field, or at least no one ought to."[61] "Managerial direction," not adjudication, optimizes "polycentric problems" like baseball assignments, where it is properly utilized, and radio frequency assignments, where it should be.[62]

Fuller warned against an excessive tilt toward legal and constitutional values as evidenced in the 1970s, which may have damaged legitimacy as well, and laid the foundation for the lurch in the other direction beginning with the Reagan administration in the 1980s.

From the vantage point of the right, much of the work of legal aid programs, funded with public tax dollars, had been to represent groups and classes, such as the poor, minorities, migrant workers, single mothers, the mentally ill, tenants, and so on in what amounted to a government-sponsored use of the legal system to intervene in the private marketplace, to influence the political process, and to create and expand the rights revolution.[63]

This perception helped elect Ronald Reagan in order to reverse those trends, which indeed he did, arguing, for example, that "if there are individuals who suffer from our economic programs, they are people who've been dropped from various things like food stamps because they weren't morally eligible for them. Maybe some instances technically, but even in many cases, weren't even technically eligible for those programs [sic]."[64]

The Rohr-Fuller synthesis achieves a balance of values, resisting either extreme: the tilt toward constitutionalism or agency "judicialization" of the 1970s, and likewise, the current excesses of managerialism. To achieve that balance today would require a strong departure from the current bias in favor of managerial values. It would demand that bureaucrats respect law; constitutional values; American history, culture, and tradition; the felt needs of the public; security and efficiency. So many variables leave a great deal indeterminate and discretionary, but nonetheless set boundaries. For example, as an expression of commitment to representative democracy, the non-delegation doctrine "continues to operate as a loose constraint on agency action."[65] Custom, history and tradition—and most important, the needs of people—justify agency power, and constrain its behavior.

For an era when public confidence in government has reached new lows, Rohr and Fuller offer guidance for bureaucrats that can revitalize the legitimacy of government agency power.

WHAT AM I SUPPOSED TO DO?

Homeland Security Directive on Immigration Policy: Administrative Action, Questionable Legislative Support

You command the Immigration and Customs Enforcement (ICE) bureau of the Department of Homeland Security (DHS). In recent years, immigration policy has generated fierce debate among the American people and among its elected representatives in Congress. President Obama and some members of Congress have urged the enactment of comprehensive legislation to reform U.S. immigration law, including legislation known as "the DREAM Act" tailored to grant citizenship to people brought illegally to the United States by their parents when they were children. To be eligible, the children have to have lived here for many years, completed college or military service, and otherwise complied with the law.

The U.S. Senate voted down the DREAM Act on December 18, 2010, 55 to 41, although the House had passed it earlier that month.[66] Thus, the laws previously enacted by Congress continue to require that "if the examining immigration officer determines that an alien seeking admission is not clearly and beyond a doubt entitled to be admitted, the alien shall be detained for a proceeding under section 1229a of this title."[67] Regulations only permit deferred detention (pending deportation) on application for employment or Social Security benefits by individual aliens.[68] They do not authorize the Secretary of DHS to defer detention for any specified *category* of aliens, or in the absence of individual applications for such benefits, although historically detention pending deportation has been deferred "for small numbers of aliens in discrete distress pending statutory or foreign policy-mandated regulatory changes."[69] In any event, DHS has the statutory authority to exercise discretion by choosing not to deport individuals under certain conditions, but it is much less clear that it has the authority to exclude the deportation of any *category* of aliens, unless Congress explicitly designated such a category as "eligible for deferred action."

However, a Directive of June 15, 2012, *Exercising Prosecutorial Discretion with Respect to Individuals Who Came to the United States as Children,* issued by Secretary of Homeland Security Janet Napolitano, ordered ICE officers to initiate such deferral actions and, in some cases, employment authorization, to eligible aliens. To be eligible, they must have arrived in the United States before they were 16 years of age; not yet reached the age of 30; never been convicted of a serious crime; pose no threat to national security; lived in the United States continuously for at least five years and were here on the date the Directive was issued; and (1) are in school; (2) graduated from high school; (3) earned a G.E.D.; or (4) have been honorably discharged from the United States Armed Forces or Coast Guard. The Directive essentially implemented the substance of the DREAM Act, which Congress had refused to enact.

Does the Directive require you "to violate federal law, as detailed below, command[] ICE officers to violate their oaths to uphold and support federal law, violate[] the Administrative Procedure Act, unconstitutionally usurp[] and encroach[] upon the legislative powers of Congress, as defined in Article I of the United States Constitution, and violate[] the obligation of the executive branch to faithfully execute the law, as required by Article II, Section 3, of the United States Constitution"?[70]

Your supervisors have ordered you to obey the Directive. What should you do?

Crane v. Napolitano provides guidance for your answer. In reality, the director of ICE did not refuse to obey the Directive, but individual ICE agents did, at least one of whom was threatened with a three-day suspension for his refusal. The ICE agents brought suit against Secretary Napolitano, the director, and another Homeland Security official, seeking a preliminary injunction preventing the Department from forcing the agents to obey the Directive and from punishing them for refusal to obey it. When the federal district court first addressed the merits of the case (after having issued an opinion holding that the plaintiffs had standing to challenge the Directive[71]), it held in *Crane v. Napolitano* that "Because Congress has the power to legislate in the area of immigration law and has expressed its intent to require the initiation of removal proceedings against aliens when the requirements of [the applicable statute] are satisfied, the Court finds that [DHS] does not have discretion to refuse to initiate removal proceedings when the requirements of [the statute] are satisfied."[72]

However, the Court dismissed the case because the Civil Service Reform Act of 1978[73] requires that federal employees first challenge disciplinary actions against them in an administrative proceeding. The ICE agents would, of course, be able to appeal to the federal courts should they lose at the administrative level. The court's dismissal was "without prejudice,"[74] meaning that should the agents appeal the results of the administrative hearing, the appellate court will not treat the dismissal as a substantive judgment against the agents' arguments.

In its 2014 memorandum outlining "the scope of the Department of Homeland Security's discretion to enforce the immigration laws,"[75] the Department of Justice noted the well-established point of law that agencies have "the discretion to decide whether a particular violation of the law warrants prosecution or other enforcement action."[76] Since the federal government only has the practical ability to deport less than five percent of those illegally present in the United States, ICE has no choice but to exercise a measure of discretion. In its legislation appropriating funding for DHS, Congress required DHS to "prioritize the identification and removal of aliens convicted of a crime by the severity of that crime."[77]

Arguing that case law clearly "allowed immigration officials to exercise enforcement discretion at any stage of the removal process, including when deciding whether to initiate removal proceedings against a particular alien," the 2014 memorandum rejected the preliminary conclusion of the court in *Crane v. Napolitano*.[78] However, the memorandum subsequently noted that Congress specifically designated "certain classes of individuals [that] should be made 'eligible for deferred action.'"[79] Congress did not include in that designation, or any other, the class of individuals described in the DREAM Act. An ancient canon of law holds that a statute's inclusion of certain items in a list implies the exclusion of other items ("*expressio unius est exclusio alterius*").[80]

Further, the memorandum acknowledged that "the Executive cannot, under the guise of exercising enforcement discretion, attempt to effectively rewrite the laws to match its policy preferences," and in particular noted that "an agency's enforcement decisions should be consonant with rather than contrary to, the congressional policy underlying the statutes the agency is charged with administering."[81] But, when the memorandum noted that "unenacted legislation is an unreliable indicator of legislative intent," in the context of a bill passed by the House that would have barred funding for deferred action for the class of individuals described in the DREAM Act,[82] it signaled another problem. While a state court decision like *Boreali v. Axelrod*, which we reviewed in Chapter 1, struck down "no smoking" regulations issued by a state agency, of course the decision does not bind the federal courts or any other part of the federal government; nevertheless, its reasoning should be instructive. As the Senate has affirmatively rejected the DREAM Act, issuing the Napolitano directive, to similar effect, is "contrary to [] the congressional policy under the statutes the agency is charged with administering."[83] Under the *Boreali* theory, courts would invalidate the directive as *ultra vires*. Even under existing federal precedents, the constitutional legitimacy of the directive is extremely questionable. When enforcement of deportation has been suspended in the past, "Congress had authorized the immigrants in question to apply for green cards; the president merely suspended enforcement against their closest family members until they, too, could get their own cards."[84]

The Department of Justice memorandum attempts to rely on the responsibility of "immigration officials to evaluate each application for deferred action on a case-by-case basis" rather than "on a class-wide basis."[85] This seems utterly unrealistic in the ordinary administration of agency action: field-level agents customarily exclude from consideration anyone in the category designated from exclusion by their superiors.[86]

But, this might be the key to resolving your own dilemma in this matter. Perhaps as the director, you should insist that your ICE agents personally decide in each case whether or not to apply the directive. More likely, the directive is simply unconstitutional and you should direct them to ignore it. "The president surely has some power to withhold prosecution, but granting legal status and work permits to millions of people most likely exceeds his discretion."[87] More generally, government employees who wish to retain the confidence of the American people should follow the example of the ICE agents in *Crane v. Napolitano*. You may well sympathize with the immigrants who would benefit from the DREAM Act. I do. I wish the DREAM Act were law. But, it is not. The ultimate loyalty of government employees should be to the Constitution and its values. If government officials issue orders in violation of their constitutional responsibility to honor the separation of powers, unless the fate of the nation is at stake, or unconscionable results on the order of magnitude of genocide will ensue, you as a public servant have a duty to refuse such orders.

[*Note*: Two decisions by the Fifth Circuit Court of Appeals came in too close to the publication of this book for further treatment here. In one, *Crane v. Johnson*, 783 F. 3d 254, 255 (5th Cir. 2015), the court upheld the lower court's dismissal in *Crane v. Napolitano*, explaining that the plaintiffs there could not show that they were likely to be punished because the Directive ostensibly gave them discretion to decide whether or not to pursue deportation on a case-by-case basis. In the other, *Texas v. United States*, 2015 WL 648579 (5th Cir. 2015), Case No. 15-40238, decided May 26, the court reaffirmed that the earlier decision was not on the merits, i.e., it had not deemed deferred action under the Directive "an exercise of prosecutorial discretion" and therefore constitutional. It addressed a different and later directive, though, "Deferred Action for Parental Accountability," or DAPA, issued by Secretary Napolitano's successor, Jeh Johnson, ordering ICE agents to defer deportation proceedings for parents of children enjoying the benefits of the previous Directive. It held that as DAPA makes such individuals eligible for various government benefits, including Social Security numbers, it cannot be characterized as mere nonenforcement. "It is the affirmative act of conferring "lawful presence" on a class of unlawfully present aliens [endnote omitted]," and therefore "is not shielded from judicial review as an act of prosecutorial discretion.]

PRACTICE PROBLEM

In 1969, the president, with the advice and consent of the Senate, approved a treaty called the Vienna Convention on Consular Relations, which among other elements provided that if a country arrests a foreign national, the arresting country must inform the consular office of the country of origin, and must inform the detainee that he or she has a right to assistance from that consular office. The treaty also includes an "Optional Protocol," which empowers the International Court of Justice (ICJ, the judicial arm of the United Nations) to hear disputes arising under the treaty. The United States had agreed to be bound by the Optional Protocol.

However, in 1997 the Texas Court of Criminal Appeals affirmed the conviction for murder and the death sentence for a Mexican citizen, Jose Ernesto Medellín, who had lived in the United States since childhood. Only after his trial and conviction, Medellín raised a claim under the Vienna Convention arguing that since he had not been informed of his rights under the treaty, the United States could not impose his sentence without first giving him the opportunity to argue his case before the ICJ. The treaty requires that the foreign national be informed of his or her rights under it within three days of arrest, but he had confessed within three hours of his arrest. The Texas courts ruled that because he had not raised the issue before his trial, and because the failure to inform him of his rights under the treaty had no impact on his conviction and sentence, the treaty imposed no bar to the imposition of his sentence.

Medellín then went to the federal courts with a *habeas corpus* petition. The federal district court agreed with the Texas courts, and denied the claim. Then, the ICJ ruled that the United States had violated the treaty by failing to inform Medellín (and others) of their rights under its provisions. In response, by means of a letter from then-Secretary of State Condoleeza Rice to then-U.N. Secretary General Kofi Annan, the United States announced that it was withdrawing from the Optional Protocol. The United States Court of Appeals once again denied Medellín's claim, rejecting the ICJ's arguments and ruling that the treaty did not empower an individual to raise claims under it. The Supreme Court then agreed to hear the case. Before it actually heard the case, President George W. Bush issued a memorandum ordering state courts in the United States to follow the rulings of the ICJ in cases, including the Medellín case. Medellín subsequently reapplied for *habeas corpus* relief in the Texas courts, but the Texas courts again rejected his application.

Did the President's memorandum reflect an attempt to abuse his power, or should the Court weigh it in Medellín's favor as within the inherent foreign policy powers the Constitution bestows on the President? If you held a managerial position in a government agency responsible for enforcing the directives implied by the memorandum, for example in the Department of Justice, would your loyalty to the constitutional principle require you to refuse to carry out such directives, to insist on enforcing them, or neither?

ENDNOTES

1. Much of this chapter is taken from Daniel Feldman, The Legitimacy of United States Government Agency Power, 75(1) *Public Administration Review*, pp. 75–84, January/February 2015, DOI: 10.1111/puar.12279.
2. See, e.g., Philip Hamburger, *Is Administrative Law Unlawful?*, (Chicago, IL: University of Chicago Press, 2014); see also Cynthia R. Farina's nuanced critique in Statutory Interpretation and the Balance of Power in the Administrative State, 89 *Columbia L. Rev.* 452 (April 1989); and Richard Epstein, Why the Modern Administrative State is Inconsistent with the Rule of Law, 3 *NYU J. of Law & Liberty* 491 (2008). The present discussion highlights the same three usual justifications identified, among others, by Jerry Mashaw in his *Due Process in the Administrative State*, (New Haven, CN: Yale University Press, 1985).
3. 71 N.Y. 2d 1, 13, 523 N.Y.S. 2d 464, 471 (1987).
4. So designated by Richard B. Stewart, The Reformation of American Administrative Law, 88 *Harv. L. Rev.* 1667, 1675 (1975), where he criticized the conventional view of "agency as a mere transmission belt for implementing legislative directives."
5. J. Lyn Entrikin Goering, Tailoring Deference to Variety With a Wink and a Nod to Chevron: The Roberts Court and the Amorphous Doctrine of Judicial Review of Agency Interpretations of Law, 36 *Journal of Legislation* 18, 27 (2010), quoting *Touby v. United States*, 500 U.S. 160, 165 (1991): "Congress may not constitutionally delegate its legislative power to another branch of government." Roman law forbade the *procurator* from delegating his powers; Bracton, in the thirteenth-century, citing the Roman maxim *delegata potestas non potest delegari*, argued that the King must not "convey[]" his powers to another. Rabbi Isaac ben Sheshet Perfet, a fourteenth-century scholar from Spain, authored a Talmudic precept to similar effect, that "authority cannot be delegated by a body required to exercise its own discretion." Richard Hooker, writing in the sixteenth century, found the principle in Bracton's work and noted it; and John Locke, in the seventeenth century, took it from Hooker and applied it to the legislature. The framers of the American constitution are presumed to have taken it from Locke. Daniel L. Feldman, *The Logic of American Government*, (New York: William Morrow & Co.. 1992), 155–156 and note 43 at 258–9, citations omitted.
6. "[C]oncerns of 'political expediency' might lead Congress to leave discreet or difficult policy choices to regulators, while taking credit for more broadly worded symbolic legislative gestures." David S. Rubenstein, Delegating Supremacy? 65 *Vanderbilt L. Rev.* 1125, 1142 (2012).
7. The Communications Act of 1934 instructed the Federal Communications Commission to grant broadcast licenses "if the public convenience, interest, or necessity will be served thereby," hardly a plausible constraint on its decision-making in this realm. Addressing a challenge to the breadth of the delegation, the Supreme Court held that a more specific standard would have "frustrate[d] the purpose for which the Communications Act was brought into being," *National Broadcasting Co. v. United States*, 319 U.S. 190, 219, 63 S. Ct. 997, 1011 (1943). The Court went further when the FCC attempted to discern the policy direction set by Congress, and therefore based a decision "in favor of competition." The Court actually chided the FCC that it should instead have relied on its *own* "independent conclusion." *Federal Communications Commission v. RCA Communications Inc.*, 346 U.S. 86, 94, 73 Sup. Ct. 998, 1004 (1953).
8. "[I]n practice, even the most broadly drawn parameters are deemed sufficient to withstand constitutional challenge." Goering, *supra* at 28, citing as example *Whitman v. Am. Trucking Ass'ns, Inc.*, *supra*, 531 U.S. at 472–6, where the Court upheld as a sufficiently "intelligible

principle;" Section 109(b)(1), 42 U.S.C. § 7409(b)(1) of the Clean Air Act, authorizing the Environmental Protection Administration to set "ambient air quality standards . . . which in the judgment of the Administrator," based on statutory provisions that really provided no significant further guidance, "are requisite to protect the public health." 531 U.S. at 475–6, 121 S. Ct. at 913–914.

9. 293 U.S. 388, 55 S. Ct. 241and 295 U.S. 495, 55 S. Ct. 837.

10. *Whitman v. Am. Trucking Ass'ns, Inc.*, 531 U.S. 457, 474, 121 S. Ct. 903, 913 (2001).

11. See Stewart, *supra*.

12. The phrase came originally from *Wayman v. Southard*, 23 U.S. (10 Wheat) 1, 19 (1825), when Chief Justice John Marshall was actually justifying the delegation of some minor power by Congress to the Supreme Court itself, not to a federal agency. The Court quoted the phrase in the more relevant context, i.e., reviewing administrative agency action, in *U.S. v. Grimaud*, 220 U.S. 506, 517, 31 S. Ct. 480, 483 (1911).

13. *Shankland v. Washington*, 30 U.S. (5 Pet.) 390, 395 (1831), in Justice Joseph Story's decision for the Court.

14. The Study of Administration, 2 *Political Science Quarterly* 197, 210 (June 1887).

15. Goering, *supra* at 24 (2010); Rubenstein, *supra* at 1142: "the sheer size of the regulatory domain staked by Congress makes it difficult for Congress to decide all the regulatory details."

16. *J.W. Hampton & Co. v. United States*, 276 U.S. 394, 409 (1928); see discussion in Farina, *supra* at 479-487.

17. 293 U.S. 388, 55 S. Ct. 241 (1935).

18. 295 U.S. 495, 55 S. Ct. 837 (1935).

19. 319 U.S. 190, 219, 63 S. Ct. 997, 1011 (1943).

20. Goering, *supra* at 26; and see Thomas W. Merrill, Rethinking Article I, Section 1: From Non-delegation to Exclusive Delegation, 104 *Columbia L. Rev.* 2097, 2151–3 (Dec. 2004).

21. As a prominent example, the Supreme Court famously said, "While agencies are not directly accountable to the people, the Chief Executive is, and it is entirely appropriate for this political branch of the Government to make such policy choices . . ." *Chevron U.S.A., Inc. v. Natural Resources Defense Council, Inc.*, 467 U.S. 837, 865, 104 S. Ct. 2778, 2793 (1984). This was in the context of upholding the technical regulation issued by the Environmental Protection Administration (EPA) under the Reagan presidency. The EPA interpreted its authorizing statute in a manner much less favorable to environmental interests than would likely have been the case under previous administrations.

22. 5 U.S.C. § 553.

23. Goering, *supra* at 32.

24. E.g., John Rohr, *To Run a Constitution*, (Lawrence, KS: University Press of Kansas 1986), 45–46; and see Merrill, *supra* at 2155, noting that while Congress is not required to hold hearings or invite public debate prior to legislating on any given issue, "Administrative rule-making, at least in its modern guise, is subject to a much more unyielding set of procedural requirements, including advance notice to the public, disclosure of studies and data on which the agency relies, extensive opportunity for public comment, and a requirement that agencies respond to and explain their disagreement with material comments submitted from any quarter [citation omitted]."

25. Mashaw, *supra* at 24; and see Mancur Olsen, *The Logic of Collective Action: Public Goods and the Theory of Groups*, (Cambridge, MA: Harvard University Press, 1965), for example at 166: "consumers are at least as numerous as any other group in society, but they have no organization to countervail the power of organized or monopolistic producers [citation omitted]."

26. Kenneth John Meier and Lloyd Nigro, Representative Bureaucracy and Policy Preferences, *Public Administration Review* 36(4):458–469 (1976); Nicole M. R. Elias, Shifting Diversity Perspectives and New Avenues for Representative Bureaucracy, *Public Administration Quarterly* 37(1):331–373 (2013).

27. Donald Rayfield, *Anton Chekhov: A Life*, (New York: Henry Holt & Company, 1997), especially Part II: Dr. Chekhov, pages 73–115; Rosamund Bartlett, *Chekhov: Scenes from a Life*, (London: Simon & Schuster, 2004), 75–82.

28. *The Cherry Orchard*, Act I; quoted, in a somewhat different translation, in Donald Rayfield, *Understanding Chekhov: A Critical Study of Checkhov's Prose and Drama*, (Madison, WI: University of Wisconsin Press, 1999), 250.

29. John Rohr taught public administration at Virginia Polytechnic Institute and State University from 1979 until his death in 2011. In several seminal books, he illuminated the importance of constitutional values in public administration and in American society.

30. Rohr, *To Run a Constitution, supra* at 188–193; *Public Service, Ethics, and Constitutional Practice*, (Lawrence, KS: University Press of Kansas, 1998), 70–75.

31. Oath of office for federal employees, 5 U.S.C. § 3331, website, U.S. Office of Personnel Management, http://www.opm.gov/constitution_initiative/oath.asp.

32. E-mail from Gary L. Wamsley to author, 6/8/12.

33. Laurence H. Tribe, *The Invisible Constitution*, (New York: Oxford University Press, 2008).

34. John Rohr, *Ethics for Bureaucrats*, (New York and Basel, Switzerland: Marcel Dekker, Inc. 1978), 66 (liberty, equality, brotherhood, replaced by work, family, county).

35. Rohr, To Run a Constitution, supra at 101, 109–110.

36. *Id.* at 193.

37. *Id.*

38. *Id.* at 84.

39. Rohr, *Civil Servants and Their Constitutions*, (Lawrence, KS: University Press of Kansas, 2002), 139.

40. *Ethics for Bureaucrats*, supra, 59–76.

41. Daniel L. Feldman, *The Logic of American Government*, (New York: William Morrow & Co., 1990), 31–2.

42. E.g., Colin Moynihan, Bollinger Defends Columbia's Treatment of Ahmadinijad, *The New York Times*, 9/26/07, http://cityroom.blogs.nytimes.com/2007/09/26/bollinger-defends-columbias-treatment-of-ahmadinejad/?_php=true&_type=blogs&_r=0, accessed 1/31/14.

43. *Hamdi v. Rumsfeld*, 542 U.S. 507, 518 and 588–9, 124 S. Ct. 2633 (2004).

44. Barack Obama, State of the Union Address, *CBS News*, 1/28/14, http://www.cbsnews.com/news/obamas-2014-state-of-the-union-address-full-text/, accessed 2/14/14.

45. *The Common Law*, (Boston, MA: Little, Brown & Co., 1881), republished by Dover Books, Mineola, New York, 1991, 1, http://www.amazon.com/The-Common-Oliver-Wendell-Holmes/dp/0486267466#reader_0486267466.

46. Expressed in more of the classic positivist terminology of H. L. A. Hart, the American people, as primary sovereign, delegates to the socially recognized authoritative institution, Congress, the power to make laws, and agencies must exercise power only as transmitted to them by Congress, under rules set by a socially recognized governing document, the Constitution, as interpreted by another institution socially recognized as authoritative for that purpose, the court system. See, e.g., H. L. A. Hart, *The Concept of Law*, (New York: Oxford University Press, 1997 [1961]), 94ff; but, see Jean Hampton, Democracy and the Rule of Law, in Ian Shapiro, ed., *The Rule of Law: Nomos XXXVI*, (New York and London, UK: New York University Press, 1994), 13–44, especially 26–28.

47. Lon Fuller taught contracts and jurisprudence at Harvard Law School from 1939 until 1972. He offered a vision of law as a tool for human purposes, but reliant on secular principles of natural law.

48. Bruce L. Benson, Reciprocal Exchange, 10 *J. of Libertarian Studies* 53, 57 (Fall 1991); and see Lon L. Fuller, *The Morality of Law*, rev. ed., (New Haven, CT: Yale University Press, 1969).

49. Lon Fuller, Human Interaction and the Law, Kenneth I. Winston, ed., *The Principles of Social Order: Selected Essays of Lon L. Fuller*, (Durham, NC: Duke University Press, 1981), 232.

50. See, e.g., James Landis, *The Administrative Process*, (New Haven, Conn.: Yale University Press, 1938), 11.

51. Fuller, *The Morality of Law*, supra, 129.

52. Peter R. Teachout, "'Uncreated Conscience': The Civilizing Force of Fuller's Jurisprudence," in Witteveen and van der Burg, *Rediscovering Fuller*, (Amsterdam, Holland: Amsterdam University Press, 1999), 229, at 241, quoting Chief Justice Shaw of the Massachusetts Supreme Judicial Court in *Norway Plains Co. v. Boston & Maine RR.*, 1 Gray 263, 167 (Mass. 1854).

53. Fuller, *The Morality of Law*, supra, 101.

54. Anne Weismann, Anne, Have We Come Full Circle? Or Unitary Executive Redux, *CREW* web-site [Citizens for Responsibility and Ethics in Washington], 8/20/13, http://www.citizensforethics.org/blog/entry/have-we-come-full-circle-or-unitary-executive-redux, accessed 12/13/13.

55. David H. Rosenbloom and Suzanne Piotrowski, Outsourcing the Constitution and Administrative Law Norms, *American Review of Public Administration* 35(2):103–121(2005).

56. *The Morality of Law*, supra, 39.

57. *Id.*

58. *Id.* at 172.

59. *Wyatt v. Aderholt*, 503 F. 2d 1305, 1317 (5th Cir. 1974).

60. The Forms and Limits of Adjudication, *Harv. L. Rev.* 92(2):353–409, 402–3 (1978) (published posthumously).

61. *Id.* at 405.

62. *Id.* at 402–3.

63. Thomas Byrne Edsall, *Chain Reaction,* (New York: W.W. Norton & Co., 1991), 189.

64. Public Papers of the Presidents of the United States, Ronald Reagan: 1984, Vol. 1. (Washington, DC: US G.P.O., 1985), 158.

65. Goering, *supra*, at 27–28.

66. Alexander Bolton, Senate rejects DREAM Act, closing door on immigration reform, *The Hill*, 12/18/10, http://thehill.com/homenews/senate/134351-dream-act-defeated-in-senate, accessed 11/26/14.

67. 8 U.S.C. § 1225(B)(2)(a).

68. See, e.g., 8 C.F.R. §§ 274a.12(c)(14) and 1.3(a)(4)(vi).

69. Complaint, *Crane v. Napolitano*, Civil Action Number 3:12-CV-03247-0 (N.D. Texas, Dallas Division, 8/23/12), https://www.numbersusa.com/content/news/august-23-2012/ice-agents-v-napolitano-read-complaint.html, paragraph 36; and see Julia Preston, Agents Sue Over Deportation Suspensions, *New York Times*, 8/24/12, A17:4.

70. *Id.* at paragraph 4.

71. *Crane v. Napolitano*, 920 F. Supp. 2d 724, 2013 U.S. DIST Lexis 10006 (N.D. Texas, Dallas Division 2013).

72. *Crane v. Napolitano* 2013 U.S. DIST Lexis 57788, *43 (N.D. Texas, Dallas Division, April 23, 2013).

73. 5 U.S.C. §§ 7501-7543, Pub. L. 95-454, 92 Stat. 1111 et seq.

74. *Crane v. Napolitano* 2013 U.S. DIST Lexis 187005, *12 (N.D. Texas, Dallas Division, July 31, 2013).

75. Karl R. Thompson, The Department of Homeland Security's Authority to Prioritize Removal of Certain Aliens Unlawfully Present in the United States and to Defer Removal of Others, Memorandum Opinion for the Secretary of Homeland Security and the Counsel to the President, Office of Legal Counsel, United States Department of Justice, 11/19/14, 1, available at http://www.google.com/url?sa=t&rct=j&q=&esrc=s&source=web&cd=2&ved=0CCcQFjAB&url=http%3A%2F%2Fwww.justice.gov%2Fsites%2Fdefault%2Ffiles%2Folc%2Fopinions%2Fattachments%2F2014%2F11%2F20%2F2014-11-19-auth-prioritize-removal.pdf&ei=o_J1VKKhC7aHsQS_3YDICA&usg=AFQjCNE3gCRyB8gkfCz-JQCLBW18ONe76g&sig2=G3GFMsRoZ-_NqQPfJYadtA&bvm=bv.80642063,d.cWc, accessed 11/26/14.

76. *Id.*, 4, citing *Heckler v. Chaney*, 470 U.S. 821, 831, 105 S. Ct. 1649 (1985).

77. *Id.*, 10, quoting Department of Homeland Security Appropriations Act, 2014, Pub. L. N0. 113-76, F, Title II, 128 Stat. 5, 251.

78. *Id.*, 11, note 4, citing *Arizona v. United States*, -- U.S. at --, 132 S. Ct. 2492, 2499 (2012); *Reno v. Am.-Arab Anti-Discrim. Comm.*, 525 U.S. 471, 483–4, 119 S. Ct. 936 (1999).

79. *Id.*, 19.

80. Clifton Williams, *Expressio Unius Est Exclusio Alterius*, 15 *Marquette L. Rev.* 191 (June 1931), available at http://www.google.com/url?sa=t&rct=j&q=&esrc=s&source=web&cd=5&ved=0CEYQFjAE&url=http%3A%2F%2Fscholarship.law.marquette.edu%2Fcgi%2Fviewcontent.cgi%3Farticle%3D4175%26context%3Dmulr&ei=aAF2VIDANdPbsAT6loGQDQ&usg=

AFQjCNHtk2uKfRLV2ZI7JFMI4VU153zztQ&sig2=LmC5cQSTxn0OiUpDBc_YUg&bvm=
bv.80642063,d.cWc, accessed 11/26/14; and see, e.g. *Leatherman v. Tarrant County*, 507 U.S.
163, 168, 113 Sup. Ct. 1160, 1163 (1993).

81. Thompson, 11/19/14, *supra*, 6, citing *Youngstown Sheet & Tube Co. v. Sawyer*, 343 U.S. 579,
    637, 72 S. Ct. 863 (1952).

82. *Id.*, 18, note 9.

83. Thompson, 11/19/14, *op. cit.* at n. 81.

84. Peter H. Schuck, Why Congress Can Impeach Obama, *The New York Times*, 11/22/14, A21, c.2,
    http://www.nytimes.com/2014/11/22/opinion/the-impeachment-of-obama-on-immigration-
    may-be-legal-but-its-wrong.html?_r=0, accessed 11/26/14.

85. Thompson, 11/19/14, *supra*, 18, note 8.

86. See, for example, the discussion of the statistics showing that the only applicants rejected for
    deferred action under the Napolitano directive were those who actually did not meet the
    criteria of the directive, had technical filing errors, lied on the form, didn't fill out the form
    correctly, committed fraud, or failed to pay required fees, in *Texas v. United States*, Civil
    Number B-14-254 (S.D. Texas, Brownsville Div. 2015), page 109, note 101, http://www.scribd
    .com/doc/255994067/Memorandum-Opinion-Texas-v-United-States , accessed 2/20/15.

87. Schuck, 11/22/14, *supra*; but see Lee C. Bollinger et al., Scholars' letter on immigration, open
    letter from ten prominent law professors arguing that "limits on the lawful exercise of prose-
    cutorial discretion are not breached here." 11/20/14, thehill.com/sites/.../files/scholars_letter_
    on_immigration_2_1.pdf, available at https://www.google.com/search?q=We+are+law+
    professors+and+lawyers+who+teach%2C+study%2C+and+practice+constitutional+law+&ie
    =utf-8&oe=utf-8&aq=t&rls=org.mozilla:en-US:official&client=firefox-a&channel=sb,
    accessed 11/26/14.

Separation of Powers—Legislative and Executive Control Over Administrative Agencies[1]

LEGISLATIVE REVIEW OF AGENCY ACTION

With the non-delegation doctrine honored mostly in the breach, Congress and the state legislatures have tried to reassert authority in other ways. While the public cannot vote out of office a bureaucrat who is obnoxious, incompetent, or committed to an unpopular policy, Congress can refuse funding, reduce funding, or abolish a problematic agency.[2] But, these actions are rare, must be based on fairly extreme circumstances, and even so cannot remedy certain kinds of agency issues.

Congressional committees, reviewing agency budgets, implicitly threaten cuts, and so have some influence. The Government Accountability Office (GAO), Congress's investigative arm, audits agencies when Congress members ask, even though the head of the GAO, the Comptroller General, is appointed by the President. Individual members of Congress sometimes themselves act as "legislative watchdogs": the late Senator William Proxmire exposed waste in Defense Department spending; former Member of Congress Elizabeth Holtzman revealed many millions of dollars lost to corruption in federally funded antipoverty programs, and investigations on behalf of state legislators have resulted in changes in state and local government agencies toward more responsible operations in road repairs, municipal real estate transactions, drug abuse treatment programs, and other matters.[3]

The Inspector General Act of 1978[4] opened another avenue of congressional control. Unlike the GAO, federal inspectors general are statutorily required to report to Congress on the agencies every six months. While the president (or agency heads appointed by the president) appoints federal inspectors general, and can remove any inspector general (IG), the president "must notify Congress first, empowering Congress to create a political problem for the president if Congress can show that the removal was unjustified."[5] And because the IG reports both to the agency and to Congress, some agencies perceive the IG as a "mole" working against them from within, more insidiously and more dangerously than the GAO. Nonetheless, despite outstanding examples of courageous and effective IGs, some believe that the average IG has been more a "lapdog" than a "watchdog," avoiding investigations that might threaten the political leadership of their agencies.[6]

Since 1978, many states and localities have also adopted and sanctioned IGs to provide a parallel measure of legislative control over agencies at those levels of government.[7]

Another vehicle for legislative control, constituent casework, has become one of the biggest functions of the elected representative. Staff for members of Congress and for state legislators spend much of their time intervening with government agencies on behalf of constituents. They remind bureaucrats of their responsibilities, and also of who supplies the funding: the citizen, with the legislator as conduit. This sometimes produces even more than fair treatment for the constituent in question, although occasionally the reverse happens, with the bureaucrat exacting revenge on the hapless citizen.[8]

Some states have institutionalized ombudsman offices, also sometimes called Citizens' Aides, or Public Counsel. In New York City, the "Public Advocate" serves as one of only three officials elected citywide. Publicity is their most potent tool.

In principle, "sunset" legislation requires elimination of agency budgets unless the agency justifies its continued existence. But, with review efforts spread too thin for effective evaluation, agency programs subject to "sunsetting" continue to be renewed more or less automatically, as before.[9]

Review of agency rules is probably even harder than review of agency budgets: it is generally too time-consuming since agencies issue far more rules than Congress enacts laws.[10] And, if the President vetoed legislation to overturn a rule, Congress might not get the two-thirds majority they need to retrieve the power granted by a mere majority vote.

THE LEGISLATIVE VETO

Instead, Congress developed the legislative veto. The original legislation creating the agency or giving it power would include a provision allowing the House of Representatives and the Senate, or sometimes only one house of Congress, to overrule an agency regulation or adjudicative decision. (Legislative vetoes could apply to agency hearing decisions as well as to rules and regulations.) The president would have no opportunity to veto this "overruling."

The use of the legislative veto started in 1918, in a law otherwise giving President Wilson more power to reorganize federal agencies. Its use blossomed under President Hoover in 1932. By 1983, more than two hundred federal statutes contained such provisions, including the War Powers Act of 1973, enabling Congress to direct the withdrawal of troops sent by a president without a formal congressional declaration of war.

The U.S. Court of Claims upheld the legitimacy and constitutionality of the legislative veto in a 1977 decision, noting in response "[t]o the plaintiff's argument that Congress cannot meddle once it has delegated power, it may be observed that legislation itself is a form of supervision. . . ."[11]

The Immigration and Nationality Act included a legislative veto provision. One section[12] allowed either house of Congress to overturn a U.S. Attorney

General's decision to let an alien remain. If either house did, the alien would be deported. Congress voted to deport Jagdish Chadha, an East Indian on a British passport. He sued, questioning the constitutionality of the legislative veto. In *INS v. Chadha*,[13] Chief Justice Warren Burger, writing for the Court in 1983, held the legislative veto unconstitutional.

The Constitution requires that the president must have an opportunity to veto every bill before it becomes law.[14] Burger reasoned that true laws are those that alter legal rights of persons "outside the legislative branch"; such acts must meet the constitutional requirement; this action indeed "altered legal rights"[15]; and was therefore unconstitutional, since it was not presented to the president.

Justice Byron White, dissenting, argued that the legislative veto really just subtracted from the power Congress would otherwise grant an agency. Since Congress did not have to give the agency any power, the president's signature on a bill, including a legislative veto, authorizes subsequent use by Congress of that veto. Therefore, when Congress uses the legislative veto it does not violate the lawmaking process described in the Constitution. In any case, the broad delegations of power to agencies we have seen, however practically necessary they may be, raise far more serious questions about adherence to constitutional theory. The legislative veto, as a congressional effort to retain policy control, looks like a good way to restore the traditional constitutional balance of power between Congress and the executive branch.[16]

With increased centralization of power in the Executive, Congress has to leave most details to the agencies. The Court's decision further reduced Congress's control of agency action. It could no longer just deal with specific problems as they came up.

The Court's decision was also bad law.[17] Pretty much every agency regulation or hearing decision "alters the legal rights of persons" without going through any legislative branch lawmaking process, much less the process specified. For example, Homeland Security (including the former Immigration and Naturalization Service), by its own decision, may order aliens to be held in detention facilities. Clearly, that power "alters the legal rights of persons," without conforming to the constitutional requirements of legislation. ". . .[T]he theoretical model of legislative action envisioned by the framers applies only in the most general sense to the 20th [or 21st!] century."[18]

Justice Powell, concurring in the result, but not the reasoning of *Chadha*, made good sense. Powell would have allowed legislative vetoes of regulations, but not of adjudications, such as the one at hand in *Chadha*: if Congress may delegate full "legislative" power, it should be able to delegate only part of that power. But, Congress has no "judicial" power (except for impeachment), so it should not be able to "reserve to itself" any part of that power.[19]

Chadha made it harder for the representative branch, Congress, to control the president and the agencies.[20] Congress made a feeble attempt to replace the legislative veto with the Congressional Review Act of 1996, delaying the implementation of a "major" agency rule until Congress has had notice for at least sixty days, during which time both houses can pass a resolution to nullify the rule, on the president's approval of the resolution.[21] But, since the resolution has no effect without presidential approval, it has only limited advantages over ordinary legislation to overrule the agency, since the president is likely to reject the move in support of his or her appointees at the agency. It was used successfully once[22]: by the time Congress presented the resolution to the president, George W. Bush had taken over from Clinton, and the new president, as hostile to the rule as the Congress that opposed it, was happy to sign the resolution.[23]

Some states allow legislative vetoes, some don't. Some have explicit constitutional provisions allowing for it (e.g., Connecticut[24]); some state courts have upheld statutory provisions (e.g., Idaho). The Idaho court, following the reasoning of Justice White's dissent in *Chadha*, held that a statute, including a legislative veto, only constituted a "conditioned grant of authority," that is less than full lawmaking power, and so overturning an agency regulation promulgated pursuant to that authority did not require presentment to the Governor as part of the process prescribed by the Idaho Constitution for enactment or repeal of a law.[25]

EXTREME SEPARATION OF POWERS THEORY

In *Bowsher v. Synar*,[26] Chief Justice Burger wrote an even worse decision than *Chadha*.[27] The Gramm-Rudman law of 1985 provided for automatic agency budget cuts if Congress passed a budget that would go more than $10 billion above a predetermined deficit level, and gave the Comptroller General the key role in identifying the excess deficit. Burger held that because Congress and the president since 1921 each had the power to remove the Comptroller General (a power Congress had never exercised), and Congress could override a presidential veto of a congressional removal with the usual two-thirds vote, giving such "executive" responsibility to an officer beholden to the legislative branch violates the congressional principle of separation of powers.[28]

This is, of course, utter nonsense. The Framers meant the separation of powers doctrine to prevent abuse, by providing that one branch would check the power of another, a process that the grant of power to the Comptroller General under Gramm-Rudman-Hollings in no way threatened. Hamilton and Madison clearly approved of overlapping powers among the branches.[29] They did draw some lines, of course: the Constitution prohibits a member of Congress or the Senate from serving simultaneously as an executive branch officer.[30]

The Court noted that the Constitution "does not contemplate an active role for Congress in the supervision of officers charged with the execution of the laws it enacts."[31] As Louis Fisher noted,

> Of course the Constitution does not contemplate a number of things, including the active role of the President in supervising the passage of laws or the ability of the President to make law unilaterally by issuing executive orders and proclamations ... For two centuries, congressional oversight of executive affairs has been a legitimate constitutional responsibility ...[32]

Tacking Back to Moderation

With Chief Justice Rehnquist's majority opinion in *Morrison v. Olson*,[33] the Court took a substantial step away from the flawed approaches of *Chadha* and *Bowsher* and toward a more sensible reading of the constitutional balance. (Rehnquist had joined in White's dissent in *Chadha*, although he joined in Burger's decision for the Court in *Bowsher*.) Alexia Morrison had been appointed by a special three-judge federal appellate court, not by the president or his appointees, to investigate possible abuses by Justice Department officials. The Independent Counsel provisions of the 1978 Ethics in Government Act authorized appointments like hers.[34]

The Justice Department, which she was investigating, however, argued that law enforcement, investigation, and prosecution are executive branch functions. Article II of the Constitution, in vesting executive power in the president, meant *all* such power, and so, the Justice Department argued and Justice Scalia agreed in his dissenting opinion, the president must have "complete control over investigations and prosecution of violations of the law."[35]

Obviously, it would be harder to trust the integrity of an investigation of the White House if the investigator depended on the president for the job. The Framers would have shared those concerns. Signaling the Court's return to sounder principles of government, Rehnquist noted that the Constitution "give[s] Congress significant discretion to determine whether it is 'proper' to vest the appointment of, for example, executive officials in the 'courts of law.'"[36] Attempting to downplay his sharp course away from the direction of *Chadha* and *Bowsher* by claiming that *Morrison* differed because Congress wasn't seeking executive-style power for itself, but vesting it in courts, Rehnquist said, "we have never held that the Constitution requires that the three branches of government 'operate with absolute independence.'"[37]

The decision in *Morrison* also turned on a somewhat technical issue. The Constitution provides that Congress may choose to have the president, the courts, or department heads appoint "Inferior Officers," but only the president, "with the Advice and Consent of the Senate," must appoint "other Officers of the United States."[38] The Court reasoned that since the special prosecutor could be "removed" by the Attorney General for good cause or when the Attorney General determines that the special prosecutor's goals have been achieved, and the special prosecutor's role, jurisdiction, and tenure in office were all limited, the special prosecutor was "an 'inferior officer' in the constitutional sense,"[39] and thus not a mandated presidential appointment.

Ultimately Congress failed to renew the Independent Counsel provisions of the Ethics in Government law when they expired in 1999, clearly influenced by Kenneth Starr's protracted and wasteful "Whitewater" investigation of President Clinton.[40] The annoyance of Republicans at an earlier Special Counsel who had cast doubt on statements by the first President Bush likely contributed to the result.[41] Instead, U.S. Attorneys General appoint special prosecutors to conduct investigations. Such special prosecutors are subject to removal by the Attorney General, limited only by such regulations as the

Justice Department—also dominated by the Attorney General—may choose to issue. This system raises questions about inappropriate political influence.

The vision behind the decisions in *Chadha* and *Bowsher*, and behind Scalia's dissent in *Morrison*, "was of a Presidency supreme and essentially unchallengeable. It was as if those who framed the Constitution at Philadelphia in 1787 had created a President on the model of King George the Third."[42] Notwithstanding the congressional decision to let the special prosecutor law expire, *Morrison* itself represented an important reaffirmation of legislative power vis-à-vis the federal executive.

EXECUTIVE CONTROL OF ADMINISTRATIVE AGENCIES

Certainly the President exercises enormous power over agencies. The power to choose the personnel to lead the agencies in itself does much to shape their direction, because the President and presidential aides will do what they can to select those who share their views. With about 3,000 political appointments, such personnel can go fairly deep into the management positions of the federal government.[43] As a vivid example, "Product seizures by the FDA decreased by more than 50 percent after the Reagan White House tapped Arthur Hull Hayes, a champion of regulatory relief for business, to lead the agency."[44]

The Civil Service Reform Act of 1978 established the Senior Executive Service, a cadre that as of 2013 included 7,910 high-level personnel[45] who may be moved by the president from agency to agency, "providing the presidential team with a pipeline into the private information that agencies might otherwise use to evade control, especially if appointees bring expertise or experience to their jobs (which is virtually guaranteed for team members within the Senior Executive Service)."[46]

Senate versus President on Appointments

However, in *National Labor Relations Board v. Noel Canning*,[47] the Supreme Court limited the President's power to appoint agency heads. The decision only affected "interim" appointments, but when faced with a hostile Senate minority that refuses to confirm presidential appointments, interim appointments often provide the President's only method of installing agency leaders who are sympathetic to the President's policy preferences.

The issue arose when an employer challenged an order of the National Labor Relations Board (NLRB) on the grounds that in the absence of a majority of its five Board members, it could not issue a valid order. The NLRB appeared to have all five of the Board members it needed. However, the employer argued that three such members had been appointed illegally by President Obama.

In appointing an "Officer of the United States," the Recess Clause of the Constitution allows the president "to fill up all Vacancies that may happen during the Recess of the Senate, by granting Commissions which shall expire at the End of their next Session."[48] Without the sixty votes then needed to cut off debate, the Democrats in the Senate were unable to prevent the Republicans from filibustering President Obama's nominees. In January 2012, Obama invoked the Recess Clause to appoint three members to the NLRB, one of whom had been awaiting Senate approval for about a year, and the others, presumably with no better prospect of prompt Senate approval, for a few weeks.[49]

A normal legislative session includes speeches, debates, and at least some apparent effort to enact legislation. An ordinary adjournment of a legislative session produces a recess. To avoid triggering the Recess Clause, the Democrats first used the tactic of holding so-called sessions of the Senate in 2007, with one Senator calling it into session and almost immediately ending the session, "to block recess appointments by President George W. Bush."[50] But, since the Constitution prohibits the Senate from adjourning for more than three days without the consent of the House, and vice versa,[51] the House leadership (Republican after 2010), was able to make the Senate hold these *pro forma* sessions as well, when they otherwise had no business to conduct. When Obama made the controversial NLRB appointments, the Senate was in a "recess" between its Tuesday *pro forma* "session" and its Friday *pro forma* session. Obama decided that this "recess" allowed him to make the appointments.[52]

The federal Court of Appeals for the District of Columbia Circuit ruled that "the Recess of the Senate" meant the recess after the end of the year's session and before the next year's session began, not any recess within a year's session.[53] Furthermore, it read the constitutional clause to mean that the president could only fill a vacancy that occurs *during* that same intersessional recess.[54]

The Supreme Court, however, disagreed. It looked to historical practice for guidance, and found that presidents filled many pre-recess vacancies with recess appointments,[55] and had made "thousands" of *intra*sessional recess appointments (appointments during recesses within a session) since 1929, and a few as early as 1867.[56] But, the Court was unable to find an appointment made in an intra-session recess of fewer than ten days.[57] So, although it did find a few inter-sessional appointments made during recesses of fewer than ten days, it decided that a recess must last for at least ten days to trigger applicability of the Recess Clause, barring some unforeseeable circumstance of national disaster that required quicker action.[58]

The Court rejected the Obama Administration's argument that the *pro forma* sessions should be ignored, and should not be considered to break up periods of recess. Although the Senate actually does no real business during such sessions, the Court concluded that it must give considerable deference to the Senate's own determinations of its status and its actions. So long as it *could* conduct business, if the Senate reports that it is in session, the law must consider it to be in session.[59] Almost two years later, the Senate changed its rules to require only a majority to confirm nominations.[60] However, when a president faces a hostile Senate majority, the problem of filling vacancies can easily recur.

When Is a Presidential Order Not Enforceable?

Scalia's dissent in *Morrison* includes his idiosyncratic view of the executive as exercising undivided power over the entire executive department.[61] However, in 1838 the Supreme Court first rejected that view (a view that we attributed in Chapter 2 to children and those who never evinced enough interest to learn further), when it instructed a postmaster, a federal executive agency employee, to follow the instructions of Congress to pay a contractor, not the contrary instructions from the President.[62]

More than one hundred years later, Justice Robert Jackson wrote a concurrence, not a decision, which courts still use to decide whether a presidential order is legitimate.[63] President Harry Truman had ordered his Secretary of Commerce to seize the steel mills during the Korean War, because the steel companies' stubborn resistance to wage increases was about to precipitate a strike. With no statute to support the executive order, the Court held that Truman could not validly issue it: his duty under the Constitution was to "take Care that the Laws be faithfully executed,"[64] not to make laws. Justice Jackson's landmark concurrence argued that the president had the most constitutional leeway when Congress explicitly or implicitly authorized his action; acted in an unclear zone when no congressional statute offered guidance; and invited constitutional defeat when acting against a congressional determination (that is itself constitutionally sound).[65] Jackson determined that Truman's order fell into the final category.[66] To survive, some independent presidential power would have to have sustained the order. Jackson disposed of various arguments of other such sources of presidential power. Regarding the strongest, the president's powers as commander-in-chief, Jackson said, "I think it is not a military prerogative, without support of law, to seize persons or property because they are important or even essential for the military and naval establishment."[67]

Naturally, the large middle zone, which Jackson called "a zone of twilight,"[68] continues to generate the most controversy. For example, under President Reagan, the White House, via executive orders, vastly increased the power of the Office of Management and Budget (OMB) over other federal agencies, forcing those other agencies to submit their proposed regulations to cost-benefit analysis by a new subdivision of the OMB, the Office of Information and Regulatory Affairs (OIRA). The proposed regulations were rendered invalid unless they earned the approval of OIRA. This new subdivision's analyses were not on-the-record, so courts could not review them, and private parties could communicate with OIRA without alerting their opponents. Some scholars argued that this kind of cost-benefit analysis could "diminish[] the role of regulation even when it was beneficial," and therefore thought the executive orders might unconstitutionally violate the president's duty to "take Care that the Laws be faithfully executed."[69] An early critic complained that no statutory authorization supported Reagan's Executive Order 12,291[70] (the initial order empowering OMB to negate regulations that did not survive its cost-benefit scrutiny); that Congress had clearly signaled that they wanted to guide the procedures governing agency policy-making itself; and that therefore "whether viewed as within Congress's exclusive domain or within the nebulous zone of concurrent authority, Executive Order 12, 291 violates the constitutional separation of powers."[71]

Although President Clinton modified OMB's mandate somewhat in this regard (now it must assure that the benefits of the rules justify, rather than exceed, its costs),[72] OMB has continued to exercise its substantial level of control over agency rulemaking.[73] Through OMB and in other ways, the President has a very substantial measure of control over agency action.

At least one state court has validated a constitutional argument against the use of executive regulatory review to halt an agency's regulatory process. The Florida court ruled that Florida's Governor Rick Scott could not order agencies to clear rules with a unit of his office before they could be promulgated. While acknowledging that the unit could properly review rules after the fact, the court held that executive orders from the Governor to cut off the rulemaking process unless the unit of his office gave advance approval violated the Florida Constitution as "an encroachment upon a legislative function."[74]

In New York, a comparable argument was reflected only in a dissenting opinion from its highest court. In that case, the Governor's Office of Regulatory Reform (GORR), the New York State version of the federal OIRA, opposed a rule proposed by the State's Department of Health requiring hospital directors of social work to have Master's in Social Work (MSW) degrees. On GORR's recommendation, the Governor's Review Committee prohibited the rule. Interestingly, while the appellate court rejected the constitutional argument on the merits as well as holding that the plaintiffs lacked standing, New York's highest court affirmed only on the standing issue, remaining silent on the constitutional merits.[75] The dissent, however, noted that the Governor should not be permitted to "'go beyond stated legislative policy and prescribe a remedial device not embraced by the policy [citations omitted].'"[76] Not only was there "no constitutional or legislative authority for the executive order's grant of veto power to the Governor's committee . . . this prohibitionary provision actually nullifies specific grants of rulemaking authority given to the agencies and divests these statutory rulemaking bodies of the discretion given them by the Legislature."[77] Therefore, the executive order should have been vacated as "violative of the doctrine of separation of powers and contrary to controlling statutory law."[78]

Beyond the constitutional concerns, a 2010 study of regulatory review at the state level across the country found it on average inefficient, inconsistent, and dangerous to significant public interests.[79]

WHAT AM I SUPPOSED TO DO?

State Department Middle East Policy: Who Decides, President or Congress?

Imagine that you are the Secretary of State. You must try to persuade the Israelis and the Palestinians to advance toward some kind of political resolution of their issues, one of the most difficult and sensitive areas of foreign policy that you must address. The President, when he appointed you, asked for your assurance that this goal would be high on your agenda. For many years, the Arab world has perceived American foreign policy as biased in favor of Israel. This perception makes it harder for you to gain the trust of the Palestinians. Accordingly, you have tried to show even-handedness to the extent possible.

In this context, the status of the city of Jerusalem stands out as even more difficult and sensitive than most of the other aspects of the conflict. Israel won the East Jerusalem area in the 1967 war, and continues to occupy it. East Jerusalem includes some of the holiest sites for Christianity, Judaism, and Islam. Both Israel and the Palestinian Authority claim Jerusalem as their state capital, but the Palestinians focus on East Jerusalem in this regard. The United Nations does not recognize Israel's annexation of East Jerusalem, but continues to regard it as occupied territory. While the United States Senate in 1990 adopted a resolution in support of Israel's view of an undivided Jerusalem as its capital, the United States has no official position on the issue.

Meanwhile, in 2002, Congress enacted a law requiring the Secretary of State to allow, on request, "a United States citizen born in the city of Jerusalem", without specifying any particular part of Jerusalem, to "record the place of birth as Israel" on a birth certificate or passport.[80] This provision was apparently intended to override the instruction of the State Department manual, which requires a person born in Jerusalem to write "Jerusalem," and not the name of a country, on a passport.[81]

American citizens, parents of a child born in Jerusalem, have asked the State Department to list the place of birth on his passport as "Jerusalem, Israel."

It is your belief, shared by the President, that this concession, if made by the State Department, would further alienate the Palestinians, making it even less likely that you would eventually be able to broker some progress toward a peaceful solution. You also know that the President, on whose authority you act, historically has been thought to have more powers independent of Congress in the foreign policy area than in the areas of domestic policy, based on a constitutional provision empowering the President to "receive Ambassadors and other public ministers."[82] If only the President, and not Congress, has such power, Congress might well have violated the Constitution by trying to exercise executive powers in enacting the statute. The question, then, is whether you should do what you are sure the President would want, and refuse to let the child's passport list Israel as place of birth, or do you follow what Congress seems to have mandated, and allow the designation of Israel on the passport, although you question whether Congress has acted unconstitutionally by enacting that statute.

As it turns out, the constitutional question proves difficult to answer, so you would be acting well within the limits of your loyalty to the American constitutional tradition whichever decision you made. The constitutional provision the courts were called on to interpret was indeed the one you cited, which only refers to the power of the President to "receive" certain visitors—which surely is not easily extended to passport matters. Further, the Constitution gives Congress power over naturalization[83] and over foreign commerce,[84] which might just as easily (or with just as much difficulty) be extended to passport matters. The philosophy behind *Chadha* and *Bowsher* seems to reflect an overly strict notion of the separation of powers, since the reality of American history demonstrates more sharing of powers than separation. Therefore, your uncertainty is well founded.

The decision in *Zivotofsky v. Clinton* provides some guidance. The Court majority decided only that the matter was a fitting one for the courts to determine, rejecting the argument that the parties were asking the courts to "decide the political status of Jerusalem." The Court calls that kind of issue, a "political question," which the text of the Constitution puts in the hands of the legislative or executive branch, or which the judicial branch has no available basis for resolving.[85] Rather, the Court held that the case posed the question of whether the child did or did not have a statutory right—the kind of question the courts certainly have the power to decide.[86] Therefore, it returned the case to the court below to address the constitutionality of the statute that the parents argued conferred the statutory right.

That court found the law that Congress passed unconstitutional.[87] As a result, the Supreme Court ultimately affirmed that decision. You should enforce the prohibition in your State Department manual, and not permit the child's passport to designate Israel as his place of birth.[88] The Court found that as early as 1818, and again in 1864, 1896, and 1919, Congress had affirmed the president's exclusive power to speak for the United States as to recognition of foreign governments.[89] On several occasions, the Supreme Court also had interpreted the "receive Ambassadors" provision of the Constitution to mean that the President has the power to extend recognition to other countries, withhold, or withdraw it, as well as to shape American foreign policy as it affects the context of recognition decisions.[90] While the Supreme Court had never *ruled* that only the President, and not Congress, had that power, it has *commented* to that effect. In conjunction with the other factors noted, the court concluded that the President does indeed hold recognition power to the exclusion of Congress.[91]

On appeal, the Circuit Court observed that the Supreme Court has affirmed the power of Congress to regulate passports, but not as an exclusive power: the Executive branch may exercise control as well, "especially if foreign policy is implicated."[92] The court framed the question as follows: Did Congress, in enacting this particular law regarding passports, invade the power that only the President can exercise regarding recognition policy toward other nations? In answering that question, it found that "Congress plainly intended to force the State Department to deviate from its decades-long position of neutrality on what nation or government, if any, is sovereign over Jerusalem."[93] The court pointedly quoted *Bowsher v. Synar* to indicate the result in such circumstances: "even the results of the constitutional legislative process may be unconstitutional if those results are in fact destructive of the scheme of separation-of-powers."[94]

[*Note:* The Supreme Court decision in *Zivotofsky v. Kerry*, 576 U.S. __, 135 S. Ct. 2076, 2015 U.S. LEXIS 3781, came in too close to the publication date of this book for further treatment. The five-to-four split suggests the difficulty of this issue. Justice Kennedy, writing for the majority, acknowledged that in requiring the State Department to list Jerusalem and not Israel on the passports of children born in Jerusalem, when a congressional statute allowed the parents to choose to have the passport list the birthplace as Israel, the President's order stood in the weakest position in Justice Jackson's *Youngstown Sheet & Tube* hierarchy. In such circumstances, the President "may rely solely on powers the Constitution grants to him alone." However, Justice Kennedy ultimately concluded that such powers were indeed sufficient to justify the President's order.]

PRACTICE PROBLEMS

PROBLEM 1: Congress gave the President the authority to remove an executive branch agency's responsibility for a particular enforcement area and to confer it on a different agency. The same statute, however, also permitted either house of Congress to nullify any such removal by voting for a resolution to such effect. Assume that the President transferred the power to enforce mine safety away from the Department of Labor and back to the Department of the Interior, where it had been prior to 1977. Congress considered using its legislative veto, but did not. A year later, the mine safety unit of the Department of the Interior began to investigate claims that the Upper Centralia Coal Mine violated safety standards. Upper Centralia argues that Interior is not empowered to enforce against age discrimination. Should the court enforce the penalties the Interior mine safety unit imposes?[95]

PROBLEM 2: You are on the White House staff. The President had run an anti-government campaign: get government off our backs, reduce regulation and make it more efficient, eliminate costly rules, and especially environmental, health, safety, and consumer protection rules. He lacks the votes in Congress to repeal or modify the underlying statutes. What else can he do?

PROBLEM 3: You are a key adviser to the Education Commissioner of a large city. For years, state aid to your school system has been about $5 billion a year lower than the leading analysts believe is necessary, and indeed your school system has suffered severely from its inability to pay enough to attract and retain qualified teachers. Teachers face overcrowded classrooms, students get out-of-date textbooks and often must share the ones they have, school buildings are decrepit. Your state constitution requires the legislature to "provide for the maintenance and support of a system of free common schools, wherein all the children of this state may be educated." The courts have interpreted that provision to require as a minimum that its schools give the state's children "the basic literacy, calculating, and verbal skills necessary to enable children to function productively as civic participants capable of voting and serving on a jury." For the most part, it is clear that the schools in your city are not meeting this standard. The

Governor and one house of the legislature have proposed an increase of about $2 billion in state aid. It is apparent that the final state budget for the year will offer aid closer to that figure than to the $5 billion most experts believe necessary. Can you tell the Commissioner that the city is likely to win in court should it seek a mandate requiring the legislature to authorize the higher amount?

ENDNOTES

1. Parts of this chapter were reproduced from Daniel L. Feldman, *The Logic of American Government*, (New York: William Morrow & Co., 1990), © Daniel L. Feldman, Chapter II: Representativeness vs. Efficiency: Legislatures vs. Agencies and Executives, 38–48.

2. "House Republicans . . . proposed a 30 percent cut in the EPA's appropriations in early 2011." William T. Gormley Jr. and Steven J. Balla, *Bureaucracy and Democracy*, 3rd ed., (Los Angeles, CA: Sage/CQ Press, 2013), 99.

3. See, e.g., Daniel L. Feldman and David R. Eichenthal, *The Art of the Watchdog*, (Albany, NY: SUNY Press, 2013).

4. 5 U.S.C. Appx. §§ 1-13, Pub. L. 95-452, 92 Stat. 1101.

5. Daniel L. Feldman and David R. Eichenthal, *The Art of the Watchdog*, (Albany, New York: SUNY Press, 2013), 106.

6. Neil Barofsky, *Bailout*, (New York: Simon & Schuster, 2012), 51–54.

7. Feldman and Eichenthal, *supra*, Chapter Nine, State Inspectors General, 139–152, and Chapter Twelve, Local Auditors and Inspectors General, 179–197.

8. An opinion column questioned the appropriateness of legislative casework. Fred A. Bernstein, A Congress for the Many, or the Few? *The New York Times*, 9/8/12, http://www.nytimes .com/2012/09/09/opinion/sunday/a-congress-for-the-many-or-the-few.html?pagewanted= all&_r=0.

9. Kenneth Davis, Review Procedures and Public Accountability in Sunset Legislation, 33 *Admin. L. Rev.* 393 (Fall 1981).

10. See Chapter 1.

11. *Atkins v. United States*, 556 F. 2d 1028 (Ct. Claims 1977), *cert. den.* 434 U.S. 1009 (1978).

12. 8 U.S.C.S. § 1254(c)(2) (Section 244(c)(2) of the Act).

13. 462 U.S. 919, 103 S. Ct. 2764.

14. Article I, Section 7.

15. 462 U.S. at 952, 103 S. Ct. at 2784–5.

16. 462 U.S. at 967, 985–7, 103 S. Ct. at 2793, 2801–3.

17. Since various United States Supreme Court justices disagree with me, you should certainly feel free to do so as well. Please look throughout this book for other controversial expressions of my opinions, and consider how I might be mistaken.

18. Louis Fisher, Judicial Misjudgments About the Lawmaking Process: The Legislative Veto Case, 45 *Public Admin. Rev.* 705 (1985).

19. 462 U.S. at 959, 103 S. Ct. at 2788.

20. However, by the end of 2006, Louis Fisher counted more than 500 legislative vetoes enacted into law *after* the *Chadha* decision. *Constitutional Conflicts Between Congress and the President*, 5th ed., (Lawrence, KS: University of Kansas Press, 2007), 152. Presidents objected, but the relationships between congressional committees and agencies that have developed over the years have produced a variety of expedited procedures that are of value to both sides, and insistence on formal procedures can have unpleasant consequences for either side, as Congress apparently made clear. *Id* at 152–3. "Congress continues to place legislative vetoes, even committee vetoes, into bills that it passes and send to the President." Jack M. Beerman, *Inside Administrative Law: What Matters and Why*, (Frederick, MD: Aspen Publishers, 2011), 54.

21. 5 U.S.C. § 801 et seq., Federal Register, National Archives website, http://www.archives.gov/ federal-register/laws/congressional-review/801.html.

22. Richard S. Beth, Disapproval of Regulations by Congress: Procedure Under the Congressional Review Act, Congressional Research Service, 10/10/01, http://www.senate.gov/CRSReports/crs-publish.cfm?pid=%270E%2C*P_%3D%22P%20%20%0A, 1, n.3.

23. Jack M. Beerman, *Inside Administrative Law: What Matters and Why*, (Frederick, MD: Aspen Publishers, 2011), 40.

24. Constitution of the State of Connecticut, Amendments to the Constitution, Article XVIII, Adopted November 24, 1982, website of the Connecticut Secretary of the State, http://www.ct.gov/sots/cwp/view.asp?A=3188&Q=392288, accessed 1/13/15.

25. *Mead v. Arnell*, 117 Idaho 660, 668, 791 P. 2d 410, 419 (1990).

26. 478 U.S. 714, 106 Sup. Ct. 3181 (1986).

27. Worse because of its logic, not its outcome. As Jennifer Farrier reminded us in Louis Fisher on Congress and the Budget: Institutional Responsibility and Other Taboos, 46 *PS* 510, 512 (July 2013) [the "Politics Science and Politics" journal of the American Political Science Association], the great constitutional scholar Louis Fisher, whose criticism of the decision is quoted below at note 32,"agreed with the outcome . . . and had previously testified against [its] budgetary delegation . . ." Fisher thought that the Gramm-Rudman law's delegation of lawmaking power was unconstitutional, because Congress should make major budgetary decisions itself and not delegate them to anyone. He rejected characterization of the role of the comptroller general as the basis for holding the law unconstitutional. Testimony, October 17, 1985, at Hearing of a Subcommittee of the Government Operations Committee, House of Representatives, 99th Cong., 1st Sess., on The Balanced Budget and Emergency Deficit Control Act of 1985, in *Deficit Control and the Gramm-Rudman-Hollings Act*, (Buffalo, NY: William S. Hein & Co., 1986), V. 2, 198 and 217.

28. 478 U.S. at 734, 106 Sup. Ct. at 3191–2.

29. See Louis Fisher, The Administrative World of *Chadha* and *Bowsher*, 47 *Public Admin. Rev.* 213, 213–4 (1987); Leonard W. Levy, *Original Intent and the Framers' Constitution*, (New York and London, UK: Macmillan Publishing Company, 1988), 31, 391.

30. Article I, Section 6, cl. 2. North Carolina's constitution has no such clause, but its court said that the separation of powers still bars state legislators from simultaneously holding executive positions; *State ex rel. Wallace v. Bone*, 304 N.C. 591, 608, 286 S.E. 2d 79, 88 (N.C. 1982).

31. 472 U.S. at 722, 106 S. Ct. at 3186.

32. Fisher, 1987, *supra*.

33. 487 U.S. 654, 108 S. Ct. 2597 (1988).

34. Public Law 95–521, 92 Stat. 1867, 28 U.S.C. §§ 591–599.

35. 487 U.S. at 697, 710, 108 S. Ct. at 2622, 2629.

36. 487 U.S. at 673, 108 S. Ct. at 2610.

37. 487 U.S. at 693–4, 108 S. Ct. at 2620.

38. Article II, Section 2.

39. 487 U.S. at 673, 108 S. Ct. at 2608–9. The Supreme Court in 2010 made it somewhat simpler to justify a non-presidential appointment, holding in *Edmond v. United States*, 520 U.S. 651, 663, 117 S. Ct. 1573, 1581 (1997) that an "inferior officer" is merely one who is supervised by and can be removed at the will of a superior.

40. John Drake, Law for independent counsel likely won't be renewed in '99, *Houston Chronicle*, 10/7/98, A7, http://www.chron.com/CDA/archives/archive.mpl/1998_3088168/law-for-independent-counsel-likely-won-t-be-renewe.html.

41. E. E. Anderson, The Demise of the Independent Counsel—Legislative Update, *American Bar Association Newsletter*, Vol. 3, Number 15, July/August 1999, http://www.americanbar.org/newsletter/publications/gp_solo_magazine_home/gp_solo_magazine_index/1999_jul_aug_anderson.html.

42. Anthony Lewis, "No to King George," *New York Times*, 6/30/88, A23:1.

43. William T. Gormley Jr. and Steven J. Balla, *Bureaucracy and Democracy*, 3rd ed., (Los Angeles, CA: Sage/CQ Press, 2013), 86, n. 33.

44. William T. Gormley Jr. and Steven J. Balla, *Bureaucracy and Democracy*, 3rd ed., (Los Angeles, CA: Sage/CQ Press, 2013), 87, citation omitted.

45. Senior Executive Service Facts and Figures, U.S. Office of Personnel Management website, undated, http://www.opm.gov/policy-data-oversight/senior-executive-service/facts-figures/#url=Demographics, accessed 1/27/14.

46. Terry M. Moe and Scott A. Wilson, Presidents and the Politics of Structure, 57 *Law and Contemporary Problems* 1, 18 (Spring 1994).

47. 2014 U.S. LEXIS 4500, 24 Fla. L. Weekly Fed. S 941, No. 12-1281 (June 26, 2014).

48. Article II, Section 2, Clause 3.

49. 2014 U.S. LEXIS 4500 at *13.

50. Michael D. Shear, Decision by Justices Opens a New Debate on the Limits of Presidential Power, *The New York Times*, 6/27/14, A.16, c.1.

51. Article I, Section 5, Clause 4.

52. Shear, *supra*.

53. Noel Canning v. National Labor Relations Board, 705 F. 3d 490, 513 (D.C. Cir. 2013).

54. 705 F. 3d at 514.

55. 2014 U.S. LEXIS 4500 at 50–1.

56. 2014 U.S. LEXIS 4500 at *27–8.

57. 2014 U.S. LEXIS 4500 at *40.

58. 2014 U.S. LEXIS 4500 at *42.

59. 2014 U.S. LEXIS 4500 at *63–71.

60. Jeremy W. Peters, In Landmark Vote, Senate Limits Use of the Filibuster, *The New York Times*, 11/21/13, http://www.nytimes.com/2013/11/22/us/politics/reid-sets-in-motion-steps-to-limit-use-of-filibuster.html?pagewanted=all, accessed 7/8/14.

61. 487 U.S. at 697, 697–99. "Justice Scalia has famously argued . . . [that the President] stands at the apex of a unitary executive department and exercises supervisory power over all subordinates within his department." Steven G. Calabresi and Gary Lawson, The Unitary Executive, Jurisdiction Stripping, and the Hamdan Opinions: A Textualist Response to Justice Scalia, 107 *Colum. L. Rev.* 1002, 1006 (May 2007).

62. *Kendall v. United States*, 37 U.S. (12 Pet.) 524, 612–3, 9 L. Ed. 1181, 1216.

63. See, e.g., Edward T. Swaine, The Political Economy of *Youngstown*, 83 *Southern Cal. L. Rev.* 263, 266 (2010): The Jackson concurrence "has become *Youngstown's* enduring legacy . . . and it is widely accepted that his opinion is one of the Court's all-time greats." Swaine, however, is skeptical of this view.

64. Article II, Section 3.

65. *Youngstown Sheet & Tube Co. v. Sawyer*, 343 U.S. 579, 635–8, 72 S. Ct. 863, 870–871 (1952).

66. 343 U.S. at 639–640, 72 S. Ct. at 872.

67. 343 U.S. at 646, 72 S. Ct. at 875.

68. 343 U.S. at 637, 72 S. Ct. at 871.

69. Article II, Section 3. See Cass R. Sunstein and Richard H. Pildes, *Reinventing the Regulatory State*, 62 U. Chi. L. Rev. 1, 4–6 (Winter, 1995); Morton Rosenberg, Beyond the Limits of Executive Power: Presidential Control of Agency Rulemaking Under Executive Order 12,291, 80 *Mich. L. Rev.* 193 (Dec. 1981), *passim*, especially 220–221.

70. 46 Fed. Reg. 13,193 (1981).

71. Rosenberg, *supra* at 234.

72. Stuart Shapiro, The Evolution of Cost-Benefit Analysis in U.S. Regulatory Decisionmaking, *Jerusalem Papers in Regulation and Governance*, Working Paper Number 5 (May 2010), 6, http://regulation.huji.ac.il/papers/jp5.pdf.

73. 136 rules submitted by the Obama administration's agencies still under review by OIRA in 2013 at one point included "24 from 2011 and three from 2010," causing the *Times'* editorialist to call for "not just a more timely and transparent review process, but a president unafraid of Republicans or corporate interests and determined to enact his regulatory agenda." Stuck in Purgatory, editorial, *The New York Times*, 7/1/13, A22, http://www.nytimes.com/2013/07/01/opinion/stuck-in-purgatory.html?hpw.

74. *Whiley v. Scott*, 79 So. 3d 702, 716–7, 2011 Fla. LEXIS 1900 at *66 (2011).

75. *Rudder v. Pataki*, 246 A.D. 2d 183, 675 N.Y.S. 2d 653 (A.D. 3d 1998), *aff'd* (on the holding that the plaintiffs lacked standing to sue) 93 N.Y. 2d 273, 689 N.Y.S. 2d 710, 711 N.E. 2d 978 (1999).
76. 246 A.D. 2d at 190, 675 N.Y.S. 2d at 659.
77. 246 A.D. 2d 193, 675 N.Y.S. 2d at 660.
78. 246 A.D. 2d at 187, 675 N.Y.S. 2d at 656.
79. Jason A. Schwartz, 52 Experiments with Regulatory Review, *Institute for Policy Integrity*, NYU School of Law, 11/16/10, available at http://policyintegrity.org/publications/detail/52-experiments-with-regulatory-review/, accessed 1/8/15.
80. Foreign Relations Authorization Act, Fiscal Year 2003, 116 Stat. 1350. 1365–6, Section 214(d).
81. 7 Foreign Affairs Manual § 1383.1, App. 127.
82. Article II, Section 3.
83. Article I, Section 8, Clause 4.
84. Article I, Section 8, Clause 3.
85. *Zivotofsky v. Clinton*, 132 S. Ct. 1421, 1427; 182 L. Ed. 2d 423, 429 (2012).
86. 132 S. Ct. at 1427, 182 L. Ed. 2d at 429–30.
87. *Zivotofsky v. Secretary of State*, 725 F. 3d 197 (2013).
88. The Supreme Court granted certiorari in *Zivotofsky v. Kerry*, 134 S. Ct. 1873; 188 L. Ed. 2d 910 (2014), so as of this writing the matter remains uncertain.
89. 725 F. 3d at 208–9.
90. E.g., *United States v. Pink*, 315 U.S. 203, 229, 62 S. Ct. 552, 565 (1942).
91. 725 F. 3d at 214.
92. 725 F. 3d at 215 (citation omitted).
93. 725 F. 3d at 220.
94. 725 F. 3d at 216, quoting *Bowsher v. Synar*, 478 U.S. 714, 769, 106 Sup. Ct. 3181 (1986).
95. Arthur E. Bonfield and Michael Asimow, *State and Federal Administrative Law* (St. Paul, MN: West Publishing Company, 1989), 495, offered a similar problem based on *Muller Optical Co. v. EEOC*, 743 F. 2d 380 (6th Cir. 1984).

4
chapter

Keeping Track of Regulations; Discretionary and Informal Agency Action

KEEPING TRACK OF REGULATIONS

Until 1936, there was no place where one could find a compilation of administrative regulations. This proved especially embarrassing to the Department of Justice in the Roosevelt administration in 1934 when it tried to defend a regulation limiting oil production and transportation before the Supreme Court in *Panama Refining Co. v. Ryan*,[1] a major case whose substantive significance was addressed in Chapter 1. Someone in the administration had neglected to send to the printer the regulation in question, an executive order issued by President Roosevelt, casting very serious doubt on its validity. In the New Deal era, when for the first time hundreds of such orders could be issued in months, "even for those working at the highest levels in government, it was often difficult or impossible to keep track of the codes."[2] As a result, Justice Louis Dembitz Brandeis, U.S. Representative Emanuel Celler, Erwin Griswold, then a young attorney in the Solicitor General's office and much later United States Solicitor General and dean of Harvard Law School, were among the central figures in using this incident to generate support for the creation of the *Federal Register* by an act of Congress in 1935 (it first came out in 1936),[3] which would daily compile the new assortment of federal regulations in its pages. Two years later, as it became even clearer that the vast array of regulations needed some rational organization to enable attorneys, bureaucrats, and scholars to locate the information they needed, Congress required codification of their regulations by each agency, and in 1938 President Roosevelt, pursuant to the congressional mandate, ordered publication of the *Code of Federal Regulations* ("CFR"), to contain in an organized and searchable fashion the entire set of federal agency regulations.[4] Since the 70th anniversary of the *Federal Register*, there is now an electronic version of the more than 200 volumes and 75,000 pages of the CFR online as well as its paper edition available in certain libraries.[5]

BOX 4-1   **Proposed Rules Federal Register 2614**

Vol. 80, No. 12

Tuesday, January 20, 2015

This section of the FEDERAL REGISTER contains notices to the public of the proposed issuance of rules and regulations. The purpose of these notices is to give interested persons an opportunity to participate in the rule making prior to the adoption of the final rules.

[1]*See* 53 FR 50381 (Dec. 15, 1988).

Farm Credit Administration

12 CFR Part 611

RIN 3052–AC72

Organization; Mergers, Consolidations, and Charter Amendments of Banks or Associations

AGENCY: Farm Credit Administration.

ACTION: Proposed rule.

SUMMARY: The Farm Credit

Administration (FCA, Agency, we, or our) proposes to amend existing regulations related to mergers and consolidations of Farm Credit System (System) banks and associations to clarify the merger review and approval process and incorporate existing practices in the regulations. The proposed rule would identify when the statutory 60-day review period begins, require that only independent tabulators be authorized to validate ballots and . . .

DATES: You may send comments on or before April 20, 2015.

ADDRESSES: We offer a variety of methods for you to submit your comments. For accuracy and efficiency reasons, commenters are encouraged to submit comments by e-mail or through the FCA's Web site. As facsimiles (fax) are difficult for us to process and achieve compliance with section 508 of the Rehabilitation Act, we do not accept comments submitted by fax. Regardless of the method you use, please do not . . .

Source: http://www.gpo.gov/fdsys/pkg/FR-2015-01-20/html/2015-00676.htm

BOX 4-2 **Code of Federal Regulations (Annual Edition)**

Title 6 - Domestic Security

Parts 5 - 1003. January 1, 2014.

Chapter X - PRIVACY AND CIVIL LIBERTIES OVERSIGHT BOARD (Parts 1000–1003)

Part 1000—Organization and Delegation of Powers and Duties of the Privacy and Civil Liberties Oversight Board

Sec.

1000.1 Purpose.

1000.2 Definitions.

1000.3 Organization.

1000.4 Functions.

1000.5 Delegations of authority.

AUTHORITY: 5 U.S.C. 552.

SOURCE: 78 FR 33689, June 5, 2013, unless otherwise noted.

§ 1000.1 Purpose.

This part describes the organization of the Board, and the assignment of authorities and the responsibilities of the Board, individual Board members, and employees.

§ 1000.2 Definitions.

As used in this part:

Board means the Privacy and Civil Liberties Oversight Board, established by the Implementing Recommendations of the 9/11 Commission Act of 2007, Public Law 110–53.

Chairman means the Chairman of the Board, as appointed by the President and confirmed by the Senate under section 801(a) of the Implementing Recommendations of the 9/11 Commission Act of 2007, Public Law 110–53.

General Counsel means the Board's principal legal adviser.

Member means an individual appointed by the President, with the advice and consent of the Senate, to be a member of the Board.

§ 1000.3 Organization.

(a)　The Board is comprised of four part-time Board members and a fulltime Chairman, each appointed by the President with the advice and consent of the Senate.

(b)　The Board's staff is comprised of the following administrative units:

(1)　Office of Management and Operations;

(2)　Office of the General Counsel; and

(3)　Office of Liaison and Oversight.

§ 1000.4 Functions.

(a)　The Board provides advice and counsel to the President and executive departments and agencies to ensure that privacy and civil liberties are appropriately considered in proposed legislation, regulations, and policies, and in the implementation of new and existing legislation, regulations, and policies, related to efforts to protect the Nation from terrorism;

Source: http://www.gpo.gov/fdsys/pkg/FR-2013-06-05/pdf/2013-13166.pdf

Just as the federal government publishes the CFR, states publish new and proposed agency regulations in what are generally monthly registers, and make available complete and codified collections of their regulations.[6] Examples of each are furnished below.[7]

With the dramatic growth of government agency responsibilities in the New Deal, concerns rose among legal scholars as well as in Congress about protecting individuals from arbitrary or unfair agency practices. Instead of the "level playing field" of a courtroom, or the democratically elected body of a legislature, private citizens and businesses now faced hearings presided over and rules issued by administrative agencies; these agencies were apparently regarded as quite fearsome by then-conservative opponents, such as the American Bar Association.[8] While some statutes empowering agencies included procedural limits on their powers, many did not, and in any event the lack of uniformity contributed to confusion and unease. Under the direction of Walter Gellhorn in the final years of the Franklin Roosevelt administration, the Attorney General's Committee on Administrative Procedure worked to create

FIGURE 4-1 **Cover of Minnesota State Register**

Minnesota
State Register

(Published every Monday (Tuesday when Monday is a holiday.))

L'ETOILE DU NORD

THE GREAT SEAL OF THE STATE OF MINNESOTA ✦1858✦

Proposed, Adopted, Emergency, Expedited, Withdrawn, Vetoed Rules;
Executive Orders; Appointments; Commissioners' Orders; Revenue Notices;
Official Notices; State Grants & Loans; State Contracts;
Non-State Public Bids, Contracts & Grants

Monday 12 January 2015
Volume 39, Number 28
Pages 1027 - 1070

Source: Department of Administration Plant Management Division, State of Minnesota

uniform rules for the operation of federal agencies. Until FDR's death, agreement was delayed by disagreements between the weaker restrictions his allies would have imposed and the stronger restrictions many in Congress and the Bar Association would have preferred. In 1946, however, toward the beginning of the Truman administration, when "[v]ituperation had . . . gone out of style,"[9] Congress reached agreement with the Attorney General and passed the Administrative Procedure Act (APA).[10]

BOX 4-3   **Example of State Code of Regulations**

FIGURE 4-2   Screen Shot of South Carolina Code of Regulations

> **South Carolina Code of Regulations**
>
> Search the Full Text of the Code of Regulations
>
> Files are current through State Register Volume 38, Issue 12, effective December 26, 2014
>
> **PLEASE NOTE:** A Microsoft Word version of the Code of Regulations is now available. For the best rendering of tables, charts and images, please refer to the PDF version.
>
> CHAPTER 1 - DEPARTMENT OF LABOR, LICENSING AND REGULATION - BOARD OF ACCOUNTANCY

FIGURE 4-3   Screen Shot of Chapter 1 of South Carolina Code of Regulations

> # CHAPTER 1
>
> ## Department of Labor, Licensing and Regulation— Board of Accountancy
>
> (Statutory Authority: 1976 Code §§ 40–1–70 and 40–2–70)
>
> **1–01.** General Requirements for Licensure as a CPA.
>
> (A) Completed application for licensure shall be submitted on forms provided by the Board. All fees must accompany the application.
>
> (B) In order for an application to be considered, it must be complete, and all questions must be answered.
>
> (C) The Board shall accept any college or university accredited by the Southern Association of Colleges and Schools and any other accrediting association having the equivalent standards or any independent senior college in South Carolina certified by the State Department of Education for teaching training.
>
> (D) Until the licensee candidate has completed twenty four (24) semester hours of acceptable accounting education as described in 40–2–35(D)(3)(a), the candidate cannot earn qualifying experience for licensure.
>
> **HISTORY:** Added by State Register Volume 31, Issue No. 5, eff May 25, 2007.

Source: South Carolina Code of Regulations

STATE ADMINISTRATIVE PROCEDURE ACTS

Every state has adopted an APA, from North Dakota, the first in 1941, to Kansas and Kentucky, the last in 1984.[11] While the federal government needs only one APA, fifty states have varying needs and desires, and so each APA may be different. But, many states adopted parts or all of a model state APA, which was drafted by scholars and expert practitioners recruited by the Uniform Law Commission, an organization supported by state government since its creation in 1892.[12] In 1946, the same year Congress enacted the federal APA, drafters completed the first Model State Administrative Procedure Act (MSAPA). Congress could amend the federal APA on an ongoing basis, but drafters of the MSAPA could only respond to changing times and concerns by occasional major revisions. By the time they issued the 1961 MSAPA, "twelve states had adopted the 1946 Act."[13] "Over one half of the states adopted the 1961 MSAPA or large parts of it,"[14] and substantial portions of the 1981 MSAPA were adopted by three states, and some provisions by a few others.[15] For the most part, this book references the 2010 MSAPA for two reasons: first, because it reflects the latest thinking of administrative law scholars on the issues it addresses, and second because it is more similar to the 1961 MSAPA rather than to the 1946 or 1981 models,[16] and thus best reflects the majority of state administrative procedure acts.

INFORMAL, "EXECUTIVE," OR DISCRETIONARY AGENCY ACTION[17]

The Administrative Procedure Act (APA) and most discussions of administrative law center on rulemaking and adjudication. One brief section of the APA, called "Ancillary Matters," appears to provide its only—and very limited—guidance for informal agency action, offering a few simple and uncontroversial rules, such as permitting people to bring their lawyers to agencies and requiring agencies to provide prompt warnings and explanations when denying an application (see Box 4.4).[18]

BOX 4-4   **5 U.S. Code Administrative Procedure Act—Section 555**

§ 555. Ancillary Matters

(a) This section applies, according to the provisions thereof, except as otherwise provided by this subchapter.

(b) A person compelled to appear in person before an agency or representative thereof is entitled to be accompanied, represented, and advised by counsel or, if permitted by the agency, by other qualified representative. A party is entitled to appear in person or by or with counsel or other duly qualified representative in an agency proceeding. So far as the orderly conduct of public business permits, an interested person may appear before an agency or its responsible employees for the presentation, adjustment, or determination of an issue, request, or controversy in a proceeding, whether interlocutory, summary, or otherwise, or in connection with an agency function. With due regard for the convenience and necessity of the parties or their representatives and within a reasonable time, each agency shall proceed to conclude a matter presented to it. This subsection does not grant or deny a person who is not a lawyer the right to appear for or represent others before an agency or in an agency proceeding.

(c)   Process, requirement of a report, inspection, or other investigative act or demand may not be issued, made, or enforced except as authorized by law. A person compelled to submit data or evidence is entitled to retain or, on payment of lawfully prescribed costs, procure a copy or transcript thereof, except that in a nonpublic investigatory proceeding the witness may for good cause be limited to inspection of the official transcript of his testimony.

(d)   Agency subpoenas authorized by law shall be issued to a party on request and, when required by rules of procedure, on a statement or showing of general relevance and reasonable scope of the evidence sought. On contest, the court shall sustain the subpoena or similar process or demand to the extent that it is found to be in accordance with law. In a proceeding for enforcement, the court shall issue an order requiring the appearance of the witness or the production of the evidence or data within a reasonable time under penalty of punishment for contempt in case of contumacious failure to comply.

(e)   Prompt notice shall be given of the denial in whole or in part of a written application, petition, or other request of an interested person made in connection with any agency proceeding. Except in affirming a prior denial or when the denial is self-explanatory, the notice shall be accompanied by a brief statement of the grounds for denial.

Source: http://www.gpo.gov/fdsys/pkg/USCODE-2011-title5/html/USCODE-2011-title5-partI-chap5-subchapII-sec555.htm

Other sections of the APA, however, provide for judicial review of any "agency action" that violates a person's rights[19] and empower federal courts to impose appropriate remedies.[20] What, then, is a truly "discretionary" action? In his momentous decision in *Marbury v. Madison*,[21] Chief Justice Marshall wrote,

> The province of the court is, solely, to decide on the rights of individuals, not to enquire how the executive, or executive officers, perform duties in which they have a discretion. Questions, in their nature political, or which are, by the constitution and laws, submitted to the executive, can never be made in this court.[22]

And yet, we see below that judicial review of major "discretionary" decisions by agencies has determined their legality, whether on the basis of provisions in their own substantive statutes or on the basis of Section 702 of the APA, providing for judicial review of any "agency action" that violates a person's rights.

The 2010 State Administrative Procedure Act (MSAPA) does not appear to include provisions comparable to APA Section 702 covering informal discretionary executive actions, but does include provisions providing for judicial review of any "final agency action" or non-final action "if postponement . . . would result in an inadequate remedy or irreparable harm that outweighs the public benefit that derives from postponing"[23] and empowering courts to remedy violative agency actions.[24]

While the federal APA might provide for judicial review of a discretionary agency action, it would not require an agency to offer a hearing to someone aggrieved by that action. But, a state APA might produce a different result. Oregon's APA shares with the 2010 MSAPA and many other states that part of its definition of "contested case" is a case that covers any adjudication where a statute or constitution requires an evidentiary hearing.[25] Unlike the 2010 MSAPA, Oregon's APA also requires a hearing for any "contested case," which it defines to include discretionary revocations of a privilege, and seems to exclude from that aspect of its definition only "proceedings in which an agency decision rests solely on the result of a test."[26] A bare majority of the Oregon court held that the award of a textbook by the Textbook Committee of its Board of Education did not qualify to give the disappointed organization a hearing, but a contractor for Oregon's school lunch program might well have won the right to a hearing to challenge its replacement by a different contractor (a "discretionary revocation[]" of a privilege"),[27] while a contractor replaced by a federal agency or the agencies of most other states would probably not succeed in getting a hearing under such circumstances.

BOX 4-5 **Oregon Administrative Procedures Act—Section 183.310**

[OREGON]

Administrative Procedures Act

(General Provisions)

183.310 Definitions for chapter. As used in this chapter: . . .

(2) (a) "Contested case" means a proceeding before an agency: . . .

(B) Where the agency has discretion to suspend or revoke a right or privilege of a person; . . .

(b) "Contested case" does not include proceedings in which an agency decision rests solely on the result of a test.

Source: http://www.oregonlaws.org/ors/183.310

BOX 4-6   **2010 Revised Model State Administrative Procedure Act**

[ARTICLE] 1

GENERAL PROVISIONS . . .

SECTION 102. DEFINITIONS. In this [act]: . . .

(7) "Contested case" means an adjudication in which an opportunity for an evidentiary 8 hearing is required by the federal constitution, a federal statute, or the constitution or a statute of this state.

Source: http://www.uniformlaws.org/shared/docs/state%20administrative%20procedure/msapa_final_10.pdf

Discretion Pluses and Minuses

Informal action, when it involves discretion, often raises difficult questions. A police officer catches a boy who threw a rock and broke a windshield. Should the officer give friendly advice, or initiate an arrest leading to trial and punishment? He arrests a second boy for the same act. We like to think that people should be treated equally under the law. But, what if the officer knows both boys, the second has been a troublemaker and the first has never been in trouble, has a dying parent, and was merely influenced by the first boy? Taking away the officer's discretion can lower the quality of street-level justice here, although it could also prevent unfairness or bias. Teachers, similarly, need discretion to decide which student to suspend—or, contrary to some currently popular notions,[28] how to shape their lessons to reach particular students most effectively.[29] But there too, discretion can also result in disservice.

It has been estimated that "more than 90 percent of the American administrative process is behind closed doors," outside the reach of the statutes requiring open, public, and reviewable procedures for rulemaking and adjudication.[30] Agencies resist structuring their discretion with public, published policy statements, plans, rules, findings, and the like for good reasons and for bad: "publishing the rules I use will only invite trouble. The lawyers for the . . . [finance companies, or fill in the blank with any subject of government concern] are very able and find flaws in almost any document or ruling."[31]

Agencies engage in informal action far more than rulemaking and adjudication, as should be immediately obvious considering the work of the Social Security Administration in sending out checks, the Veterans Administration in running hospitals, the Department of Transportation in maintaining federal highways, or virtually any other agency. The Internal Revenue Service, for example, in 2013 processed over 240 million tax returns, including more than 145 million individual returns,[32] issued over 120 million refunds,[33] audited over 1.5 million returns,[34] and resolved about

195,000 complaints from taxpayers.[35] The Social Security Administration paid benefits to more than 58 million people in 2013.[36]

The Securities and Exchange Commission's and the Justice Department's discretionary decisions as to whether to pursue penalties against bankers responsible for the financial crisis of 2007 generated considerable controversy,[37] and even an extraordinary message from a jury that acquitted one such defendant, but urged the SEC to continue to "investigate the financial industry."[38]

Agency Work Outside of Rulemaking and Adjudication

Most of the work of state and local agencies, likewise, takes place outside the realms of adjudication and rulemaking, and therefore includes "informal" decisions, with a large component subject to discretion. The vast majority of the poor do not have access to lawyers for noncriminal matters,[39] so it likely remains true that "only a small percentage of violative agency decisions are appealed" among the millions of recipients eligible for income assistance.[40] Thus, a state's Department of Social Services makes the vast majority of its benefit decisions on what is, in effect, a discretionary basis, just as the "administrative" work of federal agencies, when that work does not constitute adjudication or rulemaking, can reflect the exercise of discretionary judgment.

In principle, § 702 of the APA makes virtually any agency decision subject to judicial review,[41] and § 706(2)(A) empowers courts to redress the harm caused by an abuse of discretion. But, because § 555 of the APA, the "Ancillary Matters" section, only requires notice and a brief explanation of informal decisions, litigants have had little basis in the APA on which to challenge such decisions. Thus, challenges to "discretionary decisions" are relatively rare. Still, agency discretion has limits.

BOX 4-7   **5 U.S. Code Administrative Procedure Act—Section 702**

APA § 702 – Right of Review

A person suffering legal wrong because of agency action, or adversely affected or aggrieved by agency action within the meaning of a relevant statute, is entitled to judicial review thereof. An action in a court of the United States seeking relief other than money damages and stating a claim that an agency or an officer or employee thereof acted or failed to act in an official capacity or under color of legal authority shall not be dismissed nor relief therein be denied on the ground that it is against the United States or that the United States is an indispensable party. The United States may be named as a defendant in any such action, and a judgment or decree may be entered against the United States: Provided, that any mandatory or injunctive decree shall specify the Federal officer or officers (by name or by title), and their successors in office, personally responsible for compliance. Nothing herein

(1)   affects other limitations on judicial review or the power or duty of the court to dismiss any action or deny relief on any other appropriate legal or equitable ground; or

(2)   confers authority to grant relief if any other statute that grants consent to suit expressly or impliedly forbids the relief which is sought.

Source: http://www.gpo.gov/fdsys/pkg/USCODE-2010-title5/pdf/USCODE-2010-title5-partI-chap7-sec702.pdf

Court Challenges to Discretionary Decisions

The Supreme Court found such an abuse of discretion when the Board of Immigration Appeals based its decision to deport an alien on matters "irrelevant to the alien's fitness to reside in this country," and overruled the deportation decision.[42] The Court dispatched the argument that the Board had exercised its discretion in a similarly wide-ranging matter in the past: "Arbitrary agency action becomes no less so by dint of repetition."[43]

The Court faced a more contentious issue in dealing with a change in agency policy governing a category of discretionary decisions when the Federal Communications Commission decided to impose penalties on a television station for "indecency" on the basis of fewer violations than in the past. Justice Scalia, for the Court, decided that it is good enough for the agency to give reasons no more in depth than those used to justify the previous policy. The agency need not show "that the reasons for the new policy are *better* than the reasons for the old one [emphasis in original]."[44] Justice Breyer, dissenting, deemed the agency's failure to explain why it changed its position,[45] in the words of APA § 706, "arbitrary, capricious, and an abuse of discretion."[46]

Perhaps the most significant decision concerning the Court's review of discretionary agency action, *Citizens to Preserve Overton Park v. Volpe*, based primarily on substantive law, not the APA, involved the Secretary of Transportation's decision to approve a federally funded highway through a park without issuing findings or an explanation.[47] Federal law prohibited such harm to parkland unless there was no reasonable alternative and the Department had engaged in "all possible planning to minimize harm."[48] Local environmentalists argued that the Secretary and his Department had simply followed the lead of the Memphis City Council, and had engaged in no planning or analysis on their own.[49] The Secretary claimed that he had indeed made his own decision. Since the decision was neither one of rulemaking nor of adjudication, it did not need to be supported by findings or by "substantial evidence,"[50] the not-very-demanding test of support for adjudicative decisions.[51] The Court, however, addressed the more ambitious claim that the Secretary's decision fell under the APA's exception to judicial review for "agency action . . . committed to agency discretion by law."[52] In rejecting that claim, the Court referred to its legislative history, indicating a limit to its reach to powers exercised under "statutes . . . drawn in such broad terms that in a given case there is no law to apply."[53] Since the statute set reasonably clear criteria to guide the Secretary's decision,[54] the Court ruled that the Secretary's decision did not fall within "this . . . very narrow exception"[55] offered by the APA. The Supreme Court simply told the District Court for the Western District of Tennessee to review the record on which the Secretary had based his decision and to question Transportation Department officials further if necessary to verify the Secretary's claim that he had in fact made a reasoned decision. It warned, however, that "inquiry into the mental processes of administrative decisionmakers is usually to be avoided."[56]

Thus, while courts would not consider reviewing the vast majority of discretionary decisions involved in "the work of the Social Security Administration in sending out checks, the Veterans Administration in running hospitals, the Department of Transportation in maintaining federal highways,"[57] the "sharp dichotomy" drawn by Justice Marshall in the above quotation from *Marbury* between questions of individual rights and questions of discretionary executive duties "is at least a trichotomy . . . there exists a middle ground of discretion-under-law that characterizes the operating environment of the administrative state."[58] Thus, Professor Peter Strauss likes to tell his students that there is "AGENCY DISCRETION!!! and agency discretion."[59]

State law is generally comparable. For example, in reviewing a claim against a parole board for refusing to grant parole, the Illinois court noted that "[t]he statutory provisions do not . . . state when the Board must grant parole [citation omitted],"[60] drew an explicit comparison to aforementioned federal APA exception for "agency action . . . committed to agency discretion by law," and denied review of the refusal.[61]

Thus, the informal character of *most* agency decision-making remains relatively unfettered.

INVESTIGATION, PROSECUTION, AND IMPOSITION OF PENALTIES

Decisions not to prosecute or seek imposition of penalties, whether by a prosecutor in the criminal justice system or by other kinds of agencies in the civil context, remain almost wholly discretionary.[62] In *Heckler v. Chaney*,[63] death-row inmates sued the Food and Drug Administration for its refusal to ban injection of certain drugs to impose capital punishment as "unapproved use of an approved drug." A provision of federal Food, Drug and Cosmetic Act[64] made it clear that the FDA was not required to refer "minor violations" for prosecution or to sue civilly on such a basis.[65] So, the inmates inferred that the FDA *was* required to pursue more significant violations. The Court, however, rejecting that argument and less persuasive ones, noted that "an agency's decision not to prosecute or enforce, whether through civil or criminal process, is a decision generally committed to an agency's absolute discretion."[66] The Court explained the considerations involved justify deference to agency expertise in determining:

> whether a violation has occurred, . . . whether agency resources are best spent on this violation or another, whether the agency is likely to succeed if it acts, whether the particular enforcement action requested best fits the agency's overall policies, and, indeed, whether the agency has enough resources to undertake the action at all.[67]

As noted in Chapter 2, the Obama Administration cited *Heckler v. Chaney* in support of its 2014 executive order[68] to expand its 2012 program of "Deferred Action for Childhood Arrivals," modeled on the DREAM Act legislation, which was not enacted.[69]

For the most part, the courts have also allowed agencies to run investigations as they please. Using federal constitutional principles as guidelines in interpreting a state law, in *New York v. Berger*[70] the Supreme Court allowed a warrantless search, as a proper exercise of an agency's discretionary authority, not subject to the restrictions on rulemaking or adjudication.[71] But, that was only because the agency "pervasively regulated" the business in question, so companies involved in that business had no expectation of privacy that would bar such a search. Otherwise, an agency *would* need a warrant.[72] Similarly, the courts allowed the Federal Trade Commission (FTC), under the APA, to require companies to file detailed reports, and in 1975 to order 450 of the nation's biggest manufacturers to file Line of Business forms separating revenue, assets, and profit information for each of their respective lines. With these statistics, the FTC could target possible industry-wide antitrust or unfair trade practices. Companies objected to the high cost of preparing the reports, and many refused to file. The companies argued that since no rule or regulation required those reports, the FTC could not force them to comply. The D.C. Circuit Court of Appeals disagreed, placing investigations in the category of discretionary action, not rulemaking.[73] So long as the agency's information demand did not "transcend [its] investigatory power, . . . is not unduly burdensome or too indefinite, and the information sought is reasonably relevant,"[74] an agency may impose it under § 555(c) of the APA, the provision authorizing investigations, assuming the demand survives scrutiny under § 706 as not "arbitrary, capricious, an abuse of discretion, or otherwise not in accordance with law."

In *New York v. Berger*, although the Supreme Court allowed the warrantless search, the New York court found otherwise, ruling that under the provision of the New York State Constitution restricting search and seizure,[75] an agency *does* need a warrant even to inspect a pervasively regulated business.[76] Even if the inspections were "part of a comprehensive administrative program that is unrelated to the enforcement of the criminal laws"—and the New York court held that the inspection program here was indeed related to criminal law enforcement—the court would still require "an administrative warrant issued by a neutral Magistrate, although [the inspections] need not be based on probable cause in the traditional sense, or, alternatively, the law must provide for such certainty and regularity of application as to be a constitutionally adequate substitute for a warrant [citations omitted]."[77]

California's courts, however, hewed closer to the federal model, ruling that if the agency's enabling legislation ("authorized regulatory purpose")[78] requires regulated entities to maintain relevant records, no Fifth Amendment privilege bars the agency from inspecting such records, and so the agency does not need a warrant to do so.[79]

Arguably, Ronald Reagan's executive order empowering the Office of Management and Budget to invalidate agency rules on the basis of excessive cost to business may have been a reaction to the federal decisions empowering agencies, although the executive order did not directly affect agency investigative orders.[80] The courts, however, will rarely overturn an agency's discretionary decision.

NON-PUBLIC POLICYMAKING AND "GUIDANCE"

"Guidance" documents include agencies' policy manuals and "non-legislative" or "interpretive" and "procedural" rules, which do not command or add any obligations or burdens to affected parties, but merely explain how an agency intends to exercise its discretion in interpreting existing "legislative" rules or regulations, which do include substantive commands. Although the APA requires agencies to publish policy statements and interpretive rules in the *Federal Register*,[81] they do not provide any additional legal support for action except under rare circumstances and agencies ordinarily pay no penalty even if they fail to publish them.[82] However, the determination of whether a policy statement has "binding force" and thus whether it is truly "non-legislative" rather than "legislative" can be so difficult that the legal principles used to make that determination have been characterized as "engulfed in smog."[83]

An agency might set forth a policy in a manual for the use of its own personnel, which is not published and which was prepared without adhering to any formal processes. Although such a policy statement is not an "authoritative" statement of law, it may nonetheless require compliance as part of "a body of experience and informed judgment to which courts and litigants may properly resort for guidance."[84] Courts call this form of deference to an informal and unpublished agency policy decision "*Skidmore* deference."[85] When someone goes to court to challenge an agency action, the court often has to decide whether the agency followed the law that empowered it: did the agency interpret that law correctly in taking the action? Courts frequently defer to the agency's interpretation on the grounds that the agency that administers a statute has the advantage of significant experience in so doing. We discuss the stronger version of such deference, known as "*Chevron* deference," in Chapter 6.

In general, however, although informality need not invalidate the force of policy decisions, the absence of publication does. In *Morton v. Ruiz*,[86] the policy manual of the Bureau of Indian Affairs prohibited certain benefits to Native Americans who did not live on reservations. The Court found not only that the prohibition had not been made public, but that the Bureau by its previous actions had signaled the opposite message.[87] Further, under the Bureau's own rules, such a directive should have been published before taking effect.[88] The APA requires publication of "substantive rules of general applicability adopted as authorized by law, and statements of general policy or interpretations of general applicability formulated and adopted by the agency,"[89] in order, in the Court's view, "to avoid the inherently arbitrary nature of unpublished *ad hoc* determinations."[90] In this matter, the agency's overall record was too inconsistent for *Skidmore* deference to apply, so the Court ruled that the Bureau had to provide the assistance in controversy to the plaintiffs and to others similarly situated.[91]

INFORMAL RULEMAKING

The fact that the words of a statute seem to require a hearing does not mean the agency really has to have one, at least not in the sense most people understand the word, as requiring someone to listen.[92] Unless an agency's enabling statute requires rulemaking "on-the-record after opportunity for an agency hearing,"[93] an agency only has to give notice of the proposed rule by publication in the *Federal Register* ("The Daily Journal of the United States Government"[94]) for at least thirty days before it takes effect, allow for public comment, consider the comments, and "incorporate in the rules adopted a concise general statement of their basis and purpose."[95] Rulemaking governing "military or foreign affairs" or "agency management or personnel or . . . public property, loans, grants, benefits, or contracts" is exempt altogether.[96] Unless the enabling statute so requires, the agency does not even have to use this "notice and comment" process for "(A) . . . interpretative rules, general statements of policy, or rules of agency organization, procedure, or practice; or (B) when the agency for good cause finds [and explains in the rules] that notice and public procedure thereon are impracticable, unnecessary, or contrary to the public interest."[97] But, an agency cannot use the "interpretative rule" exception unless the rule really just explains something in an existing rule[98]; or the "procedural rule" exception unless the rule really just changes procedure[99]—not when their provisions effectuate some substantive change in the law affecting peoples' actual rights.

WHAT AM I SUPPOSED TO DO?

International Trade Commission Patent Infringement Investigation: Limits on Discretionary Action

You are a member of the United States International Trade Commission. The Commission is investigating whether *B* Company has infringed *C* Company's patent by importing a device using certain advanced technology. *B* Company has persuaded you that A-Big Company, located in Hong Kong, has documents that would show that *B* Company did not infringe the patent. The Commission does not have direct jurisdiction over A-Big Company. However, A-Big Company owns a California subsidiary, A-Little Company, and the Commission does have jurisdiction over A-Little Company.

A-Big Company makes devices similar to those sold by *B* Company. A-Little Company sells those devices in the United States. You know that the courts have given agencies a great deal of leeway in conducting investigations. Should you subpoena A-Little Company for the documents you are pretty sure that it or its parent company has? Pressure on its subsidiary could force A-Big Company to release the documents, which could answer a question vital to your investigation. On the other hand, if A-Little challenges the subpoena, as you strongly suspect it will, and if the courts uphold the challenge, you will embarrass the Commission.

A case with similar facts came to the federal Circuit Court of Appeals for the District of Columbia.[100] The court noted that in *United States v. Morton Salt Company*, the Supreme Court had held that the courts can second-guess agency tactics in their investigations to make sure that "the inquiry is within the authority of the agency, the demand is not too indefinite and the information sought is reasonably relevant,"[101] apparently implying that if the inquiry meets all three requirements, the courts will enforce the agency's demands. The situation you face seems to meet all three requirements: the Commission has the authority to investigate patent infringements in the international trade context, the demand is only for documents related to one particular narrow question, and the documents in question directly relate to the Commission's larger investigation. But, the Court in *Morton Salt* also made a broader point: judicial review of agency action must "protect against mistaken or arbitrary orders."[102] The subsidiary was only engaged in sales, and therefore quite plausibly maintained that it did not have and could not get access to the relevant documents. In the ASAT case, the Circuit Court found that on the basis of the information that the Commission had at this point, therefore, were the courts to enforce the Commission's subpoena, it would have to do so based on "the untenable position that any subsidiary whose business life may be threatened has the ability to control its parent's documents" in a situation in which that position "appears to be based on pure speculation without support in the record."[103] The court invited the Commission to find more evidence to support its theory that the subsidiary could get possession of the documents, but meanwhile it refused to enforce the subpoena.[104]

PRACTICE PROBLEM

Assume that under its enabling statute, a State Athletic Commission could, in its discretion, deny a boxing license to an applicant "convicted of one or more felonies, misdemeanors or military offenses involving moral turpitude." Assume that during the Vietnam era it did deny such a license to a boxer who had been convicted of a felony for refusing his draft notice, although it had not denied licenses to many other boxers convicted of felonies. The boxer sued the Athletic Commission, asking the court to require it to reverse its decision and grant the license. Was he successful? Would it matter if this were a case in federal court under the APA?

ENDNOTES

1. 293 U.S. 388, 55 S. Ct. 281 (1935).
2. Lotte Feinberg, Mr. Justice Brandeis and the Creation of the *Federal Register*, 61 *Public Administration Review* 359, 363 (May/June 2001).
3. *Id.*, throughout.
4. *A Brief History Commemorating the 70th Anniversary of the Publication of the First Issue of the Federal Register*, March 14, 1936, The Office of the Federal Register, National Archives and Records Administration, June 19, 2006, http://www.archives.gov/federal-register/the-federal-register/history.pdf, accessed 1/14/15.
5. *Id.*
6. Andrew Zimmerman, State Regulations and Administrative Codes, *Zimmerman's Research Guide*, LexisNexis 2015, http://law.lexisnexis.com/infopro/zimmermans/disp.aspx?z=1966, accessed 1/14/15.
7. For a sample of state registers and codes of regulations, see, e.g., Alaska Administrative Code, Barclay's Official California Code of Regulations, Colorado Code of Regulations, Rules and Regulations of the State of Georgia, Kansas Register, Louisiana Administrative Code and Louisiana Register, Code of Maine Rules, Code of Massachusetts Regulations, Minnesota State Register, Mississippi Government Register, Montana Code Annotated, Nevada Register of Administrative Regulations, New Mexico Administrative Code, NJ Administrative Code, New York Code of Rules & Regulations, S. Car. Code of Regulations, Texas Register, Utah Administrative Code, Vermont Government Register, W. Va. Code of State Rules, Wisconsin Administrative Code, Wyoming Government Register.
8. See, e.g., Walter Gellhorn, The Administrative Procedure Act: The Beginnings, 72 *Virginia L. Rev.* 219 March 1986), especially 221–3.
9. 72 *Virginia L. Rev.* at 229. See also Martin Shapiro, A Golden Anniversary? The Administrative Procedures Act of 1946, 19 *Regulation* 40, 40–1 (1996), available at http://scholarship.law.berkeley.edu/facpubs/379. Accessed 1/14/15.
10. P.L. 404, 79th Congress, Chapter 324, 2d Session, 60 Stat. 237, 1946, 5 U.S.C. §§ 500 et seq.
11. Rui J. P. de Figueiredo, Jr., and Richard G. Vanden Burgh, *Protecting the Weak: Why (and When) States Adopt an Administrative Procedure Act*, October 2001, Manuscript, Haas School of Business, U.C. Berkeley, California, 5, Table 1.
12. About the ULC, Uniform Law Commission website, http://www.uniformlawcommission.com/Narrative.aspx?title=About%20the%20ULC, accessed 1/14/15.
13. Prefatory Note, *Revised Model State Administrative Procedure Act*, National Conference of Commissioners on Uniform State Laws, 2010, 1.
14. *Id.*
15. *Id.* at 2.
16. "The 2010 MSAPA maintains continuity with the provisions of the 1961 Act, and to a lesser degree, the 1981 Act." State Administrative Procedure Act, Revised Model Summary, 2015,

website of the Uniform Law Commission, National Conference of Commissioners on Uniform State Laws, http://www.uniformlaws.org/ActSummary.aspx?title=State%20 Administrative%20Procedure%20Act,%20Revised%20Model, accessed 1/14/15.

17. Since § 551(6) of the APA defines an "order" as the result of any agency decision-making process other than rulemaking, and § 551(7) defines an adjudication as the process that results in an order, a vast array of informal agency actions, technically, are "informal adjudications." But, this terminology is confusing and misleading since many such actions consist merely of someone's quick decision, perhaps based on an application form, and do not resemble adjudication at all.

18. § 555.

19. § 702.

20. § 706.

21. 5 U.S. 137, 2 L. Ed. 60 (1803).

22. 5 U.S. at 166, 2 L. Ed. 70.

23. 2010 MSAPA § 501.

24. 2010 MSAPA § 508.

25. 2010 MSAPA § 102(7) and Oregon Revised Statutes § 183.310(2)(a)(A).

26. Oregon Revised Statutes § 183.310(2)(a)(B) and (2)(b).

27. *Oregon Environmental Council v. Oregon State Board of Education*, 761 P. 2d 1322 (Ore. 1988).

28. See, e.g., the example of Great Britain, where teachers "had a National Curriculum and national assessment forced on them without consultation," Ian Taylor, Discretion and Control in Education, 35 *Educational Management Administration and Leadership* 555, 559 (9/12/07), http://ema.sagepub.com/content/35/4/555, quoting B. P. Jeffrey Woods and G. Troman, *Restructuring Schools*, (Buckingham, UK: Open University Press, 1997), 151.

29. Michael Lipsky, *Street-Level Bureaucracy*, (New York: Russell Sage Foundation, 2010 [1980]), 13–18, http://books.google.com/books?id=WjUBulsr2OO0C&printsec=frontcover&source= gbs_ge_summary_r&cad=0#v=onepage&q&f=false; Kenneth Culp Davis, *Discretionary Justice*, (Westport, CN: Greenwood Press, 1980), 88.

30. Davis, *id.* at 282. In the present author's view, the percentage of agency decision-making "behind closed doors" is probably lower today than when Davis was writing. However, informal decision-making is still said to "comprise around 90 percent of all administrative action." William F. Fox, *Understanding Administrative Law*, 6th ed., (New Providence, NJ and San Francisco, CA: Matthew Bender, 2012), 261, citing Wendell Gardner, *The Procedures by Which Informal Action Is Taken*, 24 *Admin. L. Rev.* 155 (1972).

31. Davis, *id.*

32. 2013 Internal Revenue Service Data Book, March 2014, www.irs.gov/pub/irs-soi/13databk .pdf, 4, accessed 7/10/14.

33. *Id.*, 17.

34. *Id.*, 22.

35. *Id.*, 48.

36. *Social Security Basic Facts*, website of the Social Security Administration, http://www.ssa .gov/news/press/basicfact.html, accessed 7/10/14.

37. See, e.g., Marion Wang, Why No Financial Crisis Prosecutions?, *ProPublica*, 12/6/11, http:// www.propublica.org/article/why-no-financial-crisis-prosecutions-official-says-its-just- too-hard; Peter J. Henning, Dim Prospects for Financial Crisis Prosecutions, *New York Times*, 5/29/12, http://dealbook.nytimes.com/2012/05/29/dim-prospects-for-financial- crisis-prosecutions/; Jean Eaglesham, Financial Crimes Bedevil Prosecutors, 12/6/11, *Wall Street Journal*, http://online.wsj.com/article/SB1000142405297020408320457708079235 61440.html.

38. Peter Lattman, S.E.C. Gets Encouragement From Jury That Ruled Against It, *New York Times*, 8/3/12, http://dealbook.nytimes.com/2012/08/03/s-e-c-gets-encouragement-from- jury-that-ruled-against-it/.

39. "[M]ore than 2.3 million New Yorkers are unrepresented in civil legal proceedings in New York State courts [annually]." Helaine M. Barnett, Chair, Task Force to Expand Access

to Civil Legal Services in New York et al., Report to the Chief Judge of the State of New York, November 2010, http://www.courts.state.ny.us/ip/access-civil-legal-services/PDF/CLS-TaskForceREPORT.pdf, 4.

40. Daniel L. Feldman, Administrative Agencies and the Rites of Due Process, 7 *Fordham Urban L. J.* 229, 241 (No. 2, 1978–9), citing a 1976 study. Text at the previous footnote suggests that its findings remain valid.

41. Its exception for decisions "committed to agency discretion by law" has little impact, since the Court has interpreted it to mean when "there is no law to apply." Legislative history of the APA, S. Rep. No. 752, 79th Congress, 1st Sess., 26, 1945, cited in *Citizens to Preserve Overton Park v. Volpe*, 401 U.S. 402, 410, 91 S. Ct. 814, 821 (1971).

42. *Judalong v. Holder*, 132 S. Ct. 476, 478, 181 L. Ed. 2d 449, 454 (2011).

43. 132 S. Ct. at 488, 181 L. Ed. at 465.

44. *FCC v. Fox Television Stations*, 556 U.S. 502, 515, 129 S. Ct. 1800, 1811 (2009).

45. 556 U.S. at 549, 129 S. Ct. at 1830–1.

46. 556 U.S. at 547, 129 S. Ct. at 1829.

47. *Citizens to Preserve Overton Park v. Volpe*, 401 U.S. 402, 410, 91 S. Ct. 814, 821 (1971).

48. 49 U.S.C. § 1653(f) and 23 U.S.C. § 138 (1964 ed., Supp. V), cited at 401 U.S. at 404, 91 S. Ct. at 817, n.4.

49. 401 U.S. at 408, 91 S. Ct. at 819.

50. 401 U.S. at 414, 91 S. Ct. at 822–3.

51. 401 U.S. at 417, 91 S. Ct. at 824.

52. APA § 701(a)(2).

53. S. Rep. No. 752, 79th Cong. 1st Sess., 26 (1945), cited at 401 U.S. at 410, 91 S. Ct. at 821.

54. 401 U.S. at 411, 91 S. Ct. at 821.

55. 401 U.S. at 410, 91 S. Ct. at 821.

56. 401 U.S. at 420, 91 S. Ct. at 825, citation omitted.

57. Text above between notes 31 and 32.

58. Peter Strauss, Revisiting Overton Park: Political and Judicial Controls Over Administrative Actions Affecting the Community, 39 *UCLA L. Rev.* 1251, 1256 (1992).

59. E-mail to author, 1/24/15.

60. *Hanrahan v. Williams*, 174 Ill. 2d 268, 276, 673 N.E. 2d 251, 255 (1996).

61. 174 Ill. 2d at 281, 673 N.E. 2d at 256.

62. The European tradition does not commit such full discretion to prosecutors, although European countries now differ widely in their practices. See, e.g., Allison Marston Danner, Enhancing the Legitimacy and Accountability of Prosecutorial Discretion at the International Criminal Court, 97 *Amer. J. of Int'l Law* 510, 513 (2003).

63. *Heckler v. Chaney*, 470 U.S. 821, 105 S. Ct. 1649 (1985).

64. 52 Stat. 1040, 21 U.S.C. § 301 et seq.

65. 21 U.S.C. § 336.

66. 470 U.S. at 831, 105 S. Ct. at 1655.

67. 470 U.S. at 831, 105 S. Ct. at 1656.

68. Executive Actions on Immigration, website of the Department of Homeland Security, 11/24/14, http://www.uscis.gov/immigrationaction, accessed 11/26/14.

69. Chapter 2, text at notes 65–84.

70. *New York v. Berger*, 482 U.S. 691, 107 Sup. Ct. 2636 (1987).

71. *New York v. Berger*, 482 U.S. 691, *id.* Legitimate pursuit of the administrative goal of the agency in deterring automobile theft justified the searches of vehicle dismantlers ("chop shops"), notwithstanding potential use of the information in individual criminal prosecutions, so the Fourth Amendment challenge was unavailing.

72. *Marshall v. Barlow's*, 436 U.S. 307, 311–2, 98 S. Ct. 1816, 1820–1 (1978).

73. *In re FTC Line of Business Report Litigation*, 595 F. 2d 685, 695 193 U.S. App. D.C. 300 (D.C. Cir. 1978). The Circuit Court relied on *United States v. Morton Salt*, 338 U.S. 632, 70 S. Ct. 357 (1950): An administrative agency "has the power of inquisition . . . which is not derived from the judicial function. It is more analogous to a Grand Jury, which . . . can investigate

merely on suspicion that the law is being violated, or even just because it wants assurance that it is not." 338 U.S. at 642–3, 70 S. Ct. at 364.

74. 595 F. 2d at 703.

75. Article I, Section 12.

76. *People v. Scott*, 79 N.Y. 2d 474, 502, 593 N.E. 2d 1328, 1345 (N.Y. 1992).

77. 79 N.Y. 2d at 501–2, 593 N.E. 2d at 1345.

78. *Craib v. Bulmash*, 49 Cal. 3d 475, 478, 777 P. 2d 1120, 1121 (Cal. 1989).

79. 49 Cal. 3d at 477, 777 P. 2d at 1128.

80. See Chapter 3.

81. APA § 552(a)(1)(D).

82. See Mark Seidenfeld, Substituting Substantive for Procedural Review of Guidance Documents, 90 *Texas L. Rev.* 331, 340 (2011), citing APA § 552(a)(1) and (2).

83. *Id.* at 339, citations omitted.

84. *Skidmore v. Swift & Co.*, 323 U.S. 124, 140, 65 S. Ct. 161, 164 (1944), quoted in *Sierra Club v. United States Environmental Protection Agency*, 671 F. 3d 955, 962 (9th Cir. 2012). However, the quotation was mere *dictum* in *Sierra Club*. The actual memorandum to which the court gave "limited deference," although informal, had in fact been open to public review and comment. 671 F. 3d at 963.

85. 671 F. 3d at 962.

86. 415 U.S. 199, 94 S. Ct. 1055 (1974).

87. 415 at 228–9, 94 S. Ct. at 1071.

88. 415 U.S. at 233, 94 S. Ct. at 1073.

89. Section 552(a)(1).

90. 415 U.S. at 232, 94 S. Ct. at 1073.

91. 415 U.S. at 237–8, 94 S. Ct. at 1075–6.

92. *United States v. Florida East Coast Railway Company*, 410 U.S. 224, 241, 93 S. Ct. 810, 819 (1973).

93. Section 553(c) of the APA.

94. https://www.federalregister.gov/.

95. Section 553, throughout and quoting subsection c.

96. Section 553(a).

97. Section 553(b).

98. *Appalachian Power Co. v. EPA*, 208 F. 3d 1015, 1024 (D.C. Cir. 2005).

99. *Air Transport Association v. Dept. of Transportation*, 900 F. 2d 369, 376 (D.C. Cir. 1990).

100. *U.S. Int'l Trade Commission v. ASAT, Inc.*, 411 F.3d 245 (D.C. Cir. 2005).

101. 338 U.S. 632, 652–3, 70 S. Ct. 357 (1950).

102. 338 U.S. at 640.

103. 411 F. 3d at 255–6.

104. 411 F. 3d at 256.

chapter 5

Rulemaking

THE RULEMAKING POWER

Common parlance refers to "regulations" issued by government agencies, but "regulation-making" is an awkward phrase. Administrative law refers to "rules" and "regulations" interchangeably.

For the purpose of rulemaking, enabling legislation for an agency grants a scope of power broad enough "to deal with the unforeseen"[1]—akin to the "necessary and proper clause" of the Constitution, allowing Congress to enact such legislation as is "necessary and proper" for the fulfilment of its constitutional role.[2] While the court did not cite or discuss *McCulloch v. Maryland*,[3] the great landmark 1819 Supreme Court decision interpreting the clause broadly as giving Congress powers to do more than was "absolutely" necessary, the reference was clear enough. There, the Court held that Congress had more than the power to do what was "absolutely" necessary to carry out its constitutional functions,[4] but "that it might employ those [means] which, in its judgment, would most advantageously effect the object to be accomplished."[5] The courts also apply this standard to federal agencies and most state agencies.

However, Florida takes a different approach. There, enabling legislation allows only such rulemaking that "implement[s] or interpret[s] the specific powers and duties granted by the enabling statute."[6] "That is, an agency may not make a rule based solely on its general rulemaking authority, but must point to a specific law that is to be implemented."[7] The Division of Pari-mutual Wagering's enabling legislation authorized it to "regulate the operation of cardrooms" and to issue rules regarding licensing, cardroom operations, "recordkeeping and reporting requirements," and tax and fee collection, but not limited to those subjects. Florida's highest court held, however, that a statute limiting an agency's rulemaking power trumped the division's inclusive enabling legislation. Thus, the division could not define the game of poker to exclude a game called Big Poker 21, even though the division had concluded the game was too similar to Blackjack, which it was authorized to prohibit.[8] While the decision on appeal after remand affirmed on different grounds, the earlier decision appears to have interpreted correctly Florida's statutory restriction on rulemaking. Florida's stance resembles that suggested in the 1981 MSAPA,[9] but few if any other states found its suggestion compelling, and the 2010 MSAPA includes no such provision.

Figure 5-1, taken from The Federal Rulemaking Process: An Overview,[10] provides just what that title promises. It is fairly self-explanatory, but note that the "Congressional Review" referenced in the lower right-hand corner of the diagram refers to the Congressional Review Act of 1996, which has only overturned an agency regulation once, under extraordinary circumstances, and as explained in Chapter 3, has been almost completely ineffective.

THE PROCESS OF RULEMAKING

When government deprives a whole class of persons of property through legislation or rulemaking, that action does not trigger an individual's right to a hearing to contest it before the deprivation occurs. Justice Oliver Wendell Holmes asked, do "all individuals have a right to be heard before a matter can be decided in which all are equally concerned"? (regarding a state agency responsible for assessing the value of real estate for tax purposes) and answered "No!"[11] His answer remains good law, mostly, although the APA, as noted below, does impose some procedural requirements on rulemaking.

Of course individuals can challenge statutes or rules on constitutional and other grounds. Holmes's point was that they don't have a right to be heard "*before* [the] matter can be decided [emphasis added]."[12] When an individual challenges the constitutionality, say, of a rule or statute under which they (he or she) may be punished or harmed, they may legitimately object to the substance of the rule or statute, but not to the fact that they personally did not get a hearing before the agency issued the rule, or before the legislature enacted the statute. In contrast, it is certainly valid to complain that you did not get a hearing before YOUR license was revoked, or before YOU were barred from boxing by the State Athletic Commission.[13]

While legislatures certainly have nothing like a notice-and-comment process, and indeed are under no legal requirement to listen to others at all, rulemaking for agencies still more or less parallels passing a statute, for legislatures. The legislative process, not the trial process, provides the model.

The Electronic Freedom of Information Act of 1996[14] and the E-Government Act of 2002[15] allow citizens to "submit relevant testimony" at a computer keyboard with ease. To date their impact on public participation remains uncertain, and corporate interests appear to continue to engage in more active and effective intervention than public interest groups. Still, their mandates would appear to hold considerable potential for public empowerment. Chapter 14 includes a discussion of the implications of these acts for transparency in rulemaking.

Proper substantive rules have the full force of law. For example, when the Special Watergate Prosecutor demanded the tapes from President Richard Nixon under a regulation of the Attorney General, giving the Attorney General the authority to challenge the President's assertion of executive privilege, the President had to obey the demands of his own subordinate in the executive branch.[16]

FIGURE 5-1   **The Federal Rulemaking Process**

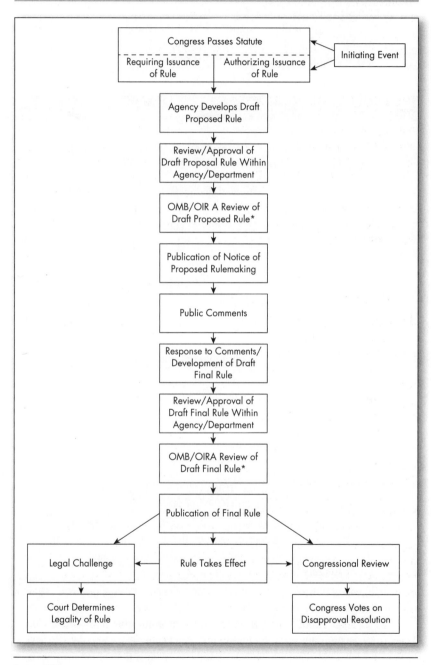

Source: CRS

* The Office of Management and Budget's (OMB) Office of Information and Regulatory Affairs (OIRA) reviews only significant rules, and does not review any rules submitted by independent regulatory agencies.

Under the APA, when agencies want to issue a substantive rule, they must

– provide notice to all affected parties;
– provide opportunity to submit relevant testimony;
– consider all the relevant data submitted; and
– offer the opportunity to petition for repeal.[17]

BOX 5-1 **5 U.S. Code Administrative Procedure Act—Section 553**

(a) This section applies, according to the provisions thereof, except to the extent that there is involved—

   (1) a military or foreign affairs function of the United States; or

   (2) a matter relating to agency management or personnel or to public property, loans, grants, benefits, or contracts.

(b) General notice of proposed rule making shall be published in the Federal Register, unless persons subject thereto are named and either personally served or otherwise have actual notice thereof in accordance with law. The notice shall include—

   (1) a statement of the time, place, and nature of public rule making proceedings;

   (2) reference to the legal authority under which the rule is proposed; and

   (3) either the terms or substance of the proposed rule or a description of the subjects and issues involved.

Except when notice or hearing is required by statute, this subsection does not apply—

   (A) to interpretative rules, general statements of policy, or rules of agency organization, procedure, or practice; or

   (B) when the agency for good cause finds (and incorporates the finding and a brief statement of reasons therefor in the rules issued) that notice and public procedure thereon are impracticable, unnecessary, or contrary to the public interest.

   (C) After notice required by this section, the agency shall give interested persons an opportunity to participate in the rule making through submission of written data, views, or arguments with or without opportunity for oral presentation. After consideration of the relevant matter presented, the agency shall incorporate in the rules adopted a concise general statement of their basis and purpose. When rules are required by statute to be made on-the-record after opportunity for an agency hearing, sections 556 and 557 of this title apply instead of this subsection.

(D) The required publication or service of a substantive rule shall be made not less than 30 days before its effective date, except—

(1) a substantive rule which grants or recognizes an exemption or relieves a restriction;

(2) interpretative rules and statements of policy; or

(3) as otherwise provided by the agency for good cause found and published with the rule.

(E) Each agency shall give an interested person the right to petition for the issuance, amendment, or repeal of a rule.

Source:http://www.gpo.gov/fdsys/pkg/USCODE-2010-title5/pdf/USCODE-2010-title5-partI-chap5-subchapII-sec553.pdf. http://www.gpo.gov/fdsys/pkg/USCODE-2011-title5/pdf/USCODE-2011-title5-partI-chap5-subchapII.pdf

Future Effect

Generally, rulemaking is future-oriented. The APA includes in its definition of a rule that it must have "future effect."[18]

BOX 5-2   **5 U.S. Code Administrative Procedure Act—Section 551**

For the purpose of this subchapter—

* * *

(4) "rule" means the whole or a part of an agency statement of general or particular applicability and future effect designed to implement, interpret, or prescribe law or policy or describing the organization, procedure, or practice requirements of an agency and includes the approval or prescription for the future of rates, wages, corporate or financial structures or reorganizations thereof, prices, facilities, appliances, services or allowances therefore or of valuations, costs, or accounting, or practices bearing on any of the foregoing;

That the APA definition refers to "general *or particular*" applicability creates some confusion, because common sense suggests that statements of particular applicability should respond to individual adjudications, not rulemaking. However, since ratemaking and certain corporate reorganizations, which are "particular" in nature, not really general, fall under the rulemaking heading for federal agencies, the definition had to cover those applications. The 2010 MSAPA makes the distinction between rulemaking and adjudication clearer with its definition of rulemaking: "the whole or part of an agency statement of *general* applicability [emphasis added] that implements, interprets, or prescribes (i) law or policy, or (ii) the organization, procedure, or practice requirements of an agency and has the force of law."[19]

The "future effect" language of the APA also bows when statutes specific to particular agencies require that result. In *Bowen v. Georgetown University Hospital*,[20] the Court said, "Retroactivity is not favored in the law," and that like congressional statutes, "administrative rules will not be construed to have retroactive effect unless their language requires this result."[21] But, sometimes their language *does* require that result, and so some rules *do* have retroactive effect. The MSAPA 2010 definition simply omits mention of future effect.[22]

Notice

"Notice" means that before an agency can affect the lives or businesses of people, those people must have knowledge and warning. Ordinarily, the agency publishes an actual proposed rule in the *Federal Register* rather than merely "a description of the subjects and issues involved," as it could under the APA.[23] "Where the change between proposed and final rule is important, the question for the court is whether the final rule is a 'logical outgrowth' of the rulemaking proceeding."[24]

The "logical outgrowth" rule can be the basis for a successful legal challenge to a rule on the basis of inadequate notice, forcing the agency to start again, with a new notice. Under a Department of Agriculture rule, chocolate milk was not an approved food item for use in the WIC program, for which federal funds assisted food purchases for poverty-stricken "Women, Infants and Children." Such "flavored milk" had been in the earlier 1979 proposed version of the rule, but Agriculture removed it in response to seventy-eight negative comments during the sixty-day comment period. After the final version of the rule was issued in 1980, the Chocolate Manufacturers Association (CMA) asked Agriculture to reopen the rulemaking to allow further comment. In 1981, Agriculture agreed, but then decided against doing so. CMA brought suit in federal district court, arguing that Agriculture had not given notice of the possibility of excluding flavored milk, and so neither CMA nor its members had been alerted to the need to submit comments in support of its inclusion in the initial proposed version of the rule. In response to the first point, Agriculture argued that the initial proposed rule was accompanied by a preamble discussion indicating concern about comestibles with high sugar content, so although it did not specifically mention flavored milk, its purveyors too should have been on notice. However, Agriculture's statement did specifically mention high-sugar cereals and juices as items of concern. The court conceded that in this matter, "whether the change in [the rule] was in character with the original scheme and whether it was a '*logical* outgrowth' [of the notice and comments—the standard by which many courts determine whether the notice was sufficient] is not easy to answer."[25] Still, because the preamble discussion explicitly warned about high-sugar cereals juices, but gave no warning at all about flavored milk, by omission it implied that it was not considering excluding the latter. Based on that language, and the fact that Agriculture had always allowed its use in the program, the court ruled that "there was insufficient notice that the deletion of flavored milk from the WIC Program would be considered if adverse comments were received" and remanded the case to Agriculture "with instructions to reopen the comment period and thereby afford interested parties a fair opportunity to comment on the proposed changes in the rule."[26]

Note, however, that the court regarded this as an unusual case. It took pains to note that: "There is no question that an agency may promulgate a final rule that differs in some particulars from its proposal. Otherwise the agency 'can learn from the comments on its proposals only at the peril of starting a new procedural round of commentary.' [But a]n interested party must have been alerted by the notice to the possibility of the changes eventually adopted from the comments [citation omitted]."[27]

In reality, federal agencies often use the APA's "good cause" exception, claiming that the notice-and-comment process would be "impracticable, unnecessary, or contrary to the public interest,"[28] and such use is rarely challenged. A study of final federal agency rules issued in 1997 found that about half of them never went through the notice-and-comment process.[29]

While federal agencies do not have to provide notice and accept comments for interpretive rules, policy statements, or internal staff manual provisions,[30] some states do. Like the APA, the 2010 MSAPA requires at least thirty days after publication for a rule to become effective, in order to give those affected time to adjust.[31]

Even when a statute requires a "hearing," the agency need not actually "hear" anyone. Unless Congress clearly intended to apply the APA's full, formal on-the-record version of a "hearing,"[32] an agency can decide a matter purely on the basis of paper, using the informal, notice-and-comment method.[33] However, the APA exempts even from notice-and-comment rulemaking requirements matters related to "military or foreign affairs" and "agency management or personnel" or to "public property, loans, grants, benefits or contracts."[34] Scholars have recognized the latter as anachronistic "as early as 1969"[35]; while the 1981 MSAPA included a number of such "proprietary function" exemptions to rulemaking procedures[36]—exemptions for government activity when government is acting as if it were a private business—no such exemptions remain in the 2010 MSAPA.

EFFICIENCY

Formal Rulemaking

As a procedure that makes law for use by large numbers of people in the future, rulemaking should be more efficient than at one a time case-by-case adjudication. Formal, on-the-record rulemaking under the APA,[37] however, has often proven much less than efficient. The Food and Drug Administration (FDA) used it to decide whether what is called "peanut butter" had to be made of peanuts by at least 87 percent or by at least 90 percent. The formal rulemaking process started in 1959, ended in 1968, and covered 7,736 pages of transcript.[38] (FDA finally decided on 90 percent.[39]) The FDA statute requiring formal rulemaking for such decisions "was repealed in 1990."[40]

Some lengthy processes for rulemaking generate less skepticism than the peanut butter case. One might expect Hazardous Material Regulations to justify lengthy attention. Even so, the length of the formal hearing process was impressive. Responding to 1908 legislation, revision started in 1981, was completed in 1990, and reached 1,400 pages in the CFR by 1994.[41]

The formal rulemaking process does not seem appropriate to most situations. Agencies use rulemaking to formulate policy. Formal rulemaking under the APA entitles each party "to present . . . evidence, to submit rebuttal evidence, and to conduct . . . cross examination . . ."[42] Such courtroom procedures help to assure fair trials, but raise barriers to the kind of creative deliberation most helpful to policymaking. For that reason, agencies far more often use informal, notice-and-comment rulemaking. The 2010 MSAPA imposes no such formal requirements on rulemaking, although of course even if a state adopts it, the state may still enact legislation that requires formal rulemaking for some particular purpose. At the federal level, quite a few statutes, especially 1970s consumer-oriented statutes, require agencies to hold hearings where they hear formal presentations, but without the full range of trial-type procedures. However, even some of these "hybrid rulemaking" hearings allow for cross examination by participants with interests adverse to one another.

Negotiated Rulemaking

Congress amended the APA in 1990 to provide for "negotiated" rulemaking.[43] It was supposed to bring together all the representatives of interests to be affected by a rule to draft a consensus proposed rule for the agency to offer for notice and comment. Even prior to the amendment formally establishing its use, it was used successfully, for example, by the Federal Aviation Administration for new flight and duty time regulations for pilots, and by the Environmental Protection Administration for penalties for illegal automobile emissions and for emergency exemptions from pesticide regulations.[44]

Under the 1990 APA negotiated rulemaking provisions, the agency must publish a thirty-day notice in the Federal Register identifying the proposed rulemaking committee members, agenda, and timetable. Anyone may apply to be on the committee, but it is generally kept to twenty-five people or fewer. The participants can of course agree not to sue to overturn a proposed rule, but the agency must in any event subject the proposal to notice and comment, so it need not adopt the rule the committee proposes.[45]

Critics have argued that negotiated rulemaking can shortchange the public interest.[46] For example, what if the consumer groups' position exactly mirrors the public interest, but consumer groups feel pressure from the agency to "negotiate" with industry groups? Does the agency thus cede power? It does not seem to be used very often, probably because it takes time and effort that have not proven cost-effective in achieving acceptance among affected interests.[47]

Informal Rulemaking

Formal rulemaking and negotiated rulemaking both remain cumbersome. Instead, agencies much more often employ the informal notice-and-comment process.[48] But, the filing of a written comment by an ordinary person in a notice-and-comment rulemaking proceeding "is much akin to dropping a feather into the Grand Canyon and trying to hear the impact."[49] When you can watch a decision-maker actually appearing to listen to your testimony, you can have somewhat more confidence that your testimony is really being considered. In contrast, the eyes of someone who has looked at your written comments, assuming someone does look at them, may well have glazed over many documents earlier, with none of your message penetrating through to the brain. Agencies can receive thousands of comments on a proposed rule. In 1995, the Food and Drug Administration received 700,000 comments on regulation of the sale of tobacco products to minors.[50] In 2002, the Department of Agriculture's notice of a proposed rule defining "organic" drew "more than 450,000 comments."[51] On the other hand, quite significant rule proposals can sometimes generate only a small number of comments. The Securities and Exchange Commission received only thirty-six comments on regulation of small companies' financial reports in 2006 and 2007.[52]

That is not to say that comments in the aggregate lack impact. But, organized interest groups—especially business groups—participate in informal rulemaking far more actively than do average citizens, and they appear to have more impact.[53] For example, the Obama Administration expected the Education Department to issue effective regulations to address scandalous practices by for-profit colleges, whose "recruiters would lure students—often members of minorities, veterans, the homeless, and low-income people—with promises of quick degrees and post-graduation jobs, but often leave them poorly prepared and burdened with staggering federal loans."[54] The regulations, as originally proposed, would have stopped or sharply limited the ability of for-profit colleges to collect money from student loans if their graduates had excessive debt and poor employment. But, of the 90,000 comments the Education Department received in the notice-and-comment period, the vast bulk were complaints about the proposals, overwhelming the relatively small number of supportive comments that came from consumers. This was no accident. The multibillion dollar industry, based on billions of dollars of federal student loans, spent more than $16 million to generate those complaints, among other tactics it used to protect its interests. Ultimately, at most about "5 percent of the schools" would face immediate penalties when they took effect in 2015; under the regulations as initially proposed, three times as many schools would have been penalized, three years earlier.[55]

However, such controversial rulemaking sessions are in the minority. More typically, the Environmental Protection Administration so often found that its notice produced no comments that it has taken to publishing rules with the announcement that they will become law unless someone comments negatively. Similarly, agencies issue "interim final rules" in the hope of eliciting comments that would help them revise them into some permanent form. Some scholars have held out hope that the advent of electronic rulemaking, allowing citizens to comment easily by e-mail, will increase public participation. Thus far, however, its impact remains uncertain.[56]

FAIRNESS IN THE PROCESS

The APA requires agencies to "consider[]" the comments, and to "incorporate in the rules adopted a concise general statement of their basis and purpose."[57]

BOX 5-3   **5 U.S. Code Administrative Procedure Act—Section 553(c)**

§ 553(c) . . . After consideration of the relevant matter presented, the agency shall incorporate in the rules adopted a concise general statement of their basis and purpose . . .

Source: http://www.gpo.gov/fdsys/pkg/USCODE-2010-title5/pdf/USCODE-2010-title5-partI-chap5-subchapII-sec553.pdf

---

REAL CONSIDERATION OF PUBLIC COMMENTS

The courts have tried to force agencies to take that statement seriously. So, the courts invalidated an FDA regulation based on a process that it held insufficient under that APA requirement when the agency "[left] vital questions, raised by comments which are of cogent materiality, completely unanswered."[58] If an agency wants to base its regulation on data it got some other way, data that were not part of the public comment process, it has to publish such data so people can respond to them as well, if not doing so could have prejudiced the final rule.[59]

Questions about the fairness of rulemaking decisions have generated much litigation. When a court investigates such a question, it must "review the whole record or those parts of it cited by a party."[60]

BOX 5-4   **5 U.S. Code Administrative Procedure Act—Section 706**

To the extent necessary to decision and when presented, the reviewing court shall decide all relevant questions of law, interpret constitutional and statutory provisions, and determine the meaning or applicability of the terms of an agency action. The reviewing court shall—

(1) compel agency action unlawfully withheld or unreasonably delayed; and

(2) hold unlawful and set aside agency action, findings, and conclusions found to be—**(A)** arbitrary, capricious, an abuse of discretion, or otherwise not in accordance with law; **(B)** contrary to constitutional right, power, privilege, or immunity; **(C)** in excess of statutory jurisdiction, authority, or limitations, or short of statutory right; **(D)** without observance of procedure required by law; **(E)** unsupported by substantial evidence in a case subject to sections 556 and 557 of this title or otherwise reviewed on-the-record of an agency hearing provided by statute; or **(F)** unwarranted by the facts to the extent that the facts are subject to trial de novo by the reviewing court.

In making the foregoing determinations, the court shall review the whole record or those parts of it cited by a party, and due account shall be taken of the rule of prejudicial error.

Source: http://www.gpo.gov/fdsys/pkg/USCODE-2011-title5/html/USCODE-2011-title5-partI-chap7-sec706.htm

COMMUNICATION BETWEEN RULEMAKERS AND PARTIES

But, in an informal rulemaking, the APA does not require any of its communication with private interests or with government officials ("*ex parte*" contacts) to be shared with opposing interests, as a court would require if it were hearing a case on the subject, or, indeed, as the APA itself requires in a formal rulemaking or adjudication. In *Sierra Club v. Costle*[61] the federal Court of Appeals for the D.C. Circuit ruled that so long as pressure on the agency, effective though it was, came from relevant considerations urged by such parties as, for example, U.S. senators, such *ex parte* contacts were permissible. "Pressure" from a legislator, so long as it was a substantive argument relevant to the factors on which the agency could properly base its decision (rather than, for example, threats to withhold funding from unrelated projects), not only do not justify invalidating the rule, but are welcome: "Americans rightly expect their elected representatives to voice their grievances and preferences concerning the administration of our laws."[62]

In that case, because the agency in question, the Environmental Protection Administration (EPA), was subject to a statute requiring creation of a "rulemaking docket" for its informal rulemaking—not required by the APA—the court warned against hiding the impact of such contacts on its decision.[63] Nevertheless, the need for confidentiality between a president and his staff, where the EPA did not base the rule in question on the substance of the meeting, persuaded the court *not* to require inclusion of a synopsis of that meeting in the record.[64] The court warned, however, that formal, on-the-record rulemaking generally requires placing any *ex parte* contacts, including presidential ones, in the rulemaking record, as can statutory requirements specific to an agency.[65]

BOX 5-5 **5 U.S. Code Administrative Procedure Act—Section 557(d)**

(1) In any agency proceeding which is subject to subsection (a) of this section, except to the extent required for the disposition of *ex parte* matters as authorized by law—

(A) no interested person outside the agency shall make or knowingly cause to be made to any member of the body comprising the agency, administrative law judge, or other employee who is or may reasonably be expected to be involved in the decisional process of the proceeding, an *ex parte* communication relevant to the merits of the proceeding;

(B) no member of the body comprising the agency, administrative law judge, or other employee who is or may reasonably be expected to be involved in the decisional process of the proceeding, shall make or knowingly cause to be made to any interested person outside the agency an *ex parte* communication relevant to the merits of the proceeding;

(C) a member of the body comprising the agency, administrative law judge, or other employee who is or may reasonably be expected to be involved in the decisional process of such proceeding who receives, or who makes or knowingly causes to be made, a communication prohibited by this subsection shall place on the public record of the proceeding:

(i) all such written communications;

Justice Scalia would have excluded from the official record even effective communications from federal legislators, arguing that agencies need "off the record" negotiations on rulemaking with legislators to reach agreements that are politically acceptable enough to survive.[66] More commonly, though, courts require that significant *ex parte* comments be included, at least in summary form, in the informal rulemaking record. In contrast, the 2010 MSAPA requires docketing only of written materials relied on, but not oral materials, unless a transcript was kept.[67]

Sometimes a dispute between two competing private interests plays out in an informal rulemaking process. Then, *ex parte* contacts invalidate the resulting rule, since what is truly at stake are individual private interests.[68] One court thought it could take the *ex parte* ban further,[69] but in *Vermont Yankee Nuclear Power Corp. v. NRDC*,[70] without explicitly overruling that decision, the Supreme Court firmly supported agencies' right to exercise a wide range of procedural discretion. It held that in the absence of clear statutory restrictions or constitutional concerns, courts may not impose additional procedural requirements on agencies. The court below tried to send the matter back to the agency with orders to undertake fact gathering proceedings sufficient to strengthen the record. But, the Supreme Court ruled that the Court of Appeals had no right to "review and overturn the rulemaking proceeding on the basis of the procedural devices employed (or not employed) by the Commission so long as the Commission employed at least the statutory minima, about which there is no doubt in this case,"[71] and should not "impose upon the agency its own notion of which procedures are 'best' or more likely to further some vague, undefined public good."[72]

The *Vermont Yankee* decision makes it unlikely that the courts will approve such extensions of the ban on *ex parte* communications to normal informal rulemaking.

RULEMAKER BIAS

What about bias among administrative decision-makers? Judges should be unbiased (as to factual issues);[73] but not legislators: people usually or at least often elect legislators because they share their constituents' views on salient issues. And administrative decision-makers, in their rulemaking capacity, are supposed to be more like legislators than judges.

A good example to consider concerns Michael Pertschuk, appointed by President Carter as chair of the Federal Trade Commission (FTC), no doubt in large part because of his history as a consumer advocate.[74]

Its statute made the FTC provide a "hybrid" proceeding before it could establish rules regulating television advertising: not quite a formal rulemaking proceeding, but still allowing for cross-examination of experts and imposing other trial-type requirements. Prior to its rulemaking hearing on television advertising directed at children, Chairman Pertschuk had made very clear his strong distaste for such advertising. After the hearing, and after the FTC proposed tough rules restricting it, the Kellogg Company and other such advertisers sued to prevent Pertschuk from participating in the final rulemaking decision, on the grounds that under the "hybrid" rules, bias that would exclude an adjudicator should exclude Pertschuk.[75] Pertschuk argued that even the adjudicative standard should not disqualify him because his prior statements implicated television advertising to children generally, and did not deal with the specific issues at the rulemaking.[76] The court, however, said that the matter was rulemaking, not adjudication, whatever procedures may have been utilized,[77] and, under *Vermont Yankee*, in such a proceeding "due process does not demand procedures more rigorous than those provided by Congress."[78] So, the Court would not disqualify the Commissioner unless he had "an unalterably closed mind on matters critical to the disposition of the hearing." Otherwise, the Court explained very clearly, "We would eviscerate the proper evolution of policymaking were we to disqualify every administrator who has opinions on the correct course of his agency's future action."[79]

State law follows the same logic. For example, the Iowa court said "taking a position, even in public, on a policy issue related to the dispute, does not disqualify a decision maker."[80] More recently, the Iowa court explicitly acknowledged consistency with the federal standard for disqualifying bias, that the decision-maker has "adjudged the facts as well as the law of a particular case in advance of hearing it."[81]

ESTOPPEL: FAIRNESS (?) IN IMPLEMENTATION

Agency rules have the force of law, with some exceptions for "rules" that merely appear in manuals or other documents intended for internal use by agency personnel.[82] As noted earlier, when the Supreme Court forced President Nixon to turn over the Watergate tapes to the Special Prosecutor, it illustrated most vividly the principle that agency regulations have the force of law.[83] The President had to obey his own Attorney General's subordinate, because that subordinate, the Special Prosecutor, acted pursuant to a proper regulation

> vest[ing] in the Special Prosecutor plenary authority to control the course of investigations and litigation related to "all offenses arising out of the 1972 Presidential Election for which the Special Prosecutor deems it necessary and appropriate to assume responsibility . . ."[84]

But then, agencies themselves, as well as everyone else, must follow agency rules. This means that when agency employees mislead citizens by giving them incorrect information, citizens have no recourse, because the rule must still be followed. Obviously, this situation can result in what appears to be cruel unfairness. In the classic case, *Federal Crop Insurance Corporation v. Merrill*,[85] Merrill, a farmer, informed the local Federal Crop Insurance Corporation (FCIC) agent that the insurance he wanted was mostly for spring wheat reseeded on winter wheat acreage. The agent accepted his application. Neither Merrill nor the agent knew that a provision in FCIC's regulations made that type of crop ineligible for insurance. Draught destroyed Merrill's crop that year, but the FCIC refused to pay him. Under a principle of law called "equitable estoppel," a private company could not have escaped liability by claiming that its agent had no real authority to offer the insurance. But government is different: it operates under rules that are law. And in a phrase so commonplace that I am confident you will understand it in Latin—which also gives you an idea of how far back the legal principle goes—"*ignorancia juris non excusat*." Like all regulations, this one was published in the Federal Register, and whether or not Merrill or anyone else actually read them, "Congress has provided that the appearance of rules and regulations in the Federal Register gives legal notice of their contents."[86]

Courts have, on rare occasions, made exceptions. Two businesswomen, Brandt and Shell, responded on June 12, 1959, to the opportunity to lease federal land for gas and oil exploration and development with a proposal giving Brandt a three-quarter interest and Shell a one-quarter interest. The Los Angeles office of the federal Bureau of Land Management thought that unequal interests were prohibited, and so they told Brandt and Shell to resubmit within thirty days without losing their priority. Alternatively, they could have appealed, but they resubmitted. The Secretary of the Interior said the Los Angeles office had no right to do this, and so by not appealing Brandt and Shell lost their priority to a Mr. Raymond Hansen, who had filed his offer on June 25. The court reinstated Brandt and Shell's right to appeal, commenting that "To say to these appellants, 'The joke is on you. You shouldn't have trusted us,' is hardly worthy of our great government." But, the court warned that it would not have found a deprivation of the appellants' right to the due process of law if doing so would have "somehow hurt the government." Here, Hansen might bear the burden of a victory by Brandt and Shell, but not the taxpayer. Otherwise, however, "Bad advice cannot ordinarily justify giving away to individuals valuable government assets."[87]

In a somewhat more recent leading case, *Office of Personnel Management v. Richmond*,[88] the federal Office of Personnel Management incorrectly advised a Navy welder that he could work overtime for extra money and then retire without losing certain pension benefits. He followed the advice, and lost the benefits. The Court again, as in *Merrill*, refused estoppel on the grounds that paying the benefits incorrectly promised would constitute an expenditure of taxpayer moneys not authorized by Congress, and would therefore violate the Constitution.[89] However, additional language in the decision creates serious doubt that the Court would allow estoppel now even in cases like *Brandt v. Hickel*, when it would not cost government assets:

> The natural consequence of a rule that made the Government liable
> for the statements of its agents would be a decision to cut back and
> impose strict controls upon Government provision of information in

order to limit liability. Not only would valuable informational programs be lost to the public, but the greatest impact of this loss would fall on those of limited means, who can least afford the alternative of private advice.[90]

Estoppel Against State Agencies

A Washington State regulation explicitly permits the use of equitable estoppel in agency hearings before its Department of Social and Health Services.[91] This seems unusual, in that while courts may on rare occasions allow its use against government, government agencies themselves should have no authority to exceed the powers granted to them by statute. More typically, in reviewing a hearing before the New York Retirement System, New York's highest court noted that the agency head (the State Comptroller) could not act favorably on an applicant's request "in the absence of statutory authority for such action."[92] An Oklahoma decision[93] dealing with a police officer who relied to his detriment on incorrect information he was given by the Oklahoma Police Pension and Retirement Board offers a clear explanation:

> The doctrine of estoppel is not ordinarily applicable to state agencies operating under statutory authority. Public officials performing acts which exceed their authority may not bind a public entity. Rather, they lack authority to expand their powers and are bound by mandatory law.[94]

A handful of cases have permitted equitable estoppel against state agencies. For example if Arkansas gets few applications for unemployment insurance from former employees of a company, that company pays a low rate of tax for unemployment insurance. When a grocery store company newly incorporated a store that had been part of a larger previous corporation, it would have paid at the low rate had it requested a transfer of the good unemployment record of the previous corporation. But, the state auditor for the agency that regulated these matters, with whom the company had always dealt, advised it that it did not need to take any action. Five years later, the State billed the company for $20,000 based on its failure to transfer the records.[95] "In most instances estoppel would not have been a justifiable defense. But in this case, except for a routine application not filed, there would have been no attempt by the State to collect the contributions."[96]

The court cited, as support for its claim that "[e]stoppel of the state is a principle of law recognized in more and more jurisdictions," a 1946 New York Court of Claims decision, a 1936 Alabama decision, a 1937 Pennsylvania decision, and a 1942 California appellate district decision.[97] The age and paucity of the citations, however, point to the rarity of success in claims of equitable estoppel against government agencies, even at the state level.

WHAT AM I SUPPOSED TO DO?

Attorney General Certification of National Security Immunity for Telephone Companies: Rulemaker Bias?

After the World Trade Center attack on September 11, 2001, President Bush authorized the National Security Agency (NSA) to engage in widespread wiretapping of American telephone calls, without having to obtain warrants, although President Bush apparently intended the surveillance only to focus on international calls. The major telephone companies cooperated with the NSA in this endeavor. In 2006, telephone customers representing the class of Americans subject to the NSA's eavesdropping sued the telephone companies for permitting the wiretapping. In 2008, Congress enacted legislation that among other things gave the telephone companies immunity for their role in the eavesdropping if the wiretapping in which they participated met certain criteria. For example, if the wiretapping was "designed to detect or prevent a terrorist attack, or activities in preparation for a terrorist attack, against the United States," and had been "authorized by the President" between September 11, 2001, and January 17, 2007, and met certain other criteria, then a lawsuit against a telephone company based on such wiretapping had to be dismissed. (The statute did not require dismissal of a lawsuit against the government for the wiretapping.)

Under law existing prior to 2008, the records of the wiretapping were classified. As Attorney General, you did not want the telephone companies to face lawsuits because of their cooperation, because they would then be less likely to want to cooperate in future efforts. If you certify that the telephone companies had indeed met the requirements for immunity, some of the basis for your certification must also be classified, because it includes evidence that the wiretapping was indeed designed to prevent terrorism, and some of that evidence would be of value to terrorists. Once you make such a certification, you would then intervene in the lawsuit on behalf of the United States government and seek its dismissal.

You are somewhat concerned about taking these steps, however, because you testified in support of the 2008 legislation, and said at the time that fairness to the telephone companies required the United States to give them a grant of immunity from liability. Therefore, you can be said to have prejudged the issue. Before issuing the certification, you would have to assess the evidence, arguably an exercise in fact finding and therefore perhaps one that could be characterized as adjudication. Could the court decide that you were a biased adjudicator, reject your certification, and therefore jeopardize immunity for the telephone companies?

In *National Security Agency Telecommunications Records Litigation v. AT&T Corporation*,[98] the court rejected the argument that the Attorney General's certification represented the kind of fact finding that would require his role to be considered adjudicative. It noted that in the foreign affairs context, such fact finding merely constitutes "executive decision making," citing a precedent explaining the need to escape the usual protections offered by the adjudicative format in especially urgent and sensitive areas of foreign policy.[99] Having rejected the argument that the Attorney General had exercised his adjudicative authority, it characterized the certification as part of his "legitimate policy role," and quoted the holding of the *Pertschuk* case that "Administrators . . . may hold policy views on questions of law prior to participating in a proceeding."[100]

You were right to be concerned. Administrative law poses many close questions, and this was one of them. The court could have decided the matter the other way. In fact, though, it allowed the Attorney General's certification to stand without further inquiry as to questions of bias, and in this regard, encouraged an activist approach in pursuit of agency missions.

PRACTICE PROBLEMS

PROBLEM 1: The Nuclear Regulatory Commission (NRC) has proposed a rule allowing nuclear power plants very wide leeway in how they must dispose of nuclear waste. The President and the industry send considerable oral and written communications to the NRC supporting the rule, arguing for the importance of continuing to build nuclear power plants (and that strict waste disposal rules would deter such construction). Many members of Congress send equally numerous communications arguing against the rule based on environmental dangers. None of these communications were placed in the record. Should the courts set aside the resulting rule?

PROBLEM 2: The federal Sexual Offenders Registration and Notification Act (SORNA) imposes a further criminal penalty on anyone with a prior conviction for a sexual offense who fails to register as a sex offender and engages in interstate travel. SORNA took effect on July 27, 2006. On February 28, 2007, pursuant to discretion permitted by statute, the Attorney General issued a regulation applying SORNA retroactively to offenders convicted prior to its effective date. (The courts have held that retroactive application of sex offender registration and notification laws does not violate the *ex post facto* clause of the Constitution.) The Attorney General issued the regulation effective immediately, citing the "good cause" exceptions of the APA for bypassing the notice-and-comment provision and the "advance publication" provision (requiring publication of the regulation at least thirty days before it can go into effect). Sex Offender X, after informing his Ohio parole officer that he intended to move to Georgia, did so in the fall of 2006. In March 2007, X was convicted of having violated SORNA. Offender X challenged the conviction on the grounds that the Attorney General did not have good cause for bypassing the notice-and-comment and advance publication procedures and that the regulation allowing for his prosecution consequently was invalid. The Attorney General argued that it was necessary to have the regulation take effect immediately on announcement (1) to avoid any period of uncertainty as to the scope of the law, and (2) to prevent any additional sex offenses resulting from delay in imposing registration requirements that facilitate the location and apprehension of offenders. As to the first point, X argued that since regulation generally is intended to clarify the applicability of statutes, were the benefit of clarification sufficient to establish "good cause" then no agency would ever have to follow the notice-and-comment or advance publication provisions. As to the second point, since the statute permitted, but did not require retroactive effect, it necessitated a period of delay for the Attorney General to take that action, and therefore itself contemplated a period of delay, so "delayed effect," implicit in the statute, also failed to constitute good cause for evading the normal requirements. And where criminal penalties are involved, the government has an especially strong responsibility to justify an approach that minimizes warnings to those affected. Will the court overturn X's conviction for violating SORNA?

ENDNOTES

1. *North American Telecommunications Association v. FCC*, 772 F. 2d 1282, 1292 (7th Cir. 1985).
2. Article I, Section 8, Clause 18.
3. 17 U.S. 316, 4 L. Ed. 579 (1819).
4. 17 U.S. at 414–5, 4 L. Ed. at 603.
5. 17 U.S. at 419, 4 L. Ed. at 604–5.
6. Fla. Stat. Ann. § 120.52(8).
7. *St. Petersburg Kennel Club v. Dep't of Bus. and Prof. Reg.*, 719 So. 2d 1210 (Fla. Dist. Ct. App. 1998), appeal after remand, 757 So. 2d 1240 (Fla. Dist. Ct. App. 2000).
8. 719 So. 2d at 1211–2.
9. 1981 MSAPA § 2-104.
10. Maeve Carey, The Federal Rulemaking Process: An Overview, *Congressional Research Service*, June 17, 2013, 7-5700, RL 32240, page 2.
11. *Bi-Metallic v. State Board of Equalization*, 239 U.S. 441, 445, 36 S. Ct. 141, 142 (1915).
12. 239 U.S. at 442, 36 S. Ct. at 145.
13. See practice problem, Chapter 4.
14. Pub. L. 104–231, 110 Stat. 3048, amending APA § 552(a)(2) and other sections.
15. Pub. L. No. 107–347, 116 Stat. 2899 (2002) (codified in scattered sections of 44 U.S.C.)
16. "So long as this regulation remains in force the Executive Branch is bound by it. . ." *United States v. Nixon*, 418 U.S. 683, 696, 94 S. Ct. 3090, 3101–3102 (1974).
17. Sections 553, 556, 557.
18. Section 551(4).
19. 2010 MSAPA § 102(30).
20. *Bowen v. Georgetown University Hospital*, 488 U.S. 204, 109 S. Ct. 468 (1988).
21. 488 U.S. at 208, 109 S. Ct. at 471.
22. 2010 MSAPA § 102(30).
23. Section 553(b)(3).
24. *United Steelworkers v. Marshall*, 647 F. 2d 1189, 1221(D.C. Cir. 1980), *cert. den.* 453 U.S. 913, 101 S. Ct. 3148 (1981), internal citation omitted.
25. *Chocolate Manufacturers Ass'n v. Block*, 755 F. 2d 1098, 1105 (4th Cir. 1985).
26. 755 F. 2d at 1107.
27. 755 F. 2d at 1103–4.
28. APA § 553(b)(B).
29. Maeve Carey, *op. cit.*, page 8, citation omitted.
30. APA § 553(b)(A).
31. APA § 553(d); 2010 MSAPA § 317(a).

32. Sections 556 and 557.

33. Section 553. See *United States v. Florida East Coast Railway*, 410 U.S. 224, 93 S. Ct. 810 (1973).

34. APA § 553(a)(1) and (2).

35. Recommendation of the Administrative Conference of the United States (regarding 1 C.F.R. 305.93–4), Florida State University School of Law website, http://www.law.fsu.edu/library/admin/acus/305934.html, 2001, accessed 1/18/15.

36. 1981 MSAPA § 3-116(3), (4), and (5).

37. Sections 556 and 557.

38. Jeffrey F. Beatty, Susan S. Samuelson, and Dean A. Bredeson, *Business Law and the Legal Environment*, 6th ed., (Mason, OH: Cengage Learning, 2010), 90–1; Citizen Carol, Federal Regulatory Accountability Act Put the Public in Harm's Way, *Public Citizen Texas Vox*, 11/19/11, http://texasvox.org/2011/11/19/federal-regulatory-accountability-act-puts-the-public-in-harm%E2%80%99s-way/; Todd R. Smyth, The FDA's Public Board of Inquiry and the Aspartame Decision, 58 *Indiana L. J.* 627, 629, note 21 (1983), citing Hamilton, Procedures for the Adoption of Rules of General Applicability, 60 *Cal. L. Rev.* 1276, 1291–3 (1972).

39. Food Standard Innovations: Peanut Butter's Sticky Standard, website of the United States Food and Drug Administration, http://www.fda.gov/AboutFDA/WhatWeDo/History/ProductRegulation/ucm132911.htm.

40. Michael Asimow and Ronald M. Levin, *State and Federal Administrative Law*, 4th ed., (St. Paul, MN: West Publishing Company, 2014), 276.

41. Cornelius M. Kerwin and Scott R. Furlong, *Rulemaking*, 4th ed., (Washington, DC: Sage/CQ Press, 2011), 39–42.

42. APA § 557(d).

43. Sections 561–570a.

44. Henry M. Perritt Jr., Negotiated Rulemaking Before Federal Agencies, 74 *Georgetown L. J.* 1625, 1667–82 (Aug. 1986).

45. *USA Group Loan Services v. Riley*, 82 F. 3d 708, 714–5 (7th Cir. 1996).

46. See, e.g., Jody Freeman, The Private Role in Public Governance, 75 *N.Y.U. L. Rev.* 543, 655 (June 2000).

47. See Cary Coglianese, *Assessing Consensus: The Promise and Performance of Negotiated Rulemaking*, Discussion Paper E-97-01, June 1997, Kennedy School of Government, Harvard University, http://belfercenter.hks.harvard.edu/publication/2808/assessing_consensus.html, accessed 2/12/15.

48. See, e.g., D. W. Brodie, *Administrative Law Glossary*, under "types of rules," http://biotech.law.lsu.edu/Courses/study_aids/adlaw/glossary/glossary_01.htm.

49. Williams, Securing Fairness and Regularity in Administrative Proceedings, 29 *Admin. L. Rev.* 1, 16 (1977), quoted in David B. Chaffin, Note: Remedies for Noncompliance with Section 553 of the Administrative Procedure Act, 1982 *Duke L. J.* 461, 472, n. 72 (1982).

50. William T. Gormley Jr. and Steven J. Balla, *Bureaucracy and Democracy*, 3d ed., (Los Angeles, CA: Sage/CQ Press 2013), 128.

51. Kerwin and Furlong, *op. cit.* at 115 (citation omitted).

52. Gormley and Balla, *op. cit.* at 128.

53. Jason Webb Yackee and Susan Webb Yackee, A Bias Toward Business? Assessing Interest Group Influence on the Bureaucracy, 68 *J. of Politics* 128 (2006).

54. Eric Lichtblau, With Lobbying Blitz, For-Profit Colleges Diluted New Rules, *The New York Times*, 12/9/11, http://www.nytimes.com/2011/12/10/us/politics/for-profit-college-rules-scaled-back-after-lobbying.html?_r=0. Accessed 1/16/15.

55. *Id.*

56. Stuart Minor Benjamin, Evaluating E-Rulemaking: Public Participation and Political Institutions, 55 *Duke L. J.* 893 (March 2006); Cynthia R. Farina et al., Rulemaking 2.0, 65 *U. Miami L. Rev.* 395 (Winter, 2011).

57. Section 553(c).

58. *United States v. Nova Scotia Food Products Corp.* 568 F. 2d 240, 252 (2d Cir. 1977).

59. *Prometheus Radio Project v. Federal Communications Commission*, 373 F. 3d 372, 412 (3d Cir. 2004), *cert. den. sub nom. Media Gen. Inc. v. FCC*, 545 U.S. 1123, 125 S. Ct. 2902 (2005). Within reason, of course: "We are mindful that the APA's notice requirements are not supposed to result in a notice-and-comment 'revolving door.'" *Id.*

60. APA Section 706.

61. *Sierra Club v. Costle*, 657 F. 2d 298 (D.C. Cir. 1981).

62. 657 F. 2d at 409.

63. 657 F. 2d at 406–7.

64. *Id.*

65. *Id.*; APA Section 557(d).

66. Antonin Scalia, Two Wrongs Make a Right: The Judicialization of Standardless Rulemaking, *Regulation*, July/August 1977, at 38, 41, http://www.unz.org/Pub/Regulation-1977jul-00038, accessed 1/8/15.

67. 2010 MSAPA §§ 302(b)(3), 306(b).

68. *Sangamon Valley Television Corporation v. United States*, 269 F. 2d 221, 224 (D.C. Cir. 1959).

69. *Home Box Office v. FCC*, 567 F. 2d 9, 57 (D.C. Cir. 1977).

70. *Vermont Yankee Nuclear Power Corp. v. NRDC*, 435 U.S. 519, 98 S. Ct. 1197 (1978).

71. 435 U.S. at 548, 98 S. Ct. at 1214.

72. 435 U.S. at 549, 98 S. Ct. at 1214.

73. As to factual issues, judges will not be disqualified for having previously expressed views on a legal issue before them. *Assoc. of National Advertisers, Inc. v. FTC*, 627 F. 2d 1151, 1172, n. 51 (D.C. Cir. 1979), *cert. den.* 447 U.S. 921 (1980).

74. See, e.g., Dolly Langdon, F.T.C. Chairman Mike Pertschuk is the Bureaucrat Who Makes Some Businessmen Turn Blue, *People*, 9/10/79, http://www.people.com/people/archive/article/0,20074544,00.html.

75. *Assoc. of National Advertisers, Inc. v. FTC*, 627 F. 2d 1151 (D.C. Cir. 1979), *cert. den.* 447 U.S. 921 (1980).

76. 627 F. 2d 1155. Even in a courtroom, such "bias" would not be disqualifying. In a memorable 19th-century decision, one judge, facing a motion to disqualify him from the trial of a defendant accused of horse theft, noted that he "was for many years attorney for the Anti-Horse Thief Association. He confesses to a strong prejudice against horse-stealing, but he has no prejudice against any individual, merely because he may be charged with this offense . . ." *Crawford v. Ferguson*, 5 Okla. Crim. 377, 386, 115 P. 278 (1911).

77. 627 F. 2d at 1161.

78. 627 F. 2d at 1165–6.

79. 627 F. 2d at 1174.

80. *Anstey v. Iowa State Commerce Commission*, 292 N.W. 2d 380, 390 (Iowa 1980).

81. *Iowa Farm Bureau Federal v. Environmental Protection Commission*, 850 N.W. 2d 403 (Iowa 2014), quoting *Cinderella Career & Finishing Schools, Inc. v. FTC*, 425 F. 2d 583, 591(D.C. Cir. 1970), quoting *Gilligan, Will & Co. v. SEC*, 267 F. 2d 461, 469 (2d Cir. 1959).

82. E.g., *Morton v. Ruiz*, 415 U.S. 199, 94 S. Ct. 1055 (1974); *First Family Mortgage Corp. of Florida v. Earnest*, 851 F. 2d 843 (6th Cir. 1988).

83. *United States v. Nixon*, 418 U.S. 683, 94 S. Ct. 3090 (1974).

84. 418 U.S. at 694, 94 S. Ct. at 3100, n.8.

85. *Federal Crop Insurance Corporation v. Merrill*, 332 U.S. 380, 68 S. Ct. 1 (1947).

86. 332 U.S. at 385, 68 S. Ct. at 3, citing 49 Stat. 502, 44 U.S.C. § 307.

87. *Brandt v. Hickel*, 427 F. 2d 53, 57 (9th Cir. 1970).

88. 496 U.S. 414, 110 S. Ct. 2465.

89. The purpose of the Appropriations Clause of the Constitution "is to assure that public funds will be spent according to the letter of the difficulty decisions reached by Congress as to the common good, and not according to the individual favor of Government agents or the individual pleas of litigants." 496 U.S. at 428, 110 S. Ct. at 2473. However, Justice Stevens, in his concurrence, thought that Congressional appropriations could well be understood to justify payments made to correct "the product of a mistaken interpretation of a statute or

regulation" that would otherwise operate unfairly to the detriment of its victim. 496 U.S. at 435, 110 S. Ct. at 2477.

90. 496 U.S. at 433-4, 110 S. Ct. at 2476.

91. WAC (Washington Administrative Code) 388-002-0495, cited in Administrative Hearings, Equitable Estoppel, on the website of the Washington State Department of Social and Health Services, Revised 1/4/12, http://www.dshs.wa.gov/manuals/eaz/sections/FHEquitEstop.shtml.

92. *Morrissey v. NYSERS*, 298 N.Y. 442, 449, 84 N.E. 2d 627, 631 (1949); and see *Daleview Nursing Home v. Axelrod*, 62 N.Y. 2d 30, 33, 475 N.Y.S. 2d 826, 827 (1984): "estoppel is not available against a government agency in the exercise of its governmental functions." The Comptroller bears fiduciary responsibility for New York's pension system, for which he is the sole trustee. The prohibition against granting a benefit not authorized by statute may therefore bind the Comptroller more absolutely than it binds other agency heads because of that obligation to safeguard the *corpus* of the trust.

93. *Strong v. Police Pension and Retirement Board*, 2000 OK 45, 115 P. 3d 889 (2005).

94. 115 P. 2d at 893.

95. *Foote's Dixie Dandy v. McHenry*, 270 Ark. 816, 607 S.W. 2d 323 (Ark. 1980).

96. 270 Ark. at 825, 607 S.W. 2d at 327.

97. 270 Ark. at 823, 607 S.W. 2d at 326.

98. *National Security Agency Telecommunications Records Litigation v. AT&T Corporation*, 671 F. 3d 881 (9th Cir. 2011). The decision dealt with many other issues in addition to the one addressed here.

99. 671 F. 3d at 900, citing *Owens v. Republic of the Sudan*, 531 F. 3d 884, 891 (D.C. Cir. 2008).

100. *Id.*, quoting *Assoc. of National Advertisers, Inc. v. FTC*, 627 F. 2d 1151, 1172, n. 51 (D.C. Cir. 1979), *cert. den.* 447 U.S. 921 (1980).

chapter 6

Preemption and Judicial Review of Agency Rulemaking

PREEMPTION

Under the Supremacy Clause of the Constitution, if state law conflicts with federal law, the state law no longer has force: federal law prevails.[1] This is called "preemption." However, courts are supposed to make such a ruling only if Congress has clearly indicated its desire for federal law to prevail, out of respect for what are called the traditional "police powers" of states.[2] By "police powers" the courts don't mean law enforcement: this is an ancient term, where the word "police" comes from the same root as "polity," meaning a governed entity. So states' "police powers" means the more internal aspects of government—not war and peace, or international diplomacy, but legislative responsibility for public health, safety, morals, and economic matters.[3] Still, if a court finds that a state law stands in the way of achieving what Congress wants, as shown by a federal law, the state law will be preempted.[4] That can happen three ways: the federal statute can obviously conflict with state law; it can say explicitly that it preempts state law; or it could regulate whatever it regulates so comprehensively that Congress obviously intended that no other regulatory scheme could continue to play a role (i.e., "field" preemption). For example, the Supreme Court in 2012 found that the federal Immigration Reform and Control Act of 1986 implied field preemption, and threw out some key provisions of a 2010 Arizona statute[5] empowering its officers to enforce laws against undocumented immigrants in a manner widely suspected of encouraging racial profiling.[6] The federal government controls immigration policy, not state governments, in part because immigration policy can be bound up with broader aspects of foreign policy, which is clearly a federal prerogative. Several aspects of Arizona's law came into conflict with the federal regulatory scheme: federal law allowed for a sentence of probation for failure to carry registration papers while Arizona's law did not; federal law did not specifically penalize efforts of an undocumented alien to find work while Arizona's law did. Federal law does permit state officials to take some measures to enforce laws against illegal immigration, so the Court found only those aspects of Arizona's law inconsistent with federal law preempted.[7]

Federal Regulations Preempting State Statutes: Airbags and Shoulder Belts

We are more concerned, however, with agency **regulations** preempting state law. For example, in *Geier v. American Honda Motor Co.*,[8] a regulation by the Department of Transportation (DOT) issued under the power Congress gave it by statute, not the statute itself, preempted a negligence lawsuit under state law. A driver, severely injured in a car crash, sued Honda for failing to install airbags in her car, although airbags had become commonplace, with well-known benefits. The federal regulation, however, only required car companies to phase in airbags gradually.

The motorist (and the dissent) argued that the federal regulation merely set a minimum standard, so state courts should be free to require a higher level of care by the car company.[9] The majority, however, ruled that a state court imposition of that higher duty of care would interfere with "the gradual . . . phase-in that the federal regulation deliberately imposed," and so would frustrate what Congress wanted (the Court assumed the regulation reflected the intent of the statute).[10]

But, the Court does not always find field preemption. A different DOT regulation required lap-and-shoulder belts on the front and side seats in minivans, but allowed manufacturers to use only lap belts, if they so chose, in middle or aisle seats. Mazda thought it could rely on *Geier* in defending itself against a negligence suit brought in the California courts by survivors of a family member who only had a lap belt in an aisle seat and died in a crash. But, the Court noted that DOT's reasons for the choices it gave car manufacturers were very different in the two cases. DOT let them phase in air bags because it expected that over time the industry would develop better passive restraints, and because of consumer worries about airbag safety and cost, they feared a possible public backlash.[11] DOT had none of those concerns about lap-and-shoulder belts when it issued the 1989 regulation, just that they might interfere with entry and exit when in use. But, "it encouraged manufacturers to address this issue through innovation."[12] DOT refrained from imposing the requirement not because it doubted the cost-effectiveness of lap-and-shoulder belts for aisle seats, but because they thought costs would fall.[13] Therefore, the Court did not agree that an ordinary common law state claim against a car manufacturer would pose an "obstacle" to the achievement of the goals of the federal law, and refused to preempt the suit under state law.[14]

Federal preemption generally reflects a logical approach to American government. If the United States is to function as a national entity, federal law should prevail over state and local law when it is intended to govern a particular category of behavior.[15]

The history we review in the next section, however, illustrates the dangers involved when courts encourage too much deference to federal agencies when they assert preemption by their regulations, and when they interpret their own authorizing statutes to allow them to issue such regulations.

THE HARM IN TOO MUCH *CHEVRON* DEFERENCE[16]

It is hard to imagine more damage than what the federal courts inflicted on the United States and perhaps the world when in 2005 they stopped Eliot Spitzer from pursuing bankers for pushing subprime mortgages in a racially discriminatory manner on homeowners unable to afford them. Four years too late, after the damage was done, the Supreme Court reversed the lower court decisions in *Cuomo v. Clearing House Association*.[17]

That decision set one limit to court deference to administrative agencies. It did not, however, change the fact that when courts defer excessively to power-grabbing federal agency interpretations of their own jurisdiction, they preempt state law and insult and threaten democratic governance, even if they do not again jeopardize the world economy.

Deference to Agency Interpretations of Unclear Statutes

In *Chevron v. Natural Resources Defense Council*,[18] the Court ruled that when the wording of a statute is unclear, courts must defer to the interpretation of that language by the agency charged with administering the statute. Within reasonable limits, the ruling made sense. Statutory interpretation can be very difficult,[19] so it usually seems sensible to follow the guidance of agency personnel who have developed expertise through experience, especially in technical areas.

Chevron itself, for example, turns on the interpretation of the phrase "stationary source" in the 1977 amendments to the Clean Air Act[20]: did Congress mean a company could not "increase the total emissions" from a particular machine, or from a whole factory? Can they have meant "stationary source" to include a whole factory, or would they have intended to limit emissions from individual "stationary" machines—machines that don't move around? The Environmental Protection Agency issued a regulation allowing the "whole factory" definition, so a state could treat all the machines within one factory as a single "stationary source," "as though they were encased within a single 'bubble.'"[21]

In the 1977 amendments, Congress had limited emissions from stationary sources in "nonattainment" states: states that had not reached certain air quality goals set forth in earlier legislation. The D.C. Circuit Court of Appeals had acknowledged that the legislative history of the 1977 amendments did not answer the question of interpretation.[22] It threw out the rule, though, reasoning that the overall legislative purpose of the statute appeared to be to bring nonattainment states up to appropriate air quality standards, and limiting emissions from individual machines would do that more quickly and effectively.[23]

The Supreme Court, however, reinstated the rule, holding that "if the statute is silent or ambiguous with respect to the specific issue, the question for the court is whether the agency's answer is based on a permissible construction of the statute"; the court should "not simply impose its own construction on the statute."[24]

The ruling annoyed environmentalists, but did reflect some logic. Congress had, in a sense, "delegated" the power to interpret an ambiguous statute, or one silent on a given issue, to the agency charged with the administration of the statute; and beyond the matter of expertise, why shouldn't the policies of the administration empowered by the nation's electorate be permitted to have some effect on decisions made by its appointees?

Self-Empowering Statutory Interpretation by an Agency

In *Cuomo v. Clearing House*, however, a federal agency, the Office of the Comptroller of the Currency (OCC), extended the logic of *Chevron* deference and federal preemption well beyond reason, in service of its own ambition. While a narrow majority of the Supreme Court ultimately rejected its particular rationale, the OCC had been encouraged in its power grab by some previous decisions of the Court,[25] among its "haphazard[]" and "inconsistent" approaches to preemption and *Chevron* deference,[26] and those decisions continue to serve as an **attractive nuisance** to other federal agencies so inclined. (The phrase "attractive nuisance" is being used metaphorically. See Glossary.) Unfortunately, the victim is again likely to be the public.

The 1863 National Bank Act established the OCC,[27] giving it "visitorial powers" over federally chartered banks to assure their solvency. Those banks pay fees to subsidize the OCC,[28] encouraging the OCC to persuade state-chartered banks to acquire federal charters: the more banks it "visits," the more money and power it accumulates.

In 1996, the OCC issued regulations claiming sole authority to enforce even state laws—including consumer protection laws—governing such banks.[29] Everyone understood that the OCC itself would seldom or never enforce such laws.[30] The regulations prohibited any visitation or inspection by state officials except for abandoned property law enforcement, and in 1999, a new amendment to the rule specifically barred state activity "prosecuting enforcement actions."[31]

Had it not made a narrow exception for zoning laws and a few other categories, in principle, this would have stopped a city from enforcing its federally chartered banks to obey its fire codes. In practice, it was worse.

In 1999, New York's Attorney General Eliot Spitzer began investigating abuses by lenders who targeted unsophisticated inner-city property owners in predominantly minority neighborhoods with scant incomes to mortgage their homes on extremely risky terms.[32] Other state attorneys general joined his effort. Spitzer won relief against Household Finance and other lenders for violating New York's laws against discrimination in lending, because those lenders had targeted minority group homeowners. Since Spitzer won judgments on behalf of the other state attorneys general as well as for New York, Household International, the parent company of Household Finance, was required to pay victims across the country $484 million in restitution.[33]

Office of the Comptroller of the Currency v. Spitzer

But, when Spitzer's investigation turned to Citibank, J. P. Morgan Chase, Wells Fargo, and HSBC, the OCC (joined by an industry trade association) sued, arguing that only *it* had the authority to enforce consumer protection laws on such banks, even state laws.[34] The federal district court for the Southern District of New York sided with the OCC,[35] as did the Second Circuit Court of Appeals.[36] As the matter slowly made its way to the Supreme Court, of course the OCC made no effort to take on the enforcement role. The enormous scale of the very practices in the subprime mortgage market Spitzer had tried to halt, magnified by the collateralization and resale of the mortgages and by complex financial instruments derived from the mortgage-backed securities, brought about the financial crisis of 2007, with calamitous results that the world continues to suffer.

In 2009, the Supreme Court reversed the Second Circuit, at last ruling that the OCC had exceeded its legitimate powers in halting Spitzer's investigation. But, it was too late.

Agencies Setting the Limits of Their Own Jurisdiction

Federal preemption and *Chevron* deference, when taken to an extreme, as it was by the Southern District and the Second Circuit in the OCC case, can mean that a federal agency can itself define the limits of its own jurisdiction. That is, when Congress does not carefully delimit the agency's enabling legislation, the agency can decide how far its power extends. Congress rarely delimits such powers narrowly, because it cannot predict what problems the agencies might have to address. (Congress may later object to an agency's action, but wants blame to fall on the agency, not on itself. See endnote 6 in Chapter 2.)

So, a federal agency might extend its powers at the expense of a state. An agency regulation, issued by unelected bureaucrats, without clear authorization by Congress, can trump a state law, enacted by the elected representatives of the public. That, in essence, is exactly what the Southern District and the Second Circuit decided in *Clearing House.*

Courts are supposed to exercise a presumption against federal preemption: " . . . the historic police powers of the States were not to be superseded by the Federal Act unless that was the clear and manifest purpose of Congress."[37] But, the presumption disappears when they find, as the Second Circuit did here, that an "entire field of regulation" has been comprehensively "occupied by federal authority."[38] The Supreme Court's actual decisions have not reliably reflected its oratorical invocation of the presumption against preemption.[39]

New York's Attorneys General argued that enforcing New York's laws against lending discrimination would not interfere with the OCC's responsibility to assure the solvency of the giant banks. (The banks' reckless lending practices ultimately threatened their solvency. The Attorney General's efforts might have lessened that threat.) But, the Second Circuit rejected the argument. Previously the Third Circuit had deferred to the OCC's interpretation of the National Bank Act to stop New Jersey from enforcing its anti-redlining statute as infringing on the OCC's visitorial powers.[40] Citing that decision,[41] the Second Circuit held that since the meaning of "visitorial powers" was unclear, it would defer to the OCC's definition to bar the Attorney General's investigation, although it acknowledged that "[t]he OCC's analysis is at or near the outer limits of what *Chevron* contemplates."[42]

Justice Scalia has usually applied *Chevron* deference very aggressively.[43] His majority opinion *Clearing House* did not reject *Chevron* deference to agency interpretations of their own jurisdictional limits. He merely wrote, "the presence of some uncertainty does not expand *Chevron* deference to cover virtually any interpretation of the National Bank Act."[44] Scalia concluded that the OCC could properly prevent the AG from "issu[ing] a subpoena on his own authority under New York's Executive Law," but not to prevent him from "bring[ing] suit to enforce state law against a national bank," which he thought was "ordinary" law enforcement, not exercising visitorial power."[45]

Scalia may have rejected the OCC's outrageous position here, but he has explicitly stated his view that it is "settled law that the rule of deference applies even to an agency's interpretation of its own statutory authority or jurisdiction."[46] Justice Thomas's partial dissent, joined by Roberts, Kennedy, and Alito, even worse, takes pains to reaffirm just such applications of *Chevron* deference.[47]

Justice William Brennan warned against this kind of deference many years ago:

> Agencies do not "administer" statutes confining the scope of their jurisdiction, and such statutes are not "entrusted" to agencies. Nor do the normal reasons for agency deference apply. First, statutes confining an agency's jurisdiction . . . reflect policies in favor of limiting the agency's jurisdiction that, by definition, have not been entrusted to the agency, and that may indeed conflict not only with the statutory policies the agency *has* been charged with advancing, but also with the agency's institutional interests in expanding its own power. Second, for similar reasons, agencies can claim no special expertise in interpreting a statute confining its jurisdiction. Finally, we cannot presume that Congress implicitly intended an agency to fill "gaps" in a statute confining the agency's jurisdiction, . . . since, by its nature, such a statute manifests an unwillingness to give the agency the freedom to define the scope of its own power. . . It is thus not surprising that this Court has never deferred to an agency's interpretation of a statute designed to confine the scope of its jurisdiction [citations omitted].[48]

Professor David S. Rubenstein of Washburn University Law School would entirely deny agencies the power to issue regulations that, via preemption, override state laws: "the framers never intended that policy choices of unelected administrative bureaucrats would reign supreme over state law."[49] Constitutional values may indeed require that radical change in administrative law. It is one thing for an agency to interpret its jurisdictional statute broadly to cover an individual situation. For example, an agency might need the power to determine whether a person or organization even falls within its jurisdiction.[50] It is quite another, and far more dangerous, to allow an agency to interpret its jurisdictional statute so broadly as to preempt vast reaches of preexisting state regulatory power.[51]

By permitting federal agencies—without congressional authorization—to override the statutory decisions of elected state representatives, based on their own interpretative power grabs, neither the majority opinion nor the dissent in *Clearing House* showed adequate concern for checks and balances.

To their credit, the dissenters in a subsequent decision, Chief Justice Roberts, joined by Justices Alito and Kennedy, would have rejected agencies' claims to powers to interpret statutory provisions unless Congress had at least implicitly "delegated lawmaking power over the ambiguity at issue,"[52] and strongly doubted that Congress would "in fact delegate[] lawmaking power" by ambiguous provisions granting jurisdiction.[53] Justice Scalia's majority opinion, however, once again emphatically approved agency interpretations of the extent of jurisdiction granted to them by their ambiguous enabling legislation.[54]

If we are to maintain a reasonable balance between state and federal power, and between agency expertise and representative democracy, we would do well to heed Brennan's warning and reverse the trend headed by Scalia.

SKIDMORE DEFERENCE AND *AUER* DEFERENCE

Chevron treated ambiguity in a statute as a signal of Congress's desire for the agency administering a statute to interpret it. In *United States v. Mead Corporation*,[55] the Court seemed to back off somewhat, over Justice Scalia's objections,[56] ruling that if a statute did not more strongly indicate Congress's intention to delegate interpretative power, then the agency's interpretation could still earn deference, but only to the extent that it was actually persuasive. Quoting *Skidmore v. Swift & Co.*,[57] a 1944 decision, the *Mead* Court held that if so, agency interpretations could offer "guidance," but only so much as warranted by "the thoroughness evident in its consideration, the validity of its reasoning, its consistency with earlier and later pronouncements, and [other persuasive] factors."[58]

The Court is now likely to use such "*Skidmore* deference" rather than *Chevron* deference only when the agency interpretation emerged out of a more informal process, for example notice-and-comment rulemaking instead of on-the-record rulemaking; when it came from lower-level employees rather than from personnel at or near the top of an agency's hierarchy; and when it reflected some fairly mechanical, perfunctory, and quotidian function rather than a somewhat unusual procedure.[59]

However, as noted above, the Court's performance on questions of deference remains inconsistent, so excessive *Chevron* deference remains as much a danger as it was prior to the Court's decision in *Clearing House*.

Of course, if there is some good reason for courts to defer to agency interpretations of ambiguous provisions of statutes they administer, a still stronger case can be made for courts to defer to agency interpretations of ambiguous provisions of regulations an agency promulgated, which is known as "*Auer* deference," from *Auer v. Robbins*,[60] "[T]he ultimate criterion is the administrative interpretation, which becomes of controlling weight unless it is plainly erroneous or inconsistent with the regulation."

A rare deviation from *Auer* deference depended to some extent on the argument that the agency had tacitly interpreted its regulations one way—the way the court ultimately decided to interpret them—despite the agency's last-minute explicit interpretation to the contrary. The Fair Labor Standards Act provided that an employer needn't pay overtime to an "outside salesman." Labor Department regulations defined an "outside salesman" as someone employed primarily to "mak[e] sales within the meaning of section 3(k) of the Act," which broadly included in its definition of "sale" such alternatives as "exchange, contract to sell, consignment for sale, shipment for sale, or other disposition."[61] Justice Alito wrote for the majority that "detailers," who urge doctors to prescribe particular medications and often elicited nonbinding commitments from the doctors to do so, but do not literally sell medications, were "outside salesmen." Thus, pharmaceutical companies did not need to pay them overtime, despite the fact that the Department of Labor interpreted its regulations to the contrary. Justice Alito argued that Labor had by virtue of "a very lengthy period of conspicuous inaction" in effect allowed that interpretation for years, so the companies would not have had adequate notice, and Labor's new regulation would have constituted an "unfair surprise."[62]

STATE COURTS AND *CHEVRON* DEFERENCE

Most states have not adopted *Chevron* deference. For example, the Ohio Environmental Protection Agency interpreted the Ohio statute requiring a business to obtain a permit to "install" an "air contaminant source" to apply when the business needed to replace a mill with a new, but otherwise identical mill.[63] The Ohio Supreme Court, reading the statute to require "a balance" between environmental protection and economic growth, held otherwise.[64] (Note: That this happens to be another environmental case, like *Chevron* itself, is purely coincidental. *Chevron* deference applies to any areas of substantive law.) The generally understood reason for the difference between the federal approach and that of many states is that state agencies often have less technical expertise than their counterparts at the federal level. A 2009 study found that sixteen states use a standard of deference to agency interpretations of statutes similar to that of *Chevron*, eighteen states provide something like *Skidmore* deference, and fourteen states do not defer at all, choosing instead to interpret ambiguous or unclear statutes without reference to the views of the administering agency.[65]

New York courts are among those who do apply a state version of *Chevron* deference. Its courts must defer to an administrative agency's interpretation of an ambiguous statute unless the "interpretation is irrational, unreasonable, or inconsistent with the governing statute."[66]

In *Robins v. Blaney*,[67] section 2509 of the New York Education Law said, "except that in the case of a teacher who has rendered satisfactory service as a regular substitute for a period of two years * * * and has been appointed to teach the same subject in day schools on an annual salary, the probationary period shall be limited to one year." The New York State Education Commissioner ruled that only substitute teaching *prior* to the first probationary period could count.

The court upheld the ruling because it was "rationally based"[68]: the statute was "intended to preserve distinctions between regular and substitute service,"[69] so regular teaching should not be interrupted by a *subsequent* period of substitute service. When a statute is ambiguous, or if its meaning is doubtful, an administrator's interpretation of an unclear statute "'takes on almost the force of judicial interpretation.'"[70]

STATE PREEMPTION AND LOCAL LAW

It would be easy to think that state law can preempt local ordinances in just the way that federal law can preempt state law, but the parallel is not exact. Legally, cities and other local governments are created by their states, and as such are not constitutionally parallel to federal and state governments as a sort of third level. The former two have constitutional status as sovereign governments; local government derives its powers from state law. States are not "arms of the federal government."[71] But, state officials actually appoint some local government officials: governors often appoint the boards and sometimes the chairs of regional public authorities, like the public authority that controls the water supply for the Lower Neches Valley in Texas,[72] or the public authority that controls most public transportation for the New York metropolitan area.[73] Incidentally, unlike the federal and state governments, all of which have APAs, local government agencies are bound only by due process and statutes relevant to particular agencies.

Preemption still operates in some ways as one would expect: state law preempts local law. However, the "home rule" principle complicates the operation of preemption doctrine. Depending on how the state constitution defines it, states can grant municipalities and other local governments the power to enact a broad range of initiatives without specific legislative authorization from the state, and/or immunity for their local laws against state legislation specifically overriding a locality's law (but not immunity from state laws affecting all such localities). Home rule provisions often require state legislatures to obtain from the local government's legislative body a majority or supermajority vote approving a "home rule message" in favor of the proposed state law that conflicts with local law, or even enters into an area of legitimate local concern. Commonly, although some states explicitly exclude from home rule powers "the power to enact private or civil laws governing civil relationships except as incident to the exercise of an independent county or city power,"[74] even in the absence of such a provision courts would not uphold local laws of such nature against private rights[75]; and "such general subjects as crime, domestic relations, wills and administration, mortgages, trusts, contracts, real and personal property, insurance, banking, corporations and many others have never been regarded by anyone, least of all the cities themselves, as appropriate subjects of local control . . . these matters are strictly of 'state control.'"[76]

Thus, when Mayor Giuliani attempted to bypass New York City's Board of Collective Bargaining because he thought the unions had too much influence there, and instead lobbied for a state agency, the Public Employment Relations Board, to take over negotiations with the police and firefighters unions, New York's Court of Appeals concluded that the legislation "was not enacted to further a matter 'of sufficient importance to the State generally' [citation omitted] [so] its enactment without a home rule message from New York City render the chapter law unconstitutional and unenforceable."[77] The "state interest" exception to home rule did not apply because the City already had its own adequate procedure for collective bargaining.[78] (The New York City Council disagreed with Giuliani, and so would not pass a home rule message authorizing the legislation.)

On the other hand, despite its acknowledgment that district attorneys had in fact become more truly local officers than state officers,[79] the New York Court upheld a state law setting the salary levels of district attorneys in certain counties at the same level as county court judges, as reasonable and related to "an appropriate level of State interest."[80]

But, even a state law of general applicability to all municipalities, purporting to require them to establish an agency in a particular manner and format, will not survive the home rule requirement unless somehow that format can be shown to be of legitimate concern to the state, and not just the reflection of someone doing someone else a political favor. Oregon's legislature tried to force each of its cities to set up a certain kind of commission to establish civil service systems. Its highest court held that "the people of a city are not 'subject to the will of the legislature in the management of purely local municipal business in which the state at large is not interested. . . .'"[81]

Whether a state has actually delegated a power to local governments under its home rule provisions actually is a somewhat different question than the question of whether the state, by legislation, has preempted a local rule. For example, a Colorado city enacted a zoning ordinance prohibiting unrelated registered sex offenders from residing in the same household, with criminal penalties for violation. Three foster children in one such home had been both victims and perpetrators of incest and were registered as sex offenders as a result.[82] The Colorado courts concluded that although the state had delegated zoning powers to its municipalities, in addition to regulating matters of local concern the ordinance also regulated a matter of statewide concern: Colorado had enacted a Children's Code reflecting the state interest in placing delinquent children in foster care homes. The local ordinance denied the children in question access to treatment best suited to their needs, in violation of the Children's Code; denied other adjudicated delinquent children in the city the expectation of consistency; and would have resulted in using up too much of the supply of available housing for such children throughout the state. Therefore, state law preempted the local ordinance both because of conflict with specific provisions ("conflict preemption"), and because to effectuate its purposes, the state legislation on the subject had to occupy the entire field of regulation, leaving no room for local law to intrude on the subject ("field preemption").[83]

The three dissenting justices argued that zoning and public safety are local concerns; the regulation and protection of juveniles are statewide concerns; and that the local ordinance could be reconciled with state law if the court had merely limited its applicability. No state law explicitly or expressly conflicted with, or "preempted," the local ordinance. The dissenting judges would have invalidated the ordinance only as it applied to "adjudicated delinquent children living in foster homes."[84]

WHAT AM I SUPPOSED TO DO?

Coast Guard Choice of Dangerous but Effective Oil Spill Clean-Up Chemical: Federal Regulations Preempt State Law–Based Health Damage Lawsuits

Go back in time to 2010, when the BP oil company's drilling rig failed and caused millions of gallons of oil to spill into the waters of the Gulf Coast. Under the Clean Water Act of 1972, subsequently amended, the President is required to prepare a "National Contingency Plan," and under circumstances like the BP oil spill must ensure "effective and immediate removal" of the spilled oil and "direct all Federal, State, and private actions to remove" the spill. The President may delegate this responsibility to perform the latter function. The National Contingency Plan provides that under these circumstances, the Coast Guard may appoint a Federal On-Scene Coordinator (FOSC) to take charge. The Coast Guard appointed you.

You are aware that the Clean Water Act gives immunity against lawsuits for damages to individuals and companies that assist you in the clean-up—other than those who caused the spill in the first place—so long as they act in accordance with the provisions of the National Contingency Plan, even if their actions do cause some additional damage to persons or property.

You now face the following problem: your experts have warned you that the longer the oil stays as concentrated as it is, the more fish, birds, and valuable vegetation it will kill. It can even threaten human life, should it catch fire. Obviously, you would prefer to remove the oil entirely, but that takes longer than dispersing it, so in the meanwhile you must disperse it as quickly as possible. The National Contingency Plan included a product called Corexit on its list of approved dispersants, and the manufacturer can provide you as much as you need and as soon as you need it. However, it contains a chemical that can cause kidney and liver damage to anyone who breathes it in or touches it too much.

On balance, it seems worth the risk in order to protect life and the environment, unless the company would also be exposed to lawsuits if you use it. If that were the case, you believe that other manufacturers of useful, but somewhat dangerous environmental clean-up products would then withdraw them from availability for use under the National Contingency Plan. While the Clean Air Act immunizes such manufacturers, they might still face product liability or other claims under state laws. Should you use Corexit?

The federal district court for the Eastern District of Louisiana addressed this question in a case of similar facts (some small changes in the facts allowed a clearer presentation of the issue here).[85] Clean-up workers who were exposed to Corexit sued, noting that they were already suffering symptoms from the exposure and would likely suffer more in the future.[86]

The plaintiff clean-up workers understood that federal preemption of state law claims would present an obstacle. Therefore, they couched their claims not against the FOSC for using Corexit, but against the manufacturer of Corexit for product liability—that the manufacturer failed in its duty, under state law, to pull it off the market as an unreasonably dangerous product, or to change its composition to make it less dangerous.[87]

However, the court explained that the logic of the Clean Water Act implied preemption of state laws that conflict with its goals. When Vermont residents sued a New York paper mill under Vermont law for the nuisance it was creating by the run-off of its pollution into Vermont waters, the Supreme Court had ruled that since the purpose of the Clean Water Act was to address the impact of water pollution on affected states, the Clean Water Act preempted remedies under Vermont law, an affected state. Remedies under Vermont law could have been inconsistent with "efficiency and predictability in the [federal] permit system [regulated by the federal law]."[88] However, the federal Clean Water Act did not preempt remedies offered by the law of New York, a "source" state. Of course, the Vermont residents could also have sued federally under certain provisions of the Clean Water Act itself.[89]

As *Geier* and *Williamson*[90] explain, analysis of the history and purpose of the federal regulatory scheme help determine the extent to which it preempts state law. Under the federal scheme here, the FOSC has the clear responsibility to direct the clean-up, including cost-benefit decisions about the use of somewhat dangerous chemicals.[91] The court, in preempting all state law causes of action in response to the use of Corexit, reflected precisely the concerns attributed to you in the hypothetical: were such a lawsuit to be allowed, a manufacturer's consequent refusal to provide that product or a comparable product "would deprive the response of a tool expressly contemplated by federal law and, consequently, impede the FOSC's ability to 'ensure effective and immediate removal' of oil and the 'efficient, coordinated, and effective' response intended by the [National Contingency Plan] [footnote omitted]."[92]

PRACTICE PROBLEMS

PROBLEM 1: A section of the Public Health Service Act provided that no federal funds appropriated under the Act for family-planning services could "be used in programs where abortion is a method of family planning." For twenty years after its enactment, doctors receiving federal funds continued to offer counseling for abortions, assuming that mere counseling did not constitute "use" under the statute. However, pursuant to that provision, the Department of Health and Human Services (HHS) then promulgated rules prohibiting family planning projects receiving such funds from engaging in counseling. Said counseling concerning, referrals for, and activities advocating abortion as a method of family planning, that is, doctors advising pregnant Medicaid patients could not discuss abortion with them, except to say such things as "the project does not consider abortion an appropriate method of family planning and therefore does not counsel or refer for abortion." Was the language of the statute sufficiently ambiguous to require deference to the agency interpretation as expressed in the rules? Assuming it was, further assume that some years later the President directed HHS not to apply the regulations in a manner that would prevent a doctor from giving abortion-related information to a patient; and in compliance with the President's wishes, HHS issued a directive (an interpretative rule, without notice and comment) to that effect. That directive was challenged in court: was it valid?

PROBLEM 2: Section 320, added in 1975 to the New York State Welfare Code, created a special welfare grant to replace clothing or furniture lost in "fire, flood, or like catastrophe." The legislative committee report with the bill explained that its purpose was to replace discretionary grants, which were often abused, and were demeaning for recipients to request. The State Department of Social Services interpreted the statute to exclude grants for losses resulting from human causes.

Ms. Howard, a welfare recipient, a single parent, lives in a slum apartment that was burglarized, and lost about $2000 of her clothing and furniture. Her application for a special grant under § 320 and her fair hearing appeal were rejected based on the manual. She appealed to the courts. What resulted?[93]

ENDNOTES

1. Federal law is "the supreme Law of the Land . . . any Thing in the Constitution or Laws of any State to the Contrary notwithstanding." Article VI, Clause 2.
2. *Rice v. Santa Fe Elevator Corp.*, 331 U.S. 218, 230, 67 S. Ct. 1146, 1152 (1947).
3. Santiago Legarre, The Historical Background of the Police Power, 9 *J. of Constitutional Law* 745, 773, 794 (2007), https://www.law.upenn.edu/journals/conlaw/articles/volume9/issue3/Legarre9U.Pa.J.Const.L.745%282007%29.pdf.
4. *Hines v. Davidowitz*, 312 U.S. 52, 67, 61 S. Ct. 399, 404 (1941).
5. *Arizona v. United States*, — U.S. at —, 132 S. Ct. 2492, 2505, 183 L. Ed. 2d 351 (2012).
6. See, e.g., Nicholas Riccardi, Racial profiling in Arizona? That's nothing new, critics say, *Los Angeles Times*, 5/1/10, http://articles.latimes.com/2010/may/01/nation/la-na-sweeps-20100501.
7. 132 S. Ct. at 2510.
8. *Geier v. American Honda Motor Co.*, 529 U.S. 861, 120 S. Ct. 1913 (2000).
9. 529 U.S. at 875, 120 S. Ct. at 1922.
10. 529 U.S. at 886, 120 S. Ct. at 1928.
11. *Williamson v. Mazda Motor of America*, 131 S. Ct. 1131, 1137, 179 L. Ed. 2d 75 (2011).
12. 131 S. Ct. at 1138.
13. 131 S. Ct. at 1139.

14. *Id.* The underlying statute included a "savings clause" providing that compliance with federal safety standards did not "exempt any person from liability under common law." 131 S. Ct. at 1135, quoting 15 U.S.C. § 1397(k). The Court in both *Geier* and *Williamson* ruled that common-law suits would therefore not be barred by any express preemption provision of a federal safety standard. 131 S. Ct. at 1135. The central issue in each case was whether such lawsuits would be barred by "field" preemption. In *Geier* the answer was yes. In *Williamson* the answer was no.

15. However, see Stephen A. Gardbaum, The Nature of Preemption, 79 *Cornell L. Rev.* 767, 769 (1994): "contrary to the standard view, the power of preemption has little if anything to do with the Supremacy Clause." 79 *Cornell L. Rev.* at 771: "Preemption is . . . a jurisdiction-stripping . . . concept, unlike supremacy which deals with conflict resolution in particular cases . . . supremacy resolves a 'true conflict' . . .; by contrast, preemption resolves a 'false conflict' . . ."

16. Much of this section is taken from Daniel Feldman, The Legitimacy of United States Government Agency Power, 75(1) *Public Administration Review*, pp. 75–84, January/February 2015, DOI: 10.1111/puar.12279.

17. *Cuomo v. Clearing House Association*, 557 U.S. 519, 129 S. Ct. 2710 (2009).

18. *Chevron v. Natural Resources Defense Council*, 467 U.S. 837, 104 S. Ct. 2778 (1984)

19. In deciding legislative intent, one might wonder how to interpret the actions of legislators who voted with their party without any attention to a bill's contents; who voted for a bill thinking and hoping it would fail; or who were part of one of several groups of legislators, none constituting a majority, each with a different understanding of the bill's implications; and so forth. Ronald Dworkin provides a good discussion of some of the difficulties of statutory interpretation in *Law's Empire*, (Cambridge, MA: Harvard University Press, 1986), especially at 342–354.

20. P.L. 95–95, 91 Stat. 685.

21. 647 U.S. at 840.

22. Natural Resources Defense Council v. Gorsuch, 685 F. 2d 718 (D.C. Cir. 1982).

23. 685 F. 2d at 27–28.

24. 647 U.S. at 843.

25. For example, in *Clearing House Association v. Cuomo*, 510 F. 3d 105 (2007) at 115–116, the Second Circuit relied on *Watters v. Wachovia Bank, N.A.*, 550 U.S. 1, 127 S. Ct. 1559 (2007), where the majority rejected Justice Stevens's dissenting opinion "that nondiscriminatory [state] laws of general application that do not 'forbid' or 'impair significantly' national bank activities should not be preempted." 550 U.S. at 24, 127 S. Ct. at 1574. Notably foreshadowing the lower courts' disastrous decisions in *Clearing House*, Stevens had also warned that is was "especially troubling that the Court so blithely pre-empts Michigan laws designed to protect consumers. Consumer protection is quintessentially a 'field which the States have traditionally occupied.'" 550 U.S. 1, 35–36, 127 S. Ct. at 1581. The *Watters* majority claimed *Chevron* deference was irrelevant because the OCC's regulation merely restated the obvious implication of the National Banking Act. 550 U.S. at 20-21, 127 S. Ct. at 1572. In the context of controversy over the OCC's interpretation of the reach of that very same regulation, the majority decision signaled even greater deference to the OCC than a *Chevron* approach could have. See Ramyn Atri, *Cuomo v. Clearing House Association*: The Latest Chapter in the OCC's Pursuit of *Chevron* Deference, 14 *North Carolina Banking Institute* 467, 481 (2/10/2010), http://www.law .unc.edu/documents/journals/articles/35.pdf.

26. Gregory M. Dickinson, Calibrating *Chevron* for Preemption, 63 *Admin. L. Rev.* 667, 669 (Fall 2011). "Even now, twenty-six years after the *Chevron* decision, it is unclear to what extent *Chevron*'s rule of deference applies in preemption cases." 63 *Admin. L. Rev.* at 680.

27. 12 U.S.C. § 484. Technically it was the National Currency Act of 1863, 12 Stat. 665, renamed the National Bank Act in 1864, 13 Stat. 99.

28. OCC Funding, web site of the Office of the Comptroller of the Currency, http://www.occ.gov/ about/what-we-do/mission/index-about.html.

29. 12 C.F.R. 7.4000.

30. Adam Liptak, "Justices to Rule on States' Bank Inquiries," *New York Times*, January 17, 2009, B3. New York State Attorney General Andrew Cuomo's brief when the case went to the Supreme Court noted that the OCC "had minimal interest in consumer protection." *Id.*

31. 64 Fed. Reg. at 60100, cited in *Clearing House Association v. Cuomo*, 510 F. 3d 105, 111 (2007).

32. Eliot Spitzer, Predatory Lenders' Partner in Crime, *Washington Post*, 2/14/08, http://www .washingtonpost.com/wp-dyn/content/article/2008/02/13/AR2008021302783.html.

33. Press Release, Refunds in Predatory Lending Case to be Mailed, Office of the New York State Attorney General website, 12/11/03, http://www.ag.ny.gov/press-release/refunds-landmark-predatory-lending-case-be-mailed.

34. Shaheen Pasha, Spitzer's Eyes Remain on Banks, *CNN/Money*, 8/24/05, http://money.cnn .com/2005/08/19/news/economy/predatory_lending/index.htm.

35. Office of the Comptroller of the Currency v. Spitzer, 396 F. Supp. 2d 383 (2005).

36. Clearing House Association v. Cuomo, 510 F. 3d 105 (2007).

37. *Rice v. Santa Fe Elevator Corp.*, 331 U.S. 218, 230, 67 S. Ct. 1146, 91 L. Ed. 1447 (1947).

38. *Clearing House Association v. Cuomo*, 510 F. 3d 105, 113 (2nd Cir. 2007).

39. Ashutosh Bhagwat, *Wyeth v. Levine* and Agency Preemption: More Muddle, or Creeping to Clarity?, 45 *Tulsa L. Rev.* 197, 221 (2009).

40. National State Bank, Elizabeth, N.J. v. Long, 630 F. 2d 981, 989 (3d Cir. 1980).

41. 510 F. 3d at 117.

42. 510 F. 3d at 119.

43. Richard W. Murphy, in Judicial Deference, Agency Commitment, and Force of Law, 66 *Ohio State L. J.* 1013, 1033 (2005) calls Scalia "that most aggressive and powerful fan of the *Chevron* doctrine."

44. 129 S. Ct. at 2715.

45. 129 S. Ct. at 2721-2.

46. *Mississippi Power & Light v. Mississippi ex rel. Moore*, 487 U.S. 354, 108 S. Ct. 2428, Scalia concurrence at 487 U.S. 377, 380, 108 S. Ct. at 2442, 2444 (1988), in direct contradiction of Brennan's statement in dissent that it is by no means settled law, and in fact the Court had never so held. Brennan dissent at 487 U.S. 354 at 383, 386, 108 S. Ct. at 2445, 2447.

47. 129 S. Ct., Thomas partial dissent at 2722, 2728–9.

48. *Mississippi Power & Light Co. v. Miss. ex rel. Moore*, 457 U.S. 354, 108 S. Ct. 2428 (1988), Brennan dissent at 457 U.S. at 383, 386–7, 108 S. Ct. at 2445, 1447.

49. Delegating Supremacy?, 65 *Vand. L. Rev.* 1125, 1129 (May 2012). (But, cf. Gardbaum, *supra*, for his technical objection to seeing preemption as an expression of federal supremacy.)

50. See, e.g., *United States v. Sing Tuck*, 194 U.S. 161, 24 S. Ct. 621 (1904); *Myers v. Bethlehem Shipbuilding Corp.*, 303 U.S. 41, 58 S. Ct. 459 (1938).

51. See Cynthia R. Farina, Statutory Interpretation and the Balance of Power in the Administrative State, 89 *Columbia L. Rev.* 452, 487–8 (April 1989): "a key assumption of Chevron's 'judicial usurpation' argument—that Congress may give agencies primary responsibility not only for making policy within the limits of their organic statutes, but also for defining those limits whenever the text and surrounding legislative materials are ambiguous—is fundamentally incongruous with the constitutional course by which the Court came to reconcile agencies and the separation of powers."

52. *City of Arlington v. FCC*, 133 S. Ct. 1863, 1880, 2013 U.S. LEXIS 3838 (2013).

53. 133 S. Ct. at 1879.

54. 133 S. Ct. at 1874.

55. *United States v. Mead Corporation*, 533 U.S. 218, 121 S. Ct. 2164 (2001).

56. 533 U.S. at 239, 121 S. Ct. at 2177.

57. *Skidmore v. Swift & Co.*, 323 U.S. 134, 65 S. Ct. 161 (1944).

58. 533 U.S. 228, 121 S. Ct. at 2171, quoting *Skidmore* at 323 U.S. at 140, 65 S. Ct. at 164.

59. Jack M. Beerman, *Inside Administrative Law*, (Frederick, MD: Aspen Publishers, 2011), 135.

60. *Auer v. Robbins*, 519 U.S. 452, 461, 117 S. Ct. 905, 911 (1997), quoting *Bowles v. Seminole Rock & Sand Co.*, 325 U.S. 410, 414, 65 S. Ct. 1215, 1217 (1945).

61. *Christopher v. SmithKline Beecham Corp.*, 132 S. Ct. 2156, 2162,183 L. Ed. 2d 153, 165 (2012).

62. 132 S. Ct. at 2168, 183 L. Ed. 2d at 171.

63. *State ex rel. Celebrezze v. National Lime & Stone Co.*, 68 Ohio St. 3d 377, 627 N.E. 2d 538 (1994).

64. 68 Ohio St. 3d at 385, 627 N.E. 2d at 544.
65. Zac Hudson, A Case for Varying Interpretive Deference at the State Level, 119 *Yale L. J.* 373, 374 (2009). The author argues that at the state level, among other factors, the different relative levels of expertise between courts and agencies, warrants much less deference to agency interpretations. 119 *Yale L. J.* at 373–4 and 378–380.
66. *Brown v. New York State Racing & Wagering Board*, 871 N.Y.S. 2d 623, 627 (2d Dept. 2009), citing *Matter of Robins v. Blaney*, 59 N.Y. 2d 393, 399, 465 N.Y.S. 2d 868 (1983); *Matter of Toys "R" Us v. Silva*, 89 N.Y. 2d 411, 418–419, 654 N.Y.S. 2d 100 (1996); and see *Espada 2001 v. New York City Campaign Finance Board*, 870 N.Y.S. 2d 293, 299 (1st Dept. 2008).
67. 59 N.Y. 2d 393, 399, 465 N.Y.S. 2d 868 (1983).
68. 59 N.Y. 2d at 399.
69. *Id.*
70. *Id.*, quoting *Town of Amherst v. County of Erie*, 256 A.D. 56, 61, 258 N.Y.S. 76 (4th Dept. 1932), *aff'd* 260 N.Y. 361, 369–370, 183 N.E. 851 (1933).
71. Richard Briffault and Laurie Reynolds, *Cases and Materials on State and Local Government Law*, 7th ed., (St. Paul, MN: Thomson/Reuters, 2009), 7.
72. Office of the Governor Rick Perry, press release, Gov. Perry Appoints Pate and Spurlock to Lower Neches Valley Authority Board of Directors, 7/25/14, http://governor.state.tx.us/news/appointment/19957/, accessed 8/19/14.
73. Andrew Cuomo, Governor, press release, Governor Cuomo Announces MTA and Transportation Appointments, 10/20/11, https://www.governor.ny.gov/press/10202011Transportation Appointments, accessed 8/19/14.
74. American Municipal League [National League of Cities], *Model Constitutional Provisions for Municipal Home Rule*, Section 4 at 19, quoted in Kenneth Vanlandingham, Constitutional Municipal Home rule Since the AMA (NLC) Model, *William & Mary L. Rev.*, 17(1):1–34, 16, 1975.
75. Vanlandingham, *id.* at 18.
76. Howard Lee McBain, *The Law and Practice of Municipal Home Rule*, (New York: Columbia University Press, 1916), 673–4, quoted in Vanlandingham, *id.* at 18, note 67.
77. *City of New York v. Police Benevolent Association*, 89 N.Y. 2d 380, 385, 676 N.E. 2d 847, 848, 654 N.Y.S. 2d 85, 86 (1996).
78. 89 N.Y. 2d at 393, 676 N.E. 2d at 853, 654 N.Y.S. 2d at 91.
79. *Kelley v. McGee*, 57 N.Y. 2d 522, 534–5, 443 N.E. 2d 908, 911–2, 457 N.Y.S. 2d 434, 437–8 (1982).
80. 57 N.Y. 2d at 540, 443 N.E. 2d at 915, 457 N.Y.S. 2d at 441.
81. *State ex rel. Heinig v. City of Milwaukie*, 231 Ore. 473, 373 P. 2d 680, 479, 684 (1962), quoting *Branch v. Albee*, 71 Ore. 188, 193, 142 P. 598, 599 (1914).
82. *City of Northglenn v. Ibarra*, 62 P. 3d 151, 153–4 (2003).
83. 62 P. 3d at 159–163.
84. 62 P. 3d at 164–167.
85. In re: Oil Spill by the Oil Rig "Deepwater Horizon" in the Gulf of Mexico, on April 20, 2010. Applies to Pleading Bundle B3, 2012 U.S. Dist. LEXIS 168755, 76 ERC (BNA) 1192 (E.D. La. 2012).
86. 2012 U.S. Dist. LEXIS 168755 at *7.
87. 2012 U.S. Dist. LEXIS 168755 at *31.
88. *International Paper Co. v. Ouellette*, 479 U.S. 481, 496, 107 S. Ct. 805 (1989).
89. 2012 U.S. Dist. LEXIS 168755 at *37, discussing *International Paper Co. v. Ouellette, supra*.
90. See discussion at notes 8–14 *supra*.
91. 2012 U.S. Dist. LEXIS 168755 at *44–6.
92. 2012 U.S. Dist. LEXIS 168755 at *48–9.
93. The relevant case law suggested a similar problem to Arthur E. Bonfield and Michael Asimow, *State and Federal Administrative Law* (St. Paul, MN: West Publishing Company, 1989), 597–8.

Adjudication

AGENCY POWER TO CONDUCT HEARINGS

When he led the Interstate Commerce Commission, Judge Thomas Cooley decided that after a hearing, an agency could not impose a penalty of more than $20, based on the Seventh Amendment guarantee of a due process of law, informed by the Ninth Amendment guarantee of jury trial "where the value in controversy shall exceed twenty dollars."[1]

BOX 7-1 **Ninth Amendment to the Constitution**

Article the ninth. . . In suits at common law, where the value in controversy shall exceed twenty dollars, the right of trial by jury shall be preserved, and no fact tried by a jury, shall be otherwise re-examined in any Court of the United States, than according to the rules of the common law.

Source: http://www.archives.gov/exhibits/charters/bill_of_rights_transcript.html

---

Today, many federal agencies conduct hearings after which penalties or other burdens cost far more than twenty dollars, including the following: Coast Guard, Commodity Futures Trading Commission, Department of Agriculture, Department of Health and Human Services/Department Appeals Board, Department of Health and Human Services/Office of Medicare Hearings and Appeals, Department of Housing and Urban Development, Department of the Interior, Department of Justice/Executive Office for Immigration Review, Department of Labor, Department of Transportation, Department of Veterans Affairs, Drug Enforcement Administration, Environmental Protection Agency, Equal Employment Opportunity Commission, Federal Aviation Administration, Federal Communications Commission, Federal Energy Regulatory Commission, Federal Labor Relations Authority, Federal Maritime Commission, Federal Mine Safety and Health Review Commission, Federal Trade Commission, Food and Drug Administration, International Trade

Commission, Merit Systems Protection Board, National Labor Relations Board, National Transportation Safety Board, Nuclear Regulatory Commission, Occupational Safety and Health Review Commission, Office of Financial Institution Adjudication, Patent and Trademark Office, Postal Service, Securities and Exchange Commission, Small Business Administration, and Social Security Administration.[2]

Hearing officers in many states work for individual agencies that parallel the federal level. However, in many other states (and some cities, including the City of New York) hearing officers are assigned to agencies as needed by a central panel. This practice is thought by some to reduce the appearance and perhaps the reality of bias in favor of the agency that employs the hearing officer. A sample list of state agencies conducting administrative hearings (i.e., only the ones that hire their own hearing officers or administrative law judges, not including the ones that use central panels), includes Alabama Department of Revenue, California Department of Consumer Affairs, California Department of Health Services, California Department of Industrial Relations, California Department of Social Services, California Employment Development Department, California Public Utilities Commission, Florida Division of Administrative Hearings, Georgia Office of State Administrative Hearings, Illinois Human Rights Commission, Industrial Commission of Arizona, Iowa Department of Corrections, Iowa Workforce Development Department, Louisiana Division of Administrative Law, Maryland Office of Administrative Hearings, Maryland Public Service Commission, Massachusetts Executive Office of Transportation, Massachusetts Department of Environmental Protection, Michigan State Office of Administrative Hearings and Rules, New York State Department of Environmental Conservation, New York State Department of Labor, Pennsylvania Department of Insurance, Pennsylvania Department of Labor and Industry, Bureau of Workers' Compensation, Pennsylvania Liquor Control Board, Pennsylvania Public Utility Commission, Texas Department of Banking, Texas Finance Commission, Texas Health and Human Services Commission, and Traffic Violations Bureau of New York State DMV.[3]

An example of state and local agencies conducting administrative hearings for people in one neighborhood (in Chicago and nearby areas outside the city limits) includes the Chicago Police Board (conducting disciplinary hearings for employees); other boards of police and fire commissioners for a smaller locality; school districts (hearing challenges to Individual Educational Plans for special education students); the Illinois Industrial Commission (conducting Workers' Compensation hearings); the Illinois Human Rights Commission; the Chicago Zoning Board of Appeals; the Chicago Department of Administrative Hearings (for parking tickets and other infractions that were at one time low-level misdemeanors heard in Criminal Court); and the Evanston Division of Administrative Hearings (for infractions by students under 21 years of age, probably primarily from Northwestern University).[4]

Power to Impose Big Fines

What happened to the Ninth Amendment guarantee? Actually, in 1856, long before Cooley's objection to administrative penalties in excess of twenty dollars, the Supreme Court acknowledged a difference between "public and private wrongs," with different "extrajudicial remedies" for each. As an example of the former, a private person may simply "recapture" goods wrongfully taken by another private person, but "an instance of redress of a particular kind of public wrong" certainly would include "the recovery of public dues by a summary process of distress, issued by some public officer authorized by law."[5] Thus, the Court implied the legitimacy of the imposition of executive agency penalties on private individuals independent of a jury determination, although of course subsequently subject to an appeal to court. Therefore, agencies continued, despite Judge Cooley's complaint, to proceed accordingly.

In 1977, the Supreme Court faced another version of the Thomas Cooley problem, when the Occupational Safety and Health Administration (OSHA) hit the Atlas Roofing Company with financial penalties for considerably more than twenty dollars. In the face of a very long history of unchallenged and substantial financial penalties imposed by government agencies, Atlas Roofing somehow thought it could still argue that the Seventh Amendment barred such penalties. This time the Court held very explicitly that the Seventh Amendment applied only to the kinds of trials conducted at the time of its adoption (perhaps, although the Court did not say so, suggested by the dollar amount explicitly set forth in the Ninth Amendment and unchanged since then), and especially did not apply to the enforcement of "public rights" created by Congress, by statute, to achieve public policy goals.[6]

Right to a Hearing

So, on the basis of hearings they conduct, agencies can impose burdens on people or on companies. But, must agencies follow the strict rules designed to protect the right to a fair trial? In a criminal trial, with life or liberty at stake, strict rules, announced in advance, bind the government. Slightly less strict rules govern civil trials because such trials should not threaten life or liberty. But, logic, experience, and compassion are supposed to play a greater role in agency decision-making. So, agencies may limit "judicialization," meaning the importation and adoption of procedures established to assure due process in the traditional court setting, but must protect rights to some extent.

There is no right to a hearing for purely arithmetical or administrative issues. Would-be motorists take a driving test. Unions must allow workers to vote their choice. The motorist and the union are not permitted to argue the merits of their position to a hearing officer instead.

Even when they have a right to a hearing, most people do not challenge administrative decisions: they accept the size of their Social Security checks; they pay their parking tickets; they send their children to the schools for which they are zoned.

But, people usually do have a right to a hearing, and that right is itself fundamental. "Even God himself did not pass sentence upon Adam before he was called upon to make his defence."[7] In addition, a party to a hearing might have certain rights, such as the right to notice of agency action, the right to present evidence and argument, the right to rebut adverse evidence through cross-examination and other means, the right to appear with counsel, the right to have the decision based only on evidence in the record, and the right to have a complete record—but not necessarily all of these rights.

RIGHT VERSUS PRIVILEGE

In the 1970s, major court decisions dealt with the question of privilege versus right. Prior to that time, citizens had no right to a hearing to challenge the loss of a "privilege," only the loss of a "right." A classic example: "in accepting charity, the appellant has consented to the provisions of the law under which the charity is bestowed"—charity, then, consisting of what we now call public assistance or welfare.[8] There was no right to appeal its termination, no matter how unfair.

That approach came under devastating attack in a 1964 article, "The New Property," by Charles Reich. Enormous concentrations of economic power in the United States from the late 19th century on threatened employees and consumers. The New Deal offset that threat with a parallel growth in government.

Reich argued that to finance the benefits it provided to individuals—by regulatory protection for workers and consumers, but even more simply and obviously by cash support through Social Security and welfare—government absorbed so much private income it left individuals less able to control their own economic destinies: "tax money is no longer available for individual savings or insurance."[9]

Therefore, individuals need "rights" to receive such government benefits previously regarded as "privileges"—not only cash support, but a wide variety of such "privileges," including drivers' licenses and professional licenses.[10] Reich sharply criticized government agencies' untrammeled discretion in conditioning or revoking such privileges.[11]

Flemming v. Nestor, a 1960 decision of the Supreme Court,[12] was his favorite illustration of the injustice resulting from the failure of the law to protect such benefits.[13] Nestor came to the United States in 1913 and contributed to the government's "old-age fund" (which became the basis for Social Security eligibility) from 1936 to 1955. He joined the Communist Party in 1933, but left it after six years. Much later, Congress passed the Smith Act, declaring that such membership was cause for deportation and requiring revocation of retirement benefits for those who had been members. In 1956, the government deported Nestor, and stopped paying benefits to his wife who was still in the United States.

The Court justified this behavior on the grounds that Social Security benefits were not an "accrued property right," they were noncontractual, they could not "be soundly analogized to that of a holder of an annuity,"[14] and it was "not irrational for Congress to have concluded that the public purse should not be utilized to contribute to the support of those deported on the grounds specified in the statute."[15]

This, said Reich, resembles feudalism: "Wealth is not 'owned' or 'vested' in the holders. Instead it is held conditionally," until the vassal displeases the lord. "No form of government largesse . . . is more obviously a compulsory substitute for private property [than Social Security] . . . is more relied on, and more often thought of as property."[16] Yet, the government could take it away. What about the tax money taken from the individual by the government to pay for public transportation, public insurance on savings deposits, public lands for parks? Should the public have rights to these things? Holders of broadcast licenses, motor carrier permits, or grazing permits for use on public lands cannot do business without those things because of government power. Should they have rights to them? If so, they should not be deprived of such new "property" in the absence of due process of law.

Reich concluded that those forms of government benefit most closely linked to status must be deemed to be held as of right. Courts should presume that a license holder will keep a license, that a Social Security recipient will keep that benefit. That presumption, if it is to be rebutted, he argued, must be rebutted on the basis of the same kind of constitutional protection that would accrue to traditional forms of property, and on the basis of fair and open procedures.[17]

"ENTITLEMENTS" AND THE MATTHEWS BALANCING TEST

In *Goldberg v. Kelly*,[18] a landmark 1970 decision requiring New York to provide greater procedural protection to a welfare recipient threatened with loss of benefits, the Court explicitly cited Reich's "The New Property," following his lead by noting that "It may be realistic today to regard welfare entitlements as more like 'property' than a 'gratuity,'" and quoted his statement from an article of his published a year after "The New Property," that "It is only the poor whose entitlements, although recognized by public policy, have not been effectively enforced."[19]

To enforce entitlement to welfare more effectively, the Court had decided that a post-termination hearing was not sufficient due process protection for a recipient of Aid to Families with Dependent Children (AFDC). Under state law, a New York City welfare official, in his or her discretion, could find a family ineligible and cut off payments. The family could appeal the decision at a hearing to be scheduled subsequently, and if they won, they would get the money they should have gotten. But, if the City cut off payments until their case could be heard, conceivably the family could not even come up with enough money to attend the hearing.

The Court acknowledged that "some governmental benefits may be administratively terminated without affording the recipient a pre-termination evidentiary hearing," but due process requires a pre-termination hearing for welfare recipients, because "His need to concentrate upon finding the means for daily subsistence . . . adversely affects his ability to seek redress from the welfare bureaucracy."[20] In addition to the opportunity to be heard, Justice Brennan's majority opinion appears to require "timely and adequate notice of the reasons" for the deprivation, the right to confront "adverse witnesses," the right to make oral presentations of arguments and evidence,[21] the right to counsel, the right to "cross-examine adverse witnesses,"[22] the right to timely disclosure of adverse evidence,[23] the right to a decision based on the record, the right to a decision logically based on the evidence, and the right to an impartial decision-maker.[24]

Other decisions by the Court in the early 1970s similarly seemed to reflect Reich's influence. Under a state law that reflected the older approach, Georgia revoked a driver's license while refusing the individual the opportunity to offer evidence that he was not liable for the accident on which the revocation was based. In 1971, the Supreme Court rejected the argument that since the license was a mere "privilege," he had no right to a hearing before it could be revoked. The Court explained its decision as "an application of the general proposition that relevant constitutional restraints limit state power to terminate an entitlement whether the entitlement is denominated a 'right' or a 'privilege.'"[25]

The courts imposed "relevant constitutional restraints" on state and federal agency "power to terminate . . . entitlement[s]" across a wide range of what had once been considered "privilege" cases: licenses, government employment, government contracts, unemployment benefits, disability payments, public housing, and so forth.[26]

Subsequently, three more Nixon appointees joined the Court after its decision in *Goldberg v. Kelly*, and Warren Burger became Chief Justice, moving its majority further to the right. This seemed to complicate, if not slow, either the procedural protection the Court was willing to impose on entitlements, or the kinds of government benefits the Court was willing to define as entitlements. The logic of the Court's greater caution in this particular area seems persuasive.

Matthews v. Eldridge [27] sets forth the essential factors used to determine the limits of procedural rights in administrative adjudication. In *Matthews*, the Social Security Administration gave a recipient notice and an opportunity to comment in writing, but terminated his disability benefits despite his written protest. Only after the termination was he given a trial-type hearing. Had he prevailed at that hearing, he would have received the benefits retroactively.

The Court said that *Matthews* was different than *Kelly v. Goldberg*, because the "brutal need"[28] of AFDC recipients meant that a wrongful termination would impose more terrible consequences than a wrongful termination of Social Security benefits; and further, that the disability determination relied

BOX 7-2   **2010 Model State Administrative Procedure Act—
Section 404**

SECTION 404. EVIDENCE IN CONTESTED CASE. The following rules apply in a contested case:

1. Except as otherwise provided in paragraph (2), all relevant evidence is admissible, including hearsay evidence, if it is of a type commonly relied on by a reasonably prudent individual in the conduct of the affairs of the individual.

2. The presiding officer may exclude evidence in the absence of an objection if the evidence is irrelevant, immaterial, unduly repetitious, or excludable on constitutional or statutory grounds or on the basis of an evidentiary privilege recognized in the courts of this state. The presiding officer shall exclude the evidence if objection is made at the time the evidence is offered.

3. If the presiding officer excludes evidence with or without objection, the offering party may make an offer of proof before further evidence is presented or at a later time determined by the presiding officer.

4. Evidence may be received in a record if doing so will expedite the hearing without substantial prejudice to a party. Documentary evidence may be received in the form of a copy if the original is not readily available or by incorporation by reference. On request, parties must be given an opportunity to compare the copy with the original.

5. Testimony must be made under oath or affirmation.

6. Evidence must be made part of the hearing record of the case. Information or evidence may not be considered in determining the case unless it is part of the hearing record. If the hearing record contains information that is confidential, the presiding officer may conduct a closed hearing to discuss the information, issue necessary protective orders, and seal all or part of the hearing record.

7. The presiding officer may take official notice of all facts of which judicial notice may be taken and of scientific, technical, or other facts within the specialized knowledge of the agency. A party must be notified at the earliest practicable time of the facts proposed to be noticed and their source, including any staff memoranda or data. The party must be afforded an opportunity to contest any officially noticed fact before the decision becomes final.

(Continued)

(Continued)

8. The experience, technical competence, and specialized knowledge of the presiding officer or members of an agency head that is a multi-member body that is hearing the case may be used in evaluating the evidence in the hearing record.

Source: http://www.uniformlaws.org/shared/docs/state%20administrative%20procedure/msapa_final_10.pdf

more heavily on medical issues that could likely be presented adequately on paper, thus also making a pre-termination hearing less crucial.

In truth, the Court seems to have been looking for excuses to revise the balance struck in *Goldberg v. Kelly*. Within the few years between *Goldberg* and *Matthews*, Justice Hugo Black's dissent in *Goldberg*[29] gained in persuasive force, where his comments had implied that cities and states would likely reduce the availability of welfare funding in order to pay for the increased costs of such extensions of due process in the administrative context.[30]

So, in *Matthews*, the Court ruled that what procedural rights would be made available in an administrative adjudication was to be based on three factors: (1) how major was the impact of the agency action on the person affected (so that Matthews was thought to be less "brutally" affected by a negative determination than was Kelly); (2) how much the likelihood of error would probably be reduced by adding the more stringently "fair" procedure (so that the medical decisions on which most Social Security disability decisions were based, the Court said, could usually be analyzed well enough on the paper record, and were unlikely to get much more accurate with a trial-type hearing as compared with, say, the income decisions at the heart of AFDC determinations); and (3) how much the additional "rights" would cost the government in terms of time, money, and effort (it is not clear that there was any significant distinction alleged between the two different administrative contexts in this regard).[31]

The 1961 MSAPA, the model for a majority of state APAs, requires formal adjudication for any proceeding "in which the legal rights, duties or privileges of a party are required by law to be determined by an agency after opportunity for a hearing,"[32] which of course eliminates the need for *Matthews* balancing and simply provides the full set of procedural protections at all hearings. The 2010 MSAPA however, limits its definition of "contested case" to one in which a statute or constitution requires an evidentiary hearing, and provides for formal hearings in such cases.[33] In such cases, it empowers the officer presiding at the hearing to limit "the opportunity to respond, present evidence and argument, conduct cross-examination, and submit rebuttal evidence" "to the extent necessary for full disclosure of all relevant facts and issues."[34]

BOX 7-3 **2010 Model State Administrative Procedure Act— Section 403(d)**

SECTION 403. CONTESTED CASE PROCEDURE

(d) In a contested case, to the extent necessary for full disclosure of all relevant facts and issues, the presiding officer shall give all parties the opportunity to respond, present evidence and argument, conduct cross-examination, and submit rebuttal evidence.

Source: http://www.uniformlaws.org/shared/docs/state%20administrative%20procedure/msapa_final_10.pdf

DUE PROCESS AND GOVERNMENT EMPLOYMENT

Even a government job today may not be taken away from its holder on the basis of the exercise of a constitutional right by that employee, the vigorous exercise of freedom of expression, for example, without due process. When Oliver Wendell Holmes Jr. served as a Justice of the Massachusetts Supreme Judicial Court, he ruled on the case of a police officer fired for violating his city's ban on political activity by police officers. The police officer argued that the ban violated his First Amendment rights. Holmes famously said, "The petitioner may have a constitutional right to talk politics, but he has no constitutional right to be a policeman."[35] While the literal meaning of Holmes's quip remains good law, the "entitlement" revolution has added considerable complexity to the analysis. A government may no longer fire an employee merely for publicly voicing opinions that the boss—whether an elected official or an agency supervisor—disagrees with, even in the absence of statutory protections like a whistleblower act.[36] "But though a private citizen is perfectly free to uninhibitedly and robustly criticize a state governor's legislative program, we have never suggested that the Constitution bars the governor from firing a high-ranking deputy for doing the same thing."[37] When a government employee's speech significantly disrupts and undermines the goals he or she was hired to achieve, the First Amendment does not bar termination of that employment.[38]

One of the most seminal Supreme Court decisions on procedural protections for government employment involved state civil servants employed under a contract that stated that they could be fired only for cause. The civil servants claimed that they were fired in violation of their right to procedural due process. They were given "post-termination administrative review," but no pre-termination opportunity to contest the charges against them in a hearing.[39]

Their complaint raised several questions: did their firing without a pre-termination hearing constitute a deprivation of property without due process, thus giving federal courts jurisdiction over their complaint? Were they entitled to a full evidentiary hearing prior to termination of their employment? Or, were they entitled at least to pre-termination notice and an opportunity to be heard?

In *Cleveland Board of Education v. Loudermill*, the Court ruled that since their contract only allowed them to be fired for cause, due process protected the right of the employees in question to have "some opportunity" to challenge the allegations against them[40]: "The governmental interest in immediate termination does not outweigh these interests."[41] *Loudermill*, an important decision, requires courts to balance the employer's "interest in immediate termination" of problematic employees by avoiding time-consuming and potential costly "red tape," against the employee's legitimate interest in avoiding termination of employment based on an error. However, the Court found that due process required no more than "notice and an opportunity to respond," not pre-termination hearings: "To require more . . . would intrude to an unwarranted extent on the government's interest in quickly removing an unsatisfactory employee."[42]

Justice Rehnquist, dissenting and arguing that the Court should have relied on the state law governing the employees' procedural rights, quoted his own opinion in a previous case: "property interests are not created by the Constitution [but by things like state law]."[43] Justice Marshall, also dissenting, would have granted the employees a full pre-termination evidentiary hearing.[44]

Chapter 13 provides a more detailed discussion of the extent to which the law protects the employment rights of government workers against their supervisors, mostly under Section 1983 of the Civil Rights Act, but also under other statutory and constitutional provisions. Chapter 12 includes a section addressing the extent to which Section 1983 protects the constitutional rights of private citizens against government workers by enabling them to impose personal liability for violations of those rights.

THE THIN EDGE OF DUE PROCESS

National Security

The Supreme Court notably imposed some additional requirements on administrative procedure in the name of due process in *Hamdi v. Rumsfeld*,[45] the American terrorist case. Shortly after the September 11th attack, Congress had passed a joint resolution signed by the President (with statutory effect) called the "Authorization for Use of Military Force"[46] (AUMF) stating that the President could "use all necessary force" against persons and entities assisting in terrorist activities against the United States. To the disappointment of the alleged terrorists, the Court in *Hamdi* did not rule on the question of whether congressional authorization was necessary for the President to order the detention of a suspected combatant who was also a U.S. citizen, but held that in any case, the AUMF would satisfy any such requirement.[47] To determine what kind of process was due Hamdi, the Court returned to the *Matthews* test.[48] On that basis, it ruled against the government: the government had to tell a "citizen-detainee" like

Hamdi why he was classified as an "enemy combatant," and had to give him "a fair opportunity to rebut the Government's factual allegations before a neutral decision-maker."[49] However, the Court also held that the procedural rules need not exclude hearsay, or a rebuttable "presumption in favor of the Government's evidence" so that the rules do not unduly "burden the Executive at a time of ongoing military conflict."[50] Justice Scalia, dissenting, with Justice Stevens, would have given Hamdi the full panoply of procedural rights.[51]

Under the Constitution, the "writ of *habeas corpus*" gives federal courts the power to bring persons before them to decide if they have been unlawfully imprisoned. Congress may suspend the writ only "when in cases of rebellion or invasion the public safety may require it."[52] In 2006, Congress passed the Military Commissions Act, Section 7 of which purported to strip any "court, justice, or judge" of the power to hear *habeas corpus* petitions from alien enemy combatants.[53] Lakhdar Boumediene and other aliens accused of being enemy combatants and held at the U.S. detention camp at Guantanamo Bay in Cuba, some for six years, were going to be tried by a military commission. Under the Act, the commission could accept hearsay evidence, including evidence that was classified and therefore unavailable for challenge by the accused, and "evidence" that had been extracted from other prisoners by "enhanced interrogation techniques."

Habeas corpus petitions for Boumediene and the others ultimately reached the Supreme Court, which invalidated Section 7 as unconstitutional.[54] The Court explained that the Constitution does not limit to citizens the protections offered by *habeas corpus*; that due process required that petitioners be offered an opportunity to prove that they were not, in fact, enemy combatants; that the procedures to be used by the military commissions did not offer them a meaningful opportunity to do so; and that according them the right to appear before a civilian court would impose no unreasonable costs on the Government, or threats to security.[55] Thus, although the Court did not reference *Matthews*, once again it applied a *Matthews*-style balancing test.

Domestic Prison Inmates

Prison inmates have liberty interests that require some, but limited, procedural protection. The Ohio prison system gave an inmate a hearing at which he could argue that his record did not merit transfer from an ordinary prison to a "supermax," where he would be kept in solitary confinement twenty-three hours day. It did not, however, provide him with the opportunity to call witnesses. The Supreme Court, using the *Matthews* test, decided that in view of the high cost of running prisons, such procedures offered sufficient safeguards against error, and "courts must give substantial deference to prison management decisions before mandating additional expenditures for elaborate procedural safeguards when correctional officials conclude that a prisoner has engaged in disruptive behavior." Further, "danger to witnesses, and the difficulty in obtaining their cooperation, make the probable value of an adversary-type hearing doubtful in comparison to its obvious costs."[56]

When certain inmates argued that parole boards essentially disregarded their record of rehabilitation, thus depriving them of meaningful hearings, the courts again deferred to criminal justice administrators in deciding that parole boards could choose virtually to exclude from consideration inmates who had been convicted of violent crimes. One judge, dissenting, restated the inmates' complaint as follows: "the former Governor of New York and the head of the Parole Commission conspired to convert hundreds of indeterminate sentences into determinate sentences of life in prison without the possibility of parole"[57]; and therefore opined that the inmates had indeed "stated a substantive due process claim."[58] The majority, however, ruled that "a policy of according substantial weight to the severity of the crime is neither arbitrary nor capricious; . . . [the Board] is entitled to give whatever weight it deems appropriate to each of the statutory factors."[59] The Second Circuit quoted the Supreme Court's warning as to the deference courts should give to such administrative agency decisions: "only the most egregious official conduct can be said to be 'arbitrary' in the constitutional sense."[60]

WHAT AM I SUPPOSED TO DO?

Police Department Drug Test Results Show Racial Disparity: Must Its Hearing Officers Allow Into Evidence Challenged Alternative Test Results?

Assume you are the Deputy Commissioner for the Police Department of a city employing about 2,000 police officers. Police Department rules require the termination of employment of any officer found to be using illegal drugs. The Department's contract with the police officers' union provides for annual tests for illegal drug use, using hair samples from the officers. The Department offers a pre-termination hearing to any officer who fails the test. An officer who loses the appeal at the Department's pre-termination hearing has a right to appeal again, although only after termination, at a hearing before the State's Civil Service Commission. In an average year, about one percent of the Department's 600 black officers fail the test, while about one fifth of one percent of the Department's 1,200 white officers fail the test.

Under Title VII of the 1964 Civil Rights Act, an employer must show a business necessity to justify "employment practices that cause[] a disparate impact on the basis of race," even if no intention to discriminate underlay the challenged practices. "Significant statistical disparity" is enough to raise the presumption, which the employer must rebut. Some officers have shared with you their theory that because on average, black officers have a higher level of melanin in their hair, and melanin bonds with certain airborne drug residues, the hair sample test may be responsible for the statistical disparity.

More recently, several Black officers whose hair samples tested positive challenged the results in their pre-termination hearings, offering negative results as evidence from other hair sample tests and urine tests from laboratories run by a different company than the one used by the Department. The Department's hearing officer refused to consider the outside company's test results on the grounds that she was not familiar with the company and therefore did not know whether their results were reliable, and ruled that the employment of the officers must be terminated. When officers have offered various outside companies' test results to the State Civil Service Commission, it has considered them.

You are worried both about potential problems with hair testing under Title VII of the 1964 Civil Rights Act and due process claims under Section 1983 of the 1871 Civil Rights Act. Should you recommend that the Commissioner overrule the hearing officer's decision, and perhaps give the officers new hearings where the results of the outside tests would be considered? Or should you recommend that the Department reconsider the use of hair sample tests altogether?

The federal Court of Appeals for the First Circuit addressed these questions in *Jones v. City of Boston*.[61] You need not have worried about the hearing officer's exclusion of outside test results. "Even in criminal trials, the state has some leeway in crafting and applying reasonable evidentiary rules," said the court, citing a Supreme Court's decision upholding a Montana law excluding evidence of intoxication as a factor in determining the mental state of the accused as an element of the crime (such as intent).[62] And administrative agencies have more "leeway" in setting their evidentiary rules than the courts.[63] The court further said that even if the Police Department's hearing officer had acted improperly in excluding the evidence—which the court refused to conclude—the Civil Service Commission's willingness to consider it would have overcome the impropriety for purposes of due process. While government employees are entitled to pre-termination hearings, the government need only provide certain procedural protections in such hearings: the availability of other protections in a post-termination hearing satisfies due process.[64]

Title VII may pose a problem, however. Even though the court conceded that the Police Department could argue against the claim of "significant statistical disparity" that "black officers and cadets were more likely than their white colleagues to test positive by just one percentage point,"[65] it found significant statistical significance on the uncontested basis of showing that they "were five times more likely to test positive."[66] That, however, did not suffice to find a Title VII violation. The Circuit Court remanded the cases to the trial court to determine whether the Department could justify the hair sample test on the basis of "business necessity": whether it produces results "'predictive of or significantly correlated' with drug use"[67]; and/or whether the plaintiffs could show that an "alternative practice would produce a smaller racial disparity in outcomes than does the department's current system."[68]

While the matter has not yet been resolved as of this writing, the plaintiffs seem unlikely to prevail. In comparable circumstances, you can probably support your agency's policies without fear of court intervention.

PRACTICE PROBLEM

The Secretary of Defense has asked you, his assistant, whether he would be subject to constitutional criticism and litigation were he to authorize the use of a drone to assassinate a fairly high-profile American citizen engaged in leading terrorist activities against the United States. Clearly, he would prefer to avoid criticism and litigation.

ENDNOTES

1. *Ethics for Bureaucrats*, (New York and Basil, Switzerland: Marcel Dekker, Inc., 1978).
2. Agencies Employing Administrative Law Judges, Association of Administrative Law Judges website, 2015, http://www.aalj.org/agencies-employing-administrative-law-judges, accessed 1/18/15.
3. *Id.*
4. Supplied by an anonymous reviewer of an early draft of the manuscript for this book for Sage/CQ Press.
5. *Murray's Lessee v. Hoboken Land and Improvement Company*, 59 U.S. 272, 283, 15 L. Ed. 372, 377 (1856).
6. *Atlas Roofing Co. v. Occupational Safety and Health Review Commission*, 430 U.S. 442, 450ff, 97 S. Ct. 1261, 1266ff.
7. *R. v. Chancellor of the University of Cambridge*, 1 Str. 566, 92 Eng. Rep. 818 (1723).
8. *Wilkie v. O'Connor*, 261 A.D. 373, 375, 25 N.Y.S. 2d 617, 620 (4th Dept. 1941).
9. *73 Yale L. J.* at 737.
10. *73 Yale L. J.* at 740.
11. *73 Yale L. J.* at 750–6.
12. *Fleming v. Nestor*, 363 U.S. 603, 80 S. Ct. 1367 (1960).
13. *73 Yale L. J.* at 768.
14. 363 U.S. at 610, 80 S. Ct. at 1372.
15. 363 U.S. at 612, 80 S. Ct. at 1373.
16. *73 Yale L. J.* at 769.
17. *73 Yale L. J.* at 783–6.
18. *Goldberg v. Kelly*, 397 U.S. 254, 90 S. Ct. 1011.
19. 397 U.S. at 295, 90 S. Ct. at 1017, n. 8, quoting Reich's Individual Rights and Social Welfare: The Emerging Legal Issues, 74 *Yale L. J.* 1245, 1255 (1965).
20. 397 U.S. at 263–4, 90 S. Ct. at 1018–9.
21. 397 U.S. at 267–8, 90 S. Ct. at 1020.
22. 397 U.S. at 268, 90 S. Ct. at 1021.
23. 397 U.S. at 270, 90 S. Ct. at 1021.
24. 397 U.S. at 271, 90 S. Ct. at 1022.
25. *Bell v. Berson*, 402 U.S. 535, 539, 91 S. Ct. 1586, 1589.
26. See, e.g., Jason Parkin, Adaptable Due Process, 160 *U. of P. L. Rev.* 1309, 1325 (2012). Note, however, that in 1996, Congress replaced Aid for Families with Dependent Children, which "entitled" those meeting statutory requirements to benefits, with Temporary Assistance for Needy Families, 42 U.S.C. § 601ff., which explicitly excluded interpretation as an entitlement program, 42 U.S.C. § 601(b). While the implications of the change on hearing rights for recipients of such assistance remain unclear, the courts of several states have ruled that their state constitutions continued to require such rights. See, e.g., *W. Va. ex rel. K.M. v. W. Va. Dept. of Health and Human Resources*, 212 W. Va. 783, 799, 575 S. E. 2d 393, 409 (2002); *Weston v. Cassata*, 37 P. 3d 469, 477, 2001 Colo. App. LEXIS 1099, *21 (2001).
27. *Matthews v. Eldridge*, 424 U.S. 319, 96 S. Ct. 893 (1976).

28. 397 U.S. at 261, 90 S. Ct. at 1017, contrasted with the less stringent circumstances typical of a Social Security recipient, such as Eldridge, 424 U.S. at 340–1, 96 S. Ct. at 905–6.

29. 397 U.S. at 271, 90 S. Ct. at 1022.

30. 397 U.S. at 278, 90 S. Ct. at 1025–6.

31. 424 U.S. at 341–9, 96 S. Ct. at 906–9.

32. 1961 MSAPA §§ 1(2), 9 and 10.

33. 2010 MSAPA §§ 102(7), 403 and 404.

34. 2010 MSAPA § 404(d).

35. *McAuliffe v. Mayor of New Bedford*, 155 Mass. 216, 220, 29 N.E. 517 (Mass. 1892).

36. *Waters v. Churchill*, 511 U.S. 661, 674, 114 S. Ct. 1878, 1887 (1994).

37. 511 U.S. at 672, 114 S. Ct. at 1886.

38. 511 U.S. at 675, 114 S. Ct. at 1888.

39. *Cleveland Board of Education v. Loudermill*, 470 U.S. 532, 535–6, 105 S. Ct. 1487, 1489–90 (1985).

40. 470 U.S. at 543, 105 S. Ct. at 1494.

41. 470 U.S. at 544, 105 S. Ct. at 1494.

42. 470 U.S. at 546, 105 S. Ct. at 1495.

43. 470 U.S. at 561, 105 S. Ct. at 1503, quoting *Board of Regents v. Roth*, 408 U.S. 564, 577, 92 S. Ct. 2701, 2709 (1972).

44. 470 U.S. at 558, 105 S. Ct., at 1501–2.

45. *Hamdi v. Rumsfeld*, 542 U.S. 507, 124 S. Ct. 2633 (2004).

46. P.L. 107-40, 115 Stat. 224. Congress acted pursuant to its power to declare war, although the resolution merely authorized, but did not require, the use of force. The President signed the resolution.

47. 542 U.S. at 518, 124 S. Ct. at 2640.

48. 542 U.S. at 529, 124 S. Ct. at 2645.

49. 542 U.S. at 533, 124 S. Ct. at 2648.

50. 542 U.S. at 533–4, 124 S. Ct. at 2649.

51. 542 U.S. at 554–579, 2660–2674.

52. Article I, Section 9, Clause 2.

53. 28 U.S.C.A. § 2241(e) (Supp. 2007).

54. *Boumediene v. Bush*, 553 U.S. 723, 128 S. Ct. 2229 (2008).

55. 553 U.S. at 769–770, 128 S. Ct. at 2261–2.

56. *Wilkinson v. Austin*, 549 U.S. 209, 228, 125 S. Ct. 2384, 2396 (2005).

57. *Graziano v. Pataki*, 689 F. 3d 110, 2012 U.S. App. LEXIS 16147, *16 (2d Cir. 2012).

58. *Id.* at *29.

59. *Id.* at *10.

60. *Id.* at *14, quoting *City of Sacramento v. Lewis*, 523 U.S. 833, 846, 118 S. Ct. 1708 (1998), internal citation omitted.

61. *Jones v. City of Boston*, 752 F. 3d 38, 2014 U.S. App. LEXIS 8560.

62. 752 F. 3d at 57, 2014 U.S. App. LEXIS at **50, citing *Montana v. Egelhoff*, 518 U.S. 37, 116 S. Ct. 2013 (1996).

63. Ernest Gellhorn, Rules of Evidence and Official Notice in Formal Administrative Hearings, *Duke L. J.* 1971(1):1–50, 6–16 (1971); as early as 1904 the Supreme Court said, "The inquiry of a board of this character [an administrative tribunal, here] the Interstate Commerce Commission should not be too narrowly constrained by technical rules as to the admissibility of proof. It . . . should not be hampered . . . by those narrow rules which prevail in trials at common law . . ." *Interstate Commerce Commission v. Baird*, 195 U.S. 25, 44, 24 S. Ct. 563, 569.

64. 752 F. 3d at 57–8, 2014 U.S. App. LEXIS at **50–1.

65. 752 F. 3d at 43, 2014 U.S. App. LEXIS at **7.

66. *Id.*; 752 F. 3d at 47, 2014 U.S. App. LEXIS at **18.

67. 752 F. 3d at 54, 2014 U.S. App. LEXIS at **42.

68. 752 F. 3d at 55, 2014 U.S. App. LEXIS at **44–5.

8
chapter

Adjudication—How Much Process Is Due?[1]

Arguably, the decision in *Goldberg v. Kelly* stressed fairness while *Matthews* sought more balance with efficiency. However, as this chapter explains later, sometimes the *Matthews* approach merely balances one kind of fairness against another kind of fairness. The tension between optimizing "fairness," exemplified by *Goldberg v. Kelly*, and balancing it with efficiency, exemplified by *Matthews v. Eldridge*, continues to inform administrative law. To illuminate this discussion, we need to look at the costs of "overjudicialization" of the administrative hearing process.

SCHOOL SUSPENSION AND EXPULSION

A judicial offspring of *Goldberg* changed the relationship between schools and students. Public, impersonal, formal proceedings were substituted for the private, personal, and informal processes that had traditionally applied to school discipline incidents. Procedural fairness may have improved, but at the expense of privacy, morale, and efficiency.

In *Goss v. Lopez*,[2] the Court ruled that the Due Process Clause requires public schools to offer at least some quasi-judicial process before depriving students of their "entitlement to a public education as a property interest."[3] The Court required schools, for a suspension of ten days or fewer, to give students "notice of the charges," "an explanation of the evidence," and a chance to argue their "side of the story,"[4] but later cases illustrate some of the costs.

Two years later, another school-related decision from a jurisdiction that had "judicialized" its school suspension procedures much earlier, illuminated the inappropriately long delays attendant to such actions, noting that "[a] child who was in the first grade when this action was begun is now ready to enter junior high school."[5] Schools now bore a new and heavy burden of providing numerous hearings. Relying on *Goss v. Lopez*, a student sued, complaining of suspension without adequate due process, although he had first been given three opportunities to explain his case to three different authorities, represented by any person of his choice. The court held that this was enough.[6] Still, providing three separate hearings is a considerable burden for a school. The spectacle of a school system "on trial" each time it attempts to suspend a student cannot be good for school morale.

Goss invited further litigation. A student brought suit to challenge her academic expulsion from medical school without having been provided an opportunity to challenge the expulsion in a formal hearing.[7] Discussions of her personal hygiene, physical appearance, "eccentric" personal conduct,[8] problematic "handwashing and grooming,"[9] and relationships with others appeared throughout the decision and concurring opinions, and in news coverage of the case.[10] The Court declined to intervene, fearing the impact on "the faculty-student relationship."[11] But, its 1978 decision applied only to expulsions on academic grounds, so judges might still intervene in disciplinary cases, even in a medical school, with such personal and psychological factors to be brought out on the record. The medical student who sued must not have minded that kind of personal publicity. Nonetheless, such "due process" requirements exact costs in privacy, as well as resources and morale.

Of course, states may choose their own particular standards to determine when their agencies must provide formal hearings, or must provide particular elements of procedural protections in their hearings. Oregon provides a formal hearing "where the agency has discretion to suspend or revoke a right or privilege of a person."[12] A dental student dismissed on the basis of "failure to 'exhibit reasonable professional development and behavior'"[13] challenged his dismissal because although he had indeed been given a hearing, he was able to show that "relevant information discussed in the closed session was not part of the record of the hearing,"[14] and therefore the dismissal decision may not have been based entirely on the record. Because the student had no opportunity to object or respond to material not in the record, the court reversed the decision and remanded it, requiring the school to reconsider.[15] The case sufficiently parallels the previous case of the medical student that the difference in outcome can probably be attributed solely to Oregon's state APA.[16]

Illustrating a different variation, Florida's Administrative Procedure Act applies its rules for formal hearings to "proceedings in which the substantial interests of a party are determined by an agency, unless the parties are proceeding under [mediation or expedited "summary hearing" provisions]"[17] as well as to those entitled to a formal proceeding because they have a right to some kind of hearing by constitutional or statutory right, as the 1961 MSAPA states, or states that choose to adopt the 2010 MSAPA would provide. When the Florida Department of Environmental Conservation gave a permit to a liquid sulphur company to build a terminal, two competitors sought a hearing to contest the permit. The competitors had no constitutional, statutory, or regulation-based right to the hearing. The Florida court ruled that since the kind of hearing they sought was intended to balance environmental and economic interests, and not to deal protect against "potential competitive economic injury," their interests were not "substantial" as that term is used in the Florida APA.[18]

WELFARE BENEFITS

Sacrificing other resources to due process becomes more painful and harder to justify when scarcity is involved. NYC issued a rule cutting off welfare payments to recipients who failed to report for interviews concerning fraud. If the recipient agreed to the interview, benefits were continued even if he or she stood mute or admitted committing fraud.[19] The 2nd Circuit Court of Appeals in 1978 allowed the attendance requirement, but not as applied to the recipient's *children*.[20] Since most or all of the money was for her children, and it would still come to her, in essence she paid no penalty. The payments could not be terminated without proper application of due-process procedures; refusal to cooperate in a fraud investigation was not enough to cease payments.

At that time of fiscal difficulty, the New York State contribution to welfare had not increased for four years,[21] and so gave recipients too little money to keep up with the rapidly increasing rate of inflation.[22] Even in a better economy, of course, states will only allocate so much to assist the poor. Hearings cost money. While in 1969, just prior to the decision in *Goldberg v. Kelly*, 1,300 welfare recipients requested hearings to appeal termination of benefits; by 1989, 150,000 hearing requests flooded the New York welfare system.[23]

The right of a recipient suspected of fraud to refuse cooperation must be weighed against the needs of other poor persons. Protecting her right to welfare benefits may mean denying some benefits to other potential recipients willing and anxious to establish the truth. This kind of decision becomes more painful as available resources diminish. Furthermore, the "rights" established have proved of little value to their intended beneficiaries when there is a shortage of poverty lawyers available to represent them.[24]

So, an exaggerated commitment of due process jeopardizes at least privacy, efficiency, and distributive justice. Courts are less efficient than agencies, because fairness should be independent of economic consequences. Thus, courts could hardly process 240 million tax returns in a year, as the IRS did in 2013,[25] or about 58 million checks a month, as the Social Security Administration did in 2013.[26]

> In almost every case, the administrative agency is, practically speaking, the only forum available; even if judicial review were freely obtainable, the amounts involved are usually too small or the parties too poor to meet the costs of court litigation.[27]

Sometimes agencies can streamline due process, reducing economic costs, without sacrificing the substance. But, some painful inequalities should not be addressed in the adjudicative mode of an administrative hearing, even if elected officials and their agents, who are otherwise properly situated to address such inequalities, refuse to do so.

MENTAL HEALTH CARE

A prominent example is Alabama's Bryce Hospital case,[28] in which representatives of mental patients sued the state for better care. No humane person could fail to rejoice when Judge Frank Johnson ruled that Alabama must rectify the horrifying conditions at the hospital, requiring drastic funding increases. Once Johnson decided that these patients had rights to much better care, he could only make his further decisions based on the evidence before him,[29] along with considerations of fairness and equity with respect to the parties. As a judge he could not properly or practically consider all the needs that Alabama had to address in its annual budget. The state estimated that Johnson's orders would cost sixty percent of its expense budget, excluding education, in addition to $75 million in capital costs.[30]

Thus, when Johnson required Alabama to spend millions of dollars more per year on Bryce Hospital, he did not, could not, and in his judicial capacity should not, have known whether shifting those dollars would, say, kill a physically ill patient somewhere else, or reduce the state's welfare grant enough for some recipients to finally starve to death. He just said, "a failure by defendants to comply with this decree cannot be justified by a lack of operating funds."[31] The suggested disasters illustrate the potential difficulties that can ensue when courts take over this kind of "polycentric"[32] decision-making, as opposed to the more typical linear decisions they make when the only interests at stake are sufficiently represented by the two parties to the case.

Johnson apparently applied the *Goldberg v. Kelly* "entitlements" theory changing public benefits from privileges easily revocable by the state to a kind of protected property right. The inmates, entitled by statute to receive treatment, therefore had a right to treatment, as Judge Johnson defined it. Johnson's definition was indeed reasonable, but the State of Alabama, at the time, did not accept it, instead tacitly accepting whatever was provided by the Bryce administrators.

If the 5th Circuit Court of Appeals had upheld Johnson's decision, Alabama could have been forced to sell state lands, or change its budget, raising major constitutional questions.[33] Instead, it ordered Johnson and the parties to the suit to reach a compromise.[34] In fact, the Bryce Hospital situation continued unresolved. Alabama tried to meet Johnson's demand for better staff-to-patient ratios by releasing about half its patients, although Johnson had not mentioned that alternative. His decrees, therefore, "may have done more harm than good,"[35] assuming those patients were worse off when deprived of custodial care than they would have been if they had stayed at Bryce.[36]

Agencies, at the instigation and on behalf of legislatures, must frequently act as economic managers. Imposing judicial values on agencies, whether directly, as in the *Bryce Hospital* case, or indirectly, when courts impose due process requirements on agency procedures, sometimes and to some extent, produces a poor fit between the task and the institution:

> To act wisely, the economic manager must take into account every circumstance relevant to his decision, and himself must assume the initiative in discovering what circumstances are relevant. His decision must be subject to change or reversal as conditions alter. The judge, on the other hand, acts upon those facts that are in advance deemed relevant under declared principles of decision. His decision

does not simply direct resources and energies; it declares rights, and rights to be meaningful must in some measure stand firm through changing circumstances. When, therefore, we attempt to discharge tasks of economic management through adjudicative forms there is a serious mismatch between the procedure to be adopted and the problem to be solved.[37]

In 1975, the Supreme Court found a due process violation in the involuntary confinement of mental patients who had not been proven dangerous to themselves or others.[38] What happened at Bryce Hospital then happened in various yet similar ways at other institutions throughout the United States that had "warehoused" mental patients in substandard conditions: most of the patients were released, with the implicit promise that they would get needed support as outpatients. In New York, for example, psychiatric hospitals housed about 100,000 people in the 1960s, but one-tenth that number by the mid-1990s. But, funds for outpatient medication and support did not follow in amounts remotely near sufficient.[39]

In 1999, after two untreated schizophrenic outpatients pushed victims onto New York City subway tracks—one fell to her death and the other suffered the loss of his legs—New York State enacted "Kendra's Law"[40] and thereby, according to one of its critics, violated the rights of mentally ill people under the 1975 Supreme Court decision.[41] The law provides that under carefully delimited conditions, a psychiatrist could in some cases force medication on a mentally ill outpatient.[42] Clearly, the law narrows the immediate scope of liberty for such patients. By returning some power to "managers"—in this case, psychiatrists at New York State hospitals—it also reduced homelessness among mentally ill patients in New York by seventy-four percent, psychiatric re-hospitalization by seventy-seven percent, arrests by eighty-three percent, and incarceration by eighty-seven percent, according to one estimate.[43]

SEEKING LESS PROCEDURAL PROTECTION

Public Pension Benefits

The imposition of procedures intended to promote fairness to individuals—to assure that individuals do not lose their entitlements except through the due process of law—exacts a price in efficiency. From time to time, government bodies have decided that the benefits of some aspects of procedural due process do not justify the costs of this "judicialization" of agency hearings. For example, the California Law Revision Commission investigated the possibility of allowing an administrative agency to hear certain private real estate disputes under the "Common Interest Development" (CID) law in order to avoid time-consuming and expensive litigation in court. It concluded that the procedural requirements of California's Administrative Procedure Act, similar to the federal Administrative Procedure Act,[44] meant that formal agency hearings would not provide any significant advantage over courtroom litigation.

However, California's legislature, on the advice of the Law Revision Commission, had amended its Administrative Procedure Act some years earlier to provide for informal hearings, imposing fewer procedural requirements and allowing more flexibility, and such hearings offered an attractive alternative: "At the hearing the presiding officer regulates the course of the proceedings and limits witnesses, testimony, evidence, rebuttal and argument. It is essentially a conference that lacks courtroom drama, but nevertheless provides assurance that the issues will be aired. . . ."[45]

As of Fiscal Year 2008, Veterans who believed the Veterans Administration shortchanged them regarding their benefits waited an average of three years from the time they sent in their appeal to the time they received a decision from the Board of Veterans Appeals.[46] Delays are attributable in large part to the heavy volume of appeals, but also to procedural protections afforded to claimants, especially their right to seek, obtain, and supply evidence to the Board throughout the process, sometimes necessitating numerous hearings, to which the claimants are entitled.[47] However, the Veterans Administration has established a procedure under which claimants can waive their procedural rights in return for a much shorter timetable, thought to be about one year.[48] If at any time they so choose, claimants can reinstate their procedural rights by returning to the normal, longer process. Advocates for the expedited program claim that under its provisions "while significantly shortening the appeal process, the claimant's due process rights are still protected."[49] The program, the Expedited Claims Adjudication initiative, originally a pilot project available only at four Veterans Administration facilities,[50] has since been expanded to every regional office of the Veterans Administration, at least for those veterans who have already been waiting at least a year for the resolution of their claim.[51]

Less Procedural Protection, More Benefits

Administrative agencies sometimes unilaterally cut back on too much procedural "due process." Retired New York government employees used the State's Retirement System hearing process to appeal when they believed their pensions should be higher. They felt "entitled" to unlimited adjournments, especially when they obtained new medical records, or their medical experts couldn't make a hearing date. Some of their attorneys argued that the System violated their clients' due process rights by introducing medical reports unfavorable to their clients without making the authors of the reports available for cross examination. By 2005, a retiree appellant could expect to wait at least three years, and often far longer, for a decision. Since many were elderly or in poor health, quite a few died first.

New York State Comptroller Thomas DiNapoli, the head of that Retirement System, would not accept the inevitability of such delays. He convened a task force.[52] It recognized that the great leeway the System offered to individuals actually hurt applicants in the aggregate. Almost certainly, the total suffering caused by the delays outweighed the benefits, when added together for each individual, attributable to the excess "rights" the System had provided.

If the System had required medical experts to show up, as opposed to merely introducing their written reports, on balance it would actually have hurt applicants. Most applicants have very limited incomes. Their medical experts do not testify for free. The Retirement System could afford the fees more easily than the applicants.

Using New York's informal notice-and-comment procedure, in 2009 the System changed its regulations governing adjournments, so applicants can get only one adjournment, and a second only for "unusual, unexpected, or unavoidable circumstances."[53] Thus, no longer could applicants with frivolous appeals be able to get four or five adjournments to find a lawyer, and then have to argue their cases themselves ("*pro se*") anyway because no responsible attorney would represent them.[54]

Applicants now have forty-five days at most after getting their hearing date to submit any new medical records; and if the hearing officer lets them bring an additional expert witness, no more than forty-five more days to tell the System if the witness will be available—or the case is closed.[55]

If an applicant simply does not show up at the scheduled hearing date—not an uncommon occurrence in the past—the case is now closed.[56]

There were reforms other than narrowing applicants' procedural rights that also contributed to the reduction of its backlog, such as greater use of teleconferencing and creation of a more intensive "pre-hearing review." But, reducing applicants' procedural rights, to some degree, if less "fair" to individuals, certainly contributed to a result that was far more "fair" to applicants in the aggregate: the backlog of administrative appeal cases, previously about 1,400, came down to 680 by the fall of 2011; and the average delay of three years was reduced to one year.

Sometimes, less process is due process.

WHAT AM I SUPPOSED TO DO?

State Medical School Expulsion: Right to a Hearing

You are the Provost of a state university. Your university offers a special six-year program leading to a joint medical degree and bachelor's degree. After the fourth year of the program, in order to proceed to the fifth year, which involves clinical work in hospitals, each student must pass a two-day rigorous test called the "NBME Part I" (National Board of Medical Examiners). The dean of the Medical School has informed you that although he has permitted many students to retake the NBME Part I after having failed it the first time, he does not intend to permit one particular student to retake the test. His decision is that he has assessed that student's particular record and found it overwhelmingly persuasive that the student does not have the ability to practice medicine at a level that would reflect favorably on the school. You are aware that the courts have found that public educational institutions, of course including your state university, must not withhold certain benefits and opportunities from students without due process, so you asked the dean for the basis on which he had made the determination that the student lacks appropriate qualifications. The dean informed you that the student received the lowest score on the NBME Part I in the school's history, that he has taken six years to complete the first four-year part of the program due to incompletes and leaves of absence, and still got mostly C grades and sometimes worse in his medicine-related studies (he got a B in Creative Writing). However, when you asked the dean about other students who were permitted to retake the examination, he acknowledged that some students had failed twice and were still permitted to take it a third time and that the student in question was the only person who had ever been denied permission to take it a second time.

It appeared likely that one faculty member who disagreed with the decision would, if asked, testify (accurately) that the established practice was that students who failed were offered another opportunity to retake the test. Also, the Medical School issued a pamphlet prior to the administration of the NBME Part I that included the following statement:

> [E]verything possible is done to keep qualified medical students in the Medical School. This even extends to taking and passing National Board Exams. Should a student fail either part of the National Boards, an opportunity is provided to make up the failure in a second exam.

Should you overrule the dean, and require the Medical School to allow the student to take the NBME Part I again? You don't want to face litigation and you especially don't want to lose such a lawsuit; on the other hand, you are very reluctant to interfere with the Medical School's handling on an academic judgment that should be within its discretion.

The Supreme Court faced this issue in *Regents v. Ewing*.[57] The Court first addressed the question of whether the student had a constitutionally protected property right in his continued enrollment, in which case an arbitrary and capricious termination of his enrollment would constitute a denial of his right to due process.

In a previous case of *Board of Curators v. Horowitz*, the Court made it clear that if the student had been expelled for disciplinary reasons rather than for academic reasons, it would have looked more favorably on her claims.[58] The present matter, unquestionably, concerned a purely academic basis for expulsion. However, the state university acknowledged that under Michigan law the student may have had the constitutionally protected right to continued enrollment; the lower courts agreed; and the Supreme Court agreed to assume that the student had such a right.[59] But, the Court made it very clear that the student's right was not to continued enrollment, but only to require the school, *if* it wished to terminate his enrollment, to have done so consistent with the students' due process rights, not on an arbitrary and capricious basis.[60]

Neither the pamphlet nor the practice establishes an absolute right to continued enrollment. The statement in the pamphlet merely recited the usual practice of the school in allowing students who fail the NBME Part I to take it again. But, neither the "usual practice," nor a custom, nor even a "mutually explicit understanding" of what is supposed to happen (in the absence of "a state statute or a university rule or [some comparable legal basis]") assures the claimed entitlement.[61]

Therefore, the Court had to determine whether the school's action had been arbitrary and capricious. In this regard, the Court returned to a theme of *Horowitz*: that a court should show considerable restraint in second-guessing an academic judgment, overruling only when there had been "such a substantial departure from accepted academic norms as to demonstrate that the person or committee responsible did not actually exercise professional judgment."[62] Here, the student had a very weak academic record and a uniquely low score on the NBME Part I test.[63] Other students with very weak academic records had been expelled without even having been permitted to take the test in the first place.[64] Under such circumstances, the Court could not deem the school's decision to dismiss him to have been arbitrary, capricious, or "a substantial departure from accepted academic norms."

As an academic administrator in a public educational institution, you can be confident that the courts will not overturn reasonable academic decisions.

PRACTICE PROBLEMS

PROBLEM 1: Under the Federal Communications Act of 1934, the Federal Communications Commission (FCC) may grant a license to broadcast on a particular frequency in a particular geographical area without a hearing, if it is persuaded that the public interest, convenience, and necessity will be served. However, after consideration if it does not reach that conclusion, before denying such license, it must give the unsuccessful applicant an opportunity to be heard.

In March, the Fetzer Broadcasting Company applied to the FCC for a license to broadcast at 1,230 kilocycles out of Grand Rapids, Michigan. In May, WKBZ of nearby Muskegon, Michigan, applied to broadcast also at 1,230 kilocycles. In June, the FCC granted the license to Fetzer, without a hearing. It also recognized and announced that "intolerable interference" would make it impossible to grant both applications. It then set the WKBZ application down for a hearing.

WKBZ appealed the license grant to Fetzer to the federal courts as an aggrieved party under APA Section 702. How should the court decide?

PROBLEM 2: The State Education Department of Jay (an imaginary 51st state) requires any person who wishes to teach in its public schools to have earned an M.E. degree (Master of Education) from a classroom-based program, pursuant to a regulation it adopted last year, which superseded its previous practice of individual reviews leading to approval for some teachers whose degrees were awarded by online programs. The Jay State Legislature enacted a statute requiring any licensing decision to be treated as a contested case, as well as the 2010 MSAPA. Article 4 of MSAPA requires agencies to provide evidentiary hearings to persons wishing to challenge their decisions in contested cases. Arthur took all his required coursework in person at Hamilton State Teachers College. His mother's serious illness required him to move back to Jay State suddenly and he used up all his savings, so he was unable to pay required fees by the Teachers College deadline, and lost the opportunity to obtain his degree. However, Jay State's Extension College, which is primarily an online program allowed him, for a nominal fee, to transfer his credits there and thus to earn an M.E. degree from them on that basis. Does Arthur have a right to a hearing to challenge the Jay Education Department's decision to deny him teaching certification as its rule precluded certification based on an online program? Would the result be any different had the federal APA applied?

ENDNOTES

1. The school, welfare, and Bryce Hospital case discussions in this chapter are taken from Daniel L. Feldman, *The Logic of American Government*, (New York: William Morrow & Co., 1991), 49–63. The first two of those case discussions, in turn, drew heavily on Daniel Feldman, Administrative Agencies and the Rites of Due Process, 7 *Fordham Urban L. J.* 229 (1978). The discussion of Kendra's Law draws on Daniel L. Feldman and Gerald Benjamin, *Tales From the Sausage Factory*, (Albany, NY: SUNY Press, 2010), 286–288. The discussion of regulatory changes by the New York State Common Retirement System is based on Deborah Richards and Daniel Feldman, Tough Love—Tightening Administrative Hearing Procedures to Get Better Substantive Justice, *The NAPPA Report*, National Association of Public Pension Attorneys, Sacramento, Cal., Nov./Dec. 2011, 7–9.
2. *Goss v. Lopez*, 419 U.S. 565, 95 S. Ct. 729 (1975).
3. 419 U.S. at 574, 95 S. Ct. at 736.
4. 419 U.S. at 581, 95 S. Ct. at 740.
5. *Chance v. Board of Education*, 561 F. 2d 1079, 1081 (2d Cir. 1977).
6. *Whiteside v. Kay*, 446 F. Supp. 716 (W.D. La. 1978).
7. *Board of Curators v. Horowitz*, 435 U.S. 78, 98 S. Ct. 948 (1978).
8. 435 U.S. at 93, 98 S. Ct. at 957.
9. Warren Weaver Jr., An Expelled Student Loses in High Court, *New York Times*, 3/2/78, A9, c.1
10. *Id.*
11. 435 U.S. at 90, 93 S. Ct. at 955.
12. Ore. 183.310(2)(a)(B).
13. *Morrison v. University of Oregon Health Sciences Center*, 68 Ore. App. 870, 873, 685 P. 2d 439, 440 (1984).
14. *Id.*
15. 68 Ore. App. at 877–8, 685 P. 2d at 444.
16. Michael Asimow and Ronald M. Levin, *State and Federal Administrative Law*, 4th ed., (St. Paul, MN: West Publishing Company, 2014), 90, suggests the comparison.
17. Florida Statutes § 120.569.
18. *Agrico Chemical Company v. Department of Environmental Regulation*, 40 So. 2d 478, 482–3 (Fla. 2d D.C.A. 1981); and see Richard M. Ellis, Standing in Florida Administrative Proceedings, 75 *The Florida Bar Journal* 49 (2001), http://www.floridabar.org/divcom/jn/jnjournal01.nsf/Author/F902E7277BC84C7285256ADB005D634A, accessed 1/18/15.
19. New York City Income Maintenance Procedure 78–76, cited in *Rush v. Smith*, 437 F. Supp. 576, 577 (S.D.N.Y. 1977).
20. *Rush v. Smith*, 573 F. 2d 110, 118 (2d Cir. 1978).
21. 18 NYCRR 352.1 (1986), cited in Daniel Feldman, *The Logic of American Government*, *supra* at 55, note 22 on page 231.

22. Edward Nelson, The Great Inflation of the Seventies: What Really Happened?, The Federal Reserve Bank of St. Louis, Working Papers Series, 1/04, http://research.stlouisfed.org/wp/2004/2004-001.pdf.
23. Cesar A. Perales, The Fair Hearing Process: Guardian of the Social Service System, 56 *Brook. L. Rev.* 889, 891 (1990).
24. See Chapter 4, note 37.
25. See Chapter 4, text at note 30.
26. Social Security Basic Facts, website of the Social Security Administration, http://www.ssa.gov/news/press/basicfact.html, accessed 7/10/14.
27. Bernard Schwartz, *Administrative Law*, (Boston, MA: Little, Brown & Co., 1976), 30.
28. *Wyatt v. Stickney*, 325 F. Supp. 781 (M.D. Ala. 1971); 334 F. Supp. 1341 (M.D. Ala. 1971); 344 F. Supp. 373 (M.D. Ala. 1972); 344 F. Supp. 387 (M.D. Ala. 1972).
29. Judges may take "judicial notice" but only of "a fact that is not subject to reasonable dispute," Rule 201, Federal Rules of Evidence, 28 U.S. C. Appendix, P.L. 93–595, 88 Stat. 1930, Legal Information Institute, Cornell University Law School, http://www.law.cornell.edu/rules/fre/rule_201, so this is a limited exception. Johnson had no way of replicating the institutional resource allocating role of the legislature, and yet by entering so deeply into this matter, he had to try to do just that.
30. *Wyatt v. Aderholt*, 503 F. 2d 1305, 1317 (5th Cir. 1974).
31. 344 F. Supp. at 377.
32. The term was used in this context, as opposed to the more linear kind of decision-making appropriate when the only interests at stake are sufficiently represented by the two parties to the case, by Lon Fuller in Collective Bargaining and the Arbitrator, 1963 *Wisconsin L. Rev.* 3, 32–3, citing M. Polanyi, *The Logic of Liberty*, (London, UK: Routledge and K. Paul, 1951), 170–84.
33. 503 F. 2d at 1318.
34. 503 F. 3d at 1319.
35. Archibald Cox, The New Dimensions of Constitutional Adjudication, 57 *Wash. L. Rev.* 791, 827 (1976).
36. Some patients should not have been confined at Bryce in the first place, Philip J. Cooper, *Hard Judicial Choices*, New York: Oxford University Press, 1988), 196, and they, at least, may have benefited from release.
37. Lon Fuller, *The Morality of Law*, rev. ed., (New Haven, CT: Yale University Press, 1969), 172.
38. *O'Connor v. Donaldson*, 422 U.S. 563, 95 S. Ct. 2486.
39. The Unfinished Promise of Willowbrook, Mental Health Association in New York State, 10/18/02, http://www.mhanys.org/policy/pp_willowbrook.htm. Note that the Supreme Court in *O'Connor v. Donaldson* did not establish a right to psychological treatment when confined, 422 U.S. at 573, 95 S. Ct. at 2492, only that "a nondangerous individual who is capable of surviving safely in freedom by himself or with the help of willing and responsible family members or friends" cannot be involuntarily confined. 422 U.S. at 576, 95 S. Ct. at 2494.
40. New York Mental Hygiene Law § 9.60, Assisted Outpatient Treatment, L.1999, c. 408.
41. Beth Haroules, Testimony: Extending Kendra's Law, website of the New York Civil Liberties Union, Before New York State Assembly Committee on Codes and Committee on Mental Health, Mental Retardation and Developmental Disabilities, 4/21/05, http://www.nyclu.org/content/testimony-extending-kendras-law. But, see *In re K.L.*, 1 N.Y. 3d 362, 806 N.E. 2d 480 (2004), upholding New York's Kendra's Law against constitutional challenge.
42. New York Mental Hygiene Law § 9.60(c).
43. Jonathan Stanley, Helping Families Deal with Mental Illness, *Health in 30.com*, 7/14/06, http://healthin30.com/2006/07/helping-families-deal-with-mental-illness/.
44. And California's Administrative Procedure Act covers an even wider range of hearings than the federal Act. See Michael Asimow, The Influence of the Federal Administrative Procedure Act on California's New Administrative Procedure Act, *Tulsa L. Rev.* 32(2):297–323 (1996), 308–310.

45. Nathaniel Sterling, Executive Secretary, Staff Memorandum 2001-54: Nonjudicial Dispute Resolution Under CID Law: Administrative Hearing Procedure, California Law Revision Commission, Study H-851, June 13, 2001, http://www.clrc.ca.gov/pub/2001/MM01-54.pdf, accessed 8/1/14.
46. Marcy W. Kreindler and Sarah B. Richmond, Expedited Claims Adjudication Initiative (ECA): A Balancing Act Between Efficiency and Protecting Due Process Rights of Claimants, *Veterans Law Review* 2:1–22, 4 (2010), http://www.bva.va.gov/docs/VLR_VOL2/Copy2--MarcyKreindlerandSarahRichmond.pdf, accessed 8/1/14.
47. *Id.* at 5.
48. *Id.* at 6–22.
49. *Id.* at 11.
50. *Id.* at 5–6.
51. Alison Hickey, Veterans Administration Undersecretary for Benefits, VA Expediting Claims Decisions for Veterans Waiting a Year or More, VAntage Point: Dispatches from the U.S. Department of Veterans Affairs, 4/19/13, http://www.blogs.va.gov/VAntage/9217/va-expediting-claims-decisions-for-veterans-waiting-a-year-or-more/, accessed 8/1/14.
52. The author served on the task force.
53. 2 NYCRR 317.5.
54. Deborah Richards and Daniel Feldman, *supra* at 8.
55. *Id.*, citing 2 NYCRR 317.6.
56. 2 NYCRR 317.7.
57. *Regents v. Ewing*, 474 U.S. 214; 106 S. Ct. 507; 88 L. Ed. 2d 523 (1985).
58. 435 U.S. at 88–9, 98 S. Ct. at 955.
59. 474 U.S. at 222, 106 S. Ct. at 511–2.
60. *Id.*
61. 474 U.S. at 223, 106 S. Ct. at 512, note 9.
62. 474 U.S. at 225, 106 S. Ct. at 513.
63. 474 U.S. at 227-8, 106 S. Ct. at 514–5.
64. 474 U.S. at 228, 106 S. Ct. at 515, note 14.

Adjudication—
Substantial Evidence Rule

T he previous two chapters explained the circumstances under which constitutional and statutory requirements require agencies to provide hearings. The APA only requires them when Congress, in its authorizing legislation, required the agency's decisions "to be determined on-the-record after opportunity for an agency hearing," and even then, military or foreign affairs and various other matters are exempt.[1]

BOX 9-1   5 U.S. Code Administrative Procedure Act—Section 554

(a) This section applies, according to the provisions thereof, in every case of adjudication required by statute to be determined on the record after opportunity for an agency hearing, except to the extent that there is involved—

  (1) a matter subject to a subsequent trial of the law and the facts de novo in a court;

  (2) the selection or tenure of an employee, except an administrative law judge appointed under section 3105 of this title;

  (3) proceedings in which decisions rest solely on inspections, tests, or elections;

  (4) the conduct of military or foreign affairs functions;

  (5) cases in which an agency is acting as an agent for a court; or

  (6) the certification of worker representatives.

Source: http://www.archives.gov/federal-register/laws/administrative-procedure/554.html

---

When they are required, however, some rules govern agency adjudications in common with ordinary courtroom trials, but some differ. Like judges, hearing officers usually permit cross-examination, but may prohibit it in any case when they think it will add nothing of value.[2] Rules concerning hearsay, however, are quite different.

BOX 9-2   **5 U.S. Code Administrative Procedure Act—Section 556(d)**

(d) Except as otherwise provided by statute, the proponent of a rule or order has the burden of proof. Any oral or documentary evidence may be received, but the agency as a matter of policy shall provide for the exclusion of irrelevant, immaterial, or unduly repetitious evidence . . .

Source: http://www.archives.gov/federal-register/laws/administrative-procedure/556.html

HEARSAY AND CROSS EXAMINATION

The Federal Rules of Evidence generally exclude hearsay at trial,[3] and state rules for the most part do as well.[4] But, those rules do not apply to most agency hearings, although some agencies use them. Those rules exclude hearsay because juries may not be able to judge the reliability of what a witness remembers someone else saying. Even ordinary judges, not usually specialists in the subject matter in question, may have trouble. A hearing officer, working for one particular agency, with more specialized knowledge, should be able to weigh the value of such statements more accurately, even in the absence of cross-examination. This argument has less persuasive value for hearing officers who work for a variety of agencies. Even so, courtroom hearsay rules usually do not apply: agencies have to balance cautious procedural rules that are supposed to help assure fairness to individuals against efficiencies that may help many people.

At one time, no court would allow an agency to base its decision solely on evidence that courts themselves would not have admitted, but would allow agency decisions if based even partly on some evidence that courts would have admitted, which is the so-called residuum rule,[5] and called the allowable evidence "substantial."

The United States Supreme Court redefined "substantial evidence" for federal courts in 1971 in *Richardson v. Perales.*[6] Social Security Disability hearing officers treated as substantial evidence (acceptable as a basis for decision) written reports of doctors who found claimants not disabled, although the claimants' own doctors testified otherwise. The other doctors did not appear— just their reports. Since they could not be cross-examined, courts would treat their reports as hearsay. But, the Court ruled that an administrative agency, exercising its judgment that the reports were reliable, could consider them substantial evidence.

In a fairly typical example, a physician's assistant, subjected to penalties by the Administrative Review Board for Professional Medical Conduct for engaging in "alcohol related criminal conduct," challenged the ruling on due process grounds. Among other things, the physician's assistant argued that the presentence report, which included and used against him a quotation of his own previous statement, was hearsay, since he did not appear as a witness at his own hearing. He admitted having made the statement, and could have subpoenaed the author of the report (as, incidentally the claimant could have in *Richardson v. Perales*[7]), so of course the court rejected this technical objection to hearsay.[8]

Admitting hearsay evidence poses far more than an academic question. A postal superintendent lost his job on that basis. He objected to the agency's acceptance as substantial evidence against him as mere hearsay, later disavowed by the source. The agency hearing officer, presumably, believed the source's initial statement, and was skeptical of the retraction. The Federal Appeals Court for the Ninth Circuit said, "Perhaps the classic exception to strict rules of evidence in the administrative context concerns hearsay evidence."[9] Of course, the administrative law judge must exclude clearly unreliable hearsay, or any form of evidence that has no significant probative value. The court mentioned, in a footnote, that it might not have agreed with the administrative decision, but it was required to respect the "trier of fact's determination of credibility. In the face of conflicting evidence that could support either outcome, it had to affirm the decision.[10]

STANDARD OF DECISION

Courts have regularly approved substitutions of the administrative proceeding's much lower threshold for proof of guilt for the "beyond a reasonable doubt" standard of the criminal courts. When New York State enacted the law that established the New York City Parking Violations Bureau, a motorist complained that substituting the special statutory standard of "clear and convincing evidence" for "proof beyond a reasonable doubt" violated his due process rights.[11] In ruling against him in 1975, New York's highest court noted that even in civil service misconduct proceedings, which have far more potential impact on defendants' lives since they can result in the loss of the employee's job, the use of a lower standard of proof of guilt rather than the standard of the criminal courts has long survived due process challenges.[12]

However, when New York State's Department of Social Services insisted on including on its public list of child abusers, those persons against whom merely stood "some credible evidence," the New York courts found that this procedure imposed an unconstitutional deprivation of a protected liberty interest, and ordered the Department to change the criterion for such listing to "a fair preponderance of the evidence."[13]

STANDARD OF PROOF

Losing parties in agencies hearings sometimes appeal the decision in court. In a criminal case, a judge or jury must decide on the basis of proof beyond a reasonable doubt. In most civil cases, the decision must be based on the preponderance of the evidence: whoever is more than fifty percent likely to be right. In an administrative hearing, the decision should also be based on the hearing officer's assessment of who is most likely to be right.

When a defendant in a criminal case appeals, the appellate court will require that the prosecution has indeed proven the defendant's guilt beyond a reasonable doubt; when the losing party in a civil case appeals, the appellate court will require that the decision reflected a preponderance of the evidence (more than fifty percent likelihood); However, when a court reviewing a hearing officer's decision decides that "substantial evidence" provides a basis for the decision, whether or not the reviewing court thinks the hearing officer decided correctly, it will uphold that decision, disappointing the complainant who had appealed the decision. "Substantial evidence" is a legal term used in the APA.[14]

BOX 9-3   **5 U.S. Code Administrative Procedure Act—
Section 706(2)(e)**

. . . The reviewing court shall—

(1) compel agency action unlawfully withheld or unreasonably delayed; and

(2) hold unlawful and set aside agency action, findings, and conclusions found to be—

* * *

(E) unsupported by substantial evidence in a case subject to sections 556 and 557 of this title or otherwise reviewed on the record of an agency hearing provided by statute;

* * *

Source: http://www.gpo.gov/fdsys/pkg/USCODE-2011-title5/pdf/USCODE-2011-title5-partI-chap7-sec706.pdf

---

STANDARD OF REVIEW

Although the federal courts have long abandoned the residuum rule of a 1938 case discussed earlier, requiring some evidence that would have been admissible in court, that decision provided a definition of substantial evidence that still seems valid: "more than a mere scintilla. It means such relevant evidence as a reasonable mind might accept as adequate to support a conclusion."[15]

"More than a scintilla," of course, means more than just a tiny bit of evidence. Clearly, however, "a reasonable mind *might* accept" less than the predominant evidence. So a citizen, with the weight of the evidence on his or her side, might nonetheless lose at an agency hearing, and lose an appeal to the courts. But, such deviation from some imagined ideal is hardly unique in our legal system. Criminal procedure has long balanced fairness and efficiency differently from civil procedure. A prosecutor has to prove guilt beyond a reasonable doubt, for example, while a civil defendant is found liable merely on a preponderance of the evidence. The civil process, as a result, enjoys proportionately more efficiency than the criminal process. Our society has lived with this trade-off for centuries. We can live equally comfortably with the still greater efficiency of administrative adjudication, at the expense of some degree of procedural due process.

The APA seemed to require that substantial evidence must support the decision in a formal adjudication,[16] while informal decisions need only pass the "arbitrary or capricious" test.[17] Then–Circuit Judge Antonin Scalia may have ended the longstanding confusion about the difference between the two tests in 1984 when he declared the latter "only a specific application" of the former, and concluded that they each require the same degree of "factual support."[18] He called the difference between the two "largely semantic," and quoted Bernard Schwartz in noting that they "converge into a test of reasonableness."[19] Although the "arbitrary and capricious" standard may take precedent into account somewhat more than does the "substantial evidence" standard,[20] "most courts appear to accept [Justice Scalia's] message . . . If the agency's action is reasonable, it must be upheld."[21]

So a reviewing court requires substantial evidence to uphold an agency's adjudication. But, hearing officers should never apply that rule. It is for court judges, not administrative law judges—a standard of review, not a standard of proof.

STANDARD OF DECISION: NOT "SUBSTANTIAL EVIDENCE"; BURDEN OF PROOF

At one time, controversies arose over the nature of the evidence used to base decisions, because as noted above the "residuum rule" required those decisions to be based on at least one element of evidence that would have been permitted in a regular courtroom, although other evidence that would be excluded in a courtroom trial could also be considered.[22] The courts called the allowable evidence "substantial." Some state courts still apply the residuum rule to determinations of substantial evidence. In fact, the 2010 MSAPA gives states a choice of the residuum rule or the modern substantial evidence rule.[23] The New Mexico court, for example, "may set aside the agency's finding or decision," no matter how credible and reliable the hearsay evidence supporting it, if hearsay that would have been inadmissible "in a jury trial" is "the only support found."[24] The Utah court restated its rule that the decision "cannot be based solely on inadmissible hearsay," noting that exceptions render certain kinds of hearsay admissible in courtroom trials.[25]

BOX 9-4   **2010 Model State Administrative Procedure Act— Section 413(f)**

Alternative A

(f) Hearsay evidence may be used to supplement or explain other evidence, but on timely objection, is not sufficient by itself to support a finding of fact unless it would be admissible over objection in a civil action.

Alternative B

(f) Hearsay evidence is sufficient to support a finding of fact if it constitutes reliable, probative, and substantial evidence.

This kind of controversy rarely arises today, because many states have abandoned the residuum rule.[26] The term "substantial evidence," however, persists and causes trouble. "The concept of substantial evidence . . . when put to use in respect to a particular determination, frequently causes difficulty and disagreement . . ."[27]

It is no wonder that the substantial evidence rule sometimes confuses hearing officers, to say nothing of law students, lawyers, and administrators. The general statutes governing hearings have provisions that are supposed to explain the basis hearing officers should use to decide the cases in front of them. For example, the Federal Administrative Procedure Act says ". . . A sanction may not be imposed or rule or order issued except on consideration of the whole record or those parts thereof cited by a party and supported by and in accordance with the reliable, probative, and substantial evidence . . ."[28] The New York State Administrative Procedure Act says ". . . No decision, determination or order shall be made except on consideration of the record as a whole or such portion thereof as may be cited by any party to the proceeding and as supported by and in accordance with substantial evidence."[29]

Until you get to the "substantial evidence" part, these statutes seem to make sense. Plainly, hearing officers should make their decisions on the basis of the most reliable evidence they find in the context of the entire record of what has been brought before them. But, as noted earlier, "substantial evidence" means only "more than a mere scintilla . . . such relevant evidence as a reasonable mind might accept as adequate . . ."[30] In the words of a New York court, "it is more than mere surmise, conjecture, or speculation, but less than a preponderance of the evidence."[31] "More than a scintilla," of course, means more than just a tiny bit of evidence. Clearly, however, "a reasonable mind *might* accept" less than the predominant evidence. A "reasonable" mind might also be a somewhat stupid mind. So, why should this be the standard a hearing officer should apply?

In fact, it is not. At issue at the hearing is the burden of proof. The Federal Administrative Procedure Act says "Except as otherwise provided by statute, the proponent of a rule or order has the burden of proof."[32] The New York State Administrative Procedure Act says "Except as otherwise provided by statute, the burden of proof shall be on the party who initiated the proceeding."[33] These statements instruct the hearing officer, not just the parties to the hearing. As the Supreme Court explained, the burden of proof under the Administrative Procedure Act "means the burden of persuasion."[34] If the credible evidence presented in the case favors one party, no honest and rational decision-maker should be persuaded by the other party, even though "a reasonable," but somewhat stupid mind might accept the less-persuasive evidence "as adequate to support a conclusion." Thus, the Supreme Court required the winning party to have proven its case by a "preponderance of the evidence," that is, by the superior weight of the evidence.

The Massachusetts Manual for Conducting Administrative Adjudicatory Hearings[35] sets forth clearly the rule of decision: "For each issue a burden of proof is assigned and the party that has that burden of proof must show by the 'clear weight' or the 'preponderance' of the credible evidence that his position is justified or else a decision on that issue will be granted in favor of the opposing party."[36] The Manual expands on the point: "presiding officers must ground their decisions on the preponderance of the reliable or credible evidence found to be relevant to the issues before their agency. This standard allows the fact finder to harbor some doubt and yet, on balance, [she] must be persuaded that a particular fact or set of facts is more likely true or probably than not."[37] Of course, agency hearings may be governed by statutes that explicitly set forth special decision rules: "While the standard of proof usually follows the 'clear weight' or, more commonly, 'preponderance of the evidence' formulation, note that such is not always the case, as in civil service proceedings [reasonable justification for the appointing authority's action] and child abuse/neglect administrative appeals ['"reasonable cause to believe' that the child was abused or neglected"].[38]

Not every state sets forth its standards as clearly. The Office of Administrative Hearings in the Department of State of New York State defines substantial evidence as "[t]he standard that the party requesting a hearing must meet in order to meet the burden of proof."[39] Of course, this makes no sense. As a party to a hearing, you have to persuade the hearing officer that you are right. You are likely to do so if the evidence as a whole, the weight of the evidence, the preponderance of the evidence, supports your side of the controversy. "Substantial evidence" is a much lower standard.

So, the hearing officer who explains that a decision is supported by substantial evidence may be announcing, "My own decision is stupid." Instead, hearing officers should base their conclusions on the weight of the evidence, or on-the-record as a whole, and say so.

The distinction between rules of decision (or burdens of proof) and rules of review has often sown confusion: for example, "The City confuses the basic concepts of scope of review and burden of proof. The confusion is understandable."[40]

Substantial evidence is a rule of review, not a rule of decision. That is, a court should apply the substantial evidence test when it reviews a hearing officer's decision to determine whether or not to uphold that decision. The hearing officer must apply a rule of decision. Under such a rule, to carry the burden of proof, a party must persuade the hearing officer that based on the record as a whole, the weight of the evidence supports a conclusion in favor of that party more than it supports a conclusion in favor of the other party. A rule of review, in contrast, tells the court the conditions under which it must affirm the hearing officer's decision. Because the hearing officer actually hears the witnesses and may also specialize in hearing cases concerned with the issues of one agency, their rule of review instructs judges to give a degree of deference to hearing officers, so even if they disagree with the hearing officer's decision, so long as that decision is based on *substantial evidence*, they must affirm it.

EX PARTE CONTACTS

In 1981, the union representing the nation's air traffic controllers (PATCO) called for a strike, which was illegal. The Federal Labor Relations Authority determined that PATCO should lose its status as the air traffic controllers' negotiating unit. During its deliberations prior to its decision to revoke, a member of the Authority, Leon B. Applewhaite, discussed the situation in a phone call with the Secretary of Transportation, Andrew Lewis, again over dinner with a leader of another union, Albert Shanker of the American Federation of Teachers, and also briefly in a meeting with some prosecutors for the Authority. Another member of the Authority, Henry B. Frazier, also talked to Lewis about the matter on the telephone.[41] An unfair labor practice hearing, such as the revocation hearing, as a formal adjudication, comes under APA requirements prohibiting *ex parte* communications like these, and allowing for (but not requiring) overturning of a decision influenced by such communications.[42]

BOX 9-5   **5: 5 U.S. Code Administrative Procedure Act—Section 557(d)**

(1)   In any agency proceeding which is subject to subsection (a) of this section, except to the extent required for the disposition of ex parte matters as authorized by law—

    (A)   no interested person outside the agency shall make or knowingly cause to be made to any member of the body comprising the agency, administrative law judge, or other employee who is or may reasonably be expected to be involved in the decisional process of the proceeding, an ex parte communication relevant to the merits of the proceeding;

    (B)   no member of the body comprising the agency, administrative law judge, or other employee who is or may reasonably be expected to be involved in the decisional process of the proceeding, shall make or knowingly cause to be made to any interested person outside the agency an ex parte communication relevant to the merits of the proceeding;

(Continued)

(Continued)

(C) a member of the body comprising the agency, administrative law judge, or other employee who is or may reasonably be expected to be involved in the decisional process of such proceeding who receives, or who makes or knowingly causes to be made, a communication prohibited by this subsection shall place on the public record of the proceeding:

(i) all such written communications;

(ii) memoranda stating the substance of all such oral communications; and

on account of such violation; and

acquisition of such knowledge.

Source: http://www.archives.gov/federal-register/laws/administrative-procedure/557.html

The APA also provides for disclosure of the communications, but the court had previously required an evidentiary hearing that resulted in a detailed report of the nature and contents of the communications.[43] If the *ex parte* communications made the process or the results unfair, courts would vacate the decision.[44] Since apparently no one even alleged that the *ex parte* communications in this matter unfairly influenced the process or the result, the court refused to vacate the Authority's decision.[45] It did say that "Mr. Shanker's purpose and conduct were improper, and . . . Member Applewhaite should not have entertained Mr. Shanker's views on the desirability of decertifying a striking union,"[46] but merely in *dicta* (as a statement of opinion considered authoritative, although not binding).

The APA prohibits *ex parte* communication with any "interested person,"[47] which according to its legislative history, was intended to cover "any individual or other person with an interest in the agency proceeding that is greater than the general interest the public as a whole may have."[48] In contrast, the 2010 MSAPA prohibits *ex parte* communication with "any person."[49]

BOX 9-6 **2010 Model State Administrative Procedure Act— Section 408**

* * *

(b) Except as otherwise provided in subsection (c), (d), (e), or (h), while a contested case is pending, the presiding officer and the final decision maker may not make to or receive from any person any communication concerning the case without notice and opportunity for all parties to participate in the communication. For the purpose of this section, a contested case is pending from the issuance of the agency's pleading or from an application for an agency decision, whichever is earlier.

Even in a case in which the court held that the State's APA did not apply, it overturned the decision of a City Council to authorize the demolition of an arguably historic building because of *ex parte* communication. The City Council had been sitting "in a quasi-judicial capacity,"[50] several of its members had received "phone calls from concerned citizens" pressing their views on the matter,[51] they kept no record of the nature or substance of the calls or the identity of the callers, and therefore there was no opportunity "to effectively respond to the arguments the callers may have advanced."[52] Thus, the City Council violated due process under Idaho law by "extend[ing] its inquiry beyond the limits of the public record."[53]

When it became clear that the staff advising the hearing examiner had not previously engaged in any activity adverse to the party in interest, a Tennessee court had an opportunity to make a point that seems applicable to most adjudications: *ex parte* advice to agency decision-makers from staff with no such history of adverse involvement is not prohibited: "Otherwise, all support staff—law clerks, court clerks, and other specialists—would be of little service to the person(s) that hire them."[54]

On the other hand, the New Jersey court strongly disapproved when a hearing officer confidentially and *ex parte*, offered his agency head, the ultimate decision-maker in the matter, the decision he planned to issue suspending the liquor license of the owner of a hotel and restaurant, setting forth its findings of fact, conclusions of law, and recommendations. Of course, the owner had no opportunity to rebut its findings or logic. The court said that the practice not only violated "the principle of the exclusiveness of the record . . . but shocks one's sense of fair play . . ."[55]

It may not be easy to reconcile the two decisions, but perhaps a hearing officer is presumed to have more influence than other staff, so when staff advise the hearing officer confidentially and *ex parte*, their advice, which may not even presume to include a recommended outcome, merely illuminates the hearing officer's considerations; while when the hearing officer confidentially and *ex parte* advises an ultimate decision-maker, the hearing officer is more likely to make and the superior officer is less likely to challenge a recommendation.

BIASED HEARING OFFICERS?

In both courts and agency adjudications, a decision-maker who has a financial interest in the outcome of the matter, or who has been personally vilified by the subject of the case, is sufficiently likely to be biased so that retaining that individual as decision-maker would violate principles of due process.[56] But, agencies, unlike courtroom judges, both investigate and decide. The fact that the same members of the Wisconsin Medical Examining Board had instigated an investigation, and then would make the decision as to whether or not to take action against the target of the investigation, did not indicate that the members of the Board had "irrevocably closed" minds on the matter,[57] and thus did not suffice to indicate a likelihood of bias violative of due process.[58] The Court noted as well that while APA § 554(d) bars an agency employee who investigates or prosecutes from participating in the decision on a matter, it exempts agency heads from that prohibition.[59]

Only personal bias so extreme that it clearly impairs fairness can justify vacating a hearing officer's decision. Apparently, such bias has surfaced frequently in immigration cases: "Time and time again we have cautioned immigration judges against making intemperate or humiliating remarks during immigration proceedings . . . * * * . . . [S]ome of our sister circuits have repeatedly echoed our concerns."[60] Under comparable conditions another federal Circuit Court of Appeals ordered the matter remanded to a different immigration judge than the one who had made the initial ruling.[61]

With no APA provision offering sufficient guidance, the Pennsylvania court resolved a similar issue by finding the same principles in its State Constitution, holding that while the same agency may both prosecute and adjudicate, the agency must create "walls of division . . . which eliminate the threat or appearance of bias"[62] so that those individuals who had been involved in the prosecution cannot participate in the adjudication.[63]

REQUIREMENTS FOR CONSISTENCY IN AGENCY ADJUDICATIONS

Prior to a particular decision against a local of the United Automobile Workers union, the National Labor Relations Board (NLRB) had regularly required "clear and unmistakable" evidence in order to find that a union (or company) had voluntarily relinquished some right it enjoyed pursuant to statute. [64] But, this time the NLRB decided that the union waived its statutory right to bargain in the face of very contradictory and unclear evidence.[65] In so doing, the NLRB had reversed the decision of its own administrative law judge. The court, in remanding the NLRB's decision for reconsideration in line with its ruling, noted "an administrative agency is not allowed to change direction without some explanation of what it is doing and why. This general principle of administrative law [citations omitted] . . . is applicable to adjudication . . ."[66]

WHAT AM I SUPPOSED TO DO?

Labor Department Work-Related Death Compensation: Will the Court Uphold the Hearing Officer's Decision?

You work for the Secretary of Labor, and must advise him as to cases coming to the Department's administrative law judges (as federal hearing offices are called) from claimants under the Defense Base Act. Under this Act, federal defense contractors overseas must pay compensation to their employees and/ or their dependents if they suffer employment-related injury or death caused by accidents or hostilities. The contractor is not liable if injury or death results from self-harm or intoxication, but the company must rebut a presumption against those causes. If the employment involved special dangers, any injury or death is presumed to be employment-related.

The widow of a deceased American military trainer filed a claim based on her late husband's death in Saudi Arabia. He had been stationed in an area where westerners had suffered terrorist attacks often enough that the deceased and his co-workers considered it quite dangerous. The deceased had been found with his neck in a noose, hanging from a beam in his room, but with his feet on the ground, wearing women's make-up and toenail polish. Shortly after he was found, cut down, and driven to a nearby hospital, a doctor pronounced him dead of asphyxiation.

The contractor will argue that suicide and autoerotic asphyxiation present themselves as reasonable hypotheses explaining the death, rebutting the presumption against self-harm and rebutting the presumption that the death was employment-related. However, the widow will testify that the deceased had been planning to return home, and other witnesses will testify that the deceased had been cheerful when last seen on the previous night. The widow will also suggest that the deceased may have been killed by someone offended by his sexual proclivities or by someone whose own illicit financial activity he was about to expose. Also, the Saudi police continue to investigate the death; at this point they have not been convinced that it was a suicide.

If the administrative law judge who hears the matter rules against the widow, the Department's Benefits Review Board will probably uphold the decision. Then, if a court reverses the Review Board, the Department could be the subject of some negative press coverage. What should you tell the Secretary about the likelihood of such an outcome?

The United States Court of Appeals for the First Circuit dealt with this issue.[67] The administrative law judge and the Benefits Review Board did indeed decide against the widow. It held that

> a reasonable factfinder could conclude, based on the record that Michael Truczinska's death could be explained by non-covered causes, thus rebutting any presumption and leaving the burden on the claimant, and that none of Terri Truczinska's suggested hypotheses that might entail coverage had any serious support in the record.[68]

The court explained that the administrative decision easily met the substantial evidence test: "Although the 'substantial evidence' test sounds demanding, it merely requires evidence that 'could satisfy a reasonable factfinder' that the claimant's injury was attributable to a non-covered cause."[69]

Agency Hearings—An Example In Practice

Some students find administrative law hard to grasp because they expect to learn the law of particular government agencies. In fact, we teach administrative law primarily to help students understand the logic that structures the way all government agencies function, or should function. The cases we review emerge from individual government agencies, of course, and so students haphazardly encounter bits of substantive agency law. But, we study administrative law for the principles that apply across the board, not for the substantive law of whatever particular agencies we use as examples.

Still, a brief immersion in the substantive law of one government agency may make it easier for students to imagine practicing in the field, and thus lead to a better understanding of administrative law.

In New York State Retirement System pension appeals, two issues arise fairly frequently. First, whether the pensioner's disability resulted from a job-related accident, for which he or she would receive more money. Often, such cases turn on whether an outside, intervening event met the *Lichtenstein v. Board of Trustees* technical definition of "accident" for this purpose: was the injury caused by a "sudden, fortuitous mischance, unexpected, out of the ordinary, and injurious in impact," or was it in fact foreseeable?[70] If it was foreseeable, it was not "unexpected" and therefore would not constitute an accident as that term is used in the New York's Retirement and Social Security Law (RSSL).

Second, decisions sometimes note discrepancies between applicants' contemporaneous written accounts of such incidents, often submitted to employers as accident or injury reports, and their subsequent testimony. The State Comptroller is the sole trustee for the New York State Retirement System. When faced with such discrepancies, reviewing courts often cite the Comptroller's authority to rule on issues of credibility, and thus to decide that earlier contemporaneous accounts probably tend to be more accurate.[71]

The following hypothetical sets the scene for a discussion of those issues. You get extra credit if you spot the jokes.

PRACTICE PROBLEM

Mr. Shelly Mazel was employed as a Fish Culturist by the New York State Department of Environmental Conservation starting on April 1, 2003. On May 28, 2008, when he applied for Article 15 Disability Retirement benefits, since he had fewer than ten years of service credit in order to qualify for such benefits, the governing statute requires him to prove that he is permanently disabled from performing the duties of the job he had, and that the disability resulted from a job-related accident (an accident "sustained in service").[72] The responsibilities of his particular position require him to assess the viability of various species of fish in the Finger Lakes, and to identify factors threatening such viability.

The Retirement System denied Mr. Mazel's application, reasoning that he had fewer than ten years of service credit, the incident of May 1, 2008 was not an accident for purposes of the governing statute, and he is not permanently incapacitated. At the hearing on his challenge to the System's decision, he testified that throughout his relatively brief career, the essential component of the duties of his employment was to use his unusually acute sense of smell to determine causes of piscine fatality. He testified that on May 1, 2008, while assessing Keuka Lake, a colleague, S. H. L. Miele, alerted him that a strong aroma indicated the presence of a deceased specimen about a half mile away.

As he approached the object of his investigation, a ferret—an animal not seen in this location in recent memory—suddenly streaked by, causing him to trip and fall directly onto the dead pickerel, nose first. The direct encounter with the powerful scent so overwhelmed his olfactory powers as to completely nullify them. When cross-examined by the System's attorney, Mr. Mazel appeared deeply disconsolate about the loss of his ability and profession.

Mr. Miele, in testimony, corroborated Mr. Mazel's account, but noted that the animal moved too quickly for him to identify its species.

In the written report of his injury, signed by Mr. Mazel and his employer on May 2, 2008, Mr. Mazel described the incident as, "I tripped over a small animal that crossed my path as I approached the dead fish." He did not identify the animal as a ferret on that occasion. Various small animals are plentiful in the Keuka Lake area.

Dr. Probosk Gogol, a board certified specialist in otorhinolaryngology, examined Mr. Mazel on behalf of the Retirement System on July 1, 2009, and reviewed his medical records. His report of that date noted that while anosmia can result from a lack of regeneration of the olfactory neuroepithelium, there are no reported cases of such results secondary to direct insult of the organ, and no objective basis for concluding that Mr. Mazel's condition is permanent, or even other than symptom magnification.

Unfortunately, on July 2, 2009, Dr. Gogol himself had a fatal encounter with a former patient who was unhappy with the results of a rhinoplasty he had performed.

Dr. Cyrano Durante, chair of the department of otolaryngology at the Mayo Sinai Clinic, who had attempted to treat applicant for this condition on at least twelve occasions, testified that the factors predisposing patients to olfactory dysfunction, or the mechanisms underlying such dysfunction, remain unclear. He further testified that throughout his treatment he had performed a number of standard tests to ascertain olfactory function, which had consistently indicated complete loss. He concluded that Mr. Mazel can no longer perform the duties of his employment, and is permanently incapacitated. Here are some questions for discussion:

1. Does applicant's contemporaneous written report negate the credibility of his later testimony?

2. Does the incident of May 1, 2008, constitute an accident as that term is used in the RSSL?

3. Can the System rely on Dr. Gogol's "hearsay" report, despite applicant's inability to cross-examine Dr. Gogol?

4. If the hearing officer determines that the May 1, 2008, incident qualifies as an accident for purposes of the Retirement and Social Security Law, but based on Dr. Gogol's report, applicant does not qualify for Article 15 Disability Retirement benefits because he is not permanently incapacitated, will a reviewing court sustain that judgment?

ENDNOTES

1. Section 554.
2. Section 556(d). Similarly, the Court in *Delaware v. Van Arsdale*, 475 U.S. 673, 683, 106 Sup. Ct. 1431, 1435 (1986) noted that trial judges may "may impose reasonable limits on . . . cross examination based on concerns about, among other things, harassment, prejudice . . . or interrogation that is repetitive or only marginally relevant."
3. Rule 802, Federal Rules of Evidence, 28 U.S. C. Appendix, P.L. 93-595, 88 Stat. 1926, Legal Information Institute, Cornell University Law School, http://www.law.cornell.edu/rules/fre/rule_802.
4. Hearsay, Legal Information Institute, Cornell University Law School, http://www.law.cornell.edu/wex/hearsay.
5. *Consolidated Edison v. NLRB*, 305 U.S. 197, 230, 59 S. Ct. 206, 217 (1938); and see *Gramaton Ave. Assoc. v. State Div. of Human Rights*, 45 N.Y. 2d 176, 180, 408 N.Y.S. 2d 54, 56, note (1978), marking the end of that requirement in New York State, noting that "the legal residuum rule and [its] doctrine . . . no longer obtain . . ."
6. *Richardson v. Perales*, 402 U.S. 389, 91 S. Ct. 1420 (1971).
7. 402 U.S. at 404, 91 S. Ct. at 1429.
8. *Matter of Chatelain v. New York State Department of Health*, 48 A.D. 3d 943, 945, 852 N.Y.S. 2d 424, 426 (3d Dept. 2008); similarly, see *Matter of Conteh v. Daines*, 52 A.D. 3d 994, 860 N.Y.S. 2d 649 (3d Dept. 2008).
9. *Calhoun v. Bailar*, 626 F. 2d 145 (1980).
10. *Id.*, quoting *Rhinehart v. Finch*, 438 F. 2d 920, 921 (9th Cir. 1971).
11. *Rosenthal v. Hartnett*, 36 N.Y. 2d 269, 274–275, 367 N.Y.S. 2d 247 (1975).
12. *Id.*, citing *Pell v. Bd. of Education*, 34 N.Y. 2d 222, 356 N.Y.S. 2d 833 (1974).
13. *Lee TT. v. Dowling*, 87 N.Y. 2d 699, 642 N.Y.S. 2d 181 (1996).
14. Section 706(2)(E).
15. *Consolidated Edison v. NLRB*, 305 U.S. 197, 229, 59 S. Ct. 206, 217.
16. Section 706(2)(E).
17. Section 706(2)(A).
18. Association of Data Processing Service Organizations v. Federal Reserve Board, 745 F. 2d 677, 683 (D.C. Cir. 1984).
19. 745 F. 2d at 684.
20. See, e.g. *North Carolina v. Brown*, 1995 U.S. Dist. LEXIS 22393 at *21 (D.C.D.C. 1995).
21. William F. Fox, *Understanding Administrative Law*, 5th ed., (Newark, NJ: Matthew Bender and Company, 2008), 309 [6th ed., 2012, 340].
22. See text at notes 5 and 6, *supra*.
23. 2010 MSAPA § § 413(f).
24. *Tallman v. ABF*, 108 N.M. 124, 128, 767 P. 2d 363, 367 (1988).
25. *Prosper, Inc. v. Department of Workforce Services*, 2007 UT. App. 281, 168 P. 3d 344, 346 (2007).
26. See, e.g., *Reguero v. Teacher Standards and Practices Commission*, 312 Ore. 402, 415, 822 P. 2d 1171, 1179 (Ore. 1991).
27. *300 Gramatan Ave. Assoc. v State Div. of Human Rights*, 45 N.Y. 2d 176,180, 408 N.Y.S. 2d 54, 56, 379 N.E. 2d 1183, 1185–6 (1978).
28. Section 556(d).
29. Section 306(1), and see *Miller v. DeBuono*, 90 N.Y. 2d 783, 789, 689 N.E. 2d 518, 520, 666 N.Y.S. 2d 548, 550 (1997).
30. Consolidated Edison v. NLRB, supra at note 12.
31. *Fernald v. Johnson*, 305 A.D. 2d 503, 503–4, 759 N.Y.S. 2d 529, 530 (2d Dept. 2003), citing *300 Gramatan Ave. Assoc. v State Div. of Human Rights*, 45 N.Y. 2d 176, 180–181, 408 N.Y.S. 2d 54, 379 N.E. 2d 1183 (1978).
32. Section 556(d).
33. Section 306(1).

34. *Dir. v. Greenwich Collieries*, 512 U.S. 267, 278, 114 S. Ct. 2251, 2258 (1994).

35. Robert J. Quinn, Jr. Assistant Attorney General, ed., Office of the Massachusetts Attorney General, *Manual for Conducting Administrative Adjudicatory Proceedings*, 2012 edition, available at http://www.google.com/url?sa=t&rct=j&q=&esrc=s&source=web&cd=8&ved=0CE0QFjAH&url=http%3A%2F%2Fwww.mass.gov%2Fago%2Fbureaus%2Fgovernment%2Ft-he-administrative-law-division%2Fadmin-adjuc-training-manual.pdf&ei=MrHfU_SEKYbnsAT9-oH4Ag&usg=AFQjCNGIi6eTHl0glCRq9vKtg8KWmYteIg&sig2=54-E6qfDJm v9gTVyHM5pEw&bvm=bv.72197243,d.cWc, accessed 8/4/14.

36. *Id*. at 4, citing *Medical Malpractice Joint Underwriting Ass'n of Mass. v. Commissioner of Insurance*, 395 Mass. 43, 46 (1985).

37. *Id*. at 29.

38. *Id*. at 55, inserts from page 55, note 34 of Quinn's Manual.

39. Glossary, website of the New York State Department of State, http://www.dos.ny.gov/ooah/glossary.html, accessed 8/4/14.

40. *Fukuda v. City of Angels Camp*, 63 Cal. App. 4th 1426, 1430; 74 Cal. Rptr. 2d 731, 733 (3d App. Dist. 1998), *rev'd*, 20 Cal. 4th 805; 977 P.2d 693; 85 Cal. Rptr. 2d 696; 1999 Cal. LEXIS 3899 (1999).

41. *Professional Air Traffic Controllers Org. (PATCO) v. Federal Labor Relations Authority*, 685 F. 2d 547, 222 U.S. App. D.C. 97 (D.C. Cir. 1982).

42. APA § 557(d).

43. 685 F. 2d at 601ff., 222 U.S. App. D.C. at 178ff.

44. 685 F. 2d at 564-5, 222 U.S. App. D.C. at 51–3.

45. 685 F. 2d at 571, 222 U.S. App. D.C. at 77.

46. *Id*.

47. APA § 557(d).

48. H.R. Rep. No. 880, Part I, 94th Cong., 2nd Sess. 19–20 (1976), quoted at 685 F. 2d at 562, 222 U.S. App. D.C. at 45.

49. 2010 MSAPA § 408(b).

50. *Idaho Historic Pres. Council Inc. v. City of Boise*, 134 Idaho 651, 654, 8 P. 3d 646, 649 (Idaho 2000).

51. *Id*.

52. 134 Idaho at 655-6, 8 P. 3d at 650-1.

53. 134 Idaho at 655, 8 P. 3d at 650.

54. *Consumer Advocate Division v. Tennessee Regulatory Authority*, 1998 Tenn. App. LEXIS 428 at *5, 1998 WL 6484536 (Tenn. Ct. App. 1998).

55. *Mazza v. Cavicchia*, 15 N.J. 498, 516, 105 A. 2d 545, 555 (N.J. 1954).

56. *Withrow v. Larkin*, 421 U.S. 35, 47, 95 Sup. Ct. 1456, 1464.

57. 421 U.S. at 48, 95 S. Ct. at 1468, quoting *FTC v. Cement Institute*, 333 U.S. 683, 701 (1948).

58. 421 U.S. at 58, 95 S. Ct. at 1470.

59. 421 U.S. at 52, 95 S. Ct. at 1467.

60. *Qun Wang v. Attorney General*, 423 F. 3d 260, 267-8 (3d Cir. 2005).

61. *Mahamed Ayunal Islam v. Gonzales*, 469 F. 3d 53 (2d Cir. 2006).

62. *Lyness v. State Bd. of Medicine*, 529 Pa. 535, 546, 605 A. 2d 1204, 1209 (Pa. 1992).

63. 529 Pa. at 547, 605 A. 2d at 1209.

64. *United Automobile Workers v. NLRB*, 802 F. 2d 969, 973 (7th Cir. 1986).

65. 802 F. 2d at 972-5.

66. 802 F. 2d at 974.

67. *Truczinskas v. Director, Office of Workers' Compensation Programs*, 699 F. 3d 672 (1st Cir. 2012).

68. 699 F. 3d at 679.

69. 699 F. 3d at 679–80.

70. *Lichtenstein v. Board of Trustees*, 57 N.Y. 2d 1010, 1012, 457 N.Y.S. 2d 472 (1982).

71. See, e.g., *Farruggio v. McCall*, 222 A.D. 2d 925, 926, 635 N.Y.S. 2d 343, 344 (3d Dept. 1995); *Esposito v. Regan*, 162 A.D. 2d 870, 871, 557 N.Y.S. 2d 773, 774 (3d Dept. 1990).

72. New York State Retirement and Social Security Law § 605.

chapter

10

Choice of
Rulemaking or Adjudication

Sometimes administrative agencies have to choose between rulemaking and adjudication as the best method of addressing a problem. Each has its advantages. Rulemaking gives notice, or "fair warning"; allows participation by all affected parties; includes all potentially relevant data; and makes for easier legislative oversight, uniformity, and in the case of informal rulemaking, speed or efficiency. Adjudication, on the other hand, lets agencies shape outcomes more flexibly depending on the circumstances. But, a person trapped by the words of a rule might feel deprived of the opportunity to show why he or she should be treated differently. Usually, agencies need to do at least some adjudication, since sometimes their rules have to be interpreted before being applied.

Generally, courts require adjudication when (1) the impact of the agency's policy falls only on one identifiable person or entity; (2) no other person or entity could ever join the described class; (3) the policy is based wholly on specific facts pertaining to that person or entity; and (4) the policy's intended burden is directed only at that person or entity. "Entity" can mean a very small identifiable group of people.

ADJUDICATION TO THE EXCLUSION OF RULEMAKING

Agencies, such as the Securities and Exchange Commission (SEC) and the National Labor Relations Board (NLRB), don't like to issue rules because rules limit their discretion. Fairness competes with flexibility: the public wants to know what to do or not to do; the government wants to be able to stop things it doesn't want even though it cannot predict exactly what those things will be.

SEC

For example, the SEC wants to prosecute anyone who cheats the public in a stock transaction, but couldn't predict every possible way that could happen. In response to stock market swindles of the 1920s, Congress passed the Securities Act in 1933 and the Securities Exchange Act in 1934 to prohibit misrepresentations or manipulative or deceptive practices in the sale or purchase of stock. Section 10b of the 1934 Act permits the Securities and Exchange Commission to issue what rules it needs to protect investors or the public.

The SEC instituted an action against the brokerage house Cady, Roberts & Co. and its broker, Robert Gintel, for violations of Rule 10b-5 and other relevant provisions of the Acts and rules issued under them. Gintel had acted very quickly after receiving a telephone call from a member of the board of the Curtiss-Wright Corporation telling him that Curtiss-Wright was about to reduce the dividend on its stock. Gintel sold shares on behalf of his clients, and sold some shares short on his own account, at 11:15 a.m. and 11:18 a.m. on November 2, 1959. The dividend announcement appeared on the Dow Jones tape at 11:48 a.m., after which the New York Stock Exchange suspended trading in Curtiss-Wright for about two hours because of the rash of sell orders.

Until the *Cady, Roberts & Co.* case,[1] the SEC had never pursued anyone for dealing in securities based on insider information, as long as they had not made any attempt to mislead anyone based on that information. The SEC never issued a rule saying that such transactions violated the Acts, nor had they decided any case that way. Gintel therefore had no official notice that what he was about to do was illegal, although it certainly can be said—and it was successfully argued—that his actions went against the spirit and the general intent of the two Securities Acts. Against criticism that it was penalizing Gintel without having given him adequate notice, the SEC decision took pains to justify itself:

> [The laws we say he broke] are broad remedial provisions aimed at reaching misleading or deceptive activities, whether or not they precisely and technically sufficient to sustain a common law action for fraud and deceit.[2] * * * [They don't specify] particular acts or practices...., but rather are designed to encompass the infinite variety of devices by which undue advantage may be taken of investors and others.[3] * * * [T]he broad language of the antifraud provisions [is] not to be circumscribed by fine distinctions and rigid classifications.... The facts here impose on Gintel the responsibilities of those commonly referred to as "insiders" [even though Gintel clearly did not meet the definition of an insider].[4]

A similar problem faced the SEC when it charged a major law firm, White & Case, and one of its partners with violations of the securities laws, because they (along with their client) failed to reveal to the parties to a merger the weakness of their clients' corporate condition.[5] The court ruled that the lawyers' loyalty to their clients did not conflict with their responsibility to the "investing public," and therefore was no defense,[6] but White & Case doubtless thought that the court's holding begged the question. Attorneys had not previously or traditionally been the targets of SEC actions based on their silence about their clients' questionable business activities, even when those clients themselves could have become targets. In the 1970s, though, the SEC changed its policy to go after the attorneys, and did so through cases like this rather than through regulations.

In what is known as "the second *Chenery* decision," the Supreme Court in 1947 allowed the SEC that kind of leeway in identifying legal requirements,—which previously had been unclear at best—by way of adjudications rather than rules:

Since the Commission, unlike a court, [can] make new law prospectively [by] rule-making . . . , it has less reason to rely on *ad hoc* adjudication to formulate new standards of conduct within the framework of the Holding Company Act [the statute generally, but certainly not clearly governing the target corporation's action in this case. The Court continued, stating that clarifications should be undertaken "as much as possible" by means of the rule-making process]. But, any rigid requirement to that effect would make the administrative process inflexible and incapable of dealing with the many specialized problems which arise . . . * * * In other words, problems may arise in a case which the administrative agency could not reasonably foresee, problems which must be solved despite the absence of a relevant general rule. Or the agency may not have had sufficient experience with a particular problem to warrant rigidifying its tentative judgment into a hard and fast rule. Or the problem may be so specialized and varying in nature as to be impossible to capture within the boundaries of a general rule . . . There is thus a very definite place for the case-by-case evolution of statutory standards . . . * * * . . . [R]etroactivity must be balanced against the mischief of producing a result which is contrary to a statutory design or to legal and equitable principles. If that mischief is greater than the ill effect of the retroactive application of a new standard, it is not the type of retroactivity which is condemned by law . . .[7]

Justice Jackson, dissenting,[8] skewered the majority's logic:

The Court's reasoning adds up to this: The Commission must be sustained because of its accumulated experience in solving a problem with which it had never before been confronted!

* * * . . . Of course, if what these parties did was really condemned "by statutory design" or "legal and equitable principles," it could be stopped without resort to a new rule and there would be no retroactivity to condone. But, if it had been the Court's view that some law already prohibited the purchases, it would hardly have been necessary three sentences earlier to hold that the Commission was not prohibited "from utilizing this particular proceeding for announcing and applying a *new standard of conduct*" (Par. 17.) [emphasis supplied].

I give up. Now I realize fully what Mark Twain meant when he said, "The more you explain it, the more I don't understand it."[9]

Jackson concluded,

This decision is an ominous one to those who believe that men should be governed by laws that they may ascertain and abide by, and which will guide the action of those in authority, as well as of those who are subject to authority. [Footnote omitted.] I have long urged, and still believe, that the administrative process deserves fostering in our system as an expeditious and nontechnical method of *applying law* in specialized fields. I cannot agree that it be used, and I think its continued effectiveness is endangered when it is used, as a method of *dispensing with law* in those fields.[10]

NLRB

But, the majority prevailed, not Jackson. If anything, the NLRB uses adjudication instead of rulemaking to proclaim new law even more than the SEC. In one of its more controversial adjudications,[11] it announced the new requirement that employers must provide lists of employees to unions engaging in elections. However, the Board applied the new rule, not to the case at hand, but only to subsequent elections. In *N.L.R.B. v. Wyman-Gordon Co.*,[12] the Supreme Court threw out the NRLB's decision as violating the Administrative Procedure Act, because it did not follow the procedure prescribed for rulemaking. But, it held that the NLRB *could* impose the new requirement in the context of an adjudication, so long as it applied it to the case on which it was ruling: "adjudicated cases may and do, of course, serve as vehicles for the formulation of agency policies, which are applied and announced therein."[13] The Court claimed that Congress's grant of statutory authority to the NLRB gave it "wide discretion to ensure the fair and free choice of bargaining representatives," even by this method.[14]

Justices Harlan and Douglas, dissenting, each said, in effect, "You want to make a rule? Use the rulemaking process!"[15]

In *NLRB v. Bell Aerospace Co.*,[16] the Court again rejected the NLRB's "rulemaking" in the course of an adjudicative proceeding, but in such a way that the NLRB, again, managed to accomplish what it wanted without using rulemaking. This time, the NLRB had decided that certain employees were managerial employees, but they were covered anyway by the National Labor Relations Act because their positions did not require them to negotiate with unions or otherwise engage in labor relations, so they could be represented by a union. The Court held that under any reasonable interpretation of the Taft-Hartley Act, managerial employees could not be covered by the National Labor Relations Act.[17] The Court ordered the matter sent back to the NLRB for a more proper ruling, under its statute, as to whether the employees in question were or were not managerial by reference to their "actual job responsibilities, authority, and relationship to management."[18] More importantly, however, the Court followed *Chenery*,[19] quoting its arguments[20] in favor of permitting agencies to "announc[e] new principles in an adjudicative proceeding."[21] The NLRB, of course, on remand decided that the employees were not, after all, managerial—so they were covered by the Act and could unionize.[22]

Still, in *Bell Aerospace* the Court may have stepped back some from its holding in *Wyman-Gordon*. It acknowledged that bypassing rulemaking and relying too much on adjudication could "amount to abuse of discretion or a violation of the Act."[23] The Court explained that it felt forced by the very fact-specific nature of the *Bell Aerospace* case to decide it as it did: whether or not the employees in question—"buyers"—were truly managerial depended on their responsibilities, which could vary considerably between buyers in one company and buyers in another. The Court therefore doubted that the NLRB could formulate a rule that would appropriately cover each situation.[24]

Although the Court has not subsequently overruled *Wyman-Gordon*, or even acknowledged that it has actually narrowed its holding,[25] in 1989 the NLRB itself for the first time used the rulemaking process to set forth categories of "appropriate bargaining units in the health care industry."[26] One can only speculate that the possibility that the Court or the country was losing patience with its total reliance on adjudication might have played a role in its decision, at long last, to use the rulemaking process.

FDA

In an interesting dissent,[27] Justice Alito complained that the Court majority ignored the holding of *Chenery* that an agency can make policy just as well through adjudication as through rulemaking. Alito noted that adjudication decisions of the Food and Drug Administration (FDA) concerning the labeling of pharmaceutical drugs contradicted state laws on that subject. The Court, however, only addressed the fact that FDA *regulations* did not conflict with the state laws in finding that the state laws were not preempted.[28] The FDA had approved the original and then the revised warning on the label of an anti-nausea drug. Although the label warned that injection of the drug could result in amputation of a limb following gangrene, it did not warn that one type of injection (the "IV-push" method) created a higher risk of this outcome than another type (the "IV-drip" method). After her doctor injected the drug using the riskier method, a patient suffered the unfortunate consequences and lost her arm (and her career as a musician). She sued under Vermont law, arguing that the inadequate risk/reward ratio for the drug rendered it too unsafe for injection altogether, and that at least the label should have warned of the greater risk of the "IV-push" method. A Vermont jury agreed, and awarded damages.[29]

The manufacturer had offered to change the warnings on its label, but the FDA had "instructed it to '[r]etain verbiage in current label.'"[30] However, it was also true that FDA regulations, as the Vermont trial judge noted to the jury, "permit a drug manufacturer to change a product label to add or strengthen a warning about its product without prior FDA approval so long as it later submits the revised warning for review and approval."[31]

The manufacturer argued that allowing the state law to prevail would create a conflict with the purposes of Congress in empowering expert decision-makers at the FDA to assure pharmaceutical safety through drug labeling rather than leaving that responsibility to juries, therefore, the federal law empowering the FDA preempts state law,[32] and so the Court should strike down the Vermont verdict.

The Court looked to the legislative history of the FDA, noting that Congress provided that FDA regulations would only invalidate state law in case of a "direct and positive conflict."[33] The preamble to the Food, Drug, and Cosmetic

Act asserts that the Act "establishes 'both a "floor" and a "ceiling"' so that 'FDA approval of labelling . . . preempts conflicting or contrary state law.'"[34] The Court, however, found that the legislative history and most of the FDA's own statements, to the contrary, reflected an intention that FDA regulations would constitute a "floor" and not a "ceiling"; and that federal and state laws should complement each other in attempting to assure patient safety.[35] Thus, the Court refused to give legal weight to the preamble,[36] rejected the preemption argument, and upheld the Vermont decision.[37]

Justice Alito noted that the FDA can make its labeling decisions through the adjudicative process, which therefore have "the force of law," whether or not the preamble to the Food, Drug, and Cosmetic Act does.[38] For that reason and others, he argued that the majority's decision wrongly disclaimed *Geier v. American Honda Motor Co.*[39] as an applicable precedent requiring preemption.[40] Therefore, he would have ruled that the Vermont judgment was preempted.

But, the majority's decision, even if Alito's criticism has merit, at most only very weakly signals a preference for policy decisions based on rulemaking. Some states exhibit more sympathy for rulemaking in this regard.

UNUSUAL STATE RESPONSES TO AGENCY AVOIDANCE OF RULEMAKING

In a rare instance of a court overruling an agency's decision to refrain from taking an action, the Washington state court required its Department of Labor and Industries to issue a regulation, in light of a state statute requiring the Department to "set a standard which most adequately assures, to the extent feasible, on the basis of the best available evidence, that no employee will suffer material impairment of health."[41] The Department's own research had already supported the need for the regulation in question, so the court held that its denial of a request for the regulation "was arbitrary"[42] and therefore subject to reversal by the court under a provision of Washington's APA.[43]

Florida has attempted to curb the use of adjudications to develop new policies by defining as a rule "each agency statement of general applicability that implements, interprets, or prescribes law or policy [among other things],"[44] and by requiring that each such rule "shall be adopted by the rulemaking procedure . . . as soon as feasible and practicable."[45]

The states generally may be more anxious to require rulemaking than the federal government, for a number of reasons. State agency adjudicative decisions are rarely published and are usually hard to find. Most states have at least some processes for legislative and/or gubernatorial review of agency rulemaking. Most people who go before federal agency adjudications have lawyers; many who go before state-level adjudications do not. Almost all state rulemaking is notice-and-comment, and therefore is relatively efficient, while a great deal of federal rulemaking remains formal or semiformal.

That said, however, the Florida effort to force agencies to provide more clarity through rulemaking has been less than entirely popular, generating considerable resentment of the proliferation of regulations.[46] A provision of the 1981 MSAPA similarly pressing agencies to provide better notice by elaborating on statutes with clarifying rules[47] has no analogue in the 2010 MSAPA.

RULEMAKING TO THE EXCLUSION OF ADJUDICATION

Agencies can generate much criticism by relying on rulemaking to the exclusion of adjudication. In *United States v. Storer Broadcasting*,[48] the Federal Communications Commission issued rules barring the issuance of any additional television broadcast licenses to an applicant who already had ownership and/or control interests in more than five stations.[49] Storer argued that since under the law that created it, the FCC was supposed to award licenses based on the "public interest, convenience and necessity,"[50] it should not have made what was in effect a predetermination against Storer by promulgating such rules. Rather, it should have given Storer an opportunity to present its case (i.e., a hearing), before it could properly deny it an additional license. The Court first held that the FCC's enabling legislation gave it "general rulemaking power," so it was indeed allowed to issue the rules to which Storer objected, based on the FCC's determination that fostering competition advanced the public interest.[51] The Court then said that Storer still did have a right to a hearing, but only to review the application of the rules to Storer, to determine whether Storer could set forth "adequate reasons why the Rules should be waived or amended."[52] Otherwise, the rules as stated would remain in force.

Twenty-seven years later, in 1983, the Court relied in part on its decision in *Storer Broadcasting* to allow the Social Security Administration to use rulemaking to bypass a degree of case-by-case adjudication in deciding whether an individual is disabled for purposes of qualifying for Social Security Disability benefits.[53] In 1978, the Department of Health and Human Services (which includes the Social Security Administration) had issued regulations identifying the number of available jobs in the United States economy in various categories. If jobs are available for individuals with an applicant's "physical ability, age, education, and work experience,"[54] then that applicant is not deemed disabled. "For example . . . a significant number of jobs exist for a person who can perform light work, is closely approaching advanced age, has a limited education, but who is literate and can communicate in English, and whose previous work has been unskilled."[55] Prior to the regulation, each applicant had received an individual assessment of his or her suitability for available jobs.

The Social Security Administration found that an applicant for disability benefits was indeed disabled by her back condition to return to her job as a chambermaid in a hotel, but was not disabled for the many jobs open to persons sharing her general characteristics.[56] The Federal Court of Appeals for the Second Circuit held that since the Social Security Administration denied the applicant benefits based on the availability of jobs in a category rather than by asserting that she qualified for a particular job, it denied her "any real chance to present evidence showing that she cannot in fact perform the types of jobs" that it claims she could perform.[57]

But, the Supreme Court citing and following the logic of *Storer* said

> even where an agency's enabling statute requires it to hold a hearing, the agency may rely on its rulemaking authority to determine issues that do not require case-by-case consideration . . . A contrary holding would require the agency continually to relitigate issues that may be established fairly and efficiently in a single rulemaking proceeding.[58]

Of course, the Social Security Administration still had to make an individual assessment of the applicant's own condition and characteristics. The regulations also provided for more individualized assessments for applicants whose characteristics do not fall clearly within the categories set forth.[59] But, the decision clearly reaffirmed an agency's choice to use rulemaking to narrow the issues even when it must take particular circumstances into account.

However, when a rule seems to aim its burden on the particular and specific characteristics of one individual person or company, that person or company (in principle) can successfully challenge the rule. Rules should be based on conditions affecting classes or categories, not individuals, usually with future application, or "legislative facts." When, on the other hand, an agency attempts to impose a burden on one individual or entity, the "adjudicative facts" underlying the decision should give rise to an adjudication, not to a rule.

Thus, in *Londoner v. City and County of Denver*,[60] the Denver City Charter provided that the assessment to pay for street paving on any given property was supposed to be based on the degree of advantage each individual property would enjoy. The charter provision affected a small number of homeowners, not just one, but the Supreme Court held, contrary to a Colorado statute, that because only a small number of homeowners was targeted, any such property owner had a right to a hearing to challenge an assessment on the basis of the particular, "adjudicative" facts the owner could adduce.[61]

The Supreme Court later issued a contrasting decision, *Bi-Metallic Investment Co. v. State Board of Equalization*,[62] also arising out of Colorado, that lawyers still pair with *Londoner* to illustrate the thin line between controversies in the administrative context calling for adjudication and those calling for rulemaking.[63] "Where a rule of conduct applies to more than a few people, it is impracticable that everyone should have a direct voice in its adoption," said the Court.[64] The Court distinguished *Londoner* as dealing with "[a] relatively small number of persons . . . who were exceptionally affected, in each case upon individual grounds."[65]

WHAT AM I SUPPOSED TO DO?

Federal Inmate Credit for Time on Parole: Does the Rule Trump Call for Individual Consideration?

The federal Parole Commission has asked you for advice regarding an inmate who, after serving his fifteen-year sentence for drug dealing, committed further offenses in violation of the conditions of his parole, was returned to prison, again released on parole, and again violated his parole conditions. Under federal regulation, an inmate who violates the condition of parole loses credit for the time he spent on parole, so he must face further imprisonment for the same total period of time he would otherwise have been on parole. The statute empowering the Parole Commission to issue the regulation provided that "the Commission shall determine . . . whether all or any part of the unexpired term being served at the time of parole shall run concurrently or consecutively with the sentence imposed for the new offense . . . "

You are faced with the problem that the statute seems to request you to assess the inmate's situation individually, and come up with a specific rationale as to whether he or she should get credit for the time spent on parole, while the regulation clearly forbids you to give the inmate credit for time spent on parole. Of course, statutes trump regulations, so if the regulation is inconsistent with the statute, it must fail as *ultra vires* or "outside the power" granted to the Commission, and therefore is invalid.

How should you advise the Commission? Does the inmate simply go back to prison for all the time he or she would otherwise have been on parole, or must you write a justification for any such decision—which the inmate could then challenge in court?

The Federal Appeals Court for the Sixth Circuit addressed this issue (along with several other issues) in *Edwards v. Dewalt*.[66] As had the Supreme Court in an earlier decision,[67] the court quoted the great administrative law scholar Kenneth Culp Davis, who said

> the mandate to decide "in each case" does not prevent the Board from supplanting the original discretionary chaos with some degree of order, and the principal instruments for regularizing the system of deciding "in each case" are classifications, rules, principles, and precedents. Sensible men could not refuse to use such instruments and a sensible Congress would not expect them to.[68]

The court explained that the interpretation of "in each case," as explained by Davis and as followed by the Supreme Court in *Storer Broadcasting* and other decisions, fully informs the interpretation of the "shall determine" language in the regulation at issue. Thus, "the Commission is permitted to make its determination on an across-the-board basis, if in its discretion it decides to do so."[69]

PRACTICE PROBLEMS

PROBLEM 1: Assume that for its 25,000 welfare recipients, instead of granting a welfare benefit of $5,000 a year, terminable for cause, the state of West Dakota decided to grant a benefit of $6,000 a year, but reserved the right to suspend it for any one month out of six at will, without cause, and therefore with no reason for or right to a hearing. It has suspended the grant to Joe

Jones. Will he win his lawsuit, based on the principle established in *Londoner*, to overturn the statutory provision denying his right to a hearing?

PROBLEM 2: A statute of Jay State provided for the loss of license for "unprofessional conduct" in the practice of dentistry. The state Board of Dental Examiners had not used its rulemaking authority to interpret the statute, but on the basis of the statute itself revoked the license of a dentist who had purchased malpractice coverage for other dentists he employed in Kay State by pretending that they worked in Jay. Can the dentist's case succeed on the basis of the statute the Board of Dental Examiners used to revoke the dentist's license? The matter raised the question of whether "unprofessional conduct," as that term was used in the statute, covered his behavior. Did the Board violate the dentist's due process rights in penalizing him under the statute, without having previously issued regulations clarifying the terms of the statute? Would the results be different under the federal APA?

ENDNOTES

1. 40 S.E.C. 907 (1961).
2. 40 S.E.C. at 910, citations omitted.
3. 40 S.E.C. at 911, footnote and citations omitted.
4. 40 S.E.C. at 912, citations omitted.
5. *S.E.C. v. National Student Marketing Corporation*, 457 F. Supp. 682, 714 (D.C.D.C. 1978)
6. 457 F. Supp. at 715–6.
7. *SEC v. Chenery Corp.*, 332 U.S. 194, 202–3, 67 S. Ct. 1575, 1580 (1947).
8. 332 U.S. at 209, 67 S. Ct. at 1584.
9. 332 U.S. at 213–4, 67 S. Ct. at 1584.
10. 332 U.S. at 217–8, 67 S. Ct. at 1584.
11. *Excelsior Underwear Inc.*, 156 N.L.R.B. 1236 (1966).
12. *N.L.R.B. v. Wyman-Gordon Co.*, 394 U.S. 759, 764, 89 S. Ct. 1426, 1429 (1969).
13. *Id.*
14. 394 U.S. at 767, 89 S. Ct. at 1430.
15. See Douglas at 394 U.S. at 775, 89 S. Ct. at 1434; Harlan at 394 U.S. at 780, 89 S. Ct. at 1437.
16. *N.L.R.B. v. Bell Aerospace Co.*, 416 U.S. 267, 94 S. Ct. 1757 (1974).
17. 416 U.S. at 289, 94 S. Ct. at 1769.
18. 416 U.S. at 290, 94 S. Ct. at 1769, n. 19.
19. The *Chenery* decision reviewed in text was the second in that matter. In the first, the Supreme Court held that when an agency is challenged in court, it must defend the decision on the basis of the reasoning it used when it made the decision, not on the basis of some other argument, although on remand to the agency, it can issue a new decision with the same result based on a different argument. *SEC v. Chenery Corp.*, 318 U.S. 80 (1943).
20. 416 U.S. at 292–3, 94 S. Ct. at 1771.
21. 416 U.S. at 294, 94 S. Ct. at 1771.
22. *Bell Aerospace*, 219 N.L.R.B. 384 (1975).
23. 416 U.S. at 294, 94 S. Ct. at 1771.
24. 416 U.S. at 294, 94 S. Ct. at 1771–2.
25. William F. Fox, *Understanding Administrative Law*, 6th ed., (New Providence, NJ: Matthew Bender & Co., 2012), 158–161.
26. 29 C.F.R. 1030.
27. *Wyeth v. Levine*, 555 U.S. 555, 604, 129 S. Ct. 1187, 1217 (2009).

28. 555 U.S. at 623, 129 S. Ct. at 1228.

29. 555 U.S. at 558-560, 129 S. Ct. at 1190–2.

30. 555 U.S. at 562, 129 S. Ct. at 1192.

31. 555 U.S. at 562, 129 S. Ct. at 1193.

32. 555 U.S. at 563–4, 129 S. Ct. at 1193–4, and 555 U.S. at 573, 129 S. Ct. at 1199.

33. 555 U.S. at 567, 129 S. Ct. at 1196, quoting 21 U.S.C. § 202 of the Federal Food, Drug, and Cosmetic Act as amended in 1962; and see 555 U.S. at 574–5, 129 S. Ct. at 1200.

34. 555 U.S. at 575, 129 S. Ct. at 1200.

35. 555 U.S. at 577–8, 129 S. Ct. at 1201–2.

36. 555 U.S. at 577, 129 S. Ct. at 1201.

37. 555 U.S. at 581, 129 S. Ct. at 1204.

38. 555 U.S. at 623, 129 S. Ct. at 1228.

39. 529 U.S. 861, 120 S. Ct. 1913 (2000).

40. 555 U.S. at 623, 129 S. Ct. at 1228. See Chapter 6, text at notes 8 through 10, for a discussion of *Geier*.

41. RCW 49.17.050(4), quoted by *Rios v. Department of Labor & Industries*, 145 Wn. 2d 483, 507–8, 39 P. 2d 961, 973–4 (2002).

42. 145 Wn. 2d at 507, 39 P. 2d at 973.

43. RCW 34.05.570(4)(c)(iii), cited at 145 Wn. 2d at 505, 39 P. 2d at 972, n. 15.

44. 2012 Florida Statutes, Title X, § 120.52(16), http://www.leg.state.fl.us/Statutes/index.cfm?App_mode=Display_Statute&Search_String=&URL=0100-0199/0120/Sections/0120.52.html.

45. 2012 Florida Statutes, Title X, § 120.54(1)(a), http://www.leg.state.fl.us/Statutes/index.cfm?App_mode=Display_Statute&Search_String=&URL=0100-0199/0120/Sections/0120.54.html.

46. See, e.g., John R. Smith, The number of Florida laws, rules, and regulations is excessive, *Sun-Sentinel*, 8/3/11, http://articles.sun-sentinel.com/2011-08-03/news/fl-jscol-florida-laws-rules-smith-08020110803_1_new-laws-legal-system-rules, accessed 1/19/15.

47. 1981 MSAPA § 2-104(3).

48. *United States v. Storer Broadcasting*, 351 U.S. 192, 76 S. Ct. 763 (1956).

49. 351 U.S. at 196, 76 S. Ct. at 767, n.1, quoting Section 3.636 of the FCC rules.

50. 47 U.S.C. § 309(a).

51. 351 U.S. at 203–4, 76 S. Ct. at 770–1.

52. 351 U.S. at 205, 76 S. Ct. at 771.

53. *Heckler v. Campbell*, 461 U.S. 458; 103 S. Ct. 1952 (1983).

54. 461 U.S. at 461–2, 103 S. Ct. at 1954–5.

55. 461 U.S. at 462, 103 S. Ct. at 1955, note 4.

56. 461 U.S. at 462–3, 103 S. Ct. at 1955.

57. 461 U.S. at 464, 103 S. Ct. at 1956, quoting *Campbell v. Secretary of Dept. of Health and Human Services*, 665 F. 2d 48, 53 (1981).

58. 461 U.S. at 467, 103 S. Ct. at 1967.

59. 461 U.S. 462, 103 S. Ct. at 1955, note 5.

60. *Londoner v. City and County of Denver*, 210 U.S. 373, 28 S. Ct. 708 (1908).

61. 210 U.S. at 385–6, 28 S. Ct. at 714.

62. *Bi-Metallic Investment Co. v. State Board of Equalization*, 239 U.S. 441, 36 S. Ct. 141 (1915).

63. See, e.g., *Iowa Farm Bureau Federal v. Environmental Protection Commission*, 850 N.W. 2d 403, 417 (Iowa 2014).

64. 239 U.S. at 445, 36 S. Ct. at 142.

65. 239 U.S. at 445–6, 36 S. Ct. at 142–3.

66. *Edwards v. Dewalt*, 681 F.3d 780 (6th Cir. 2012).

67. *Am. Hosp. Assn. v. NLRB*, 499 U.S. 606, 612, 111 S. Ct. 1539, 1543 (1991).

68. 681 F. 3d at 786, quoting *Administrative Law Text*, § 6.04, page 145, 3d ed., (St. Paul, MN: West Publishing Co., 1972).

69. 681 F. 3d at 786.

Availability of Judicial Review

I n general, the operating presumption is that parties may challenge agency decisions in court. This reverses the nineteenth-century presumption to the contrary, that agency action is not reviewable unless Congress explicitly signaled its intent that it should be.

This chapter, explaining how to determine whether people can get a court to review and possibly overrule an agency action, or reverse a decision by a company regulated by an agency, involves more technical aspects of law than we encounter in any other part of this book. However, these issues are too important to ignore.

The "case" and "controversies" language of Article III Section 2 of the Constitution has been understood to mean that courts in the United States can only deal with matters that are real conflicts, between real parties, who have real interests that are really at stake. Certain legal doctrines that flesh out this understanding must be considered in determining whether an agency decision can be reviewed by the court.

Sometimes complaints that people think they can take straight to court must come to agencies for resolution first; sometimes agencies must take certain final steps before courts can hear appeals of their decisions. Various terms of art—standing, primary jurisdiction, ripeness, finality, exhaustion of administrative remedies, mootness—describe elements of these realities, which are explained below.

STANDING: HAS ACTUAL HARM OCCURRED?

The Supreme Court correctly said, "We have no power *per se* to review and annul acts of Congress on the ground that they are unconstitutional. The question may be considered only when the justification for some direct injury suffered or threatened [not merely . . . in common with people generally], presenting a justiciable issue, is made to rest upon such an act."[1] And, of course, the Court's lack of unilateral power applies to acts of agencies well.

Direct Personal Injury or Interest

In order to obtain court review, a plaintiff must have "standing": some direct personal interest, "some particularized injury that sets him apart from the man in the street."[2] For generations, this test was a bar to most consumer suits, environmental suits, and the like. That bar has been lowered, to some extent. The key questions remain: is the matter a "case or controversy"? Is there a statutory basis for or bar against judicial review? Are there special circumstances leading a court to deny standing?

So, if a doctor refuses to challenge the revocation of his medical license, revoked because the licensing board believed that he or she improperly prescribed narcotic drugs to patients, who else if anyone can challenge the revocation—his family, employees, patients, fellow physicians? If he won't challenge, courts will most likely not look kindly on challenges by others.

For many years, *Frothingham v. Mellon*,[3] a 1923 decision of the Supreme Court, stood as the last word on the subject: a mere taxpayer lacks standing to challenge the constitutionality of a federal expenditure. A successful challenge can only come from one who "has sustained or is in immediate danger of sustaining some direct injury as the result of its enforcement, and not merely that he suffers in some indefinite way in common with people generally."[4]

However, in *Flast v. Cohen*[5] the Court allowed the first exception to the *Frothingham* rule. Frothingham's effort "to be free of taxing and spending" by Congress in violation of some constitutional limitation was not enough, but Flast had a more personal claim. Flast challenged a congressional authorization of funds as a violation of the establishment clause of the First Amendment, protective of individual rights. Frothingham's complaint that an expenditure violated the Tenth Amendment's reservation of powers to the states was an "attempt[] to assert the States' interest," not her own.[6] Thus, the Court claimed to distinguish *Flast* from *Frothingham*, not to overrule the latter.

But, in *Hein v. Freedom from Religion Foundation*,[7] the Court closed the door to taxpayers at least part of the way that *Flast* had opened it. *Hein* challenged only a discretionary executive expenditure,[8] albeit again one alleged to violate the religious freedom provisions of the First Amendment. Justice Alito's majority opinion claimed that because *Flast* only offered standing to challenge a congressional expenditure authorization, the new situation did not fall under the *Flast* precedent. Justice Scalia, with whom Justice Thomas agreed, concurred in the result, but would have preferred to overrule *Flast* outright,[9] as granting standing for what he called "Psychic Injury," instead of the "Wallet Injury" that he thought should be required.[10] He summarized the point nicely: "Is a taxpayer's purely psychological displeasure that his funds are being spent in an allegedly unlawful manner ever sufficiently concrete and particularized to support Article III standing? The answer is plainly no."[11]

Taking the opposite view, Justice Brennan earlier said that "Although *Flast v. Cohen* was not a case challenging agency action, its determination of the basis for standing should resolve that question for all cases," in his concurrence in the result, but dissent to the reasoning of the 1970 *ADP* decision.[12] That decision allowed private providers of data processing services to challenge a ruling by government agency (the Office of the Comptroller of the Currency) permitting federally chartered banks to compete in that field. The

Court thought the relevant statute "arguably [included the private providers] within the zone of interests protected by it."[13] The *Flast* plaintiffs had challenged congressional action on constitutional grounds; if anything, plaintiffs challenging agency action on statutory grounds, like those in *ADP*, should have an easier time winning standing, since the Administrative Procedure Act appears to assure standing to anyone "aggrieved by agency action within the meaning of a relevant statute."[14] But, the Court's actual behavior in such cases is more complicated, as shown most clearly in its decisions on standing in environmental cases.

Environmental Cases

In 1972, the Court denied standing to the Sierra Club when it challenged a federal Forest Service decision to allow a resort to be built on federal parkland, in violation of various statutes protecting the environment, because the Sierra Club could not show that it or its members particularly and individually suffered an injury, notwithstanding its "special interest" in the matter.[15] The following year, however, in an eight-to-zero decision, probably the "high water mark" of liberal jurisprudence on standing, the Court held that an environmental group did have standing to sue based on their allegations of actual use by its members of the natural resources in the geographical area threatened by a decision by the Interstate Commerce Commission.[16]

A unanimous Court, per Justice Scalia, also granted standing in an environmental case in 1997—but to the commercial interests that, based on their economic interests, opposed the federal Fish and Wildlife Service's protection of endangered species.[17] But, Scalia, Thomas, and Alito joined Chief Justice Roberts' dissenting opinion[18] when in 2007 the Court held that Massachusetts' ownership of coastal property threatened by rising sea levels attributed to global warming gave it standing, as a "landowner" "alleg[ing] a particularized injury" to challenge the decision of the Environmental Protection Administration not to regulate emissions exacerbating such global warming.[19] To be fair, Massachusetts' argument suffered from two weaknesses: the emissions in question might have too little effect on sea levels to be noticeable in the State,[20] and courts will rarely invite challenges to an agency decision *not* to take action.[21]

Widening Access to Standing?

Furthermore, thirty years after *Flast*, the Court opened another significant door to standing, ruling that a mere voter could challenge a decision by the Federal Elections Commission (FEC).[22] The FEC's ruling that the American Israel Public Affairs Committee (AIPAC) was not a political committee as defined in the Federal Election Campaign Act of 1971 meant that it did not have to disclose its "membership, contributions, and expenditures."[23] The Court therefore ruled that voters suffered a particularized injury distinguishing them from citizens in general, because the resulting deprivation of information harmed their ability to make informed voting choices.[24]

Like *Frothingham, Flast,* and *Hein, United States v. Windsor*[25] was not primarily a matter of administrative law, but a constitutional decision with significant implications for standing. The Court's decision in that high-profile case, holding unconstitutional the Defense of Marriage Act (DOMA), further weakened traditional requirements for standing. The United States Department of Justice argued in the federal District Court for the Southern District of New York that Windsor was not entitled to a refund of estate taxes as a surviving spouse of the deceased because DOMA prohibited recognition of same-sex marriages. After the District Court ruled in Windsor's favor, the Justice Department appealed the decision to make it possible for the case to be reviewed by higher courts, but informed Congress that while it would continue to enforce DOMA, it would no longer defend it. In response, a group of members of Congress intervened to replace the Justice Department as appellant. Justice Scalia, dissenting from the Supreme Court's decision, very credibly accused the Justice Department of disingenuously "enforcing" DOMA by withholding the tax refund from Windsor only to create the illusion of a continuing "controversy," that is to create an artificial basis for standing, since the real party in interest, the United States government, no longer truly opposed Windsor.[26]

Justice Kennedy, however, writing the majority opinion for the Court, argued that the technical contest over the refund met the Article III requirement of "case" or "controversy," while the question of whether the particular members of Congress were truly a party with a "particularized interest sufficient to show 'injury in fact,'"[27] was merely "prudential," and thus could be outweighed by other important reasons to decide the matter.[28]

It is hard, therefore, to summarize just where the present Court stands on standing, so to speak. In some respects, it seems to have narrowed access, but on balance it seems to have continued the liberalization of standing requirements that the Warren Court initiated.

The 2010 MSAPA appears to suggest a more liberal approach to standing, in simply offering it to "a person aggrieved or adversely affected by the agency action" and "to anyone with standing under any other state law."[29] Justice Brennan had objected to the federal "zone of interests" test when used to bar standing for a plaintiff who had met the requirement of "injury in fact." Brennan argued that passing the "case" or "controversy" test sufficed to justify standing, and no more should be required. Whether the applicable statute actually protected against the harm the plaintiff suffered should only be a question as to the merits of the plaintiff's claim, to be answered in the course of a trial, and not a test that the court could use to avoid hearing the case.[30] While the 2010 MSAPA would appear to exclude such a test, some states use it.[31]

PRIMARY JURISDICTION

Sometimes a person or company may wish to sue without bringing the controversy before an agency. Allegheny Airlines "bumped" Ralph Nader off a flight it had overbooked. This was a bad mistake. Nader, probably "the foremost consumer advocate in the United States,"[32] sued them for fraud for accepting his payment for the original booking without warning him of the possibility that he might be forced off the flight. A federal agency, the Civil Aeronautics Board (CAB), in those days regulated the airline business, so Allegheny Airlines argued that Nader had to take the dispute to the agency for initial resolution, in other words, the agency had "primary jurisdiction." If the Board then found that the deliberate overbooking without warning was not a deceptive practice under the Board's rules, even if Nader subsequently appealed the agency's decision to a court, the court probably would have to accept the Board's finding and therefore could not hold the airline liable.[33] Congress established the agency so that it could apply its expertise to such matters. Ignoring the agency, and allowing Nader to take his case directly to court, would violate the intent of the agency's enabling legislation, argued the airline.

The Court disagreed. Often, if courts were to allow plaintiffs the sanctuary of their jurisdictions without subjecting themselves to agency procedures first, defendant companies could be squeezed between decisions of agencies that regulate them and contrary court decisions. Here, though, the Court found that no such conflict could arise, because the CAB had no rules regulating airlines overbooking anyway.[34] Even more important, in the Court's view, the CAB's enabling statute did not and could not cut off a plaintiff's ancient common-law right to seek court protection against fraud. The CAB's power to regulate "supplement[s]" but does not replace "compensatory private-law remedies" for "a breach of duty under the common law."[35]

The *Nader* decision seemed in sharp contrast with the Court's decision only three years earlier in *Ricci v. Chicago Mercantile Exchange.*[36] There, the Court refused to let the courts hear a plaintiff's antitrust claim until the Commodities Exchange Commission determined whether the defendant's action in unilaterally excluding him from its membership violated the laws the Commission was created to enforce. If the Mercantile Exchange did not violate those laws, the exclusion might be "insulated from antitrust attack."[37] The Court ruled that the Commission, an entity "especially familiar with the customs and practices of the industry and of the unique marketplace involved in this case,"[38] should make its determination before the courts could hear the antitrust claim, and stayed the court action until a court could have the benefit of the Commission's determination.[39]

Some believe that the Court legitimately distinguished *Nader* in that the CAB had no special competence to assess Nader's cause of action although they would have had special competence to assess his cause of action had it been simply for his damages resulting from the "bumping."[40] However, agencies have no more competence to assess antitrust actions than courts do; prior to court review, the CAB could have added just as much value by determining whether "bumping" was not a deceptive practice. It seems more likely, then, that a particular clause in the CAB's enabling legislation, guaranteeing that it would not "abridge or alter the remedies now existing at common law or by statute," accounted for the difference.[41] Even so, the *Nader* decision may have been merely aberrational.

In *AT&T v. Central Office Telephone*,[42] the Court required Central Office Telephone, a small telephone company, to have its complaint assessed by the Federal Communications Commission before it could seek court review. The Court claimed that the "filed-rate doctrine," dealing with rates telephone companies could charge, covered all aspects of the contractual relationship between telephone rates and services provided, and this gave the FCC primary jurisdiction.[43] In reality, though, Central Office Telephone tried to sue partly because AT&T tried to steal its customers by telemarketing to them, a practice known as "slamming." Central Office Telephone made a very strong argument that the legal nature of its claim for intentional interference with its business relationships constituted a tort claim, entirely independent of any contractual relationship between itself and AT&T. Justice Stevens, dissenting, cited *Nader* in support of its argument that the FCC should not have primary jurisdiction over that tort claim.[44] With the majority's refusal to acknowledge *Nader*'s relevance, its holding now appears to have been entirely dependent on the savings clause in the relevant statute; but, even when enabling statutes for other agencies include a similar clause, the Court is likely to continue to ignore *Nader*.

"RIPENESS" FOR REVIEW

Assuming, as is usually the case, that the relevant agency has primary jurisdiction, and the complainant has standing, when can the complainant appeal the agency's decision to a court?

In 1962, Congress required generic names on drug labels. Pursuant to that statute, the Food and Drug Administration (FDA) issued a regulation requiring a generic name to be used every time a drug's trade name was used. Abbott Laboratories sued on behalf of a class of pharmaceutical manufacturers, seeking to enjoin the FDA from enforcing the rule, arguing that it exceeded the agency's authority.[45]

The requirement that a case must be "ripe for review" before a court may hear it means that agencies' actions must first have adverse effect, concreteness, and imminence. If rights or obligations have been determined by the agency action, or legal consequences will flow from it, then a court will hear the complaint. In the *Abbott Laboratories* case, Justice Harlan for the Court, explained that the ripeness doctrine was intended

> to prevent the courts, through avoidance of premature adjudication, from entangling themselves in abstract disagreements over administrative policies, and also to protect the agencies from judicial interference until an administrative decision has been formalized and its effects felt in a concrete way by the challenging parties.[46]

Here, though, laboratories must "change all their labels, advertisements, and promotional materials; . . . and . . . invest heavily in new printing type and new supplies"; or else risk "serious criminal and civil penalties."[47] So the case was "ripe for review."

The same day, though, in *Toilet Goods Association v. Gardner*, the Court refused review of another FDA rule, this time allowing the FDA to stop the sale of color additives to food by suspending certification of the additive, if its manufacturer refused to allow FDA inspectors access to its premises. In the Court's view, requiring pharmaceutical manufacturers to allow FDA inspectors into their factories did not impose a heavy burden on them: all they had to do was to let the inspectors in. And if they refused, and lost access to the market when the FDA suspended certification, they could "promptly challenge[]" the suspension "through an administrative procedure, which in turn is reviewable by a court."[48]

Sixteen years later, over a strong dissent, the Court majority held that the petitioners' case in *National Park Hospitality Assn. v. Dept. of Interior* did not meet the standards for ripeness set by the *Abbott Laboratories* and *Toilet Goods Association* decisions.[49] In 1978, Congress had enacted a law providing that a government contractor unhappy with the relevant agency's dealings regarding the contractor and unhappy with the response of the agency's contract officer to its complaints, could appeal the decision either to the federal Court of Claims or to the agency's administrative appeals board. If still dissatisfied, the contractor could appeal a decision by either of those bodies to the federal Court of Appeals for the District of Columbia Circuit. In 1998, the National Park Service issued a regulation purporting to exclude disputes with those companies it permitted to sell concessions in national parks from the reach of that law. A trade association representing such concessionaires and a few of its members sued the Department of the Interior (of which the National Park Service is a bureau), seeking a declaratory judgment that the regulation violated the terms of the law and was therefore invalid.[50]

The Court distinguished the situation of the concessionaires from that of the pharmaceutical manufacturers in *Abbott Laboratories*: the National Park Service regulation did not actually require the concessionaires to do anything, while the FDA regulation required the manufacturers to change the labels on their drugs and take other costly measures. The Court opined that the "concessionaires suffer no practical harm" from the regulation and thus were not even as burdened as the food manufacturers in *Toilet Goods Association*, who themselves were found to suffer too little immediate or irreversible harm to meet the ripeness requirements for judicial review.[51]

The dissent, however, cited the findings of a congressional committee that application of the 1978 law lowered costs for contractors and even the perception of its applicability influenced potential contractors to offer lower bids. Thus, the stance of the National Park Service in asserting that the 1978 law did not apply to its concession contracts meant that concessionaires seeking renewal of contracts would face increased costs[52]—an "immediate concrete harm," rendering the matter "ripe for judicial review."[53]

The majority, however, characterized the dissent's view as claiming that "mere uncertainty as to the validity of a legal rule constitutes a hardship for purposes of the ripeness analysis," and rejected it,[54] concluding that "judicial resolution of the question presented here should await a concrete dispute about a particular concession contract."[55]

The D.C. Circuit Court nicely summarized the balancing test for ripeness, pitting "the petitioner's interest in prompt consideration of alleging unlawful agency action" against "the agency's interest in crystallizing its policy before that policy is subjected to judicial review" and "the court's interest in avoiding unnecessary adjudication and [in] deciding issues in a concrete setting."[56]

FINAL ORDER RULE: HAS THE AGENCY TAKEN ITS FINAL STEP?

In 1973, the Federal Trade Commission issued a complaint against Standard Oil of California (Socal) for unfair competition. Within the FTC's own administrative process, Socal argued that the FTC had no grounds for its allegation and should drop the complaint. The FTC disagreed, and proceeded with charges against Socal in a hearing before one of its administrative law judges. Socal exhausted all administrative remedies available to get the FTC to withdraw its complaint (the exhaustion requirement is explained in further detail below), and then sought judicial review. The APA permits judicial review for "final agency action for which there is no other adequate remedy in a court," and for other agency actions only in the context of review of final agency action.[57]

The Court explained that exhaustion of administrative remedies does not satisfy the APA's finality rule: the FTC initiated proceedings against Socal, but until the FTC's administrative law judges made their decision, and the FTC's commissioners affirmed or reversed that decision after an appeal by the losing party, the FTC's decision could not be deemed "final." Issuing a complaint, or "complaining," isn't final; the FTC's action would be final only if it ruled in favor of its staff's complaint. In *Abbott Laboratories* and even in its companion cases, the agency actions in question—the promulgation of regulations—were clearly final.[58] The FTC initiated proceedings against Socal based on its "reason to believe" it was violating the applicable statute; but Socal's ability to challenge that belief within the agency's own procedures distinguished its situation from that of Abbott Labs, who truly faced "final" agency action.[59] (Although the Court did not address ripeness *per* se, it also noted that, while responding to charges clearly imposed some burden on Socal, it did not impose nearly as heavy a burden as the FDA's regulation imposed on Abbott Labs.[60]) The Court offered a succinct summary of the rationale behind the final order rule:

> Judicial intervention into the agency process denies the agency an opportunity to correct its own mistakes and to apply its expertise . . . Intervention also leads to piecemeal review which at the least is inefficient and upon completion of the agency process might prove to have

been unnecessary ... Furthermore, unlike the review in Abbott Laboratories, judicial review to determine whether the Commission decided that it had the requisite reason to believe would delay resolution of the ultimate question whether the Act was violated. Finally, every respondent to a Commission complaint could make the claim that Socal had made. Judicial review of the averments in the Commission's complaints should not be a means of turning prosecutor into defendant before adjudication concludes. [Citations omitted.][61]

The 2010 MSAPA uses the phrase "final agency action," excludes from its definition "agency action that is a failure to act," and makes it prerequisite to judicial review,[62] consistent with federal case law.

EXHAUSTION OF ADMINISTRATION REMEDIES: HAS THE PRIVATE PARTY USED EVERY KIND OF RECOURSE THE AGENCY MAKES AVAILABLE?

Ordinarily, when a party is involved in a case before an agency, the party must exhaust all appeal rights at the agency before bringing the agency's final determination to a court for appeal. But, sometimes the plaintiff claims that the agency lacks legal jurisdiction altogether and that it is therefore unfair to require the plaintiff to go through what may be an expensive and time-consuming process of exhausting the administrative process. Over a century ago, in *U.S. v. Sing Tuck*, persons of Chinese descent claiming citizenship argued that immigration officers had no authority to determine whether they should be excluded from the United States. The Court, however, decided that the initial question of whether they were indeed citizens was properly within the jurisdiction of the immigration officers. Holmes wrote for the majority that "even fundamental questions should be determined in an orderly way."[63] Similarly, in *Myers v. Bethlehem Shipbuilding Corp.*, the Court insisted on a hearing before the National Labor Relations Board despite an employer's argument that he did not engage in interstate or foreign commerce and therefore did not fall under NLRB jurisdiction.[64]

The exhaustion rule serves to "avoid[] ... premature interruption of the administrative process" so as to "allow the agency to make a factual record [which would be helpful to a court should it eventually review the agency's decision], or to exercise its discretion or apply its expertise." Further, it reflects respect for the somewhat independent role of agencies pursuant to congressional intent, giving them a chance to "discover and correct [their] own errors"; and reduces the judicial caseload to the extent that many agency decisions will ultimately satisfy the parties, without necessitating recourse to courts.[65]

But, courts have refused to apply the exhaustion rule in cases unlike *Sing Tuck* and *Myers* when they agree with the petitioner that the agency in question lacks jurisdiction; if there is no meaningful possibility that the agency will or can grant the relief sought; if the petitioner will otherwise suffer irreparable harm; if administrative handling will unduly prejudice later court action (for example by imposing too much delay); or if the central question rests on the constitutionality of the agency's enabling statute.

In *McCarthy v. Madigan*, for example, McCarthy sued the federal prisons for damages, claiming violations of the Eighth Amendment's prohibition of cruel and unusual punishment on the basis of indifference to his medical needs. The government argued that he had not exhausted his administrative remedies. The Court, however, ruled that since the administrative process offered no real opportunity for a prisoner to win "money damages," it would allow his court case to proceed.[66]

In view of the heavy volume of prisoner lawsuits, Congress subsequently enacted legislation explicitly imposing exhaustion prerequisite to federal court review. It left open, however, the question of whether the federal courts could review a particular claim for which administrative remedies were exhausted when other claims in the lawsuit were not. The Court ruled that they could.[67]

Further, when no statute or agency rule requires exhaustion of administrative remedies, so long as the challenger meets the final order requirement, courts cannot withhold judicial review on the argument that the challenger should have availed himself or herself of an internal agency appeals process. Since under the rules of the Department of Housing and Urban Development a decision by one of its administrative law judges becomes final if it is not appealed within fifteen days, the Court permitted judicial review of HUD's decision to exclude a real estate developer from its housing programs despite his failure to appeal the result of its hearing process.[68]

However, the mere presence of a constitutional claim among others will not qualify a challenger for an exception to the exhaustion requirement. To qualify, the challenger must show that otherwise "the agency would violate a clear right of the petitioner by disregarding a specific and unambiguous statutory, regulatory, or constitutional directive."[69]

MOOTNESS: HAS THE MATTER BEEN RESOLVED?

A party may have had standing at one time, because he or she could allege a particularized injury resulting from the behavior of the defendant. However, at a later time the injury could cease to exist. Thus, a taxpayer sued the IRS claiming that it wrongfully assessed her for unpaid taxes and withheld a tax refund due her. By the time the courts resolved the matter, the IRS had abandoned its claim against her and was under court order to pay her refund. The Fifth Circuit therefore dismissed her claims against the IRS in this regard as moot.[70]

However, courts find an exception to the mootness requirement when a particular type of harm is "capable of repetition, but evad[es] review" because no individual complainant will likely continue to experience it before a court can resolve the issue. Thus, the Second Circuit refused to dismiss a lawsuit by female prison inmates (individually and on behalf of other female inmates) seeking to compel the New York State Department of Correctional Services to institute measures to protect them against sexual abuse and harassment, even though those particular inmates had been released from prison.[71]

IMPORTANCE OF THESE LEGAL "TECHNICALITIES"

To discern whether or when a course may hear a complaint about an agency-related matter, it may be necessary to delve into the legal "thicket." These technical legal issues often determine whether or not you will have your day in court. Thus, while they demand more "lawyerly" analysis than non-lawyers may ordinarily wish to apply, the importance of the result justifies the effort.

WHAT AM I SUPPOSED TO DO?

State Inmate Assault Victim: Will Failure to Exhaust Administrative Remedies Defeat Inmate's Claim Against State?

Once again, imagine yourself as a prison official, this time as deputy to a state Commissioner of corrections (the criminal justice system also generates a great deal of civil litigation, often in the administrative context). That State Department of Correction includes only one prison facility, which is filled to capacity. A few days after his incarceration at the facility, an inmate told his caseworker that he feared assault by another inmate. The caseworker told him that there was no alternative space available to relocate him at that time, but he should apply for a transfer to a different location, and meanwhile the staff member would warn the sergeant in his location of the possible danger. Two days afterward, he was indeed assaulted, and suffered serious head injuries. After spending a few days in the prison infirmary, he was then moved to a special unit where he was not in danger of assault, but where he also lacked access to the prison handbook. The manual detailed the procedure for filing grievances, including a provision requiring such a filing no later than fifteen days after the incident that is the subject of the complaint, and a provision requiring the inmate to solve the problem through informal means before filing the grievance.

The inmate filed his grievance about six weeks after his initial expression of concern to the staff member and the subsequent assault. Anticipating the objection that he had not filed in a timely manner, he noted that the assault having occurred shortly after his arrival, he had not had time to familiarize himself with the contents of the prison handbook. The grievance officer nevertheless rejected the filing, claiming that the inmate failed to meet the requirements of the two provisions of the handbook cited above. The inmate appealed, but the appeals unit upheld the grievance officer's ruling. At the next level of appeal, the prison warden also upheld the ruling. The inmate has now appealed the decision to the Commissioner, his final internal level of appeal. If the Commissioner upholds the ruling as well, the inmate will likely file a Section 1983 Civil Rights Act complaint in court, alleging Eighth Amendment violations. If so, the Commissioner would seek summary judgment—an immediate dismissal of the claim—based on the inmate's failure to exhaust administrative remedies (as prescribed in the prison handbook), as required under the Prison Litigation Reform Act of 1996.

However, should the court refuse summary judgment, the case would proceed to trial. Even if the court ultimately ruled against the inmate, such a trial would illuminate prison administration difficulties to the discomfort of the Commissioner and the Department. How should you advise the Commissioner? How much risk of a trial will he incur if he upholds the ruling? Is avoiding that risk worth demoralizing the warden and the staff by reversing their decisions, and setting a bad precedent in bypassing the requirements of the prison handbook?

The federal District Court for the District of Maine faced that issue in 2014. While the ultimate outcome of the case remains uncertain as of this writing, the U.S. Magistrate Judge for the District recommended that the court deny the motion for summary judgment.[72] The inmate presented an issue of fact in asserting that his placement in the special unit following the attack gave him no access to the prison handbook; it is unclear without further evidence whether that "placement prevented him from filing the grievance within the applicable 15-day period."[73] If it did, then the inmate might successfully argue that he did not have access to the administrative remedies he was supposed to exhaust. The Prison Litigation Reform Act only requires inmates to exhaust "such administrative remedies *as are available* [emphasis added]."[74] If administrative remedies are not available, the Act does not bar lawsuits based on the alleged grievance. However, in a footnote, the Magistrate recommended a pretrial conference on certain issues, and made some references to the potential for a motion to dismiss the case.[75] Thus, while it is by no means certain that the Department will be subjected to a trial, it is equally certain that the Commissioner cannot simply count on summary judgment or a motion to dismiss under such circumstances.

PRACTICE PROBLEM

Under federal anti-discrimination laws and its own regulatory Code, the Internal Revenue Service was supposed to deny tax exempt status to racially discriminatory private schools in school districts subject to court-ordered desegregation. Plaintiffs were parents of black public school students who alleged that the tax exemption allowed tax-deductible contributions supporting such schools, attracting white students out of the public schools, and thus thwarting federal school integration policy. The children of these plaintiffs had not themselves applied for admission to the schools that discriminated against black children. Do their parents have standing to sue for enforcement of federal law against the private schools?

ENDNOTES

1. *Frothingham v. Mellon*, 262 U.S. 447, 488, 43 S. Ct. 597 (1923).
2. *U.S. v. Richardson*, 418 U.S. 166, 194, 94 S. Ct. 2940, 2955 (1974).
3. 262 U.S. 447, 43 S. Ct. 597.
4. 262 U.S. at 488, 43 S. Ct. at 601.
5. *Flast v. Cohen*, 392 U.S. 83, 88 S. Ct. 1942 (1968).
6. 392 U.S. at 105, 88 S. Ct. at 1955.
7. *Hein v. Freedom from Religious Foundation*, 551 U.S. 587, 127 S. Ct. 2553 (2007).
8. 551 U.S. at 609, 127 S. Ct. at 2568.
9. 551 U.S. at 618, 127 S. Ct. at 2573–4.
10. 551 U.S. at 619–20, 127 S. Ct. at 2574–5.
11. 551 U.S. at 633, 127 S. Ct. at 2583.
12. *Association of Data Processing Services v. Camp*, 397 U.S. 150, 90 S. Ct. 827 (1970). Brennan's opinion actually appears as part of a companion case, *Barlow v. Collins*, 397 U.S. 159, 90 S. Ct. 832, at 397 U.S. at 167, 170, 90 S. Ct. at 838.
13. 397 U.S. at 156, 90 S. Ct. at 831.
14. Section 702.
15. *Sierra Club v. Morton*, 405 U.S. 727, 738–9, 92 S. Ct. 1361, 1367–8 (1972).
16. *United States v. Students Challenging Regulatory Agency Procedures*, 412 U.S. 669, 683–4, 93 S. Ct. 2405, 2414 (1973).
17. *Bennett v. Spear*, 520 U.S. 154, 166, 117 S. Ct. 1154, 1163 (1997).
18. *Massachusetts v. EPA*, 549 U.S. 497, 535, 127 S. Ct. 1438, 1463 (2007).
19. 549 U.S. at 522–3, 127 S. Ct. at 1456.
20. The majority acknowledges these weaknesses at 549 U.S. at 523–4, 127 S. Ct. at 1457; the dissent argues that they should compel a different result at 549 U.S. at 541–2, 127 S. Ct. at 1467–8.
21. The majority acknowledges this weaknesses at 549 U.S. at 527, 127 S. Ct. at 1459; Scalia's separate supplemental dissent argues that it should compel a different result at 549 U.S. at 549, 127 S. Ct. at 1471–2.
22. *FEC v. Atkins*, 524 U.S. 11, 118 S. Ct. 1777 (1998).
23. 524 U.S. at 13, 118 S. Ct. at 1780–1.
24. 524 U.S. at 21, 118 S. Ct. at 1784. Justice Souter, dissenting in the later *Hein* decision (see text above at notes 7 through 11), thought that the logic of *FEC v. Atkins* ("where the harm is concrete, though widely shared, the Court has found 'injury in fact.'" 524 U.S. at 24, 118 S. Ct. at 1786) should have required the Court to find standing for the Freedom from Religion Foundation in *Hein*. Souter's dissent, quoting *FEC v. Atkins*, in *Hein*, 551 U.S. at 642, 127 S. Ct. at 2587, note 3.
25. *United States v. Windsor*, 570 U.S. ___, 133 S. Ct. 2675, 186 L. Ed. 2d 808 (2013).
26. 133 S. Ct. at 2699, 186 L. Ed. 2d at 834.
27. 133 S. Ct. at 2687–8, 186 L. Ed. 2d at 820–2.
28. 133 S. Ct. at 2867, 186 L. Ed. 2d at 821.
29. 2010 MSAPA § 505.
30. Dissent in *Barlow v. Collins*, 397 U.S. 159, 168–9, 90 S. Ct. 832, 838 (1970).
31. Michael Asimow and Ronald M. Levin, *State and Federal Administrative Law*, 4th ed., (St. Paul, MN: West Publishing Company, 2014), 759.
32. Morgan Pehme, Corporate America's Worst Nightmare: A Q&A With Ralph Nader, *City and State*, 5/30/14, http://www.cityandstateny.com/2/92/interviews-and-profiles/corporate-americas-worst-nightmare-a-q-and-a-with-ralph-nader.html#.U-PVaaOHjYU, accessed 8/7/14.
33. *Nader v. Allegheny Airlines, Inc.*, 426 U.S. 290, 298, 96 Sup. Ct. 1978, 1984 (1976).
34. 426 U.S. at 299–300, 96 S. Ct. at 1984–5.
35. 426 U.S. at 301–2, 96 S. Ct. at 1986.
36. *Ricci v. Chicago Mercantile Exchange*, 409 U.S. 289, 93 S. Ct. 573 (1973).
37. 409 U.S. at 303, 93 S. Ct. at 581.

38. 409 U.S. at 305, 93 S. Ct. at 582.

39. 409 U.S. at 307–8, 93 S. Ct. at 583.

40. William F. Fox, *Understanding Administrative Law*, 6th ed., (New Providence, NJ: Matthew Bender, 2012), 315.

41. 426 U.S. at 298, 96 S. Ct. at 1984.

42. *AT&T v. Central Office Telephone*, 524 U.S. 214, 118 S. Ct. 1956 (1998).

43. 524 U.S. at 223, 118 S. Ct. at 1963.

44. 524 U.S. at 231, 233-4, 118 S. Ct. at 1967, 1967–8.

45. *Abbott Laboratories v. Gardner*, 387 U.S. 136, 87 S. Ct. 1507 (1967).

46. 387 U.S. at 148–9, 87 S. Ct. at 1515.

47. 387 U.S. at 152–3, 87 S. Ct. at 1517.

48. *Toilet Goods Association v. Gardner*, 387 U.S. 158, 165, 87 S. Ct. 1520, 1525 (1967).

49. *National Park Hospitality Assn. v. Dept. of Interior*, 538 U.S. 803, 123 S. Ct. 2026 (2003).

50. 538 U.S. at 804–7, 103 S. Ct. at 2028–9.

51. 538 U.S. at 810, 103 S. Ct. at 2031. The decision, along with the concurrence by Justice Stevens and the dissent by Justice Breyer, joined by Justice O'Connor, also engages in a controversy concerning standing, which only the concurrence would deny.

52. 538 U.S. at 818–9, 103 S. Ct. at 2035–6.

53. 538 U.S. at 819, 103 S. Ct. at 2036.

54. 538 U.S. at 811, 103 S. Ct. at 2032.

55. 538 U.S. at 812, 103 S. Ct. at 2032.

56. *Better Government Association v. Department of State*, 780 F. 2d 86, 92 (D.C. Cir. 1986).

57. Section 704.

58. See, e.g., 387 U.S. at 162, 87 S. Ct. at 1524.

59. *FTC v. Standard Oil Company of California*, 449 U.S. 232, 241, 101 S. Ct. 488, 493–4 (1980).

60. 449 U.S. at 242, 101 S. Ct. at 494.

61. 449 U.S. at 242–3, 101 S. Ct. at 494.

62. 2010 MSAPA § 501.

63. 194 U.S. 161, 168, 24 S. Ct. 621, 623 (1904).

64. *Myers v. Bethlehem Shipbuilding Corp.*, 303 U.S. 41, 58 S. Ct. 459 (1938).

65. *McKart v. United States*, 395 U.S. 185, 193–5, 89 Sup. Ct. 1657, 1662–3 (1969).

66. *McCarthy v. Madigan*, 503 U.S. 140, 156, 112 S. Ct. 1081, 1092 (1992).

67. *Jones v. Bock*, 549 U.S. 199, 127 S. Ct. 910 (2007).

68. *Darby v. Cisneros*, 509 U.S. 137, 113 S. Ct. 2539 (1993).

69. *Hunt v. CFTC*, 591 F. 2d 1234, 1236 (7th Cir. 1979).

70. *Looney v. United States*, 336 Fed. Appx. 434, 436 (5th Cir. 2009).

71. *Amador v. Andrews*, 655 F. 3d 89, 101 (2nd Cir. 2011).

72. *Bean v. Barnhart*, 2014 U.S. Dist. LEXIS 66277 (D. Maine).

73. 2014 U.S. Dist. LEXIS 66277 at *18.

74. 42 U.S.C. § 1997e(a).

75. 2014 U.S. Dist. LEXIS 66277 at *19, note 6.

12

Suing Government Agencies and Employees

"**P**rivate actions constitute a kind of control on action of administrative agencies,"[1] so any review of the sources and limits of agency power must include a discussion of sovereign immunity and officer tort liability.

SOVEREIGN IMMUNITY—THE KING (U.S. GOVERNMENT?) CAN DO NO WRONG?

By resolution, the Pennsylvania "state congress" ordered goods useful to the British to be hidden. The effort failed: the British found and seized the plaintiff's "hidden" 227 barrels of flour, for which he subsequently sued the Commonwealth of Pennsylvania. The court reminded those who might read its decision that "The Lord Mayor of London, in 1666, when the city was on fire, would not give directions for, or consent to, the pulling down of forty wooden houses, or to removing the furniture, &c. belonging to the Lawyers of the Temple, then on the Circuit, for fear he should be answerable for a trespass; and in consequence of this conduct half that great city was burnt."[2] The court was making the point, of course, that those government officials who must make decisions, especially in perilous times, must not hesitate for fear of losing a lawsuit, and therefore should not be held liable in such circumstances. The court did not use the words "sovereign immunity," but that was the principle it applied, so the plaintiff lost.[3]

It strikes some people as odd that the United States, born out of democratic revolution against a monarchy, retained in its law the doctrine of sovereign immunity, originally based on the idea that the King can do no wrong. Although courts usually justified it on the grounds that fear of lawsuits could deter appropriate government action, and actual lawsuits could unacceptably interfere with or delay government action, distinguished legal scholars have argued that "it is inconsistent with the United States Constitution" and should be abolished[4]; and that "[i]t simply does not mesh well with the rule of law."[5] Nonetheless, as early as 1821 Chief Justice Marshall wrote that "[t]he universally received opinion is, that no suit can be commenced or prosecuted against the United States; that the judiciary act does not authorize such suits" (although the federal government remained liable in the context of certain legal actions, not technically considered lawsuits).[6] Indeed, Justice Iredell wrote in 1793 that there was no provision authorizing lawsuits against a state "when the Constitution was adopted, or at the time the judicial act was passed."[7] A 1999 decision reaffirmed the sovereign immunity of states, throwing out provisions of the federal Fair Labor Standards Act that would have allowed state employees to sue their states for unpaid overtime compensation.[8] Although Iredell had made his comment in a dissent, the 1999 decision relied on it in part, as did the majority opinion in an 1890 decision, which noted that "The suability of a state without its consent was a thing unknown to law."[9] Thus, despite its anachronistic character, sovereign immunity remains firmly ensconced in American law.

Exceptions to Sovereign Immunity

However, from the very beginning Congress found ways to compensate private parties injured by their dealings with government. At the beginning, it just used "private" legislation—bills enacted each with the purpose of reimbursing individuals for their losses. Later, in 1887, under the Tucker Act, Congress established the federal Court of Claims, waiving sovereign immunity in situations where the government violated its contractual obligations,[10] presumably so that private contractors would agree to do business with the federal government. Congress created that court under its Article I powers, and can limit or abolish it at will.

Congress enacted the 1946 Federal Tort Claims Act to escape the burden of private bills it was still enacting to compensate individuals for injuries not covered by the 1884 legislation allowing lawsuits by contractors. Thus, the 1946 Act permitted certain suits against the federal government in Article III courts for certain tortious actions (wrongful actions, like negligent or purposeful infliction of damage against persons or property) of its employees if committed within the scope of their employment. However, numerous exceptions to the Tort Claims Act leave the federal government immune from huge categories of lawsuits, including claims based on discretionary functions, policymaking, military combat, and such torts as assault, battery, libel, slander, misrepresentation, and interference with contract, among others.[11]

The Administrative Procedure Act was amended in 1976 to bar sovereign immunity as a defense against suits for relief against the United States government, but limits the waiver to suits **not** seeking money damages, and also explicitly denies that it "confers authority to grant relief" forbidden by any other statute.[12] Article III courts, those under the judicial power, handle such suits as well.

Innocent Victims of Government Policy Cannot Win

Sovereign immunity retains its importance. Supreme Court decisions in key cases under the Federal Tort Claims Act implicate important policy decisions. In *Laird v. Nelms*,[13] for example, homeowners sued the government for damage to their homes caused by the sonic booms from military aircraft. The Court found that the Federal Tort Claims Act was intended to allow compensation for injuries resulting from "intentionally wrongful or careless conduct of Government employees," but not from "the ultrahazardous nature of an activity undertaken by the Government,"[14] on the theory that government officials had determined, as a matter of policy, that the interest of the country required them to allow such activity. Justice Stewart, dissenting,[15] argued that the words "negligent or wrongful act or omission" in the statute could indeed include such ultrahazardous activity. He further noted that the Act provides for liability when under the law of the state in which it occurred a private party would have been liable for the activity; and under the law of North Carolina, the state in question, a private party would indeed have been liable.[16] Stewart, in essence, urged no-fault social insurance by the government for victims of administrative accidents: absolute liability at least for those actions for which private parties would be liable. If government has acted on the belief that society as a whole benefits from its actions, a small number of private parties should not have to bear the cost. As the benefits are spread over the population, so should be the costs. If government bore the burden of liability, it would spread the costs over the population by taxation.[17]

But, unlike France and Germany, the United States and Great Britain have not adopted this approach.[18]

The majority in *Laird v. Nelms* had cited *Dalehite v. United States,*[19] in support of its rejection of the imposition of strict liability on the federal government. Stewart noted that *Dalehite* depended for its logic on the need to protect the exercise of "policy judgment and decision" from the chilling effect of liability, but here the question was simply one of fairly allocating the financial burden, not "whether Government officials acted irresponsibly or illegally," and therefore should have had no bearing on the decision.[20]

In *Dalehite*, the majority had characterized the cause of the massive damage (hundreds of deaths, thousands of injuries, and vast property damage from an explosion of fertilizer about to be shipped from a port in Texas as part of a foreign aid program) as a policy decision, thus coming under the "discretionary function" exception to the Federal Tort Claims Act. The trial court found that the disaster resulted from negligence. The decision in *Dalehite* had drawn a stinging dissent from Justice Jackson, joined by Black and Frankfurter.[21] The dissent argued that the cause was negligent behavior, not negligent "policy decisions." Clearly, were this kind of negligence the fault of private parties, it would incur liability. Therefore, said the dissent, so should this.[22]

Two years thereafter, Frankfurter wrote a decision (in which he was joined by Black; Jackson had died in 1954) implicitly validating the dissent in *Dalehite*, although he claimed that the difference in facts justified the difference in outcome from that case.[23] When a ship ran aground and suffered damage to its cargo because the Coast Guard did not properly check or maintain the light at a lighthouse or issue a warning that it was not functioning, the Court held that although the government must escape liability for the negligent "exercise of judgment" under the Federal Tort Claims Act exceptions, it cannot escape liability for negligence at "the 'operational level' of government activity," as in the matter at hand.[24]

The Line Between Government Negligence and Government Policy

But, the Court drew a fine line between cases when the "operational level" of government activity includes the negligent "exercise of judgment" and when it does not. In the *Varig Airlines* case, the Court held that the Federal Aviation Administration's "spot check" safety inspection of airplanes, where its inspectors cannot inspect everything and must make choices as to where they will inspect, requires the exercise of policy discretion and thus falls under the exception[25]; in *Berkovitz v. United States*,[26] it held that FDA regulators had no discretionary authority to fail to test the particular lot of vaccines which resulted in a child's contracting polio and therefore were not immune from liability.[27]

Even Kenneth Culp Davis, the giant of administrative law scholarship who wrote the influential law review article Sovereign Immunity Must Go,[28] acknowledged that it must be retained for the results of policy decisions. As a more recent scholar put it, "government must be able to make difficult political choices without the threat that any resulting loss will be charged to the public purse by court order [citation omitted]."[29] Nevertheless, sovereign immunity continues to draw courts into troubling decisions.[30] Where the government may well have been negligent in failing to repair or warn about a hole in a federally owned pier causing injury, the courts applied the discretionary function exception to the results of this "public policy" decision that it was too expensive to fix the pier surface.[31] Similarly, where the Occupational Safety and Health Administration inspectors appeared to have negligently failed to inspect a defective machine during their tour of a plant, and the defect later caused serious injuries to a worker, OSHA's decision to do a less-than-thorough inspection fell under the discretionary function exception as well, as the result of a decision based in "policy considerations."[32]

Between the 1950s and the 1980s, the states are said to have virtually abandoned the doctrine of sovereign immunity.[33] However, that's what the federal government was said to have done when it enacted the Federal Tort Claims Act. Clearly, the doctrine still lives.

OFFICER TORT LIABILITY OR IMMUNITY

The government employee, classically, has not been given personal immunity from liability for behavior "outside the scope" of the employee's authority. The underlying logic of this premise is sound: the mere fact of holding government employment should not create liability for otherwise illegal acts. But, at one time determinations as to the scope of authority were made very narrowly. In the famous old case of *Miller v. Horton*,[34] members of a local board of health found that a horse had the disease called "glanders," and ordered it destroyed. The court found that the horse in fact did not have glanders and held that the plaintiff, the horse's owner, could therefore collect damages from the board. Oliver Wendell Holmes Jr., writing for the Supreme Judicial Court of Massachusetts, said that the defense of legality did not apply because the statute limited the powers of the board to a horse "actually having the glanders."[35]

This sort of decision, with its obviously inhibiting effect on the enthusiasm with which government officials pursue their responsibilities in making good faith decisions, has gradually been abandoned. Now, if the official was without fault, the action would be considered within the scope of duty, not *ultra vires*, legal, and therefore not actionable. This modern approach has been extended to cover cases even where the officer was negligent. But, such liability did not apply to judges, perhaps ever. Long before Holmes found the board of health liable, courts gave themselves immunity from liability for actions performed in the course of their work, as "a general principle of the highest importance to the administration of justice . . ."[36] Of course, in addition to self-interest, logic does support the point, in its usefulness in promoting "a fearless administration of the law."[37] Legislators and government officials who make policy have long enjoyed immunity from liability for torts committed in the exercise of their authority.[38]

In *Barr v. Mateo*,[39] for example, the Acting Director of the Office of Rent Stabilization put defamatory material in a press release he issued. However, the Court found his action "absolutely privileged," since such officials should not be inhibited in their function by fear of liability for damages, even, as in that case, in the "outer perimeter"[40] of their duties. The plurality opinion by Justice Harlan quoted Learned Hand's explanation from a decision ten years earlier. Hand had argued for the protection of officials who at least thought they were acting within the scope of their official duties. Otherwise, "the burden of a trial" to determine whether the complaints against them were or were not truly justified, and "the inevitable danger of its outcome, would dampen the ardor of all but the most resolute, or most irresponsible, in the unflinching discharge of their duties."[41]

But, lower-level government employees, those who simply carried out the policies determined by others, with merely "ministerial" responsibility, did not enjoy such immunity. In 1952, taking pity on one such longtime government employee, the 82nd Congress enacted Private Law 820 to reimburse a Post Office employee who had to pay the victim of his negligence in driving a mail truck.[42] Two years later, though, the Supreme Court signaled a different direction in *United States v. Gilman*.[43] The federal government had paid damages to the private citizen who suffered damage from a collision with a car driven by a government employee for the U.S. Coast and Geodetic Survey. The Court refused to let the federal government reimburse itself by collecting from its employee. The Court ostensibly rested its decision on the grounds that the Federal Tort Claims Act did not impose such liability (or preclude it), and Congress, not the Court (or the agency), was the proper institution to make the judgment as to whether such liability should be imposed.[44] It may well have reflected, however, *inter alia*, Professor Davis's argument that in the course of many years of driving for the government, one negligent error could happen to anyone, and should not result in potential personal liability that could wipe out years of savings.[45] Professor Davis suggested that a fairer rule would leave the government liable, not the individual. Only if the individual had acted maliciously (in vehicular or non-vehicular cases) should the government be able to recover against its own officers for what it paid out.[46] A federal statute enacted in 1961 does protect drivers of federal government vehicles and other negligent federal employees by creating a tort remedy against the government and precluding individual liability if the negligence occurred "while acting within the scope of the [employee's] office or employment."[47]

The question becomes more complicated in the case of police officers, who may be lower-level government employees, but who exercise discretion to an important degree. "The old cases uniformly assume that policemen are not immune from tort liability . . . "[48] Generally, however, "state and local government units," not individual officers, are now "liable for such torts as false arrest and false imprisonment,"[49] just as (under 1974 amendments to the Federal Tort Claims Act), the federal government now accepts liability for such violations.[50]

ACTING "UNDER COLOR OF LAW"

However, under the 1871 Civil Rights Act,[51] state officers, or persons acting "under color of" state law, who deprive persons of clearly established federal constitutional rights are liable, as individuals, in federal court, in actions known as Section 1983 lawsuits, after the relevant section of the United States Code, unless there is an adequate remedy under state tort law.[52] Defendants have tried to argue that if they acted illegally, they were not acting "under color of" law, but the Court rejected the argument, holding that actionable behavior "under color of state law" would include illegal abuse of authority by a government official "clothed with the authority of state law."[53]

A prison doctor under contract with the State of North Carolina rather than on the State payroll, still "acted under color of state law" for purposes of liability under Section 1983,[54] although he might not have been a "state officer." His "function within the state system, not the precise terms of his employment . . . determines whether his actions can be fairly attributed to the State."[55] The state has the obligation to provide medical care to its prison inmates. "If an individual is possessed of state authority and purports to act under that authority, his action is state action."[56]

On the other hand, the federal Court of Appeals for the Seventh Circuit refused to characterize a security guard employed by a company under contract to the Chicago Housing Authority (CHA) as a state actor for purposes of Section 1983. The victim of a shooting by the security guard brought a Section 1983 action against him for violating his Fourth and Fourteenth Amendment rights. The security guard "was employed to provide security for

CHA residents and was thereby authorized to carry a handgun, to arrest people for criminal trespass pending the arrival of the police, and use deadly force in self-defense."[57] The court explained its refusal to find that he had acted under color of law in part because "[a]lthough all of these powers have traditionally been exercised by the sovereign via the police, none has been *exclusively* reserved to the police [emphasis in the original]."[58] The court cited citizens' arrests, security guards in retail stores who hold shoplifters, and security guards who protect other private company property as illustrations.[59] To deem the action of a private individual or entity "state action," the court must be persuaded that the action "may be fairly treated as that of the State itself."[60] That may be because the actions took place at least in part as the result of the government's influence (nexus), or because the state turned over responsibility for one of its functions to the private individual or entity (state function).[61] Here, the victim alleged the latter, but the court insisted that serving the public does not transform the private actor into a state actor unless the performance of that service is "traditionally the *exclusive* prerogative of the State [emphasis added]."[62]

However, a federal court justified a different result when a guard working for the private security company engaged under contract with the Metropolitan Government of Davidson County (Metro) to guard a courthouse, insisted that an observant practitioner of Islam remove his *kufi* (skullcap) as a condition of entering the building where he was scheduled for a hearing. The practitioner refused, and the guard refused to let him enter. Unlike the Chicago Housing Authority case, here a statute required the provision of security. Under Tennessee state law a courthouse is entrusted to protection by the sheriff, a public officer "unless some other person is specially appointed by the county legislative body for that purpose . . . "[63] Thus, the government (Metro) is directly responsible for guarding the courthouse. It delegated that responsibility to the security company, which was therefore "performing an exclusive state function."[64] Even if the Section 1983 action had not met that "state function" test, the court noted that it would have survived scrutiny under the "nexus" test, because a government officer, Metro's security director, had issued a memorandum noting that he had instructed the security company to enforce "the prescribed policy" concerning the removal of headwear.[65] Thus, the court denied the defendant's motion to dismiss the claim, and let the case proceed on the merits.

OTHER FACTORS

Although generally plaintiffs need not exhaust administrative remedies before suing under the 1871 Civil Rights Act,[66] the Prison Litigation Reform Act of 1996 made an exception for prison inmates, who do have to exhaust their administrative remedies first.[67]

Ordinarily, a Section 1983 plaintiff must sue the officer or official who personally violated his or her constitutional rights. The officer's boss may have more personal wealth, and may be in a better position actually to pay should the plaintiff win a big verdict, but the legal doctrine of *respondeat superior*—"let the master answer"—does not apply here, since the lawsuit must be brought against the wrongdoer in his or her individual capacity.[68] However, a supervisor can be held liable for violating a plaintiff's federal constitutional rights if the supervisor got personally involved by causing or reinforcing the street-level officer's abusive behavior in certain ways:

- having actual knowledge of the wrongdoing, failed to take remedial action
- was responsible for instituting or continuing the conditions leading to the abusive behavior
- so negligently supervised the abusive officer so as to allow the abuse.[69]

Even if a supervisor might have prevented the employee's abuse by taking some particular action, the courts will not necessarily deem the supervisor's failure to that action sufficient to incur personal liability. For example, in a matter in which the court denied qualified immunity to a state trooper who surreptitiously photographed a volunteer who was changing her clothes to participate in a training video, the court granted qualified immunity to his supervisor, who had neglected to review his personnel file, which included references to previous occurrences of inappropriate gender-related behavior, and so might have suggested that he not be given the training video assignment.[70]

A Supreme Court decision, not a statute, began to provide the analog to the Civil Rights Act for federal officers. In *Bivens v. Six Unknown Agents of the Federal Bureau of Narcotics,*[71] the Court held that the Fourth Amendment creates a cause of action for damages from an unlawful search and seizure. Since then, other constitutional provisions have been held to give rise to other rights of action against individual government officers.[72]

IMMUNITY REVISITED

In *Butz v. Economou,*[73] the Court made explicit the absolute immunity enjoyed by judges and prosecutors,[74] and even to "agency officials performing certain functions analogous to those of a prosecutor."[75] Such absolute immunity means that even with bad motives, so long as the official engaged in the challenged behavior in the course of performing official duties, lawsuits based on that official action will be dismissed before trial. As noted above,[76] legislators have absolute immunity. Absolute immunity also attaches to all agency officials with "functions analogous" to other officials whose functions would be compromised "if their immunity from damages was less than complete," including those engaging in the rulemaking process, because in that role they are analogous to legislators.[77]

Although after *Barr v. Mateo*, policy-making officials seemed to have too much immunity from liability, actually *Barr v. Mateo* applied only a qualified immunity to those whose *function* would not be compromised "if their immunity from damages was less than complete."[78] In 1978, almost twenty years later, in *Butz v. Economou*, the Court clarified the limits of immunity. Absolute immunity did not depend on rank: those whose function would not be compromised, and so do not enjoy absolute immunity, included Secretary of Agriculture Earl Butz. Even Cabinet officers are liable if they knew or should have known that their actions violated plaintiffs' constitutional rights.[79]

The Secretary of Agriculture would still enjoy qualified immunity, and therefore would not suffer personal liability unless the plaintiff could prove that the Secretary (or any other government official enjoying qualified immunity) acted maliciously, or violated a clear constitutional right. However, in *Harlow v. Fitzgerald* the Court once again increased the level of protection for government officials afforded by immunity, ruling that merely alleging malicious intent would not suffice to penetrate the defense of qualified immunity. That is, the Court would not allow a suit to go forward based on such an allegation,[80] because such allegations are too "subjective" and "inquiries of this kind ["in which there often is no clear end to the relevant evidence"] can be peculiarly disruptive of effective government."[81] By ensuring that complaints based on such "subjective" terms would be dismissed before trial, the Supreme Court substantially reduced the likelihood that officials would be distracted from their duties by lawsuits.

The standard thus moved to a determination of whether the defendant could have had an objectively reasonable belief that he was not violating constitutional rights. In other words, instead of inquiries about what was in the defendant's head at the time—was he acting maliciously?—the appropriate inquiry, instead, was whether a reasonable person would think he was acting legally. At the same time, plaintiffs had to show that the constitutional right allegedly violated was "clearly established" rather than a right whose existence courts and legal scholars still debated. As one court put it, "If the district judges in the Southern District of New York, who are charged with ascertaining and applying the law, could not determine the state of the law with reasonable certainty, it seems unwarranted to hold prison officials to a standard that was not even clear to the judges . . ."[82] Ultimately, the courts began to merge the two questions: if the law is indeed clearly established, then a reasonable person would know when it was being violated.[83]

The Court held that the President enjoys absolute "immunity from damages liability for acts within the 'outer perimeter' of his official responsibility,"[84] in a lawsuit brought by Ernest Fitzgerald, the legendary whistle-blower who suffered years of punishment for his exposure of about $2 billion in wasteful overspending by the Defense Department in a contract with Lockheed for aircraft. Nixon had ordered that he be fired. Since a constant prospect of personal liability could well distract a president from the optimal performance of his duties, and since press scrutiny, the possibility of impeachment, a desire for reelection (when possible), and other factors serve as deterrents to "misconduct on the part of the Chief Executive,"[85] the Court ruled that the same kind of functional analysis it applied in *Butz v. Economou* justified the decision here.

WHAT AM I SUPPOSED TO DO?

State Prison Commissioner Follows State Law Imposing Supervision On Released Inmates: Does Contrary Case Law Result in Personal Liability for Commissioner?

Let's say you are the Acting Commissioner for the State Department of Corrections, having previously served as Counsel for the Department. A few years ago, your State legislature, in an attempt to appear tough on crime, "abolished" parole, but immediately replaced it with mandatory "post-release supervision," which amounted to much the same thing. Primarily, the two systems differ in that the former resulted from "indeterminate" sentences so that a criminal defendant, if sentenced by a judge to a term of five to ten years, might have served as little as one third of the sentence before being paroled for good behavior and other factors, serving the rest of the sentence under parole supervision. Under the new system, the criminal defendant would serve a mostly "determinate" sentence, such as ten years, with the ability to reduce it only by one-seventh at most, and would then serve the "new" term of post-release supervision. For a second violent felony offense, the statute required five years of post-release supervision after the prison term; for other felony offenders, the statute offered judges a range of options for post-release supervision, up to three years in some cases and up to five years in others, just as it offered a range of choices for the length of the prison sentence.

The problem you face is that some judges failed to specify any period of post-release supervision. You are aware of a court decision holding that a legislative enactment does not suffice and that only a judge can constitutionally impose a sentence. However, you believe that the court erred: that legislatures make the law, and as the head of an agency, you must uphold that law. Should you instruct your assistants to impose periods of post-release supervision on those cases where the judges had failed to do so? You certainly do not want to be the target of a Section 1983 lawsuit alleging that you violated the constitutional rights of those inmates. However, it seems hard to believe that a court would find that the inmates had a "clearly established constitutional right" as justification for you to ignore the law the legislature had enacted.

In fact, the New York State courts had ruled on this very question, and had concluded that "because the PRS [post-release supervision] term is mandatory under New York law, Earley's [the subject of the administratively imposed supervision term] request to eliminate it from his sentence could not be granted."[86] Earley then submitted a habeas corpus petition (having violated the conditions of his post-release supervision, he was back in prison). The federal magistrate who first reviewed it pointed out that the Department of Corrections "had no authority, nor affirmative legal duty, much less a clearly established one," to remove post-release supervision terms it had applied or to alert the initial sentencing judges to the problem, until a few years later, when the legislature changed the law to so alert the relevant judges.[87] The federal district court to which Earley then submitted his habeas corpus petition agreed, and rejected Earley's petition.[88]

In 1936 the Supreme Court, in rejecting an additional condition of confinement imposed by a court clerk, included a statement that was not at all necessary to that decision, but went much further and would bear on the appellate decision in Earley's case: "The only sentence known to the law is the sentence or judgment entered upon the records of the court."[89] (Lawyers call this kind of comment in a decision *dictum*, as opposed to the "holding." Holdings have real precedential effect; *dicta* much less so.) Still, when the federal Court of Appeals heard Earley's appeal of the district court decision, notwithstanding the state law, it analogized the 1936 situation: "If . . . an erroneous order of commitment prepared by the clerk of court with the court's knowledge cannot alter the sentence imposed by the court, then plainly a later addition to the sentence by an employee of the executive branch cannot do it."[90] The court then concluded that a decision by the Department of Corrections to impose a period of post-release supervision is "contrary to clearly established federal law . . ."[91] In rejecting the petition for rehearing, the Court of Appeals strengthened its holding somewhat. It ruled that the administrative imposition of the supervision condition "violated [Earley's] rights under the Due Process Clause of the United States Constitution."[92] It went on to acknowledge that the judge's original sentence, having omitted the post-release supervision, may be "unlawful," "but it remains the sentence to be served until and unless it is lawfully modified,"[93] (by the judge).

A subsequent decision assessed the case against the Acting Commissioner. It acknowledged that prior to the federal Court of Appeals decision in Earley's case in 2006, the Acting Commissioner could not have been expected to have considered his Department's imposition of post-release supervision to be "contrary to clearly established federal law."[94] It acknowledged that the Acting Commissioner disagreed with that decision,[95] and therefore apparently felt that it was not a good or accurate statement of the applicable law. It also affirmed the ruling of the trial court below that the Acting Commissioner's codefendants merited qualified immunity from the lawsuit, accepting the argument of the codefendants that until the State's highest court (as opposed to the federal courts) a few years later decided that the Correction Department could not impose post-release supervision, the law was not clear to them.[96] But, it treated the Acting Commissioner differently: he had been Counsel to the Department, and therefore the court held him to a different standard, because he should have been more sensitive to the development of the law.[97]

The Supreme Court seemed to have ruled in *Harlow v. Fitzgerald* that courts should not delve into the mind-set of the defendant government official: it called for the application of an objective standard to determine whether the official was violating a clearly established law, not the subjective attitude of the particular official.

The federal Court of Appeals left the Acting Commissioner the opportunity to demonstrate that he had made "reasonable efforts either to seek resentencing of such persons or to end their unconstitutional imprisonment and excise [post-release supervision] from their prison records,"[98] and remanded the case to the trial court for further proceedings to make that determination.[99] But, the qualified immunity that one would have thought protected the Acting Commissioner against the hazards, burdens, and pressures of office apparently did not apply.

It can be very difficult to be a Commissioner.

PRACTICE PROBLEMS

PROBLEM 1: Assume that in 2014, the Governor of a northeastern state appointed you as chair of a commission to study and report on the advisability of permitting fracking in the regions of the State under which lay natural gas deposits known to be accessible by techniques of horizontal as well as vertical drilling and injection of pressurized fluids to fracture the shale rock layers to expose the gas. Much controversy has arisen over the tension between the economic benefits of fracking and its environmental risks.

Assume further that your commission report identified Behemoth Energy as a company whose careless fracking practices increase environmental risk to an unacceptable level for your State, based on a study by a university professor. After the press gave wide coverage to this finding, two other states announced that they would bar Behemoth. Subsequently, however, a competing study by an equally qualified expert cast significant doubt on the validity of the earlier finding, and suggested that there were no significant differences in risk among fracking companies. Behemoth's CEO has let it be known that it is exploring the possibility of suing you on the basis of what it claims are false statements in your commission report. Does this prospect constitute a serious enough threat for you to hire a lawyer to prepare a defense? Would it make a difference to your analysis had it been a federal Commission to which you were appointed?

PROBLEM 2: A state court judge presiding over cases brought against juvenile offenders, regularly sentenced those offenders to incarceration in detention facilities even for uttering a curse word, getting into a minor traffic accident, or creating a parody of a teacher's MySpace page on the Internet. The judge had a financial incentive to impose these sentences. He had used his influence to bring about the closing of an older, existing juvenile detention facility, and secretly received millions of dollars from the companies who built two new detention centers in return for his commitment to keep it occupied. The judge often sentenced the offenders after hearings lasting under two minutes, and alerted the detention centers as to the number of new inmates coming on a given day prior to those hearings.

Judicial immunity extends to all of a judge's judicial actions so long as they were taken with some claim to jurisdiction, notwithstanding malicious or corrupt motivation.[100] Plaintiffs who had been incarcerated as juveniles as a result of the judge's sentences brought a civil rights suit against him under 42 U.S.C. § 1983. Can they recover?

ENDNOTES

1. William F. Fox, *Understanding Administrative Law*, 6th ed., (New Providence, NJ: Matthew Bender, 2012), 363.
2. *Respublica v. Sparkhawk*, 1 U.S. (Dall) 357, 363, 1 L. Ed. 174, 177 (1788).
3. *Id.*
4. Erwin Chemerinsky, Against Sovereign Immunity, 53 *Stanford L. Rev.* 1201, 1202 (2001). But, see Gregory S. Sisk, The Inevitability of Federal Sovereign Immunity, 55 *Villanova L. Rev.* 899 (2010).
5. Richard J. Fallon, Claims Court at the Crossroads, 40 *Cath. U. L. Rev.* 517, 519 (1991).
6. *Cohens v. Virginia*, 19 U.S. 264, 412–3, 6 Wheat 264, 412–3 (1821).
7. *Chisholm v. Georgia*, 2 U.S. 419, 434–5, 2 Dall 419, 434–5 (1793).
8. *Alden v. Maine*, 527 U.S. 706, 119 S. Ct. 2240 (1999).
9. *Hans v. Louisiana*, 134 U.S. 1, 16, 10 S. Ct. 504, 507 (1890), cited at 527 U.S. at 715–6, 119 S. Ct. at 2247–8.
10. Fallon, 40 *Cath. U. L. Rev.* at 520. See, e.g., *Bowen v. Massachusetts*, 487 U.S. 879, 108 S. Ct. 2722 (1988), illustrating plaintiffs' preference for Article III courts over what is now called the United States Court of Federal Claims.
11. 28 U.S.C. § 2680.
12. Section 702.
13. *Laird v. Nelms*, 406 U.S. 797, 92 S. Ct. 1899 (1972).
14. 406 U.S. at 801, 92 S. Ct. at 1901–2.
15. 406 U.S. at 803, 92 S. Ct. at 1903.
16. 406 U.S. at 804, 92 S. Ct. at 1903.
17. 406 U.S. at 809-10, 92 S. Ct. at 1905–6.
18. Cees van Dam, Chapter Four: European Tort Law and the Many Cultures of Europe, in Thomas Wilhelmsson, ed., *Private Law and the Cultures of Europe*, The Netherlands: Kluwer International Law BV, 2007, 53, at 59, http://www.ceesvandam.info/default.asp?fileid=393.
19. *Dalehite v. United States*, 346 U.S. 15, 73 S. Ct. 956 (1953).
20. 406 U.S. at 812, 92 S. Ct. at 1907.
21. 346 U.S. at 47, 73 S. Ct. at 975.
22. 346 U.S. at 60, 73 S. Ct. at 980.
23. *Indian Towing Co. v. United States*, 350 U.S. 61, 69, 76 S. Ct. 122, 127 (1955).
24. 350 U.S. at 64–5, 76 S. Ct. at 124.
25. *United States v. S.A. Impresa de Viacao Aerea Rio Grandense (Varig Airlines)*, 467 U.S. 797, 819–820, 104 S. Ct. 2755, 2767–8 (1984).
26. *Berkovitz v. United States*, 486 U.S. 531, 108 S. Ct. 1954 (1988).
27. 486 at 547–8, 108 S. Ct. at 1964.
28. 22 *Admin. L. Rev.* 383, 386 (1970).
29. Jonathan R. Bruno, Immunity for "Discretionary" Functions: A Proposal to Amend the Federal Tort Claims Act, 49 *Harv. J. on Legislation* 411, 437 (2012). But, Bruno argues that the discretionary function exception to the Act overreaches, and that its valid purposes would be served most of the time by judges legitimately finding that in the circumstances where it applies, the government owed no duty of care to the plaintiffs anyway. *Id.* at 439–440.
30. Bruno, *id.* at 443 describes the two following decisions.
31. *Reichert v. United States*, 695 F. Supp. 2d 8, 15 (W.D.N.Y. 2010).
32. *Irving v. United States*, 162 F. 3d 154, 168 (1st Cir. 1998).
33. Loren K. Robel, Sovereignty and Democracy: The States' Obligations to their Citizens Under Federal Statutory Law, 78 *Indiana L. J.* 543, 548 (2003).

34. *Miller v. Horton*, 152 Mass. 540, 26 N.E. 100 (Mass. 1891).

35. 152 Mass. at 547, 26 N.E. at 103.

36. *Bradley v. Fisher*, 13 Wall. (80 U.S.) 335, 347 (1872), quoted in Kenneth Culp Davis, Administrative Officers' Tort Liability, 55 *Mich. L. Rev.* 201, 202 (1956). Davis also notes an exception to the rule, when the Sixth Circuit allowed a Civil Rights Act case to go forward against a justice of the peace in *McShane v. Moldovan*, 172 F. 2d 1016 (1949), cited at 229.

37. *Booth v. Fletcher*, 101 F. 2d 676, 680 (D.C. Cir. 1938), cert. den. 307 U.S. 628 (1939), quoted in Davis, *id.*

38. Davis, *id.* at 230.

39. *Barr v. Mateo*, 360 U.S. 564, 79 S. Ct. 1335 (1959).

40. 360 U.S. at 575, 79 S. Ct. at 1341.

41. 360 U.S. at 571, 79 U.S. at 1339, quoting *Gregoire v. Biddle*, 177 F. 2d 579, 581 (2d Cir. 1949).

42. Davis, *supra* at 209.

43. *United States v. Gilman*, 347 U.S. 507, 74 S. Ct. 695 (1954).

44. 347 U.S. at 511–2, 74 S. Ct. at 697–8.

45. Davis, *supra* at 208.

46. *Id.* at 211.

47. 28 U.S.C. § 2679(b).

48. Davis, *id.* at 213.

49. Davis, *id.* at 217, citing, for example, *Bonnau v. State*, 278 A.D. 181, 104 N.Y.S. 2d 364 (4th Dept. 1951), aff'd 303 N.Y. 721, 103 N.E. 2d 340.

50. 28 U.S.C. § 2680(h).

51. 42 U.S.C. § 1983.

52. E.g., *Harlow v. Fitzgerald*, 457 U.S. 800, 818, 102 S. Ct. 2727, 2738 (1982).

53. *Monroe v. Pape*, 365 U.S. 167, 184, 81 S. Ct. 473, 482 (1961).

54. *West v. Atkins*, 487 U.S. 42, 67, 108 S. Ct. 2250, 2260 (1988).

55. 487 U.S. at 55–6, 108 S. Ct. 2259.

56. 487 U.S. at 57, 108 S. Ct. at 2260, quoting *Griffin v. Maryland*, 378 U.S. 130, 135, 84 S. Ct. 1770 (1964).

57. *Wade v. Byles*, 83 F. 3d 902, 906 (7th Cir. 1996), *cert. den.* 519 U.S. 935, 117 S. Ct. 311.

58. *Id.*

59. *Id.*

60. 83 F. 3d at 905, quoting *Blum v. Yaretsky*, 457 U.S. 991, 1004, 102 S. Ct. 2777 (1982), itself quoting *Jackson v. Metropolitan Edison Co.*, 419 U.S. 345, 351, 95 S. Ct. 449 (1974).

61. 83 F. 3d at 905.

62. 83 F. 3d at 905, quoting *Jackson*, 419 U.S. at 353.

63. *Al-Qadir v. G4S Secure Solutions (USA) Inc.*, 2013 U.S. Dist. LEXIS 548 (M.D. Tenn.), *10, quoting Tenn. Code. Ann. § 5-7-108(a)(1)(2011).

64. *Id.* at *11.

65. *Id.* at 13–14.

66. 365 U.S. at 183, 81 S. Ct. at 482.

67. 42 U.S.C. § 1997(e)(a), enacted by Pub. L. No. 104–134, 110 Stat. 1321.

68. *Monell v. Dept. of Social Services*, 436 U.S. 658, 691, 98 S. Ct. 2018, 2036 (1978)

69. *Colon v. Coughlin*, 58 F. 3d 865, 873 (2d Cir. 1995).

70. *Poe v. Leonard*, 282 F.3d 123, 134 (2d Cir. 2002).

71. *Bivens v. Six Unknown Agents of the Federal Bureau of Narcotics*, 403 U.S. 388, 91 S. Ct. 1999 (1971).

72. See, e.g., *Carlson v. Green*, 446 U.S. 14, 100 S. Ct. 1468 (1980), where the Supreme Court held that prison officials could face personal liability under *Bivens* and the government could face liability under the Federal Tort Claims Act for Eighth Amendment violations.

73. *Butz v. Economou*, 438 U.S. 478, 98 S. Ct. 2894 (1978).

74. 438 U.S. at 511–2, 98 S. Ct. at 2913.

75. 438 U.S. at 515, 98 S. Ct. at 2915. Absolute immunity applies to legislative activity by legislators. *Gravel v. United States*, 408 U.S. 606, 92 S. Ct. 2614 (1972). Absolute immunity attaches

to all agency officials with "functions analogous" to other officials whose functions would be compromised "if their immunity from damages was less than complete," including those engaging in the rulemaking process, because in that role they are analogous to legislators.

76. See text at note 38, *supra*.
77. See *Supreme Court of Virginia v. Consumers Union of the United States, Inc.*, 446 U.S. 719, 734, 100 S. Ct. 1967, 1976 (1980): "in this case . . . the Virginia Court is exercising the State's entire legislative power [as an agent of the Legislature] with respect to regulating the Bar, and its members are State legislators for the purpose of issuing the Bar Code. Thus the Virginia Court and its members are immune from suit when acting in their legislative capacity."
78. 438 U.S. at 515, 98 S. Ct. at 2915.
79. 438 U.S. at 507, 98 S. Ct. at 2911.
80. 457 U.S. 800,817–8, 102 S. Ct. 2727, 2738.
81. 457 U.S. at 817, 102 S. Ct. at 2737–8, footnote omitted.
82. *Richardson v. Selsky*, 5 F.3d 616, 623 (2d Cir. 1993).
83. See especially *Okin v. Village of Cornwall*, 577 F. 3d 415, 433, n. 11 (2d Cir. 2009), citing *Saucier v. Katz*, 533 U.S. 194, 202, 121 S. Ct. 2151, 2156 (2001) and *Pearson v. Callahan*, 555 U.S. 223, 243–4, 129 S. Ct. 808, 822 (2009). However, in at least one subsequent decision the court continued to separate to two tests. *Cornejo v. Bell*, 592 F. 3d 121, 128 (2d Cir. 2010).
84. *Nixon v. Fitzgerald*, 457 U.S. 731, 756, 102 S. Ct. 2690, 2704 (1982).
85. 457 U.S. at 757, 102 S. Ct. at 2705.
86. *Earley v. Murray*, 451 F. 3d 71, 73 (2d Cir. 2006).
87. *Vincent v. Yelich*, 718 F. 3d 157, 165 (2d Cir. 2013).
88. *Earley v. Annucci*, 2012 U.S. Dist. LEXIS 10892 (N.D. N.Y.), 9:08-CV-669.
89. *Hill, Warden v. United States ex rel. Wampler*, 298 U.S. 460, 464, 56 S. Ct. 760, 762 (1936).
90. 451 F. 3d at 75.
91. 451 F. 3d at 76.
92. *Early v. Murray*, 462 F. 3d 147, 148 (2d Cir. 2006).
93. 462 F. 3d at 149.
94. 718 F. 3d at 171.
95. 718 F. 3d at 168.
96. 718 F. 3d at 170.
97. 718 F. 3d 171–2.
98. 718 F. 3d at 174.
99. 718 F. 3d at 178.
100. See, e.g. *Bradley v. Fisher*, 80 U.S. 335, 20 L. Ed. 646 (1871); *Mireles v. Waco*, 502 U.S. 9, 112 S. Ct. 286 (1991).

13

Government Employment Rights and Due Process

Government employee rights have come a long way from Oliver Wendell Holmes' ruling in *McAuliffe v. Mayor of New Bedford* that "The petitioner may have a constitutional right to talk politics, but he has no constitutional right to be a policeman."[1] With some exceptions, federal government employees can appeal punishments ranging from firing to negative evaluations[2] to the Merit Systems Protection Board using an electronic "e-appeal" process.[3] State and local governments have comparable procedures,[4] including some that are also available online.[5] The Washington State Municipal Services and Research Center, in its discussion of civil service protection for local government employees in that state, summarizes well one of the main points of civil service protection: "Civil service in local government seeks to curb political favoritism and remove the coercive pressures that once caused public employees to contribute money and time to partisan political candidates, to the detriment of the work for which they were paid."[6] Disappointed employees can go to court to appeal civil service commission and Merit Systems Protection Board decisions. Some of these procedures overlap grievance processes established by collective bargaining between unionized government employees and governments at every level, often ultimately leading to a hearing before "a professional neutral arbitrator" who renders a "final and binding" decision, which generally cannot be subjected to further appeal.[7]

The courts have come a long way too. Although administrative law mostly strives to teach to general principles and procedures of agencies, not so much the specific policy content of laws and court rulings relating to agencies, this chapter gives more attention to the substantive law than is usual, but an understanding of personnel policy in public administration requires some familiarity with its legal dimensions. Of course, the chapter can do no more than provide illustrative examples of certain areas of government employment law.[8] However, the selected illustrations will convey a sense of the logic of the field. The first three sections of this chapter address government employment rights under Section 1983 of the Civil Rights Act; the following three sections address government employment rights under other constitutional and statutory provisions.

FREEDOM OF SPEECH

The main thrust of Section 1983, in allowing lawsuits only against "persons," provides remedies against government officials in their individual capacities, and if found liable they must pay damages personally. In 1978, the Supreme Court decided that cities—"municipal corporations"—were "persons" for purposes of allowing Section 1983 actions against them,[9] although to be liable some actual policy of the city must have caused the abuse; they could not be sued merely as the employer of a person who committed the abuse.[10] Section 1983 plaintiffs cannot sue states or the federal government—they are not "persons,"—but remedies for successful plaintiffs against individual officers of states or the federal government may include injunctions, orders requiring the official to take a particular action.[11]

While government employees no longer necessarily lose their "right to be a policeman" for exercising their "constitutional right to talk politics," as Holmes would have it, they do face serious limits on the simultaneous exercise of those "rights." In *Garcetti v. Ceballos*,[12] a prosecutor in the Los Angeles District Attorney's office who himself had supervisory responsibilities, reviewed a search warrant, did some personal investigation, and concluded that it was based on lies by the police. He argued against using the results of the search warrant in writing and in a heated meeting that included police officers from the sheriff's department, but was overruled. He was then reassigned, transferred, and denied promotion. Consequently, he sued under Section 1983, claiming that his First Amendment rights were violated.

In ruling against him, the Court majority denied that it did so because Ceballos spoke out within the office rather than to the public—although that might have helped convince the Court that he had spoken out as a citizen on a matter of public concern rather than as an employee, and thus allowed him more leeway; denied that it did so because his comments bore on professional concerns of the District Attorney's office for which he worked—although, of course, had it not been a matter of such character it would have been harder to conclude that it interfered with his job responsibilities; but claimed that it did so because he wrote his memorandum and made his arguments pursuant to his specific responsibilities as calendar deputy. Having done so, his supervisors could have acted entirely within their rights in deciding that he had performed poorly, and treated him as they did in consequence.[13] Had it ruled in Ceballos's favor, the Court argued, it would have "commit[ted] state and federal courts to a new, permanent, and intrusive role, mandating judicial oversight of communications between and among government employees and their superiors in the course of official business."[14]

In dissent, Justice Stevens, joined by Justices Souter and Breyer, wrote, "Of course a supervisor may take corrective action when [an employee's] speech is 'inflammatory or misguided' [citations to majority opinion omitted]. But, what if it is just unwelcome speech because it reveals facts that the supervisor would rather not have anyone else discover?"[15] Also in dissent, Justice Souter, joined by Justice Stevens and Justice Ginsburg, pointed out that the majority drew a line between criticisms voiced by an employee about some office matter outside his personal job responsibilities, which the majority would have protected, and criticism voiced about a matter within the employee's job responsibilities. Justice Souter wrote, "This is an odd place to draw a distinction [and one without justification]."[16] While Justice Souter did acknowledge the need for the larger distinction the majority drew between speech as a citizen and speech as an employee, he argued "private and public interests in addressing official wrongdoing and threats to health and safety can outweigh the government's stake in the efficient implementation of policy, and when they do public employees who speak on these matters in the course of their duties should be eligible to claim First Amendment protection."[17]

Both the majority and the dissenters in *Garcetti* were attempting to apply the "*Pickering*" test, essentially the version of *Matthews* balancing applicable to First Amendment cases, based on the 1968 Supreme Court decision in *Pickering v. Board of Education*: Has the employer made a reasonable assessment of the disruptive effect of the speech in question? Is the value of the speech indeed outweighed by its disruptive potential? And, was the action taken to the detriment of the employee retaliatory, or to minimize the potential for disruption?[18]

The answers to four other questions help courts answer the preceding three: (1) Were the comments made in the employee/speaker's capacity as an employee, or as a citizen? Justice Souter noted ironically that had Ceballos first made his comments in a "separate, public forum or in a letter to a newspaper," he would have merited greater protection under the majority's logic,[19] as the public forum would have weighed toward viewing his speech as made in his capacity as a citizen. (2) Is the subject matter of the comments of concern to the public, or merely to the government agency where the speaker works?[20] (3) Did the speaker suffer significant enough penalties to discourage other potential speakers from speaking out?[21] (4) If so, were such penalties in consequence of the speech, or would they have been imposed anyway, for other reasons?[22]

The Supreme Court found a different *Pickering* balance, this time unanimously, in *Lane v. Franks*.[23] Lane, the director of a youth training program, hired in 2006 only on a probationary basis, quickly found that a state legislator on the program's payroll was not showing up for work. The organization's president warned him not to fire the legislator, but after she refused to change her behavior, Lane fired her anyway, attracting the attention of the FBI, and thereafter resulting in her indictment. Lane testified against her first before a grand jury and later at the trial at which she was convicted in 2008. In 2009, the new president of the organization fired Lane.[24]

The federal Circuit Court of Appeals, affirming the trial court's decision, denied Lane's suit for damages and reinstatement, reasoning that even if testifying was not actually part of his job, it was close enough to come under the holding of *Garcetti*. But, if it were not for his job, Lane would never have known about the legislator or come into contact with the issue. Therefore, the court ruled, Lane spoke as an employee, not as a mere citizen.[25]

This was too much even for Thomas, Scalia, and Alito, who concurred with Justice Sotomayor's opinion for the majority that when a public employee "gives '[t]ruthful testimony under oath . . . outside the scope of his ordinary job duties,' . . . he spoke 'as a citizen,' not as an employee,"[26] and therefore enjoys First Amendment protection.

CHOICE OF APPEARANCE

Two police officers had less success when bringing a Section 1983 Civil Rights Act action on the basis of a claim that by reprimanding and demoting them for wearing earrings, their police department superiors violated their First Amendment rights. They began wearing ear studs in December 1986, and received reprimand letters the next month (also based on accusations of public intoxication and failure to complete assignments). The senior of the two was the only supervisor other than the police chief. He was demoted from sergeant to patrol officer, with a decrease in salary.[27] A departmental policy manual prohibited ornamental items, although it said nothing specifically about ear-rings or ear studs.[28] Depositions of the police chief, the Police Committee, and the village trustees (all named as defendants) expressed the view that ear studs had a detrimental effect on morale and public perceptions of the police force.[29] The federal Court of Appeals for the Seventh Circuit noted that

> although state employment cannot be conditioned on surrender of first amendment rights, the state, nevertheless, has interests in regu-lating the speech of its employees. Those interests differ significantly from those the state possesses in connection with the regulation of the speech of the citizens in general.[30] [In the small community involved,] even some family members and officers colleagues were disturbed by the ear studs [and thus] plaintiffs not only caused an adverse impact on police discipline . . . but caused great public dis-satisfaction as well. Plaintiffs totally fail to meet the burden . . . of showing no rational connection between the male ear stud prohibi-tion and their police responsibilities.[31]

On the other hand, in *Pence v. Rosenquist*[32] the same court held that the suspension of a school bus driver for refusing to shave off a neatly trimmed mustache did indeed violate his First and Fourteenth Amendment rights, and therefore did constitute a violation under Section 1983, because "choice of appearance is an element of liberty," and here there was "no rational relationship between the rule and a public purpose."[33]

POLITICAL AFFILIATION

The Supreme Court upheld Section 1983 claims that being fired or punished for the "wrong" political party affiliation violated First Amendment rights in three decisions, *Elrod v. Burns* (1976),[34] *Branti v. Finkel* (1980),[35] and *Rutan v. Republican Party of Illinois* (1990).[36] Justice Rehnquist joined strong dissents in each case, all essentially pointing to role of partisanship and political patronage in facilitating disciplined commitment to the policies advanced by the head of the office in question, and the long American tradition of accepting that role. None of them quoted the prominent Tammany Hall leader of the early twentieth century, "Boss" Richard Croker, but his comments concerning "mugwumps," the reformers of his day, which he also called "the minority of cultured leisured citizens" and "silk stockings," supplement their argument as well:

> All your high principles will not induce a mugwump to take more than a fitful interest in an occasional election . . . Why, then, when mugwump principles won't even make mugwumps work, do you expect the same lofty motives to be sufficient to interest the masses in politics? . . . And so we need to bribe them with spoils . . . Here they take the shape of offices [jobs]. But you must have an incentive to interest men in the hard daily work of politics . . .[37]

The Court was not persuaded. In *Elrod*, Justice Brennan, writing the Court's decision for a plurality (not a majority), doubted "that the mere difference of political persuasion motivates poor performance . . . [and in any event,] employees may always be discharged for good cause, such as insubordination or poor job performance, when those bases in fact exist."[38] But, the Court did acknowledge "a need to ensure that policies which the electorate has sanctioned are effectively implemented," and noted that it would allow government officials to fire employees in "policymaking positions" (unlike the employees who brought this action) on the basis of party affiliation.[39] However, in *Branti* the Court moved beyond the policymaking versus non-policymaking distinction, holding that "the question is whether the hiring authority can demonstrate that party affiliation is an appropriate requirement for the effective performance of the public office involved,"[40] as it might be, for example, for a governor's speechwriter or press officer. At its core, the decision held that

> If the First Amendment protects a public employee from discharge based on what he said, it must also protect him from discharge based on what he believes [and so] unless the government can demonstrate "an overriding interest" "of vital importance," requiring that a person's private beliefs conform to those of the hiring authority, his beliefs cannot be the sole basis for depriving him of continued public employment.[41]

In *Rutan*, Justice Brennan, for the majority, extended the principles of *Elrod* and *Branti* to "determine that promotions, transfers, and recalls after layoffs based on political affiliation or support are an impermissible infringement on the First Amendment rights of public employees," because "there are deprivations less harsh than dismissal that nevertheless press state employees and applicants to conform their beliefs and associations to some state-selected orthodoxy."[42]

RESIDENCY REQUIREMENTS

Various local jurisdictions have imposed residency requirements for some or all categories of their government employees. Such requirements often generate serious controversy in legal as well as in political arenas.[43] A New Orleans ordinance required all city employees to have a domicile in that city. As enacted in 1973, it included a grandfather clause exception and exceptions granted on the basis of special applications. A 1990 revision removed the grandfather clause, and required all city employees, without exception, to establish domicile by the beginning of 1994. Another revision in 1992 reinstated the grandfather clause and the special applications, and also allowed employees who were hired on or after December 10, 1973 to keep their non–New Orleans domiciles, although they would have to establish New Orleans domiciles to qualify for promotion. This meant that only employees hired between August 27, 1973 and December 10, 1990, unless their applications were approved, needed to have New Orleans domiciles.[44]

The New Orleans police and firefighters associations each brought suit under the equal protection and due process provisions of the Louisiana Constitution to declare the statute unconstitutional. They also alleged that the ordinance was preempted by State law establishing the New Orleans Civil Service Commission and thus also exceeded the home rule powers of New Orleans (see discussion of state preemption and home rule in Chapter 6), but the court rejected both arguments because "such domicile requirements are unrelated to the promotion of public employees on the basis of merit, fitness and qualifications," which are the only concerns of the Civil Service Commission.[45]

The court also rejected the equal protection challenge to the grandfather clause in the ordinance, in that the "discrimination" it created did not affect a "suspect" category, such as race, ancestry, or gender, and did not infringe fundamental rights like freedom of speech or the right to vote, and therefore "need only be rationally related to a legitimate government interest."[46] The preamble to the ordinance set out its purposes, including for example that those domiciled in the city "have a stronger and more direct interest and a greater stake in the City's general welfare and in [its] quality of life," and the court agreed that those were "certainly legitimate government interests" the furthering of which the requirements of the ordinance could be said to be "rationally related,"[47] and so did not violate the state's (or federal) equal protection or due process guarantees.

As to the grandfather clause generally, the court held that as a method of gradual implementation, it also "suitably further[ed] an appropriate governmental interest and therefore does not violate equal protection."[48] But, it found no logical rationale for letting only some employees get promotions without living in New Orleans, based only on when they joined the force. The court found that particular provision in violation of Louisiana's equal protection guarantee and ordered it stricken as unconstitutional.[49]

SEXUAL HARASSMENT

Twin brothers who took summer jobs working for a small Illinois city performing basic horticultural tasks suffered verbal and physical sexual harassment by coworkers, apparently in large part because one of them wore an earring. Although neither the victims nor the harassers were gay, the harassers abused the victims as they apparently would have abused gay coworkers, to the point that the victims left their jobs prior to the normal termination of their employment. They sued the city under Title VII of the Civil Rights Act and the Equal Protection Clause of the U.S. Constitution. The federal Court of Appeals for the Seventh Circuit noted that the Supreme Court had interpreted Title VII's prohibition of discrimination on the basis of gender to include the creation, through such discrimination, of a "hostile or abusive work environment."[50] A guideline issued by the Equal Employment Opportunity Commission states, in relevant part, that " . . . verbal or physical conduct of a sexual nature constitutes sexual harassment when . . . such conduct has the purpose or effect of unreasonably interfering with an individual's work performance or creating an intimidating, hostile, or offensive work environment."[51] Although the Fifth Circuit had refused to consider male-on-male harassment as "gender discrimination," and therefore rejected it as a violation of Title VII,[52] none of the other Circuits took that position.[53] The Seventh Circuit concluded that one of the brothers "was harassed 'because of' his gender": "it can be inferred from the harassers' evident belief that in wearing an earring, H. Doe did not conform to male standards."[54] It therefore reversed the district court's grant of summary judgment to the defendant city as to the plaintiffs' Title VII hostile environment and Equal Protection claims, and remanded the case for further proceedings consistent with its judgment.[55]

PROTECTION AGAINST PRIVATIZATION

A Hawaiian county entered into contract with Waste Management of Hawaii to privatize a landfill previously staffed by civil servant members of the United Public Workers union. In response to litigation by the former workers alleging violations of Hawaii's civil service and collective bargaining laws, the court voided the contract as a violation of civil service laws and merit principles. Privatization purports to increase efficiency. Civil service purports to eliminate the "spoils system" of awarding jobs on the basis of political loyalty, and therefore also might increase efficiency by avoiding the hiring of "patronage hacks"—employees who were given their jobs as a reward for political service, but who do little or no work in those jobs. Civil service claims to be characterized by openness (public announcements, open applications, public notice of qualifying requirements); merit (competitive examination); and independence (with job security, employees can speak out against unlawful activities). The court set forth three different tests or approaches used by state courts to determine whether civil service laws permit the contracting out of a service hitherto provided by government employees. Some states do not allow the privatization of a type of service customarily and historically provided by civil servants, unless for some reason a continuation of its provision by civil servants is impossible. Other states permit the privatization of a new service, even if it does fall within a general category historically provided by civil servants. Finally, yet other states reject privatization if undertaken by the government employer in an attempt to circumvent civil service laws, assuming that the courts can see through bad faith and dishonest claims that economic efficiency motivated the effort.[56]

Hawaiian civil service

> comprises all positions in the public service of each county . . . and embraces all personal services performed for each county, [except when specifically exempted by some other statute, and] except the following: * * * [when the Civil Service Commission has certified] that the service is special or unique, is essential to the public interest, and [due to circumstances] personnel to perform the service cannot be recruited through normal civil service procedures; provided that no contract pursuant to this paragraph shall . . . exceed[] one year . . .[57]

Given the language of the statutes, broad in its sweep, the Hawaiian Supreme Court decided that it was most consistent with the first kind of state test. Since the former landfill employees were certainly capable of continuing to perform their service, which they had "customarily and historically provided," the court held that the civil service law applied.[58] No matter that the county might characterize the service as in some way new, and no matter that the workers could not prove bad faith on the county's part: the court invalidated the privatization contract, and ordered the return of the landfill to operation by the county, and not by its private contractor.[59]

The Louisiana court read the powers of that state's civil service law more narrowly. The New Orleans Civil Service Commission had promulgated a rule that required its approval for any privatization contract to be valid. The Louisiana court held that the Commission did not exceed its constitutional authority in issuing the rule, because it was sufficiently related to its constitutional authority for "selection, hiring, promotion, demotion, suspension and removal of public employees."[60] It should indeed determine whether under a privatization contract New Orleans civil service employees will be involuntarily displaced, and if so whether the contract was entered into for reasons of efficiency and economy and not for political reasons. But, the Commission's "review is limited to that . . . necessary to [protect] merit [selection], and to protect classified employees [against] religious or political motivated [dismissals or disciplinary action]," and its authority therefore does not extend beyond actions necessary to reflect those concerns. Therefore, it has no authority to determine whether a governmental function should or should not be provided by civil service, whether a contract is in the best interest of the city, or whether fiscal constraints presented by the city can justify privatization.[61] While the dissent claimed that the decision merely gave "lip service to the broad powers granted to the Mayor and Council over operation of City government," and that by its ruling the majority was in reality ceding too much of that power to the Civil Service Commission,[62] clearly the majority distinguished its reading of Louisiana law from the reading of the Hawaiian court of Hawaiian law. It warned the New Orleans Commission not to reject privatization contracts unless they reflected some kind of inconsistency with merit principles, while the Hawaiian Commission could reject privatization simply because the jobs affected were "customarily and historically" performed by civil servants. These decisions exemplify part of the range of various views of courts interpreting various civil service laws, a range surveyed in part by the Louisiana court.[63]

WHAT AM I SUPPOSED TO DO?

Police Commissioner Removes Towing Company From List for Contract Approval: Does Civil Rights Act Protect Government Contractors Against Political Retaliation?

You are an assistant to your city's police commissioner. The commissioner's responsibilities include deciding which towing companies get contracts from the city to tow away disabled cars on its roadways. The owner of one towing company, which had performed well under city contracts for years, had publicly supported the mayor's opponent during the election campaign. In the past, companies had lost their city contracts only on the basis of poor performance. The commissioner would like to please the mayor by removing the offender towing company from the list of those approved for city contracts, and asked you whether she would be on safe ground, legally, if she did so. What is your advice?

The Supreme Court addressed this issue in *O'Hare Truck Service v. City of Northlake*.[64] The decisions in *Elrod*, *Branti*, and *Rutan*, barring retaliation against government employees for their political affiliations in the absence of a rational relationship between those affiliations and their job requirements, had not previously been extended to independent contractors. On that basis, the lower courts had held that no such First Amendment protection applied, and that therefore O'Hare could not state a valid claim of infringement via Section 1983 of the Civil Rights Act.[65]

The Supreme Court recognized that unlike government employees, many contractors depend on government only for a small fraction of their income, and therefore would not feel coerced to renounce their political views in the face of the threat of loss of their government contract, at least not nearly to the same extent as would government employees. However, the only relevant statistics available to the Court indicated that towing companies do not fall into that category: on the contrary, they tend to rely quite heavily on government contracts for their economic survival.[66] Therefore, the Court rejected "the proposition . . . that those who perform the government's work outside the formal employment relationship are subject to what we conclude is the direct and specific abridgement of First Amendment rights described in this complaint."[67]

Similarly, in *Bd. of Commissioners, Wabaunsee County v. Umbehr*,[68] the Court ordered the reinstatement of a trash-hauling contractor if he could prove that the county's governing board retaliated for his public criticism of its competence by ending its contract, unless the board could prove that its interest in controlling the assignment of the trash-hauling contract outweighed the First Amendment interests involved.[69] The Court ruled that a government's decision to use a contractor rather than a direct employee does not allow it to escape the *Pickering* test.[70]

In one dissenting opinion simultaneously addressing the majority in both *O'Hare* and *Umbehr*, Justice Scalia pointed to his earlier objections to the Court's decisions in *Elrod*, *Branti*, and *Rutan*, based on his reading of the historical role of political patronage in American government.[71] But, he raised even stronger objections to the extension of Section 1983 liability based on applying First Amendment protection to government contractors, suggesting that such protections might prohibit the Department of Housing and Urban Development, when deciding upon the award of a contract to provide security in public housing projects, to take into account the racist political views of a bidder, and to reject the bidder on that basis.[72] Scalia argued that while in *Umbehr* the Court encouraged the use of the *Pickering* test regarding expressions of opinion, in *O'Hare* it seemed more absolutely to bar exclusions of contractors based on political affiliations, and thus undermined any assurance of applicability of the *Pickering* test (because expressions of opinion and political affiliations are not easily distinguished from each other).[73] Nevertheless, it seems unlikely that Court would have had any difficulty finding that the Department's rejection of such a bidder would pass the *Pickering* test.

PRACTICE PROBLEM

Plaintiff's supervisors fired the deputy counsel at a state's Office of Mental Retardation and Developmental Disabilities. In his Section 1983 lawsuit, he alleges that they did so not because of his political affiliations, but because his wife's wrongful termination lawsuit against the State Attorney General claiming improper discrimination embarrassed the administration of his agency, which, on its own and through the Governor, had a close relationship with the Attorney General. Does the former deputy counsel have a legitimate claim that his First Amendment rights of free association were violated if the agency fired him based on his wife's action? What if the courts find that he was indeed fired because of his political affiliations? Will the courts order his reinstatement?

ENDNOTES

1. *McAuliffe v. Mayor of New Bedford*, 155 Mass. 216, 220, 29 N.E. 517 (Mass. 1892)
2. Prohibited personnel practices, 5 U.S.C. § 2302.
3. U.S. MSPB e-Appeal online, website of the Merit Systems Protection Board, https://e-appeal .mspb.gov/default.aspx, undated, accessed 1/27/15.
4. See, e.g., Civil Service Rules, Michigan Civil Service Commission, October 1, 2013, 146–155, available at http://www.michigan.gov/mdcs/0%2C1607%2C7-147-6877---%2C00.html, accessed 1/27/15.
5. See, e.g., Appeals Resource Guide, California State Personnel Board website, August 2014, 2, spb.ca.gov/content/appeals/Appeals_Resource_Guide.pdf, accessed 1/27/15.
6. Civil Service, Washington State MRSC website, December 1, 2014, http://www.mrsc.org/Home/ Explore-Topics/Personnel/Beginning-Employment/Civil-Service.aspx, accessed 1/27/15.
7. AFSCME Steward Handbook, American Federation of State, County, and Municipal Employees website, 23, www.afscme.org/steward-handbook-2013, accessed 1/27/15; and see AFGE Stewards Manual, American Federation of Government Employees website, 21, www .afge.org/Documents/Steward.pdf, accessed 1/27/15.
8. Estreicher, Samuel, and Zev J. Eigen, in The Forum for Adjudication of Employment Disputes, in M. L. Wachter and C. L. Esdund (Eds.), *Research Handbook on the Economics of Labor and Employment Law*. (Northampton, MA: Edward Elgar Publishing, 2010), address concerns that mandatory binding arbitration agreements have reduced the role of adjudication of employee discipline cases, but argue that adjudication may be equally problematic and that "improve[d] employer-promulgated ADR [alternative dispute resolution]" *id.* at 13, can provide optimal recourse.
9. *Monell v. Dep't of Social Services*, 436 U.S. 658, 690, 98 S. Ct. 2018, 2035–6 (1978).
10. *Id.*at 691, 2036.
11. E.g., *Sullivan v. Little Hunting Park*, 396 U.S. 229, 238 90 S. Ct. 400, 405 (1969); *Davidson v. Scully*, 148 F. Supp. 2d 249 (S.D.N.Y. 2001), where such a remedy may be imposed even on an official who was not personally involved in the deprivation of rights, but who could correct it, 148 F. Supp. 2d at 254.
12. *Garcetti v. Ceballos*, 547 U.S. 410, 126 S. Ct. 1951 (2006).
13. 547 U.S. at 420–3, 126 S. Ct. at 1959–61.
14. 547 U.S. at 423, 126 S. Ct. at 1961.
15. 547 U.S. at 426, 126 S. Ct. at 1962.
16. 547 U.S. at 430, 126 S. Ct. at 1965.
17. 547 U.S. at 428, 126 S. Ct. at 1963.
18. *Pickering v. Bd. of Education*, 391 U.S. 563, 568–72, 88 S. Ct. 1731, 1735–7 (1968), cited by Kennedy for the majority at 547 U.S. at 415, 126 S. Ct. at 1956, cited by Souter, dissenting, 547 U.S. at 429ff, 126 S. Ct. at 1969ff.
19. 547 U.S. at 430, 126 S. Ct. at 1964, n.1.
20. 391 U.S. at 569–575, 88 S. Ct. at 1735–8.
21. *Zelnik v. Fashion Inst. of Technology*, 464 F. 3d 217, 225 (2d Cir. 2006).
22. *Mt. Healthy City Bd. of Ed.v. Doyle*, 429 U.S. 274, 287, 97 S. Ct. 568, 576 (1977).
23. *Lane v. Franks*, 189 L. Ed. 2d 312, 2014 U.S. LEXIS 4302.
24. 189 L. Ed. 2d at 319, 2014 U.S. LEXIS 4302 at **7.
25. 189 L. Ed. 2d at 321, 2014 U.S. LEXIS 4302 at **12.
26. Thomas, joined by Scalia and Alito, concurring, 189 L. Ed. 2d at 329, 2014 U.S. LEXIS 4302 at **31–2, and quoting the majority opinion at 189 L. Ed. 2d at 323, 2014 U.S. LEXIS 4302 at **18.
27. *Rathert v. Village of Peotone*, 903 F. 2d 510, 511 (7th Cir. 1990), *cert. den.* 498 U.S. 921, 111 S. Ct. 297.

28. 903 F. 2d at 513.
29. *Id.*
30. 903 F. 2d at 514–5.
31. 903 F. 2d at 516.
32. *Pence v. Rosenquist,* 573 F. 2d 395 (7th Cir. 1978).
33. 573 F. 2d at 399.
34. *Elrod v. Burns,* 427 U.S. 327, 96 S. Ct. 2673.
35. *Branti v. Finkel,* 445 U.S. 507, 100 S. Ct. 1287.
36. *Rutan v. Republican,* 497 U.S. 62, 110 S. Ct. 2729.
37. M.R. Werner, *Tammany Hall,* (New York: Doubleday, Doran & Co., 1928), 449.
38. 427 U.S. at 365, 96 S. Ct. at 2685–6.
39. 427 U.S. at 372, 96 S. Ct. at 2689.
40. 445 U.S. at 518, 110 S. Ct. at 1295.
41. 445 U.S. at 515–6, 110 S. Ct. at 1293, citations omitted.
42. 497 U.S. at 75, 110 S. Ct. at 2737.
43. See, e.g., Connie Hager, Residency Requirements for City Employees: Important Incentives in Today's Urban Crisis, *Urban Law Annual* 18(1):197–222.
44. *Police Association of New Orleans v. City of New Orleans,* 649 So. 2d 951 (La. 1995).
45. 649 So. 2d at 959.
46. 649 So. 2d at 961.
47. 649 So. 2d at 962.
48. 649 So. 2d at 964.
49. 649 So. 2d at 965.
50. *Doe v. City of Belleville, Illinois,* 119 F. 3d 563, 569 (1997), quoting *Meritor Savings Bank, FSB v. Vinson,* 577 U.S. 57, 66, 106 S. Ct. 2399 (1986).
51. 29 C.F.R. § 1604.11(a), quoted at 119 F. 3d at 571, note 3.
52. 119 F. 3d at 571, discussing and citing *Garcia v. Elf Atochem, N.A.,* 28 F. 3d 446, 451–2 (5th Cir. 1994).
53. 119 F. 3d at 570–1 and see 573–4.
54. 119 F. 3d at 575.
55. 119 F. 3d at 597.
56. *Konno v. County of Hawaii,* 85 Haw. 61, 69–70, 937 P. 2d 397, 405–6 (1997).
57. 85 Haw. at 70, 937 P. 2d at 406, quoting Hawaii Revised Statutes 76–77.
58. 85 Haw. at 72, 937 P. 2d at 408.
59. 85 Haw. at 79, 937 P. 2d at 415.
60. *Civil Service Commission of City of New Orleans v. City of New Orleans,* 854 So. 2d 322, 330, 335 (2003).
61. 854 So. 2d at 335.
62. 854 So. 2d at 337.
63. 854 So. 2d at 333.
64. 518 U.S. 712, 116 S. Ct. 2353 (1996).
65. O'Hare Truck Service v. City of Northlake, 47 F. 3d 883, 885 (7th Cir. 1995).
66. 518 U.S. at 722–3, 116 S. Ct. at 2359–60, citing Brief for Towing and Recovery Assn. of America, Inc., as *Amicus Curiae* 9.
67. 518 U.S. at 721, 116 S. Ct. at 2358.
68. *Bd. Of Commissioners, Wabaunsee County v. Umbehr,* 518 U.S. 668, 116 St. Ct. 2342 (1996).
69. 518 U.S. at 685, 116 S. Ct. at 2352.
70. 518 U.S. at 678–9, 116 S. Ct. at 2349–50; and see text at notes 11 through 19 above.
71. 518 U.S. 686–9, 135 L. Ed. 2d 858–9.
72. 518 U.S. at 700, 135 L. Ed. 2d at 867.
73. 518 U.S. at 703–4, 135 L Ed. 2d at 869.

14

"Transparency"

Public Access to Government Information

THE FREEDOM OF INFORMATION ACT

The Freedom of Information Act (FOIA), signed into law by President Lyndon Johnson in 1966, amended the Administrative Procedure Act.[1] Prior to 1966, under the APA, agencies could withhold documents from the public more or less at will. At that time, its Section 3 allowed agencies to withhold official records and documents on their own determination that requesters were not "properly and directly concerned" with the subjects of their inquiries, or on their own determination that they had "good cause" to keep the documents confidential, unless some other statute happened to guarantee public access to the records of the agency in question.[2]

Now, under FOIA, disclosure is supposed to be the rule, not the exception. Every state and many local governments have also enacted their versions of FOIA,[3] although details differ. Reaction against the Watergate scandal inspired another move toward greater transparency in government, this time in terms of the public's ability to see and hear the deliberations of participants in meetings where agency leaders made policy. In 1976, Congress enacted the Open Meeting, or Government in the Sunshine, Act, signed into law by President Gerald Ford, requiring agencies headed by at least two people to allow the public to observe meetings of its leadership.[4] The Act has exceptions mostly parallel to the exceptions to FOIA.[5]

When then-Attorney General Ramsay Clark issued the first memorandum to "Executive Departments and Agencies" explaining their responsibilities under the Act, he wrote, "Nothing so diminishes democracy as secrecy. Self-government . . . is meaningful only with an informed public."[6] But, presidential administrations have not been reliable in matching that sentiment with performance.

PRE-FOIA INFORMATION ACCESS REQUIREMENTS OF THE ADMINISTRATIVE PROCEDURE ACT

The first part of Section 552 had antecedents even prior to the Administrative Procedure Act of 1946, to say nothing of FOIA. Prior to 1935, agencies were not even required to publish copies of their own regulations. Chapter 1 noted *Panama Refining Co. v. Ryan*[7] as one of only two decisions in which the Supreme Court struck down a delegation of power by Congress as overbroad, but did not mention the fact that the government agency involved had tried to enforce a regulation that did not exist, because "No one—not the government, not the defendants, not the lower courts—was aware that the regulation had been eliminated."[8] The ensuing embarrassment, when the lapse was discovered, prompted Supreme Court Justice Louis Brandeis to call for legislation, introduced by Member of Congress Emanuel Celler, resulting in the Federal Register,[9] the monthly compilation of proposed and adopted federal agency regulations, along with notices of federal grants, presidential orders, and other timely federal documents[10] (previously discussed in Chapter 4). That legislation, requiring publication of agency regulations and proposed regulations in the Federal Register, eventually became Section 552(a)(1) of the Administration Procedure Act. Section 552(a)(2) requires agencies to "make available for public inspection and copying" opinions in agency adjudications, policy statements, interpretations, instructions to staff that have impact on the public, records released under FOIA that "become or are likely to become" popular subjects of public requests, and an index of such "popular" records.

HOW FOIA EMPOWERS CITIZENS TO OBTAIN GOVERNMENT DOCUMENTS

Subsection (a)(3) of Section 552 is where the Administration Procedure Act truly begins to reflect the way FOIA amended it.

BOX 14-1   **5 U.S. Code Administrative Procedure Act— Section 552(a)(3)**

(A) Except with respect to the records made available under paragraphs (1) and (2) of this subsection, each agency, upon any request for records which (i) reasonably describes such records and (ii) is made in accordance with published rules stating the time, place, fees (if any), and procedures to be followed, shall make the records promptly available to any person.

(B) In making any record available to a person under this paragraph, an agency shall provide the record in any form or format requested by the person if the record is readily reproducible by the agency in that form or format. Each agency shall make reasonable efforts to maintain its records in forms or formats that are reproducible for purposes of this section.

(Continued)

(Continued)

(C) In responding under this paragraph to a request for records, an agency shall make reasonable efforts to search for the records in electronic form or format, except when such efforts would significantly interfere with the operation of the agency's automated information system.

(D) For purposes of this paragraph, the term "search" means to review, manually or by automated means, agency records for the purpose of locating those records which are responsive to a request.

Source: http://www.archives.gov/federal-register/laws/administrative-procedure/552.html

Even if an agency can use an exemption to withhold some information in a document, it must release the other information in the document if it can separate one from the other.[11] Before electronic editing, agencies ordinarily did this by blacking out the information that it wanted to withhold. After agencies began redacting electronically, citizens receiving the documents could not even tell how much had been deleted—a few words, or many pages. Amendments in 1996 required agencies to show the location of deletions, unless even that information is protected by an exemption.[12]

When an agency claims that all information responsive to a request falls under an exemption, the courts still require the agency to offer a list of those responsive documents, called a "*Vaughn* index," unless such a list is itself protected by an exemption.[13]

In enacting FOIA, Congress took into account the likely effort by recalcitrant agency personnel to use one of the oldest and easiest methods of resistance: foot-dragging. To some extent, Congress itself faced and faces resistance from agencies in its quests for information, so the original statute gave the agencies only ten days to accept or deny the request, and twenty days to resolve the requester's appeal of a denial. Of course, the requester may challenge in court an adverse ruling in the administrative appeal, having thus exhausted administrative remedies (see Chapter 11). If the agency fails to meet the time limit for responding to the initial request, the requester is deemed to have exhausted administrative remedies, and may appeal to court.[14] Unlike ordinary proceedings, where the Federal Rules of Civil Procedure give the government sixty days to respond, a government agency must respond to a court challenge to FOIA request denial within thirty days, or else must submit the documents.[15] When a court reviews an agency decision to withhold the information under one of the exemptions in FOIA, the agency has the burden of proof that the exemption truly applies.[16] And unlike other court reviews of agency action, the courts are not expected to defer to agency findings, but must review the controversy *de novo* ("as if new").[17] The

1996 amendments eased the pressure on the agencies somewhat, extending to twenty days the basic deadline for initial responses,[18] and giving agencies more flexibility in adjusting response times to the degree of burdensomeness of the request.[19] The amendments also provided for electronic requests and responses.[20]

When courts find that agencies have improperly withheld information, they may award attorney fees and other litigation costs to the requester, instruct Special Counsel[21] to determine whether disciplinary action should be initiated against recalcitrant agency employees (and the agency must take any such action if recommended), and "In the event of noncompliance with the order of the court . . . may punish for contempt the responsible employee."[22]

HOW FOIA EMPOWERS AGENCIES TO WITHHOLD INFORMATION TO PREVENT ABUSE

Some exceptions to FOIA ("exemptions from the FOIA") and some related protective statutes are intended to prevent requesters from obtaining information with which they could abuse others. For example, federal law requires manufacturers of pesticides to reveal their composition formulae to the Department of Agriculture.[23] Such a manufacturer would have invested money, often considerable sums, in the research that resulted in any one such formula. Allowing competitors access to the information, and thus allowing them to copy and compete with the initial pesticide, would promote an unfair method of competition, in essence stealing the first company's work product. FOIA doubly protects such information from disclosure: its fourth exemption protects "trade secrets and commercial or financial information obtained from a person and privileged or confidential"[24]; its third exemption protects information "specifically exempted from disclosure by statute [other than the FOIA itself],"[25] such as formulae under the Trade Secrets Act.[26]

BOX 14-2   **5 U.S. Code Administrative Procedure Act—Section 552(b)(3)-(6)**

(b) This section does not apply to matters that are—

* * *

(3) specifically exempted from disclosure by statute (other than section 552b of this title), provided that such statute (A) requires that the matters be withheld from the public in such a manner as to leave no discretion on the issue, or (B) establishes particular criteria for withholding or refers to particular types of matters to be withheld;

(Continued)

(Continued)

(4) trade secrets and commercial or financial information obtained from a person and privileged or confidential;

(5) inter-agency or intra-agency memorandums or letters which would not be available by law to a party other than an agency in litigation with the agency;

(6) personnel and medical files and similar files the disclosure of which would constitute a clearly unwarranted invasion of personal privacy;

Source: http://www.archives.gov/federal-register/laws/administrative-procedure/552.html

Under the Trade Secrets Act, a government official who releases information that should be withheld under the fourth exemption can be prosecuted criminally.[27] However, Exemption 4 does not *require* the agency to withhold trade secret information, and while the Trade Secrets Act can result in prosecution, this prospect offers little consolation to a company whose trade secrets have already been revealed. In *Chrysler Corp. v. Brown*,[28] the Court suggested that a company might claim that under the Trade Secrets Act or under a FOIA provision, an agency's release of secret information would be "arbitrary, capricious, an abuse of discretion, or otherwise not in accordance with law," thus authorizing court intervention under Section 706 of the APA and permitting the court to enjoin (prevent) the release of the information under Section 702 of the APA.[29]

The federal government also collects data that could prove personally embarrassing to individuals, ranging from medical information held by the Veterans Administration or the Centers for Medicare and Medicaid Services of the U.S. Department of Health, to the federal Bureau of Alcohol, Tobacco, Firearms, and Explosives, which among other things requires an application from a family producing wine for its own use "not exceeding 200 gallons per annum."[30] While the sixth exemption, for "information of a personal nature where disclosure would constitute a clearly unwarranted invasion of personal privacy,"[31] has generated difficult-to-decide cases,[32] the courts have gone so far as to prohibit the disclosure of the family wine list.[33] The Privacy Act of 1974[34] significantly supplemented the FOIA exemption. Although lengthy and full of its own exceptions, at its core it prohibits the dissemination of records about an individual to anyone except that individual, and makes the records available to the subject individual upon request. With its enactment, therefore, Congress made some headway in preventing agencies from releasing private information to others, and in preventing agencies from withholding "information"—which was sometimes mistaken—from the individual in question. For example, the FBI under J. Edgar Hoover notoriously kept records falsely identifying persons as communists.[35] Under the Privacy Act, all agencies, including the FBI must have procedures to correct records based on information provided by individuals who have reviewed their own files and found errors.[36]

Exemption 6 makes specific reference to personnel files as an example of information protected against FOIA disclosure. But, the Supreme Court did not accept the argument by the Air Force that suitably redacted summaries of decisions in cases of student honor code violations could be considered "personnel files" for that purpose when they "name no names except in guilty cases, are widely disseminated for examination by fellow cadets, contain no facts except such as pertain to the alleged violation of the Honor or Ethics Codes, and are justified by the Academy solely for their value as an educational and instructional tool the better to train military officers for discharge of their important and exacting functions."[37]

We discuss most of Exemption 7, protecting the confidentiality of law enforcement–related information on a variety of grounds after Box 14.5, but Part C of Exemption 7, allowing agencies to withhold law enforcement information that "could reasonably be expected to constitute an unwarranted invasion of personal privacy," obviously overlaps Exemption 6 in its focus on privacy. However, the Supreme Court has held that Exemption 7(D) provides a stronger basis for withholding information than Exemption 6, because the latter allows withholding only "when disclosure would constitute a clearly unwarranted invasion," while 7(D) allows withholding even when disclosure might merely "be expected to constitute an unwarranted invasion."[38] On this basis, the Court explained that even though arrest records were public documents, "Plainly there is a vast difference between the public records that might be found after a diligent search of courthouse files, county archives, and local police stations throughout the country and a computerized summary located in a single clearinghouse of information."[39] Further, in the matter under consideration, the individual's arrest record would shed no light on potential government misbehavior; FOIA was not intended to enhance the disclosure of information about private individuals[40]; and therefore, the disclosure of the computerized summary of the individual's arrest record was indeed an "unwarranted" invasion of his personal privacy.[41]

It is very tempting to believe that Exemptions 8 and 9, respectively excluding from the purview of FOIA requests information in the files of government agencies that regulate or supervise financial institutions, and "geological or geophysical information and data, including maps, concerning wells," resulted from the powerful political influence of banks and oil companies. According to the official legislative history, however, Congress intended Exemption 8 to prevent "a run on the banks" in the event that some document reflecting bank weakness might cause a public crisis of confidence, where sudden withdrawals of deposits in consequence might create a far worse situation, and also to avoid frightening bankers into withholding documents from regulators for fear they would be released[42]; and oil companies thought that the maps they made showing actual or likely oil deposits, reflecting the explorations, were not covered by Exemption 4, which excludes trade secrets, so they needed this additional protection.[43]

BOX 14-3   **5 U.S. Code Administrative Procedure Act—**
            Section 552(b)(8) and (9)

(b) This section does not apply to matters that are—

* * *

(8) contained in or related to examination, operating, or condition reports prepared by, on behalf of, or for the use of an agency responsible for the regulation or supervision of financial institutions; or (9) geological and geophysical information and data, including maps, concerning wells.

Source: http://www.archives.gov/federal-register/laws/administrative-procedure/552.html

---

HOW FOIA EMPOWERS AGENCIES TO WITHHOLD INFORMATION TO SAFEGUARD OTHER SUBSTANTIVE INTERESTS

National Security

Exemption 1 allows agencies to withhold "properly classified" information[44] "specifically authorized under criteria established by an Executive order to be kept secret in the interest of national defense or foreign policy."[45] Under the original version of FOIA, the mere fact that a document had been classified sufficed to allow an agency to withhold it.[46] The current language, adopted in 1974, persuaded at least one scholar to conclude that "properly classified" at least "arguably" should mean that classification of a document "only after an FOIA request is received" would make the document *not* exempt from release.[47] The Obama Administration has taken a different view.

BOX 14-4   **U.S. Code Administrative Procedure Act—**
            Section 552(b)(1)

(b) This section does not apply to matters that are—

(1) (A) specifically authorized under criteria established by an Executive order to be kept secret in the interest of national defense or foreign policy and (B) are in fact properly classified pursuant to such Executive order;

Source: http://www.archives.gov/federal-register/laws/administrative-procedure/552.html

In 2006, federal district court judge Alvin Hellerstein ordered the Bush Administration to release about 2,000 photographs of detainee abuse by U.S. soldiers at Abu Ghraib and other sites in Iraq and Afghanistan, and his decision was affirmed on appeal in 2008.[48] Before the decision could be implemented, the Bush Administration was succeeded by the Obama Administration. President Obama said that he would release the photographs. Shortly thereafter, the Iraqi Prime Minister asked that the photographs not be released, and Congress passed the Protected National Security Document Act (PNSDA) permitting a delay for three years of FOIA requirements for any document that the Secretary of Defense certified as endangering American lives. President Obama then changed his mind about the release of the photographs, and his then-Defense Secretary Robert Gates made the requisite certification in 2009. The federal court faced with a lawsuit seeking release accepted the Secretary's decision, and Obama's next Defense Secretary, Leon Panetta, recertified the documents in 2012.[49] However, as the *New York Times* editorialized, "the greatest threat to [the safety of American citizens and soldiers] lies not in the photographs of horrific behavior; it lies in the fact of the behavior itself . . . America reinforces its values and thus its security by being transparent about even the worst abuses of those values, not by hiding the evidence deep in a file drawer."[50]

In 2014, Judge Hellerstein, who had accepted Secretary Gates's decision in 2009, again reviewed the motion by the American Civil Liberties Union to order the release of the photographs. The Obama Administration argued that under the PNSDA the judge did not have the authority even "to review the basis for the Secretary of Defense's position."[51] Neither the language of the statute nor its legislative history included any clear statement by Congress that it intended the basis for the Secretary's certification to be subject to judicial review, or not.[52] However, since FOIA itself provides for judicial review of agency justifications for exceptions, since Congress can be presumed to have been aware of the underlying statute (FOIA) it was amending when it enacted PNSDA, and since American law presumes judicial review in the absence of explicit statutory language to the contrary, Judge Hellerstein rejected the Administration's claim that he had no authority to determine whether the Secretary's certification had a valid basis in fact and law.[53] Finally, Judge Hellerstein required the government to show why the release of the photographs, appropriately redacted to prevent individual identification, still constituted a danger to American citizens, military personnel, or other government employees,[54] and to make such a showing for each individual photograph, not simply for the photographs *en masse*.[55]

The second Bush administration, which may even initially have been unsympathetic to disclosure,[56] reacted to the 2001 terrorist attack with a memorandum by Attorney General Ashcroft on October 12, 2001 and a later memorandum by White House Chief of Staff Andrew Card on March 19, 2002 "revers[ing] the Clinton Administration's 'presumption of disclosure' approach to releasing information . . . and caution[ing] agencies to consider withholding [sensitive but unclassified] information if there was a 'sound legal basis' to do so."[57] This new "Sensitive But Unclassified" category effectively created a new basis for restricting public access to government information. When Congress pushed back against it,[58] the Bush Administration in December 2005 urged agencies to create protocols for withholding "controlled unclassified information," and formalized the use of the category close to the end of its term, in May 2008.[59]

The Obama Administration reversed course by ordering federal officials on 1/21/09 to "adopt a presumption in favor" of FOIA requests,[60] and Attorney General Eric Holder's memorandum of 3/19/09 overruled the Bush Administration memorandum of October 12, 2001, and called for a "presumption of openness," and noted that the Justice Department would defend agency denials of requests for information only for disclosures reasonably foreseen to "harm an interest protected by one of the FOIA exemptions" and for disclosures "otherwise prohibited by law."[61] But, the exercise of executive power by the Obama Administration seemed to generate a tendency to restrict information.

As noted above, the Obama Administration vigorously opposed release of the prisoner abuse photographs. In a brief filed with the U.S. Supreme Court in November, 2009, Obama's then-Solicitor General Elena Kagan and Defense Department General Counsel Jeh Johnson defended the Defense Department's refusal to release the photographs.[62] An ACLU spokesperson, Alex Abdo, characterized the Administration's argument as setting a precedent "that the government can conceal evidence of its own misconduct precisely because the evidence powerfully documents gross abuses of power and of detainees."[63]

In many ways, the Obama Administration exhibited a weird duality, swerving back and forth from openness to secrecy in its information policies. It initiated more than twice as many prosecutions under the Espionage Act of 1917 as all other administrations in United States history put together, often against individuals like reporters and government employee "leakers" whose efforts to publicize facts embarrassing to the government could well be justified.[64] It allowed its agencies to classify documents *after* receiving FOIA requests for those documents.[65] On the other hand, the same Executive Order so providing also instructed agencies that "if there is significant doubt about the need to classify information, it shall not be classified."[66] It ordered far more government information to be made easily accessible online, announced that the "default" stance of its agencies should be "open and machine readable" information, and continued to argue in favor of open information policies.[67] Under the Obama Administration, intelligence agency budgets were declassified, agencies spending on classification decreased,[68] and the President supported declassification of parts of the Senate Intelligence Committee's Report on "the CIA's detention and interrogation programs."[69]

Law Enforcement

(b) This section does not apply to matters that are—

* * *

(7) records or information compiled for law enforcement purposes, but only to the extent that the production of such law enforcement records or information (A) could reasonably be expected to interfere with enforcement proceedings, (B) would deprive a person of a right to a fair trial or an impartial adjudication, (C) could reasonably be expected to constitute an unwarranted invasion of personal privacy, (D) could reasonably be expected to disclose the identity of a confidential source, including a State, local, or foreign agency or authority or any private institution which furnished information on a confidential basis, and, in the case of a record or information compiled by criminal law enforcement authority in the course of a criminal investigation or by an agency conducting a lawful national security intelligence investigation, information furnished by a confidential source, (E) would disclose techniques and procedures for law enforcement investigations or prosecutions, or would disclose guidelines for law enforcement investigations or prosecutions if such disclosure could reasonably be expected to risk circumvention of the law, or (F) could reasonably be expected to endanger the life or physical safety of any individual;

Source: http://www.archives.gov/federal-register/laws/administrative-procedure/552.html

Exemption 7 protects a wide range of law enforcement interests by permitting the withholding of certain "records or information compiled for law enforcement purposes."[70] Part A exempts information that might notify a target that he or she is under investigation, and might therefore encourage the target to flee, destroy evidence, intimidate witnesses, or otherwise take action to thwart the investigation. Part B exempts information that "would deprive a person of a right to a fair trial or an impartial adjudication." In the early 1980s, the Department of Justice began to investigate whether the Eli Lilly pharmaceutical corporation had hidden information about one of its arthritis drugs that had apparently killed a number of people. Lilly had submitted its own report to the Department of Justice on the assurance that it would remain confidential. The *Washington Post* made a FOIA request to Justice. Justice denied it on the basis of Exemption 7B, among other exemptions.[71] The court held that to sustain Justice's denial, Justice would have to show "that a trial or adjudication is truly imminent," and that releasing the information really would impair the fairness of the trial or the impartiality of the adjudication.[72] As always, the agency (here, Justice) had the burden of proof "that the information [fell] under the claimed exemption."[73]

Part C, allowing the withholding of information for reasons of personal privacy, was previously addressed, both before and after Box 14.5. Part D includes a provision related to Exemption 1, in that it covers information that might reveal the identity of a confidential source of national security intelligence. Otherwise, Part D exempts information revealing the identity of confidential law enforcement sources. Part E exempts information about law enforcement techniques that, if disclosed, could compromise their effectiveness; and Part F exempts information that could endanger life or physical safety.

HOW FOIA EMPOWERS AGENCIES TO WITHHOLD INFORMATION TO SAFEGUARD PROCEDURAL INTERESTS

BOX 14-6 **5 U.S. Code Administrative Procedure Act— Section 552(b)(2) and (5)**

(b) This section does not apply to matters that are—

* * *

(2) related solely to the internal personnel rules and practices of an agency;

* * *

(5) inter-agency or intra-agency memorandums or letters which would not be available by law to a party other than an agency in litigation with the agency;

Source: http://www.archives.gov/federal-register/laws/administrative-procedure/552.html

Exemption 5 allows the withholding of "inter-agency or intra-agency memorandums or letters which would not be available by law to a party other than an agency in litigation with the agency."[74] In part, this exemption derives from the "deliberative process privilege," explained by retired Supreme Court Justice Stanley Reed while sitting as a federal Court of Claims judge as follows: "Free and open comments on the advantages and disadvantages of a proposed course of governmental management would be adversely affected if the civil servant or executive assistant were compelled by publicity to bear the blame for errors or bad judgment properly chargeable to the responsible individual with power to decide and act."[75] More simply, "the quality of administrative decision-making would be seriously undermined if agencies are forced to operate in a fishbowl [citation omitted] ... the purpose of Exemption 5 is to encourage 'the frank discussion of legal and policy issues' [citation omitted]."[76]

However, agencies may not use Exemption 5 to withhold documents reflecting a decision and the reasons it was adopted: once the decision has been made, the "deliberative process" has ended.[77] Matters covered by the attorney–client privilege, the attorney work-product privilege, and other documents not available in litigation are of course also exempt from disclosure requirements under Exemption 5.[78]

Exemption 5 has come under considerable criticism, and was the major focus of legislation intended to curb its frequent abuse by agencies legally withholding information under its provisions,[79] but in violation of constitutional values as explained in Chapter 2.[80] The legislation passed the Senate in 2014, but not the House. For example, Exemption 5 has apparently allowed the CIA to "block the release of internal reports on the Bay of Pigs invasion simply because the decades-old document is still marked 'draft.'"[81]

Exemption 2 allows an agency to withhold information "related solely to [its] internal personnel rules and practices ... "[82] However, the Court has limited the reach of this exemption to "matter[s] in which the public could not reasonably be expected to have an interest [citations omitted] ... matter[s] with merely internal significance ... [and] routine matters."[83] Therefore, in the case referenced above when previously discussing Exemption 6, the Air Force also could not rely on Exemption 2 to justify the withholding of summaries of decisions in cases of suitably redacted student honor code violations.[84] One may presume that Exemption 2 was adopted for reasons similar to those underlying Exemption 5: the release of information that risks disruption to agency operation is not warranted or justified when the public has no significant interest in that information.

OPEN MEETINGS LAWS

As of 2008, there were 917 Federal Advisory Committees,[85] generally appointed by heads of federal agencies, which they advise. In 1973, seventy-two percent of the nation's "largest 50 financial corporations and largest 150 non-financials ... had an executive on at least one advisory committee ... "[86] Although the percentage decreased subsequently, the corporate linkage remained powerful: In 1998, during the Clinton Administration, Dick Cheney, then–chair of Halliburton, and Kenneth Lay, then–president of the Enron Corporation, both served on the National Petroleum Council, one such committee, and Lay also served on the President's Council for Sustainable Development, another. Both of those committees advised the Department of Energy.[87] Corporate-dominated advisory committees "played a key role in formulating the North American Free Trade Agreement."[88]

Suspicion of the power of these advisory committees, "an opinion punctuated by the closed-door meeting policies of many committees,"[89] prompted Congress to pass the Federal Advisory Committee Act (FACA) in 1972,[90] although obviously these committees continued to exercise significant influence. If an advisory committee has at least one non-federal employee, but is dominated by federal executive branch employees, it must meet the requirements of the Act. The Act, as subsequently amended, requires (with some exceptions and among other things) that notice of meetings must be published in the Federal Register at least 15 days in advance[91]; meetings must be open to the public[92]; documents must be available to the public except for the same exemptions as under FOIA[93]; and membership must be "fairly balanced."[94]

In any event, the Court's decision in *Cheney v. U.S. Dist. Court for Dist. of Columbia*[95] reflects the ease with which a government official can evade the requirements of FACA. First, even if a committee falls under its provisions, no private individual can bring a successful suit to require enforcement of those provisions, such as the release of documents.[96] Second, if private citizens participate in a committee without official status as members of the committee, the committee may be able to escape the purview of FACA altogether,[97] so long as the courts do not deem them "de facto" members.[98]

Congress enacted FACA *prior* to the Watergate scandal. Congressional suspicions of executive and agency decision-making only increased thereafter, whether or not that process included private participants. Therefore, in 1976 Congress required that when a group of people heads an agency, and thus may make executive decisions in the course of a meeting, that meeting must be open to the public,[99] and communications between any of the decision-makers and any individual or entity affected by their decisions must be included in the public record.[100] This legislation, known as the Sunshine Act,[101] governs the SEC, FTC, and dozens of other presidentially appointed committees and commissions. As with FACA, its exceptions track the exceptions to FOIA,[102] with variations logically implied by the fact that it governs meetings, not documents.[103] To deal with matters covered by the exceptions, commission members may vote for, and then hold, a closed session, which must be transcribed,[104] in case a federal district court hears a challenge and needs the transcript to review the propriety of closure, with the burden of proof on the agency.[105]

BOX 14-7 **5 U.S. Code Sunshine Act—Section 552b**

(a) For purposes of this section—

   (1) the term "agency" means any agency, as defined in section 552 (e) [1] of this title, headed by a collegial body composed of two or more individual members, a majority of whom are appointed to such position by the President with the advice and consent of the Senate, and any subdivision thereof authorized to act on behalf of the agency;

(2) the term "meeting" means the deliberations of at least the number of individual agency members required to take action on behalf of the agency where such deliberations determine or result in the joint conduct or disposition of official agency business, but does not include deliberations required or permitted by subsection (d) or (e); and

(3) the term "member" means an individual who belongs to a collegial body heading an agency.

(b) Members shall not jointly conduct or dispose of agency business other than in accordance with this section. Except as provided in subsection (c), every portion of every meeting of an agency shall be open to public observation.

Source: http://www.gpo.gov/fdsys/pkg/USCODE-2011-title5/pdf/USCODE-2011-title5-partI-chap5.pdf

While the Sunshine Act was intended to increase accountability,[106] and presumably also to decrease the hidden influence of special interest groups, it may not have been as effective as proponents had hoped. Informal freewheeling discussion may be inhibited.[107] The only statistical analysis available on the Act dates from the early 1980s, but it indicates that the Sunshine Act appears to have resulted in a thirty-one percent decrease of official decision-making meetings among the federal agencies affected over the five-year period studied.[108] Staff briefings sometimes substitute for public meetings. Later, the public meeting merely serves as the forum to announce the decision.

Notwithstanding its weaknesses, the value of "sunshine" laws can be seen perhaps best where they do not apply. The Port Authority of New York and New Jersey was notorious in 2013 for the "Bridgegate" scandal in which appointees of New Jersey Governor Christie, apparently thinking they were representing his political interests, purposely caused massive traffic jams in Fort Lee by closing entrance lanes to the George Washington Bridge.[109] However, the bistate agency has long been regarded as a secretive "patronage mill" for the governors of its two states. Its twelve commissioners, appointed by those governors, "rarely give either the public or the media notice that a vote is going to be taken, and little inkling of the final outcome."[110] Opening their meetings to the public would at least subject them to some additional measure of accountability.

All states have "Open Meetings" laws similar to the Sunshine Act.[111] Also similarly, their boards and commissions attempt to evade the requirements of those laws, for example by telephone call discussions in which key policy decisions are made, which may or may not survive legal challenges, taking the place of official meetings.[112]

The federal statute strongly suggests that courts should require publication of the hidden information, such as by release of a transcript of the proceedings, as the remedy for a Sunshine Act violation rather than interfering in any way with the substantive decision of the commission in question,[113] and the courts have so ruled.[114] Unlike FACA, the Sunshine Act allows for private individuals and entities to sue for enforcement of its provisions.[115]

ELECTRONIC TRANSPARENCY IN RULEMAKING

The Electronic Freedom of Information Act of 1996[116] and the E-Government Act of 2002[117] have changed the nature of rulemaking. For the most part, they have vastly increased the transparency of the process. At present, "Regulation.gov.," a joint venture among various federal government entities, although housed in the Environmental Protection Agency, makes it easy to review proposed regulations and their background material, and comment on the proposals and respond to the comments of others.[118] Every federal agency now has an electronic "reading room," allowing the public to review all of its documents in electronic form. Agencies must now "make all their guidance materials that did *not* have to be published in the Federal Register available in their electronic reading rooms, if the agencies wished them to have any impact on private conduct . . . [and] the electronic docket it mandates for all rulemaking is to be comprehensive, containing *all* materials relevant to the rulemaking process [citations omitted]."[119] Such a wealth of information greatly facilitates informed comment, and therefore presumably more effective comment. Whether its effect will be beneficial on the balance of power between agencies and other government actors like the Office of Management and Budget (OMB) may be in the eye of the beholder, depending on one's view of the virtue of strong executive control of agency policy.

The 2010 MSAPA gives states the option to require electronic rulemaking,[120] and some states have adopted electronic rulemaking.[121]

Professor Peter Strauss has warned of one troubling exception to this dramatic increase in transparency. Agencies incorporate by reference industry standards often developed by organizations associated with the American National Standards Institute (ANSI). However, although like other substantive regulations these standards have the force of law, agencies do not reproduce them in the Federal Register or the Code of Federal Regulations, but simply reference them. For example, the Occupational Safety and Health Administration (OSHA) requires certain colors to be used in caution signs at work locations. A worker who wants to check compliance by the employer, or the employer who wants to comply, cannot find this information in the *Federal Register* or the Code of Federal Regulations. If the seeker cannot travel to Washington, D.C., to engage in personal inspection of the standards, ANSI, the holder of the copyright on the standards, charges the employee and the employer what price it chooses for a copy. The cost of the complete set of Underwriters Laboratories' referred to in its "Standard for Manual Signaling Boxes for Fire Alarm Systems," needed to fully understand that standard, costs more than $10,000.[122]

The APA permits agencies to "incorporate[] by reference" rather than spelling out or reprinting, "matter reasonably available to the class of persons affected thereby," so long as the Director of the *Federal Register* approves,[123] and so long as the doing so "substantially reduces the volume of material published in the *Federal Register*."[124] The Office of the Federal Register (OFR) has promulgated regulations requiring that an agency "must provide the OFR with one physical copy of the material to be incorporated [to be] stored in the National Archives where the public might find it [citations omitted]."[125] The OFR regulations further require that the agency regulation must include a statement explaining how the public can gain access "with maximum convenience to the user,"[126] but the practices of the directors have made it clear that the existence of a copy in the offices of the National Archives and Records Administration "and another in the incorporating agency's Washington, D.C.-area reading room [citation omitted]"[127] suffices to constitute "maximum convenience to the user" under the OFR regulation and "reasonably available" under the statute.

Worse, perhaps, again unlike the situation with normal regulations, the affected public has very limited opportunity to make meaningful comments on these proposed standards. Agencies need alert the OFR of a proposed incorporation only "twenty working days before its submission for publication in the Federal Register as a *final* rule [emphasis in original],"[128] and such access as the public has to review data underlying the adoption of the standards owes more to judicial intervention than to the OFR regulations.[129]

Professor Strauss, among others, "filed a petition for rulemaking with the OFR" [cite petition for rulemaking provision of APA] calling for "revision of the federal practice to identify standards that would effect compliance with regulations independently stated rather than constituting the standards themselves as law [citation omitted]."[130]

OFR has recently proposed some mild steps in the direction of more transparency, and the Administrative Conference of the United States (ACUS) has also proposed some reforms,[131] but these "fall[] short of requiring disclosure of the standards themselves" and continue to "fail[] to suggest a definition of 'reasonably available' . . . "[132]

WHAT AM I SUPPOSED TO DO?

Favoritism by Immigration Officials Toward Applicants for Certain Visas: Can Immigration Inspector General Use Exemptions to FOIA to Avoid Releasing Related Documents?

You are an assistant to the Inspector General of the Department of Homeland Security, which has jurisdiction of Immigration and Customs Enforcement (ICE). An investigation by the Inspector General had determined that a former ICE official had gone into business under a provision of the immigration law that makes special visas available to foreign nationals who have invested at least $500,000 in businesses that employ ten or more American workers.

The business involves making loans to foreign investors with only $150,000 so that they can become eligible for special visas. The investigation showed that current ICE employees gave special and favorable attention to the applications for the visas put forward by their particular former ICE official, and other former ICE officials involved in the business.

A crusading immigration attorney, suspicious that this kind of behavior had taken place, filed a FOIA request for a copy of the investigation report. The Inspector General is reluctant to release it, but if she will be required to release it eventually she would prefer to do so immediately, so as not to appear defensive of the agency, and thereby make herself look worse. Do you advise her to release it now, or is it more likely that she can continue to withhold it under Exemption 6 (personnel, medical, and "similar" files jeopardizing personal privacy) and/or under Exemption 7(c) (law enforcement files that "could reasonably be expected to constitute an unwarranted invasion of personal privacy")?

The Second Circuit Court of Appeals faced this question in *Perlman v. United States Department of Justice*,[133] although since at the time ICE was the Immigration and Naturalization Service, it used that older terminology. The trial court held that the report fell under the protection of the two exemptions. As to "witnesses and third parties" mentioned in the report, the Supreme Court agreed that the report fell under the protection of Exemption 6, quoting the language of the exemption that included "any detailed Government records on an individual that can be identified as applying to that individual" as arguing that it was "similar" to a personnel file, and Exemption 7(c), because the report was clearly "compiled for a law enforcement purpose," and exposure of those persons would subject them to embarrassment for having played a role—whether as someone under scrutiny or someone who provided damaging information, or both—without giving the public material information about the policies and practices of ICE (then INS) or the Inspector General's office that investigated it.[134]

However, the former INS official had held high rank in the organization, so understanding his role would in fact provide information that would enlighten the public about the behavior of the agency; the strong evidence of serious wrongdoing on his part weighs similarly; the information concerns the way he performed his public duties, not the way he conducted his personal life; and the public has no other source of information about the investigation other than the report. Based on these factors, the court held that the public interest in the information outweighed the invasion of his personal privacy, and thus warranted the release of the report, redacted to avoid identifying the other persons mentioned.[135]

PRACTICE PROBLEMS

PROBLEM 1: The FBI investigated the suicide of a member of the White House staff. The investigation included taking photographs of the deceased. Journalists anxious to provide coverage of the story, doubting that the death truly resulted from suicide, and hoping to find an aspect of the story embarrassing to the

President, filed a FOIA request with the FBI for the photographs. Should they succeed?

PROBLEM 2: The Secretary of Defense had asked you, his assistant, whether he would be subject to constitutional criticism and litigation were he to authorize the use of a drone to assassinate a fairly high-profile American citizen engaged in leading terrorist activities against the United States. Now he wants to know how much of the documentation surrounding such a decision, including legal analysis, would be available to news organizations and others under FOIA, the statutory structure making government records available to the public, with important exceptions. He would prefer to keep confidential as much as possible of the documentation needed for any such decision.

ENDNOTES

1. 5 U.S.C. § 552(d), repealed by the Freedom of Information Act, 5 U.S.C. § 552, Pub. L. 89-554, 80 Stat. 383 (1966).
2. The Freedom of Information Act emerged out of a somewhat convoluted legislative process. A review of that process does not enhance the understanding of the Act itself, but those who are interested should consult Joshua Tauberer's Blog, 11/6/13, http://razor.occams.info/blog/2013/11/06/the-original-text-of-the-freedom-of-information-act/, accessed 8/31/14.
3. House Report 106-050: A Citizen's Guide on Using the Freedom of Information Act and the Privacy Act of 1974 to Request Government Records, 106th Congress (1999–2000), Section VI. A, http://thomas.loc.gov/cgi-bin/cpquery/?&dbname=cp106&sid=cp106BXnTS&refer=&r_n=hr050.106&item=&&sel=TOC_24963&, accessed 9/3/14.
4. 5 U.S.C. § 552b, Pub. L. 94-409, 90 Stat. 1241 (1976).
5. 5 U.S. C. § 552b(c).
6. Celebrating FOIA's Forty-Fifth Anniversary & Assessing This Past Year's Progress in Implementing Attorney General Holder's Guidelines, website of the U.S. Department of Justice, undated but presumably 2011, http://www.justice.gov/oip/blog/foia-post-8, accessed 8/31/14.
7. *Panama Refining Co. v. Ryan*, 293 U.S. 388 (1935).
8. Amy Bunk, Federal Register 101, *Proceedings*, United States Coast Guard, Spring 2010, 55, http://www.uscg.mil/proceedings/spring2010/, accessed 9/3/14.
9. Cindy Skrzycki, The Federal Register Turns 70, *The Washington Post*, 3/7/06, http://www.washingtonpost.com/wp-dyn/content/article/2006/03/06/AR2006030601757.html, accessed 9/3/14.
10. Bunk, *supra* at 56.
11. Section 552(b).
12. FOIA Exemptions, FOIA Advocates, 2014, http://www.foiadvocates.com/exemptions.html, accessed 9/3/14; Pub. L. 104–231, 110 Stat. 3048 (hereafter "1996 Electronic FOIA Amendments"), amending 5 U.S.C. § 552(a)(2).
13. *Vaughn v. Rosen*, 484 F. 2d 820 (D.C. Cir. 1973), *cert. denied* 415 U.S. 977, 94 S. Ct. 1564 (1974).
14. 5 U.S.C. § 552(a)(6)(C).
15. FOIA Appeals and Litigation, FOIA Advocates, 2014, http://www.foiadvocates.com/appeals_litigation.html, accessed 9/4/14, citing Federal Rule of Civil Procedure 36(a).
16. 5 U.S.C. § 552(a)(4)(B).
17. *Id.*
18. 1996 Electronic FOIA Amendments, amending 5 U.S.C. § 552(a)(6)(A)(i).
19. 1996 Electronic FOIA Amendments, adding subparagraphs 5 U.S.C. § 552(a)(6)(D) and (E).

20. 1996 Electronic FOIA Amendments, 5 U.S.C. § 552(a)(2) and other sections.
21. The Office of Special Counsel, an independent federal agency whose head is appointed by the President, enforces against FOIA abuses, among other responsibilities. See U.S. Office of Special Counsel website, https://osc.gov/Pages/about.aspx, accessed 2/14/15.
22. APA § 552(a)(4)(E), (F), and (G).
23. See, e.g., *Ruckelshaus v. Monsanto Co.*, 467 U.S. 986, 991, 104 S. Ct. 2862, 2867 (1984).
24. Section 552(b)(4).
25. Section 552(b)(3).
26. Under the Federal Insecticide, Fungicide, and Rodenticide Act, as amended by the Federal Pesticide Act of 1978, 7 U.S.C. § 136, Section 10; and also under the Trade Secrets Act of 1974, 18 U.S.C. § 1905, which prohibits the disclosure of confidential information received by a government employee in his or her official capacity.
27. Trade Secrets Act, *id.*
28. *Chrysler Corp. v. Brown*, 441 U.S. 281, 99 S. Ct. 1705 (1979).
29. 441 U.S. at 317–9, 99 S. Ct. at 1725–6. In a more recent reverse-FIOA case, Chiquita Brands International had submitted documents to the Securities Exchange Commission "related to payments Chiquita had made to terrorist organizations in Columbia." *Chiquita Brands International v. U.S. Securities and Exchange Commission*, Civil Case Number 130435 (RJL) (D.C. Dist. and Bankruptcy Courts, November 18, 2013), 3. The National Security Archive submitted FOIA requests to the SEC for the documents. Chiquita brought a reverse-FOIA suit to enjoin the release of the documents—not, of course, under the trade secrets exemption or Act, but under Exemption 7(b), claiming that it would deprive Chiquita of a fair trial, in a different litigation. The federal district court for the District of Columbia rejected Chiquita's argument on the grounds that Chiquita had failed to show that the release of the information would actually deprive the company of a fair trial. *Id.* at 7–10.
30. *Wine Hobby U.S.A. Inc. v. United States Internal Revenue Service*, 502 F. 2d 133, 134 (3d Cir. 1974), citing 26 U.S.C. § 5042(a)(2).
31. Section 552(b)(6).
32. See, e.g., *Department of the Air Force v. Rose*, 425 U.S. 352, 96 S. Ct. 1592 (1976).
33. *Wine Hobby U.S.A. Inc. v. United States Internal Revenue Service*, above at note 43.
34. 5 U.S.C. Section 552a.
35. See, e.g., David Wallis, For Your FBI File, Take a Number (15,001), *The New York Times*, 8/11/96, http://www.nytimes.com/1996/08/11/weekinreview/for-your-fbi-file-take-a-number-15001.html, accessed 9/18/14.
36. See National Archives and Records Administration Guide to Making a Privacy Act Request, National Archives, undated, http://www.archives.gov/foia/privacy-program/guide.html, accessed 9/18/14; FBI Records: Freedom of Information/Privacy Act, 63 FR 8659, 2/20/98, http://www.fbi.gov/foia/privacy-act/63-fr-8659, accessed 9/18/14.
37. *Dep't of the Air Force v. Rose*, 425 U.S. 352, 377, 96 Sup. Ct. 1592, 1606–7 (1976).
38. *Dep't of Justice v. Reporters Committee for Freedom of the Press*, 489 U.S. 749, 756, 109 S. Ct. 1468, 1473 (1989).
39. 489 U.S. at 764, 109 S. Ct. at 1477.
40. 489 U.S. at 774; 109 S. Ct. at 1482.
41. 489 U.S. at 780, 109 S. Ct. at 1485.
42. House Report 89-813 (1966), at 10, cited in Thomas M. Susman and David C. Vladeck, Freedom of Information, Sunshine, Advisory Committees, Section of Administrative Law and Regulatory Practice, American Bar Association, 69–70, 6/01.
43. House Report 89-1497 (1966), at 11, cited in Federal FOIA Appeals Guide, Exemption 9, Reporters Committee for Freedom of the Press, http://www.rcfp.org/federal-foia-appeals-guide/exemption-9, 2012, accessed 9/19/14.
44. 5 U.S.C. Section 552(b)(1)(B).
45. 5 U.S.C. Section 552(b)(1)(A).
46. *Environmental Protection Agency v. Mink*, 410 U.S. 73, 84, 93 S. Ct. 827, 834 (1973).
47. William F. Fox, *Understanding Administrative Law*, 6th ed., (New Providence, NJ: LexisNexis, 2012), 385.

48. *American Civil Liberties Union v. Department of Defense*, 543 F. 3d 59 (2d Cir. 2008).

49. Order and Opinion Granting, In Part, Plaintiffs' Motion for Partial Summary Judgment and Denying Defendants' Motion for Partial Summary Judgment, *American Civil Liberties Union v. Department of Defense*, 04 Civ. 4151 (AKH) (S.D.N.Y. 8/27/14), available via a link in Kevin Gosztola, Judge: Government's Justification for Keeping Detainee Abuse Photos Secret is 'Not Sufficient,' 8/27/14, https://dissenter.firedoglake.com/2014/08/27/judge-govern ments-justification-for-keeping-detainee-abuse-photos-secret-is-not-sufficient/, accessed 8/31/14; and see Dan McCue, More Abu Ghraib Photos May Come to Light, *Courthouse News Service*, 8/28/14, http://www.courthousenews.com/2014/08/28/70869.htm, accessed 8/31/14.

50. Stop Hiding Images of American Torture, editorial, *The New York Times*, 8/31/14, SR 10, c. 1.

51. Order and Opinion, above at 9.

52. *Id.* at 14.

53. *Id.* at 15–16.

54. *Id.* at 17.

55. *Id.* at 18–19.

56. See, e.g., Danielle Bryan, The Transparent Obama Administration?, *Public Administration Review* 74(1):8–9 (January/February 2014), 8; Controlled Unclassified Information, Recommendations for Information Control Reform, website, OMB Watch, 7/09, available via http://www.google.com/url?sa=t&rct=j&q=&esrc=s&source=web&cd=1&ved=0CCAQ FjAA&url=http%3A%2F%2Fwww.foreffectivegov.org%2Ffiles%2Finfo%2F2009cuirpt. pdf&ei=x6MDVO_NL421ggSU_oH4Bw&usg=AFQjCNHKqWFkyAgh4v-dLwEDB1fYenw XxQ&sig2=1IGllDi97MWkbIocT2OonA&bvm=bv.74115972,d.eXY, accessed 8/31/14, 4.

57. Genevieve J. Knezo, "Sensitive But Unclassified" Information and Other Controls: Policy and Options for Scientific and Technical Information, updated 12/29/06, Congressional Research Service, Order Code RL 33303, Summary [introductory pages]; and The Ashcroft Memo: "Drastic Change" or "More Thunder than Lightning?," The National Security Archive, 3/14/03, http://www2.gwu.edu/~nsarchiv/NSAEBB/NSAEBB84/methodology .htm, accessed 9/1/14.

58. See, e.g., Secrecy in the Bush Administration, U.S. House of Representatives Committee on Government Reform—Minority Staff, Prepared for Rep. Henry A. Waxman, 9/14/04, 6.

59. George W. Bush, Memorandum for the Heads of Departments and Agencies: Designation and Sharing of Controlled Unclassified Information (CUI), 5/7/08, available via New Executive Order Reforms Controlled Unclassified Information, website, Center for Effective Government, 11/9/10, http://www.foreffectivegov.org/node/11360, accessed 8/31/14.

60. Barack Obama, Memorandum to Heads of Executive Departments and Agencies: Freedom of Information Act, 1/21/09, http://www.whitehouse.gov/the-press-office/freedom-information-act, cited in Bryan, above at note 15.

61. President Obama's FOIA Memorandum and Attorney General Holder's FOIA Guidelines, Department of Justice Office of Information Policy, website, Department of Justice, undated, http://www.justice.gov/oip/blog/foia-post-2009-creating-new-era-open-government, accessed 9/1/14.

62. Jeh Charles Johnson and Elena Kagan, Supplemental Brief for Petitioners, *United States Department of Defense v. American Civil Liberties Union*, No. 09-160 in the Supreme Court of the United States, 11/09, http://www.justice.gov/osg/briefs/2009/2pet/7pet/2009-0160.pet .sup.html, accessed 9/1/14.

63. Secretary Of Defense Says Americans Should Not See Torture Photos, press release, website of the American Civil Liberties Union, 11/14/09, https://www.aclu.org/national-security/ secretary-defense-says-americans-should-not-see-torture-photos, accessed 9/1/14.

64. See, e.g., Daniel Politi, Obama has Charged More Under Espionage Act Than All Other Presidents Combined, *Slate*, 6/22/13; Cora Currier, Charting Obama's Crackdown on National Security Leaks, *Pro Publica*, 7/30/13, http://www.propublica.org/special/sealing-loose-lips-charting-obamas-crackdown-on-national-security-leaks, accessed 9/1/14; Bryan, 8. http://www.slate.com/blogs/the_slatest/2013/06/22/edward_snowden_is_eighth_ person_obama_has_pursued_under_espionage_act.html, accessed 9/1/14.

65. Executive Order 13526: Classified National Security Information, Section 1.7(d), http://www.whitehouse.gov/the-press-office/executive-order-classified-national-security-information, 12/29/09, accessed 9/16/14.

66. *Id.*, Section 1.1(b).

67. Obama Administration Releases Historic Open Data Rules to Enhance Government Efficiency and Fuel Economic Growth, press release, Office of the White House, website of the White House, 5/9/13, http://www.whitehouse.gov/the-press-office/2013/05/09/obama-administration-releases-historic-open-data-rules-enhance-governmen, accessed 9/1/14; Barack Obama, Executive Order 13642: Making Open and Machine Readable the New Default for Government Information, 5/9/13, http://www.whitehouse.gov/the-press-office/2013/05/09/executive-order-making-open-and-machine-readable-new-default-government-, accessed 9/1/14.

68. Bryan, 9.

69. Steven Dennis and Niels Lesniewski, Intelligence Committee Votes to Declassify CIA Report (Updated), *Roll Call*, 4/3/14, http://blogs.rollcall.com/wgdb/intelligence-committee-votes-to-declassify-cia-report/, accessed 9/1/14.

70. Section 552(b)(7).

71. *Washington Post Company v. U.S. Dep't of Justice*, 863 F. 2d 96, 99 (D.C. Cir. 1988).

72. 863 F. 2d at 102.

73. *Id.* Apparently the trial judge only required release of records concerning the drug, Oraflex, after Lilly's witnesses testified in praise of the company's handling of the drug. But, Lilly "cut[] a secret deal with victims' attorneys to pay them and their clients not to introduce the damaging Oraflex evidence." Evelyn Pringle, Big Pharma's Big Graveyard, *Counterpunch*, 6/26/06, http://www.counterpunch.org/2006/06/26/big-pharma-s-big-graveyard/, accessed 2/14/15.

74. Section 552 (b)(5).

75. *Kaiser Aluminum Chemical Corp. v. United States*, 157 F. Supp. 939, 945–6 (Ct. Cl. 1958), quoted in Michael N. Kennedy, Escaping the Fishbowl: A Proposal to Fortify the Deliberative Process Privilege, *Northwestern Univ. L. Rev.* 99(4):1769–1815, 1780.

76. *Wolfe v. Dep't of Health and Human Services,* 839 F. 2d 768, 773. 268 U.S. App. D.C. 89 (D.C.D.C. 1988).

77. *Renegotiation Board v. Grumman Aircraft Engineering Corp.*, 421 U.S. 168, 184, 95 S. Ct. 1491, 1500 (1975).

78. See, e.g., Thomas M. Susman and David C. Vladeck, Freedom of Information, Sunshine, Advisory Committees, Section of Administrative Law and Regulatory Practice, *American Bar Association*, 50–53, 6/01.

79. See, e.g., Kelly J. O'Brien, FOIA reform dies while the press looked the other way, *Columbia Journalism Review*, 12/12/14, http://www.cjr.org/behind_the_news/foia_reform_dies_while_the_pre.php, accessed 2/14/15.

80. See Chapter 2, text at notes 39–44.

81. Matthew Rumsey, FOIA Improvement Act clears Senate hold, heads to House, Sunlight Foundation website, 12/8/14, http://sunlightfoundation.com/blog/2014/12/08/foia-improvement-act-clears-senate-hold-heads-to-house/, accessed 1/14/15.

82. Section 552(b)(2).

83. *Dep't of the Air Force v. Rose*, 425 U.S. 352, 369–70, 96 Sup. Ct. 1592, 1603 (1976).

84. *Id.*

85. Wendy R. Ginsberg, Federal Advisory Committees: An Overview, *Congressional Research Service*, R40520, 4/16/09, 1.

86. G. William Domhoff, The Corporate Community, Non-Profit Organizations, and Federal Advisory Committees: A Study in Linkages, *Who Rules America?* website, 4/05, http://www2.ucsc.edu/whorulesamerica/power/federal_advisory_committees.html, accessed 9/24/14.

87. *Id.*

88. *Id.*

89. Ginsberg, *supra*, at "Summary" (front matter, not paginated); similar comment at 2.

90. Pub. L. 92–463, 86 Stat. 770, 5 U.S.C. App. II (1972).

91. U.S.C. App. Section 10(a)(2).
92. U.S.C. App. Section 10(a)(1).
93. U.S.C. App. Section 10(b).
94. U.S.C. App. Section 5(b)(2).
95. 542 U.S. 367, 124 S. Ct. 2576 (2004).
96. 542 U.S. at 374, 124 S. Ct. at 2583 ("The court acknowledged FACA does not create a private right of action").
97. 542 U.S. at 373, 124 S. Ct. at 2583.
98. *Association of American Physicians & Surgeons v. Clinton*, 997 F. 2d 898, 915, 302 U.S. App. D.C. 208 (D.C. Cir. 1993).
99. Section 552b(b).
100. Section 557(d)(1).
101. Sunshine Act, P.L. 94–409, 90 Stat. 1241.
102. Section 552b(c)(1–10).
103. See, e.g., Section 552b(c)(9)(A) and (B); Section 552b(c)(10).
104. Section 552b(d).
105. Section 552b(h)(1).
106. P.L. 94–409, Section 2.
107. Grover Starling, *Managing the Public Sector*, 9th ed., (Boston, MA: Wadsworth, Cengage Learning, 2010), 70.
108. Richard K. Berg, Stephen H. Klitzman, and Gary J. Edles, *An Interpretive Guide to the Government in the Sunshine Act*, 2nd ed., (Chicago, IL: American Bar Association Book Publishing, 2005), 70, note 15, citing a 1986 report by the Congressional Research Service.
109. See, e.g., Jessica Durando, The Backstory of Christie's 'Bridgegate' Scandal, *U.S.A. Today*, 1/10/14, http://www.usatoday.com/story/news/politics/2014/01/09/christie-bridge-scandal-what-happened/4392155/, accessed 1/27/15.
110. Port Authority: The Lavish, Secretive Workings of the PA, *Edmecka.com: Hoboken's Activist Community*, 10/8/06, http://www.edmecka.com/articles/port-authority--the-lavish-secretive-workings-of-the-pa----5b-agency-cuts-deals-far-from-the-public-eye.html, accessed 1/27/15.
111. See State open meetings laws, website of *Ballotpedia*, undated, http://ballotpedia.org/State_open_meetings_laws, accessed 10/1/14.
112. See, e.g., Jeffrey L. Rabin, MTA May Have Broken Law on Open Meetings, Experts Say, *Los Angeles Times*, 11/15/00, http://articles.latimes.com/2000/nov/15/local/me-52063, accessed 10/1/14.
113. Section 552b(h)(2).
114. *Pan American Airways Inc. v. Civil Aeronautics Board*, 684 F. 2d 31, 36, 221 U.S. App. D.C. 257 (D.C. Cir. 1982).
115. Section 552b(h)(2).
116. Electronic Freedom of Information Act of 1996, Pub. L. 104–231, 110 Stat. 3048, amending APA § 552(a)(2) and other sections.
117. E-Government Act of 2002, Pub. L. No. 107–347, 116 Stat. 2899 (2002) (codified in scattered sections of 44 U.S.C.).
118. Participate Today, at Regulations.gov. website, http://www.regulations.gov/#!home; and About Us, *id.*, http://www.regulations.gov/#!aboutProgram, undated, accessed 1/27/15.
119. Peter L. Strauss, Private Standards Organizations and Public Law, 22 *William & Mary Bill of Rights Journal* 497, 523–4 (Dec. 2013).
120. 2010 MSAPA § 201(b).
121. See, e.g., Guide to Rule Making, website of the Secretary of State of Maine, http://www.maine.gov/sos/cec/rules/guide.html, accessed 1/27/15; Rulemaking and Licensing Procedures by State Agencies, website of the Secretary of State of Colorado, Colorado Revised Statutes 24-4-103(3)(b), requiring electronic notification of proposed rules to persons who so request, http://www.sos.state.co.us/pubs/info_center/laws/Title24Article4.html, accessed 1/27/15.

122. 22 *Wm & Mary Bill of Rights J.* at 509, citing the Underwriters Laboratories website, http://www.comm-2000.com.
123. APA § 552(a)(1)(E).
124. 1 C.F.R. § 51.7(a)(3).
125. 22 *Wm & Mary Bill of Rights J.* at 521.
126. 1 C.F.R. § 51.9(b)(4).
127. 22 *Wm & Mary Bill of Rights J.* at 522.
128. *Id.* at 519, citing 1 C.F.R. § 51.5(a)(1).
129. *Id.* at 520, citing *Portland Cement Ass'n v. Ruckelshaus*, 486 F. 2d 375, 393 (D.C. 1973), *cert. den.* 417 U.S. 921 (1974).
130. *Id.* at 530–1.
131. *Id.* at 538; and see Paul Verkuil and Emily Bremer, Final ACUS Comments on OFR NPRM (letter to Charles A. Barth, Director, Office of the Federal Register, January 31, 2014).
132. *Id.* at 538.
133. *Perlman v. United States Department of Justice*, 312 F. 3d 100, 2002 U.S. App. LEXIS 24070 (2nd Cir. 2002).
134. 312 F. 3d at 105–6.
135. 312 F. 3d at 107–9.

INDEXES

CASE INDEX

Note: Unlike the General Index, this list includes references in the endnotes to the listed item, because so many case names appear only in the endnotes and not in the main text.

300 Gramatan Ave. Assoc. v State Div. of Human Rights, 45 N.Y. 2d 176, 408 N.Y.S. 2d 54, 379 N.E. 2d 1183 (1978). 150n

Abbott Laboratories v. Gardner, 387 U.S. 136, 87 S. Ct. 1507 (1967). 168–171, 176n

Agrico Chemical Company v. Department of Environmental Regulation, 40 So. 2d 478 (Fla. 2d D.C.A. 1981). 133n

Air Transport Association v. Dept. of Transportation, 900 F. 2d 369, 376 (D.C. Cir. 1990). 70n

Alden v. Maine, 527 U.S. 706, 119 S. Ct. 2240 (1999). 189n

Al-Qadir v. G4S Secure Solutions (USA) Inc., 2013 U.S. Dist. LEXIS 548 (M.D. Tenn.) 190n

Am. Hosp. Assn. v. NLRB, 499 U.S. 606, 612, 111 S. Ct. 1539, 1543 (1991). 162n

Amador v. Andrews, 655 F. 3d 89 (2nd Cir. 2011). 176n

American Civil Liberties Union v. Department of Defense, 543 F. 3d 59 (2d Cir. 2008). 223n

American Insurance Company v. 356 Bales of Cotton, 26 U.S. (1 Pet.) 511, 545, 7 L. Ed. 242, 257. 16n

American Trucking Association v. EPA, 531 U.S. 457, 474, 121 S. Ct. 903, 913 (2001). 15n

Anstey v. Iowa State Commerce Commission, 292 N.W. 2d 380, 390 (Iowa 1980). 91n

Appalachian Power Co. v. EPA, 208 F. 3d 1015, 1024 (D.C. Cir. 2005). 70n

Arizona v. United States,—U.S. at—, 132 S. Ct. 2492, 2505, 183 L. Ed. 2d 351 (2012). 78n, 105n

Assoc. of National Advertisers, Inc. v. FTC, 627 F. 2d 1151 (D.C. Cir. 1979), *cert. den.* 447 U.S. 921 (1980). 91n, 92n

Association of American Physicians & Surgeons v. Clinton, 997 F. 2d 898, 302 U.S. App. D.C. 208 (D.C. Cir. 1993). 225n

Association of Data Processing Service Organizations v. Federal Reserve Board, 745 F. 2d 677, (D.C. Cir. 1984). 150n

Association of Data Processing Services v. Camp, 397 U.S. 150, 90 S. Ct. 827 (1970). 175n

AT&T v. Central Office Telephone, 524 U.S. 214, 118 S. Ct. 1956 (1998). 168, 176n

Atkins v. United States, 556 F. 2d 1028 (Ct. Claims 1977), *cert. den.* 434 U.S. 1009 (1978). 46n

Atlas Roofing Co. v. Occupational Safety and Health Review Commission, 430 U.S. 442, 97 S. Ct. 1261 (1977). 16n, 111, 122n

Auer v. Robbins, 519 U.S. 452, 461, 117 S. Ct. 905, 911 (1997). 100, 107n

Barlow v. Collins, 397 U.S. 159, 90 S. Ct. 832 (1970). 175n

Barr v. Mateo, 360 U.S. 564, 79 S. Ct. 1335 (1959). 181, 185, 190n

Bean v. Barnhart, 2014 U.S. Dist. LEXIS 66277 (D. Maine). 176n

Bell Aerospace, 219 N.L.R.B. 384 (1975). 155, 161n

Bell v. Berson, 402 U.S. 535, 91 S. Ct. 1586 (1971). 122n

Bennett v. Spear, 520 U.S. 154, 166, 117 S. Ct. 1154, 1163 (1997). 175n

Berkovitz v. United States, 486 U.S. 531, 108 S. Ct. 1954 (1988). 180, 189n

Better Government Association v. Department of State, 780 F. 2d 86, 92 (D.C. Cir. 1986). 176n

STATUTES INDEX

*Note: This statute 5 U.S.C. § 552b, is codified differently than provisions of the Freedom of Information Act at 5 U.S.C. §§ 552(a) and 552(b). The "b" in the latter is in parentheses, unlike the "b" in the former.

CONSTITUTIONAL PROVISIONS INDEX

GENERAL INDEX

Peanut butter 78
Pertschuk, Michael 83–4
Political culture 20
Policy manuals 64–5, 195
Preemption, federal 93–8, 103–4,
    157; state 101, 103, 197 and
    home rule powers 101–3
President 3–6, 17, 19, 20, 22, 27–8, 34–45,
    53, 82, 88, 103, 105, 118, 185, 215–6,
    22; appointment powers 38–40, "on the
    model of King George the Third" 39;
    presidents Bush, George H.W. 38, Bush,
    George W. 23, 28, 37, 40, 87, 211–2,
    Carter 83, Clinton 37–8, 42, 211, 215,
    Ford 204, Hoover 35, Jefferson 21,
    Johnson 204, Lincoln 21, Madison 37,
    Nixon 21, 72, 84, 114, 185, Obama
    22–4, 39–40, 63, 79, 210–2, Reagan
    24, 39, 41, 64, Roosevelt, Franklin 18,
    21, 50, 53, Truman 21, 41, 54; Wilson
    18–9, 35, recess appointments 40
Primary jurisdiction 163, 167–8
Private rights 101
Prosecution 9, 26–7, 38, 63, 88,
    139, 146, 208, 212–3
Proxmire, William 34
Public rights 9, 111

Regime values 21–3, see also Constitution,
    constitutional values
Regulations. See Rulemaking;
    regulatory review 42
Reich, Charles 112–4
Representativeness 3, 9, 21
Residuum rule 137, 139–141
Respondeat superior 184
Revolutionary War 3
Rice, Condoleeza 28
Ripeness 163, 168–170
Rohr, John 19–24
Rubinstein, David 98
Rulemaking 2, 19, 42, 56, 59, 65, 71–84,
    94–105, 152–161, 218–9, bias 83–4,
    87–8, docket 82–3, 218, *ex parte*
    contacts 81–3, exemptions from or
    exceptions to requirements of 74–5,
    77–8, fair warning 154, formal 77–9,
    81–2, 157, future-oriented 75–8, 159,
    general or particular applicability
    65, 76, 157, guidance documents
    (interpretive rules, policy statements,
    staff manuals) 64–5, hearings 19,
    78, hybrid 78, 83–4, informal 65,
    78–83, 99, 152, interim final rules 80,

"logical outgrowth" 76–7, negotiated
    78–9, notice 73–4, 76, 80, 85,
    88–9, 100, 105, 152–3, notice-and-
    comment 72, 77–9, 88–9, 99, 130,
    157, good cause exception 65, 74–5,
    77, 88–9; retroactivity 76, 88–9
Rules, estoppel against 84–6, See also
    Equitable estoppel; interpretive 64,
    77, legislative 64, non-legislative 64,
    procedural 64–5, states 71, 77–8

Schechter brothers 5
Schwartz, Bernard 140
Senate, U.S. 3–4, 10, 17, 25, 27–8, 35, 37–8,
    43, 52–3, 212, 215–6; adjournment
    39–40; Senator, U.S. 2, 40, senators 81
Social Security benefits or checks 1, 3, 25, 28,
    59–60, 62, 111–3, 116, 126, eligibility
    28, disability benefits 137, 158–9
"Soft power" 20
Sovereign immunity 177–180
Spitzer, Eliot 95–7
Standing 26, 42, 163–6, 168, 172, 174
Starr, Kenneth 38
State agencies (long list) 110, Civil
    Service Commission, Hawaii 199,
    Correctional Services Department,
    New York 173, 186–7, Division
    of Pari-mutual Wagering, Florida
    71, Education Department,
    New York 101, Environmental
    Conservation Department, Florida
    125, Environmental Conservation
    Department, New York 110, 148,
    Environmental Protection Agency, 100,
    Governor's Office of Regulatory Reform,
    New York 42, Health Department,
    New York 42, Labor and Industries
    Department, Washington State 157,
    Medical Examining Board, Wisconsin
    145, Municipal Services and Research
    Center, Washington State 192, Police
    Pension and Retirement Board,
    Oklahoma 86, Public Health Council,
    New York 9–12, Retirement System,
    New York State 86, 129–130, 148–9,
    Social and Health Services Department,
    Washington State 86, Social Services,
    Department of (any state) 60
State and local agencies, Chicago area (long
    list) 110, local agencies, Board of Health,
    NYC 7–8, Bryce Hospital of Alabama
    23, 126–8, Civil Service Commission,
    New Orleans 197, 199–200, Collective